Fodor's 97
Washington, D.C.

"When it comes to information on regional history, what to see and do, and shopping, these guides are exhaustive."

—*USAir Magazine*

"Usable, sophisticated restaurant coverage, with an emphasis on good value."

—Andy Birsh, *Gourmet Magazine* columnist

"Valuable because of their comprehensiveness."

—*Minneapolis Star-Tribune*

"Fodor's always delivers high quality...thoughtfully presented...thorough."

—*Houston Post*

"An excellent choice for those who want everything under one cover."

—*Washington Post*

D0281404

Fodor's Travel Publications,
New York • Toronto • London • Sydney • Auckland
http://www.fodors.com/

Fodor's Washington, D.C.

Editor: Neil Chesanow

Contributors: Rob Andrews, Holly Bass, Bob Blake, Anna Borgman, Mary Case, Michael Dolan, John F. Kelly, Deborah Papier, Betty Ross, Nancy Ryder, Linda K. Schmidt, Mary Ellen Schultz, Dinah Spritzer, M. T. Schwartzman, Bruce Walker, Jan Ziegler

Creative Director: Fabrizio La Rocca

Cartographer: David Lindroth

Cover Photograph: Steve Weber

Text Design: Between the Covers

Copyright

Special Sales

Fodor's Travel Publications are available at special discounts for bulk purchases for sales promotions or premiums. Special editions, including personalized covers, excerpts of existing guides, and corporate imprints, can be created in large quantities for special needs. For more information, contact your local bookseller or write to Special Markets, Fodor's Travel Publications, 201 East 50th Street, New York, NY 10022. Inquiries from Canada should be directed to your local Canadian bookseller or sent to Random House of Canada, Ltd., Marketing Department, 1265 Aerowood Drive, Mississauga, Ontario L4W 1B9. Inquiries from the United Kingdom should be sent to Fodor's Travel Publications, 20 Vauxhall Bridge Road, London SW1V 2SA.

PRINTED IN THE UNITED STATES OF AMERICA

10 9 8 7 6 5 4 3 2 1

CONTENTS

ON THE ROAD WITH FODOR'S

A GOOD TRAVEL GUIDE IS LIKE A wonderful traveling companion. It's charming, it's brimming with sound recommendations and solid ideas, it pulls no punches in describing lodging and dining establishments, and it's consistently full of fascinating facts that make you view what you've traveled to see in a rich new light. In the creation of *Washington, D.C. '97,* we at Fodor's have gone to great lengths to provide you with the very best of all possible traveling companions—and to make your trip the best of all possible vacations.

About Our Writers

The information in these pages is a collaboration of several extraordinary writers.

John F. Kelly, who originally wrote most of this guide, is the editor of *The Washington Post's* "Weekend" section. A new dad, Kelly passed the updating torch to his *Post* colleague, **Bruce Walker.** A D.C.-area resident for most of his life, Walker has perfect credentials for a Fodor's revisor: He's old enough to be a seasoned journalist with an eagle eye for detail, yet hip enough to be up on the latest trends and hot spots about town. Walker, who has been with the *Post* since 1981, updated Chapters 2, 3, 7, and 8.

Holly Bass, who updated Chapter 4, has the perfect credentials for a restaurant reviewer. In addition to being a journalist, she has years of experience working in her family's restaurant. She writes for the *Washington CityPaper,* teaches creative writing in public schools in the Capitol, and lives in the ever-changing neigborhood of Adams Morgan.

Ironically **Anna Borgman,** who conceived of "So You Want to Be a Washington In-

sider" in Chapter 10, is one reporter at *The Washington Post* who usually tries to avoid writing about politics. Her insider knowledge, however, is encyclopedic. Pumpkins? Guatemalan immigrants? Assorted disasters? The federal budget crisis? She's covered them all.

Editor **Neil Chesanow** is also a New York–based journalist, author, and writing instructor at Baruch and Marymount Manhattan colleges. His very first trip away from home, at age 10, was a family visit to Washington, where he caught the travel bug.

New This Year

New Takes on History

We've added a list of U.S. presidents and a historical time line to this edition—a welcome refresher for those whose memories of American history classes are hazy. While researching presidents, the editor learned a fun fact he'd like to share: The S. in Harry S. Truman doesn't stand for anything.

A New Design

If this is not the first Fodor's guide you've purchased, you'll immediately notice our new look. More readable and easier to use than ever? We think so—and we hope you do, too.

How to Use This Guide

Organization

Up front is the **Gold Guide,** comprising two sections on gold paper that are chockfull of information about traveling within your destination and traveling in general. Both are in alphabetical order by topic. **Important Contacts A to Z** gives addresses and telephone numbers of organizations and companies that offer destination-related services and detailed information or publications. Here's where you'll find information about how to get to Washington, D.C., from wherever you are. **Smart Travel Tips A to Z,** the Gold Guide's second section, gives specific tips on how to get the most out of your travels, as well as information on how to accomplish what you need to in Washington, D.C.

At the end of the book you'll find Portraits: a historical timeline—a chronology of Washington's history; a list of U.S. presidents; quotes about the nation's capitol from famous Washingtonians, past and present; anecdotes about Washington's many inscriptions; and a description of how our government works. These are followed by suggestions for pretrip reading, both fiction and nonfiction. Here we also recommend movies you can rent on videotape to get you in the mood for your travels.

Icons and Symbols

★ Our special recommendations
✕ Restaurant
🏨 Lodging establishment
✕🏨 Lodging establishment whose restaurant warrants a detour
⚠ Campground
🐤 Rubber duckie (good for kids)
☞ Sends you to another section of the guide for more information
✉ Address
☎ Telephone number
🕐 Opening and closing times
💰 Admission prices (those we give apply only to adults; substantially reduced fees are almost always available for children, students, and senior citizens)

Numbers in white and black circles—② and ❷, for example—that appear on the maps, in the margins, and within the tours correspond to one another.

Restaurant and Hotel Criteria and Price Categories

Restaurants and lodging places are chosen with a view to giving you the cream of the crop in each location and in each price range.

Hotel Facilities

Note that, in general, you incur charges when you use many hotel facilities. We wanted to let you know what facilities a hotel has to offer, but we don't always specify whether or not there's a charge, so when planning a vacation that entails a stay of several days, it's wise to ask what's included in the rate.

Hotel Meal Plans

Assume that hotels operate on the **European Plan** (EP, with no meals) unless we note that they use the **American Plan** (AP, with all meals), the **Modified American Plan** (MAP, with breakfast and dinner daily), or the **Continental Plan** (CP, with a Continental breakfast daily).

Credit Cards

The following abbreviations are used: **AE,** American Express; **D,** Discover; **DC,** Diners Club; **MC,** MasterCard; and **V,** Visa.

Please Write to Us

Everyone who has contributed to *Washington, D.C. '97* has worked hard to make the text accurate. All prices and opening times are based on information supplied to us at press time, and the publisher cannot accept responsibility for any errors that may have occurred. The passage of time will bring changes, so it's always a good idea to call ahead and confirm information when it matters—particularly if you're making a detour to visit specific sights or attractions. When making reservations at a hotel or inn, be sure to mention if you have a disability or are traveling with children, if you prefer a private bath or a certain type of bed, or if you have specific dietary needs or any other concerns.

Were the restaurants we recommended as described? Did our hotel picks exceed your expectations? Did you find a museum we recommended a waste of time? We would love your feedback, positive and negative.

If you have complaints, we'll look into them and revise our entries when the facts warrant it. If you've happened upon a special place that we haven't included, we'll pass the information along to the writers so they can check it out. So please send us a letter or postcard (we're at 201 East 50th Street, New York, New York 10022.) We'll look forward to hearing from you. And in the meantime, have a wonderful trip!

Karen Cure
Editorial Director

Washington, D.C.

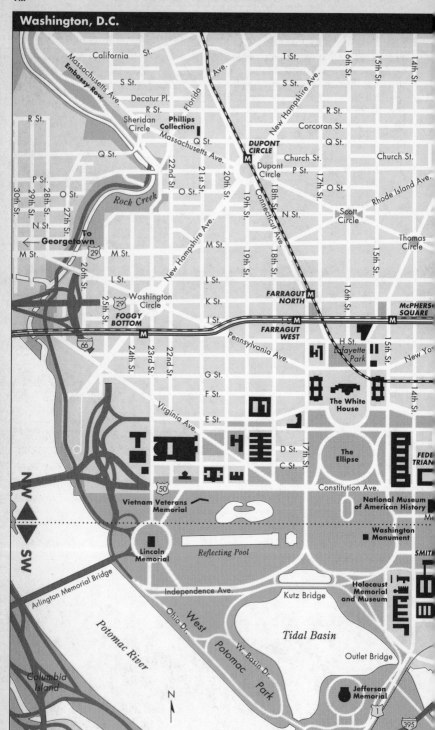

Washington, D.C. Area

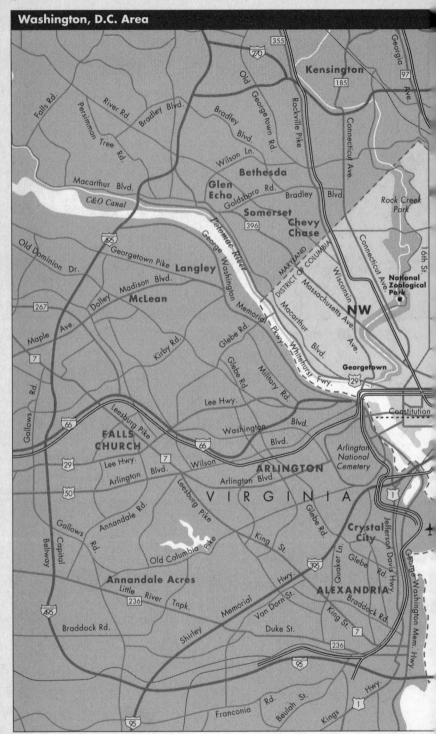

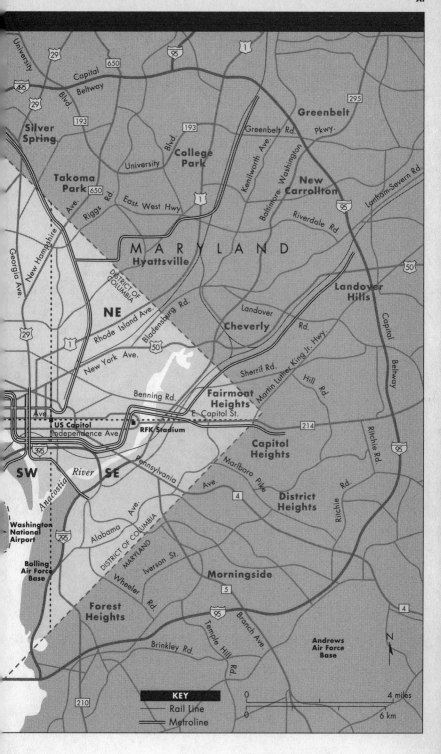

Silver Spring

Takoma Park

College Park

Greenbelt

New Carrollton

M A R Y L A N D

Hyattsville

NE

Landover Hills

Cheverly

Landover

Fairmont Heights

Capitol Heights

US Capitol

RFK Stadium

SW

River

SE

Anacostia

Washington National Airport

Bolling Air Force Base

District Heights

Morningside

Forest Heights

Andrews Air Force Base

Capital Beltway
Capital Blvd.
University Blvd.
Greenbelt Rd.
Pkwy.
Kenilworth Ave.
Baltimore-Washington
East-West Hwy.
Riggs Rd.
Ave.
New Hampshire Ave.
Georgia Ave.
Riverdale Rd.
Lanham-Severn Rd.
DISTRICT OF COLUMBIA
Rhode Island Ave.
Bladensburg Rd.
New York Ave.
Sherrif Rd.
Martin Luther King Jr. Hwy.
Hill Rd.
Benning Rd.
E. Capitol St.
Ave.
Independence Ave.
Pennsylvania Ave.
Marlboro Pike
Ritchie Rd.
Capital Beltway
Ritchie Rd.
Alabama Ave.
DISTRICT OF COLUMBIA
MARYLAND
Iverson St.
Wheeler Rd.
Brinkley Rd.
Temple Hill Rd.
Branch Ave.

KEY
—— Rail Line
══ Metroline

0   4 miles
0   6 km

Washington, D.C. Metro System

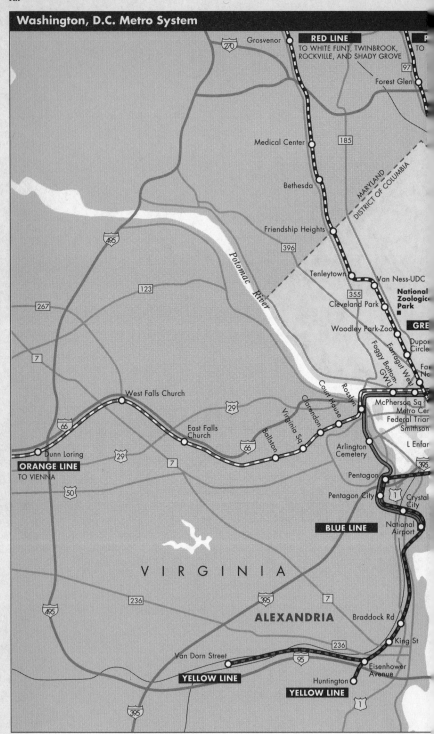

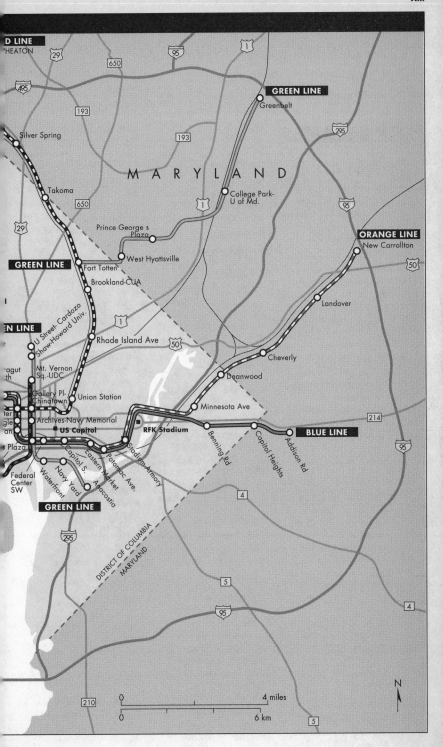

IMPORTANT CONTACTS A TO Z

*An Alphabetical Listing of Publications,
Organizations, and Companies that Will Help You
Before, During, and After Your Trip*

A

AIR TRAVEL

FLYING TIME

Flying time is one hour from New York, two hours from Chicago, and five hours, 40 minutes from Los Angeles.

The major gateways to Washington, D.C., include **National Airport** (☎ 703/419–8000), in Virginia, 4 miles south of downtown Washington; **Dulles International Airport** (☎ 703/661–2700), 26 miles west of Washington; and **Baltimore-Washington International (BWI) Airport** (☎ 410/859–7100), in Maryland, about 25 miles northeast of Washington.

CARRIERS

To NATIONAL AIRPORT➤ Contact **Air Canada** (☎ 800/776–3000), **America West** (☎ 800/235–9292), **American Airlines** (☎ 800/433–7300), **Continental** (☎ 800/525–0280), **Delta** (☎ 800/221–1212), **Midway** (☎ 800/446–4392, **Northwest** (☎ 800/225–2525) **TWA** (☎ 800/221–2000), **United** (☎ 800/241–6522), and **USAir** (☎ 800/428–4322).

To DULLES➤ Contact **Air Canada** (☎ 800/776–3000), **American Airlines** (☎ 800/433–7300), **Continental** (☎ 800/525–0280), **Delta** (☎ 800/221–1212),

Northwest (☎ 800/225–2525), **TWA** (☎ 800/221–2000), **United** (☎ 800/241–6522), and **USAir** (☎ 800/428–4322), and **Western Pacific** (☎ 800/930–3030).

To BWI➤ Contact **America West** (☎ 800/235–9292), **American Airlines** (☎ 800/433–7300), **Continental** (☎ 800/525–0280), **Delta** (☎ 800/221–1212), **Northwest** (☎ 800/225–2525), **Southwest** (☎ 800/435–9792), **TWA** (☎ 800/221–2000), **United** (☎ 800/241–6522), and **USAir** (☎ 800/428–4322).

For inexpensive, no-frills flights, contact **MarkAir** (☎ 800/627–5247), **Midwest Express** (☎ 800/452–2022), **Prestige Airlines** (☎ 800/299–8784); **Private Jet** (☎ 404/231–7571, 800/546–7571, or 800/949–9400), and **ValuJet** (☎ 404/994–8258 or 800/825-8538).

COMPLAINTS

To register complaints about charter and scheduled airlines, contact the U.S. Department of Transportation's **Aviation Consumer Protection Division** (✉ C-75, Washington, DC 20590, ☎ 202/366–2220). Complaints about lost baggage or ticketing problems and safety concerns may also be logged with the **Federal Aviation Administration**

(FAA) Consumer Hotline (☎ 800/322–7873).

PUBLICATIONS

For general information about charter carriers, ask for the Department of Transportation's free brochure **"Plane Talk: Public Charter Flights"** (✉ Aviation Consumer Protection Division, C-75, Washington, DC 20590, ☎ 202/366–2220). The Department of Transportation also publishes a 58-page booklet, **"Fly Rights,"** available from the Consumer Information Center (✉ Supt. of Documents, Dept. 136C, Pueblo, CO 81009; $1.75).

For other tips and hints, consult the Consumers Union's monthly **"Consumer Reports Travel Letter"** (✉ Box 53629, Boulder, CO 80322, ☎ 800/234–1970; $39 1st year).

AIRPORT
TRANSFERS

BY BUS

National and Dulles airports are served continuously by **Washington Flyer** (☎ 703/685–1400). The ride from National to downtown takes 20 minutes and costs $8 ($14 round-trip); from Dulles, the 45-minute ride costs $16 ($26 round-trip). The bus takes you to 1517 K Street NW, where you can board a free shuttle bus that serves downtown hotels. The shuttle bus will also transport you from your hotel to the K Street address to catch the main airport bus on your return journey. Washington Flyer also provides service to Maryland and Virginia suburbs. Fares may be paid in cash or with Visa or Master-Card; children under age six ride free.

BWI SuperShuttle buses (☎ 800/809–7080) leave BWI every hour for 1517 K Street NW. The 65-minute ride costs $15 ($25 round-trip); drivers accept traveler's checks and major credit cards in addition to cash.

Some hotels provide van service to and from the airports; check with your hotel.

BY LIMOUSINE

Call at least a day ahead and **Diplomat Limousine** (☎ 703/461–6800) will have a limousine waiting for you at the airport. The ride downtown from National or Dulles is about $75; it's $90 from BWI. **Private Car** (☎ 800/685–0888) has a counter at BWI Airport and charges $63 from there to downtown; or call ahead to have a car waiting for you at National ($45) or Dulles ($73).

BY SUBWAY

If you are coming into Washington National Airport, have little to carry, and are staying at a hotel near a subway stop, it makes sense to take the Metro downtown. The station is within walking distance of the baggage claim area, but a free airport shuttle stops outside each terminal and brings you to the National Airport station. The Metro ride downtown takes about 20 minutes and costs either $1.10 or $1.40, depending on the time of day.

BY TAXI

Expect to pay about $13 to get from National Airport to downtown, $45 from Dulles, and $50 from BWI. Unscrupulous cabbies prey on out-of-towners, so if the fare strikes you as astronomical, get the driver's name and cab number and threaten to call the **D.C. Taxicab Commission** (☎ 202/645–6018). A $1.25 airport surcharge is added to the total at National.

BY TRAIN

Free shuttle buses carry passengers between airline terminals and the train station at BWI Airport. **Amtrak** (☎ 800/872–7245) and **Maryland Rail Commuter Service** (MARC, ☎ 800/325–7245) trains run between BWI and Washington's Union Station from around 6 AM to midnight. The cost of the 40-minute ride is $10 on an Amtrak train, $4.50 on a MARC train (weekdays only).

B
BETTER BUSINESS BUREAU

Contact the **Better Business Bureau of Washington, D.C.** (1012 14th Street NW, 9th Floor, Washington, DC 20005, ☎ 202/393-8000). For other local contacts, consult the **Council of Better Busi-** ness Bureaus (✉ 4200 Wilson Blvd., Suite 800, Arlington, VA 22203, ☎ 703/276–0100, FAX 703/525–8277).

BUS TRAVEL

Washington is a major terminal for **Greyhound Bus Lines** (1005 1st St. NE, ☎ 202/289–5160 or 800/231–2222). The company also has stations in nearby Silver Spring and Laurel, Maryland, and in Arlington and Springfield, Virginia. Check with your local Greyhound ticket office for prices and schedules.

WITHIN WASHINGTON

For schedule and route information, contact the **Washington Metropolitan Area Transit Authority** (WMATA, ☎ 202/637–7000, TTY 202/638–3780; open daily 6 AM–11:30 PM).

C
CAR RENTAL

The major car-rental companies represented in Washington, D.C., are **Alamo** (☎ 800/327–9633; in the U.K., 0800/272–2000), **Avis** (☎ 800/331–1212; in Canada, 800/879–2847), **Budget** (☎ 800/527–0700; in the U.K., 0800/181181), **Dollar** (☎ 800/800–4000; in the U.K., 0990/565656, where it is known as Eurodollar), **Hertz** (☎ 800/654–3131; in Canada, 800/263–0600; in the U.K., 0345/555888), and **National InterRent** (☎ 800/227–7368; in the U.K., where National is known as Europcar InterRent, 0345/222525). Rates in Washington begin at

$40 a day and $149 a week for an economy car with unlimited mileage. This does not include tax on car rentals, which is 8%.

RENTAL WHOLESALERS

Contact **Auto Europe** (☎ 207/828–2525 or 800/223–5555).

FLYING

Look into **"Flying with Baby"** (✉ Third Street Press, Box 261250, Littleton, CO 80163, ☎ 303/595–5959; $4.95 includes shipping), cowritten by a flight attendant. **"Kids and Teens in Flight,"** free from the U.S. Department of Transportation's Aviation Consumer Protection Division (✉ C-75, Washington, DC 20590, ☎ 202/366–2220), offers tips on children flying alone. Every two years the February issue of *Family Travel Times* (☞ Know-How, *below*) details children's services on three dozen airlines. **"Flying Alone, Handy Advice for Kids Traveling Solo"** is available free from the American Automobile Association (AAA) (✉ send stamped, self-addressed, legal-size envelope: Flying Alone, Mail Stop 800, 1000 AAA Dr., Heathrow, FL 32746).

KNOW-HOW

Family Travel Times, published quarterly by Travel with Your Children (✉ TWYCH, 40 5th Ave., New York, NY 10011, ☎ 212/477–5524; $40 per year), covers destinations, types of vacations, and modes of travel.

LOCAL INFORMATION

A Kid's Guide to Washington, D.C. (Gulliver Books/Harcourt Brace Jovanovich, 111 5th Ave., New York, NY 10003; $6.95) includes games, photographs, maps, and a travel diary. *Kidding Around Washington, D.C., A Young Person's Guide to the City,* by Anne Pedersen (John Muir Publications, Box 613, Santa Fe, NM 87504, ☎ 800/888–7504; $9.95) highlights the sights in each neighborhood that are of most interest to children; it includes maps of the major sectors of the city.

TOUR OPERATORS

Contact **Grandtravel** (✉ 6900 Wisconsin Ave., Suite 706, Chevy Chase, MD 20815, ☎ 301/986–0790 or 800/247–7651), which has tours for people traveling with grandchildren ages 7–17.

CANADIANS

Contact **Revenue Canada** (✉ 2265 St. Laurent Blvd. S, Ottawa, Ontario K1G 4K3, ☎ 613/993–0534) for a copy of the free brochure **"I Declare/Je Déclare"** and for details on duty-free limits. For recorded information (within Canada only), call 800/461–9999.

U.K. CITIZENS

HM Customs and Excise (✉ Dorset House, Stamford St., London SE1 9NG, ☎ 0171/202–4227) can answer questions about U.K.

customs regulations and publishes a free pamphlet, **"A Guide for Travellers,"** detailing standard procedures and import rules.

COMPLAINTS

To register complaints under the provisions of the Americans with Disabilities Act, contact the U.S. Department of Justice's **Disability Rights Section** (✉ Box 66738, Washington, DC 20035, ☎ 202/514–0301 or 800/514–0301, FAX 202/307–1198, TTY 202/514–0383 or 800/514–0383). For airline-related problems, contact the U.S. Department of Transportation's **Aviation Consumer Protection Division** (☞ Air Travel, *above*). For complaints about surface transportation, contact the Department of Transportation's **Civil Rights Office** (✉ 400 7th St., SW, Room 10215, Washington DC, 20590 ☎ 202/366–4648).

ORGANIZATIONS

Travelers with Hearing Impairments➤ The **American Academy of Otolaryngology** (✉ 1 Prince St., Alexandria, VA 22314, ☎ 703/836–4444, FAX 703/683–5100, TTY 703/519–1585) publishes a brochure, "Travel Tips for Hearing Impaired People."

Travelers with Mobility Problems➤ Contact the **Information Center for Individuals with Disabilities** (✉ Box 256, Boston, MA 02117, ☎ 617/450–9888; in MA,

800/462–5015; TTY 617/424–6855); **Mobility International USA** (✉ Box 10767, Eugene, OR 97440, ☎ and TTY 541/343–1284, FAX 541/343–6812), the U.S. branch of a Belgium-based organization (☞ *below*) with affiliates in 30 countries; **MossRehab Hospital Travel Information Service** (☎ 215/456–9600, TTY 215/456–9602), a telephone information resource for travelers with physical disabilities; the **Society for the Advancement of Travel for the Handicapped** (✉ 347 5th Ave., Suite 610, New York, NY 10016, ☎ 212/447–7284, FAX 212/725–8253; membership $45); and **Travelin' Talk** (✉ Box 3534, Clarksville, TN 37043, ☎ 615/552–6670, FAX 615/552–1182) which provides local contacts worldwide for travelers with disabilities.

TRAVELERS WITH VISION IMPAIRMENTS➤ Contact the **American Council of the Blind** (✉ 1155 15th St. NW, Suite 720, Washington, DC 20005, ☎ 202/467–5081, FAX 202/467–5085) for a list of travelers' resources or the **American Foundation for the Blind** (✉ 11 Penn Plaza, Suite 300, New York, NY 10001, ☎ 212/502–7600 or 800/232–5463, TTY 212/502–7662), which provides general advice and publishes "Access to Art" ($19.95), a directory of museums that accommodate travelers with vision impairments.

IN THE U.K.

Contact the **Royal Association for Disabil-**

ity and Rehabilitation (✉ RADAR, 12 City Forum, 250 City Rd., London EC1V 8AF, ☎ 0171/250–3222) or **Mobility International** (✉ rue de Manchester 25, B-1080 Brussels, Belgium, ☎ 00–322–410–6297, FAX 00–322–410–6874), an international travel-information clearinghouse for people with disabilities.

PUBLICATIONS

Several publications for travelers with disabilities are available from the **Consumer Information Center** (✉ Box 100, Pueblo, CO 81009, ☎ 719/948–3334). Call or write for its free catalog of current titles. The Society for the Advancement of Travel for the Handicapped (☞ Organizations, *above*) publishes the quarterly magazine **"Access to Travel"** ($13 for 1-year subscription).

Fodor's **Great American Vacations for Travelers with Disabilities** (available in bookstores, or ☎ 800/533–6478; $18 plus $4 shipping) details accessible attractions, restaurants, and hotels in U.S. destinations. The 500-page **Travelin' Talk Directory** (✉ Box 3534, Clarksville, TN 37043, ☎ 615/552–6670, FAX 615/552–1182; $35) lists people and organizations who help travelers with disabilities. For travel agents worldwide, consult the **Directory of Travel Agencies for the Disabled** (✉ Twin Peaks Press, Box 129, Vancouver, WA 98666, ☎ 360/694–2462 or 800/637–2256, FAX 360/696–3210; $19.95 plus $3 shipping).

The **Smithsonian Institution** (☎ 202/786–2942, TTY 202/357–1729) offers a somewhat out-of-date booklet "Smithsonian Institution: A Guide for Disabled Visitors." **Baltimore/Washington International Airport** (Marketing and Development Office, Box 8766, BWI Airport, MD 21240, ☎ 410/859–7100) publishes the free brochure "BWI Special Services & Access Guide."

TRAVEL AGENCIES & TOUR OPERATORS

The Americans with Disabilities Act requires that all travel firms serve the needs of all travelers. That said, you should note that some agencies and operators specialize in making travel arrangements for individuals and groups with disabilities, among them **Access Adventures** (✉ 206 Chestnut Ridge Rd., Rochester, NY 14624, ☎ 716/889–9096), run by a former physical-rehab counselor.

TRAVELERS WITH MOBILITY PROBLEMS➤ Contact **Hinsdale Travel Service** (✉ 201 E. Ogden Ave., Suite 100, Hinsdale, IL 60521, ☎ 708/325–1335), a travel agency that benefits from the advice of wheelchair traveler Janice Perkins; and **Wheelchair Journeys** (✉ 16979 Redmond Way, Redmond, WA 98052, ☎ 206/885–2210 or 800/313–4751), which can handle arrangements worldwide.

TRAVELERS WITH DEVELOPMENTAL DISABILITIES➤ Contact the nonprofit **New Directions** (✉

5276 Hollister Ave., Suite 207, Santa Barbara, CA 93111, ☎ 805/967–2841) and **Sprout** (✉ 893 Amsterdam Ave., New York, NY 10025, ☎ 212/222–9575), which specializes in custom-designed itineraries for groups but also books vacations for individual travelers with developmental disabilities.

TRAVEL GEAR

The **Magellan's** catalog (☎ 800/962–4943, FAX 805/568–5406), includes a section devoted to products designed for travelers with disabilities.

DISCOUNTS & DEALS

AIRFARES

For the lowest airfares to Washington, call 800/FLY–4–LESS. Also try 800/FLY–ASAP.

CLUBS

Contact **Entertainment Travel Editions** (✉ Box 1068, Trumbull, CT 06611, ☎ 800/445–4137; $28–$53, depending on destination), **Great American Traveler** (✉ Box 27965, Salt Lake City, UT 84127, ☎ 800/548–2812; $49.95 per year), **Moment's Notice Discount Travel Club** (✉ 7301 New Utrecht Ave., Brooklyn, NY 11204, ☎ 718/234–6295; $25 per year, single or family), **Privilege Card** (✉ 3391 Peachtree Rd. NE, Suite 110, Atlanta, GA 30326, ☎ 404/262–0222 or 800/236–9732; $74.95 per year), **Travelers Advantage** (✉ CUC Travel Service, 49 Music Sq. W, Nashville, TN 37203, ☎ 800/548–1116 or 800/648–

4037; $49 per year, single or family), or **Worldwide Discount Travel Club** (✉ 1674 Meridian Ave., Miami Beach, FL 33139, ☎ 305/534–2082; $50 per year for family, $40 single).

HOTEL ROOMS

For discounts on hotel rates, contact the **Hotel Reservations Network** (☎ 800/964–6835) or **Quickbook** (☎ 800/789–9887).

PASSES

See Subway Travel in Smart Travel Tips A to Z, *below.*

STUDENTS

Members of Hostelling International–American Youth Hostels (☞ Students, *below*) are eligible for discounts on car rentals, admissions to attractions, and other selected travel expenses.

PUBLICATIONS

Consult *The Frugal Globetrotter,* by Bruce Northam (✉ Fulcrum Publishing, 350 Indiana St., Suite 350, Golden, CO 80401, ☎ 800/992–2908; $16.95 plus $4 shipping). For publications that tell how to find the lowest prices on plane tickets, *see* Air Travel, *above.*

E

EMERGENCIES

Dial 911 for **police, fire,** or **ambulance** in an emergency.

DOCTOR

Prologue (☎ 202/362–8677) is a referral service that locates doctors, dentists, and urgent-care clinics in the greater Washington area. The hospital

closest to downtown is **George Washington University Hospital** (901 23rd St. NW, ☎ 202/994–3211, emergencies only).

DENTIST

The **D.C. Dental Society** (☎ 202/547–7615) operates a referral line weekdays 8–4.

24-HOUR PHARMACY

CVS Pharmacy operates 24-hour pharmacies at 14th Street and Thomas Circle NW (☎ 202/628–0720) and at 7 Dupont Circle NW (☎ 202/785–1466).

G

GAY & LESBIAN TRAVEL

ORGANIZATIONS

The **International Gay Travel Association** (✉ Box 4974, Key West, FL 33041, ☎ 800/448–8550, FAX 305/296–6633), a consortium of more than 1,000 travel companies, can supply names of gay-friendly travel agents, tour operators, and accommodations.

PUBLICATIONS

The premier international travel magazine for gays and lesbians is **Our World** (✉ 1104 N. Nova Rd., Suite 251, Daytona Beach, FL 32117, ☎ 904/441–5367, FAX 904/441–5604; $35 for 10 issues). The 16-page monthly **"Out & About"** (☎ 212/645–6922 or 800/929–2268, FAX 800/929–2215; $49 for 10 issues and quarterly calendar) covers gay-friendly resorts, hotels, cruise lines, and airlines.

TOUR OPERATORS

Toto Tours (⊠ 1326 W. Albion Ave., Suite 3W, Chicago, IL 60626, ☎ 312/274–8686 or 800/565–1241, FAX 312/274–8695) offers group tours to worldwide destinations.

TRAVEL AGENCIES

The largest agencies serving gay travelers are **Advance Travel** (⊠ 10700 Northwest Fwy., Suite 160, Houston, TX 77092, ☎ 713/682–2002 or 800/292–0500), **Islanders/Kennedy Travel** (⊠ 183 W. 10th St., New York, NY 10014, ☎ 212/242–3222 or 800/988–1181), **Now Voyager** (⊠ 4406 18th St., San Francisco, CA 94114, ☎ 415/626–1169 or 800/255–6951), and **Yellowbrick Road** (⊠ 1500 W. Balmoral Ave., Chicago, IL 60640, ☎ 312/561–1800 or 800/642–2488). **Skylink Women's Travel** (⊠ 2460 W. 3rd St., Suite 215, Santa Rosa, CA 95401, ☎ 707/570–0105 or 800/225–5759) serves lesbian travelers.

I
INSURANCE

IN CANADA

Contact **Mutual of Omaha** (⊠ Travel Division, 500 University Ave., Toronto, Ontario M5G 1V8, ☎ 800/465–0267 (in Canada) or 416/598–4083).

IN THE U.S.

Travel insurance covering baggage, health, and trip cancellation or interruptions is available from **Access America** (⊠ 6600 W. Broad St., Richmond, VA 23230, ☎ 804/285–3300 or 800/334–7525), **Carefree Travel Insurance** (⊠ Box 9366, 100 Garden City Plaza, Garden City, NY 11530, ☎ 516/294–0220 or 800/323–3149), **Near Travel Services** (⊠ Box 1339, Calumet City, IL 60409, ☎ 708/868–6700 or 800/654–6700), **Tele-Trip** (⊠ Mutual of Omaha Plaza, Box 31716, Omaha, NE 68131, ☎ 800/228–9792), **Travel Guard International** (⊠ 1145 Clark St., Stevens Point, WI 54481, ☎ 715/345–0505 or 800/826–1300), **Travel Insured International** (⊠ Box 280568, East Hartford, CT 06128, ☎ 203/528–7663 or 800/243–3174), and **Wallach & Company** (⊠ 107 W. Federal St., Box 480, Middleburg, VA 22117, ☎ 540/687–3166 or 800/237–6615).

IN THE U.K.

The **Association of British Insurers** (⊠ 51 Gresham St., London EC2V 7HQ, ☎ 0171/600–3333) gives advice by phone and publishes the free pamphlet **"Holiday Insurance and Motoring Abroad,"** which sets out typical policy provisions and costs.

L
LODGING

For information on hotel consolidators, *see* Discounts, *above*.

APARTMENT & VILLA RENTAL

Among the companies to contact is **Rent-a-Home International** (⊠ 7200 34th Ave. NW, Seattle, WA 98117, ☎ 206/789–9377 or 800/488–7368, FAX 206/789–9379, rentahomeinternational£msn.com). Members of the travel club **Hideaways International** (⊠ 767 Islington St., Portsmouth, NH 03801, ☎ 603/430–4433 or 800/843–4433, FAX 603/430–4444, info@hideaways.com; $99 per year) receive two annual guides plus quarterly newsletters and arrange rentals among themselves.

HOME EXCHANGE

Some of the principal clearinghouses are **HomeLink International/Vacation Exchange Club** (⊠ Box 650, Key West, FL 33041, ☎ 305/294–1448 or 800/638–3841, FAX 305/294–1148; $78 per year), which sends members five annual directories, with a listing in one, plus updates; **Intervac International** (⊠ Box 590504, San Francisco, CA 94159, ☎ 415/435–3497, FAX 415/435–7440; $65 per year), which publishes four annual directories.

M
MONEY

ATMS

For specific **Cirrus** locations in the United States and Canada, call 800/424–7787. For U.S. **Plus** locations, call 800/843–7587 and enter the area code and first three digits of the number from which you're calling (or of the calling area in which you want to locate an ATM).

N

NATIONAL MONUMENTS & BATTLEFIELDS

While there are no national parks in the Washington vicinity, national monuments and battlefields abound. A variety of passes is available for senior citizens, travelers with disabilities, and frequent visitors. The passes can be purchased at any park that charges admission or obtained by mail from the **National Park Service** (✉ Dept. of the Interior, Washington, DC 20240).

P

PACKING

For strategies on packing light, get a copy of *The Packing Book,* by Judith Gilford (✉ Ten Speed Press, Box 7123, Berkeley, CA 94707, ☎ 510/559–1600 or 800/841–2665, FAX 510/524–4588; $7.95 plus $3.50 shipping).

PASSPORTS & VISAS

U.K. CITIZENS

For fees, documentation requirements, and to request an emergency passport, call the **London Passport Office** (☎ 0990/210410). For U.S. visa information, call the **U.S. Embassy Visa Information Line** (☎ 01891/200–290; calls cost 49p per minute or 39p per minute cheap rate) or send a self-addressed, stamped envelope to the **U.S. Embassy Visa Branch** (✉ 5 Upper Grosvenor St., London W1A 2JB). If you live in Northern Ireland, write to the **U.S.**

Consulate General (✉ Queen's House, Queen St., Belfast BTI 6EO).

PHOTO HELP

The **Kodak Information Center** (☎ 800/242–2424) answers consumer questions about film and photography. The *Kodak Guide to Shooting Great Travel Pictures* (available in bookstores; or contact Fodor's Travel Publications, ☎ 800/533–6478; $16.50 plus $4 shipping) explains how to take expert travel photographs.

S

SAFETY

"Trouble-Free Travel," from the AAA, is a booklet of tips for protecting yourself and your belongings when away from home. Send a stamped, self-addressed, legal-size envelope to Trouble-Free Travel (✉ Mail Stop 75, 1000 AAA Dr., Heathrow, FL 32746).

SENIOR CITIZENS

EDUCATIONAL TRAVEL

The nonprofit **Elderhostel** (✉ 75 Federal St., 3rd Floor, Boston, MA 02110, ☎ 617/426–7788), for people 55 and older, has offered inexpensive study programs since 1975. Courses cover everything from marine science to Greek mythology and cowboy poetry. Fees for programs in the United States and Canada, which usually last one week, run about $300, not including transportation.

ORGANIZATIONS

Contact the **American Association of Retired**

Persons (✉ AARP, 601 E St. NW, Washington, DC 20049, ☎ 202/434–2277; annual dues $8 per person or couple). Its Purchase Privilege Program secures discounts for members on lodging, car rentals, and sightseeing, and the AARP Motoring Plan (☎ 800/334–3300) furnishes domestic triprouting information and emergency road-service aid for an annual fee of $39.95 ($59.95 for a premium version). Senior citizen travelers can also join the AAA for emergency road service and other travel benefits (☞ Discounts & Deals *in* Smart Travel Tips A to Z).

Additional sources for discounts on lodgings, car rentals, and other travel expenses, as well as helpful magazines and newsletters, are the **National Council of Senior Citizens** (✉ 1331 F St. NW, Washington, DC 20004, ☎ 202/347–8800; annual membership $12) and Sears's **Mature Outlook** (✉ Box 10448, Des Moines, IA 50306, ☎ 800/336–6330; annual membership $14.95).

SIGHTSEEING

ORIENTATION TOURS

Tourmobile buses (☎ 202/554–7950 or 202/554–5100), authorized by the National Park Service, stop at 18 historic sights between the Capitol and Arlington National Cemetery; the route includes the White House and the museums on the Mall. Tickets are $10 for adults, $5 for children 3–11.

Old Town Trolley Tours (☎ 301/985–3021), orange-and-green motorized trolleys, take in the main downtown sights and also foray into Georgetown and the upper northwest, stopping at out-of-the-way attractions such as Washington National Cathedral. Tickets are $16 for adults, $8 for children 3–12, free for children under three.

BOAT TOURS

D.C. Ducks (1323 Pennsylvania Ave. NW, ☎ 202/966–3825) offers 90-minute tours in their converted World War II amphibious vehicles. After an hour-long road tour of prominent sights, the tour moves from land to water, as the vehicle is piloted into the waters of the Potomac for a 30-minute boat's-eye view of the city. Tours run continuously from 10 AM to 4 PM from March through November. Prices are $16 adults, $14 senior citizens, $8 ages 12 and younger.

The enclosed boat **The Dandy** (Prince St., between Duke and King Sts., Alexandria, VA, ☎ 703/683–6076 or 703/683–6090) cruises up the Potomac past the Lincoln Memorial to the Kennedy Center and Georgetown. Lunch cruises board weekdays starting at 10:30 AM and weekends starting at 11:30 AM. Dinner cruises board Monday–Thursday at 6 PM, Friday at 7:30 PM, and Sunday at 7:15 PM. A $21 "midnight cruise" boards at 11:30 PM April–October at Washington Harbour in Georgetown or in

Alexandria. Prices are $26–$30 for lunch and $48–$56 for dinner.

The **Spirit of Washington** (Pier 4, 6th and Water Sts. SW, ☎ 202/554–8000), offers lunch cruises Tuesday–Saturday at 11:30 AM and a Sunday brunch cruise at 1. Evening cruises board at 6:30 PM and include dinner and a floor show. Adult "Moonlight Party" cruises board Friday and Saturday at 11:15 PM. Prices range from $21 per person for the moonlight cruise to $55 for dinner on Friday or Saturday night. A sister ship, the **Potomac Spirit**, sails to Mount Vernon, mid-March–October, Tuesday–Sunday. During peak tourist season (mid-June–August), boats depart at 9 AM and 2 PM. From mid-March through mid-June and September through October, boats leave at 9 AM only. Prices are $22 adults, $19.75 senior citizens, $13.25 children 6–12.

BUS TOURS

All About Town, Inc. (519 6th St. NW, ☎ 202/393–3696) has half-day, all-day, two-day, and twilight bus tours that drive by some sights (e.g., memorials, museums, government buildings) and stop at others. Tours leave from the company's office at 7:45 AM March–September and at 8:15 AM October–February. An all-day tour costs $30 for adults, $15 for children.

Gray Line Tours (☎ 301/386–8300) has a four-hour tour of Washington, Embassy Row, and Arlington National

Cemetery that leaves Union Station at 8:30 AM and 2 PM (at 2 PM only November–March; adults $22, children 3–11 $11); tours of Mount Vernon and Alexandria depart at 8:30 AM (adults $20, children $10). An all-day trip combining both tours leaves at 8:30 AM (adults $36, children $18).

PERSONAL GUIDES

Personal tour services include **Guide Service of Washington** (733 15th St. NW, Woodward Bldg., Suite 1040, Washington, DC 20005, ☎ 202/628–2842); **A Tour de Force** (Box 2782, Washington, DC 20013, ☎ 703/525–2948), and **Guide Post, Inc.** (11141 Georgia Ave., Suite A-8, Wheaton, MD 20902, ☎ 301/946–7949). **Sunny Odem** (2530D South Walter Reed Dr., Arlington, VA 22206, ☎ 703/379–1633) offers custom photography tours.

SPECIAL-INTEREST TOURS

Special tours of government buildings—including the Archives, the Capitol, the FBI Building, the Supreme Court, and the White House—can be arranged through your representative's or senator's office. Limited numbers of these so-called VIP tickets are available, so plan up to six months in advance of your trip. With these special passes, your tour will often take you through rooms not normally open to the public.

Government buildings and offices that have

regularly scheduled tours include: The **Government Printing Office** (H and North Capitol Sts. NW, ☎ 202/512–1995), which offers free tours Tuesday–Thursday at 10 AM; the **Old Executive Office Building** (Pennsylvania Ave. and 17th St. NW, ☎ 202/395–5895), which is open for tours Saturday 9–noon; and the **Naval Observatory** (34th St. and Massachusetts Ave. NW, ☎ 202/653–1507 or 202/653–1541 for group reservations), which offers tours every Monday night, except on Federal holidays. In addition, tours of the opulent 18th-and early-19th-century **State Department Diplomatic Reception Rooms** (23rd and C Sts. NW, ☎ 202/647–3241) are given weekdays at 9:30, 10:30, and 2:45; the **Voice of America** (330 Independence Ave. SW, ☎ 202/619–3919) offers free 45-minute tours Tuesday–Thursday at 10:40, 1:40, and 2:40; and the **Washington, D.C., Post Office** (Brentwood Rd. NE between Rhode Island and New York Aves., ☎ 202/636–1200) has free tours weekdays between 9 and 4, and does not admit children under 7.

Reservations are required for tours of all of these sites except the Naval Observatory, which admits the first 90 people in line at the observatory's south gate across from the New Zealand Embassy. It's wise to make your reservations a few weeks before your visit.

The Washington Post (1150 15th St. NW, ☎ 202/334–7969) offers free 50-minute guided tours for ages 11 and up on Monday from 10 to 3. Make reservations well in advance of your trip.

Every second Saturday in May, a half-dozen embassies in Washington open their doors as stops on a self-guided **Goodwill Embassy Tour** (☎ 202/636–4225). The cost is $25, which includes refreshments, a tour booklet, and free shuttle bus transportation between embassies.

Scandal Tours (☎ 800/758–8687) offers a 90-minute tour of Washington's seamier locales. Tours leave from the Pavilion at the Old Post Office Building on Saturday at 1. The cost is $27 per person, and reservations are required.

WALKING TOURS

The **Black History National Recreation Trail** links a group of sights within historic neighborhoods illustrating aspects of African-American history in Washington, from slavery days to the New Deal. A brochure outlining the trail is available from the National Park Service (1100 Ohio Dr. SW, Washington, DC 20242, ☎ 202/619–7222).

The National Building Museum (☎ 202/272–2448) sponsors several architecture tours including the **"Construction Watch Tour"** ($7), which accompanies architects and construction-project managers to buildings in various stages of completion, and **"Site Seeing"** tours

($60 including bus transportation and a boxed lunch), which are led by architectural historians and visit various Washington neighborhoods and well-known monuments, public buildings, and houses.

The **Smithsonian Resident Associate Program** (☎ 202/357–3030) routinely offers guided walks and bus tours of neighborhoods in Washington and communities outside the city. Many tours are themed and include sights that illustrate such things as Art Deco influences, African-American architecture, or railroad history.

The **D.C. Foot Tour** (Box 9001, Alexandria, VA 22304, ☎ 703/461–7364) is a walking tour of major historic sites.

Capital Entertainment Services (3629 18th St. NE, Washington, DC 20018, ☎ 202/636–9203) offers African-American history tours.

GROUPS

A major tour operator specializing in student travel is **Contiki Holidays** (✉ 300 Plaza Alicante, Suite 900, Garden Grove, CA 92640, ☎ 714/740–0808 or 800/266–8454) .

HOSTELING

In the United States, contact **Hostelling International–American Youth Hostels** (✉ 733 15th St. NW, Suite 840, Washington, DC 20005, ☎ 202/783–6161 for reservations worldwide or 800/444–6111 for reservations at U.S. hostels using a

credit card, FAX 202/
783–6171); in Canada,
**Hostelling Interna-
tional–Canada** (✉ 205
Catherine St., Suite 400,
Ottawa, Ontario K2P
1C3, ☎ 613/237–
7884); and in the
United Kingdom, the
**Youth Hostel Association
of England and Wales**
(✉ Trevelyan House,
8 St. Stephen's Hill, St.
Albans, Hertfordshire
AL1 2DY, ☎ 01727/
855215 or 01727/
845047). Membership
(in the U.S., $25; in
Canada, C$26.75; in
the U.K., £9.30) gives
you access to 5,000
hostels in 77 countries
that charge $5–$40 per
person per night.

ORGANIZATIONS

A major contact is the
**Council on International
Educational Exchange**
(✉ mail orders only:
CIEE, 205 E. 42nd St.,
16th Floor, New York,
NY 10017, ☎ 212/
822–2600, info@ciee.
org). The **Educational
Travel Centre** (✉ 438
N. Frances St., Madi-
son, WI 53703, ☎ 608/
256–5551 or 800/747–
5551, FAX 608/256–
2042) offers rail passes
and low-cost airline
tickets, mostly for
flights that depart from
Chicago.

In Canada, also contact
Travel Cuts (✉ 187
College St., Toronto,
Ontario M5T 1P7,
☎ 416/979–2406 or
800/667–2887).

SUBWAY TRAVEL

For schedule and route
information, contact the
**Washington Metropoli-
tan Area Transit Author-
ity** (WMATA; ☎ 202/
637–7000, TTY 202/
638–3780; open daily 6
AM–11:30 PM).

T

TAXIS

Two major companies
serving the District are
Capitol Cab (☎ 202/
546–2400) and **Dia-
mond Cab** (☎ 202/
387–6200). *See* Taxis
in Smart Travel Tips A
to Z for information on
rates.

TOUR OPERATORS

Among the companies
that sell tours and
packages to Washing-
ton, the following are
nationally known, have
a proven reputation,
and offer plenty of
options.

GROUP TOURS

DELUXE➤ **Globus** (✉
5301 S. Federal Circle,
Littleton, CO 80123,
☎ 303/797–2800 or
800/221–0090, FAX 303/
795–0962), **Maupintour**
(✉ Box 807, 1515 St.
Andrews Dr., Lawrence,
KS 66047, ☎ 913/
843–1211 or 800/255–
4266, FAX 913/843–
8351), and **Tauck Tours**
(✉ Box 5027, 276 Post
Rd. W, Westport, CT
06881, ☎ 203/226–
6911 or 800/468–2825,
FAX 203/221–6828).

FIRST-CLASS➤ **Brendan
Tours** (✉ 15137 Califa
St., Van Nuys, CA
91411, ☎ 818/785–
9696 or 800/421–8446,
FAX 818/902–9876),
Collette Tours (✉ 162
Middle St., Pawtucket,
RI 02860, ☎ 401/728–
3805 or 800/832–4656,
FAX 401/728–1380),
Gadabout Tours (✉ 700
E. Tahquitz Canyon
Way, Palm Springs, CA
92262, ☎ 619/325–
5556 or 800/952–
5068), and **Mayflower
Tours** (✉ Box 490, 1225
Warren Ave., Downers
Grove, IL 60515, ☎

708/960–3793 or 800/
323–7604, FAX 708/
960–3575).

BUDGET➤ **Cosmos**
(☞ Globus, *above*).

PACKAGES

Independent packages
are available from major
tour operators and
airlines. Contact **Adventure Vacations** (✉ 10612
Beaver Dam Rd., Hunt
Valley, MD 21030-
2205, ☎ 410/785–3500
or 800/638–9040, FAX
410/584–2771), **Certi-
fied Vacations** (✉ Box
1525, Fort Lauderdale,
FL 33302, ☎ 954/
522–1440 or 800/233–
7260), **Continental
Vacations** (☎ 800/634–
5555), **Delta Dream
Vacations** (☎ 800/872–
7786), **SuperCities** (139
Main St., Cambridge,
MA 02142, ☎ 617/
621–0099 or 800/333–
1234), **United Vacations**
(☎ 800/328–6877), and
USAir Vacations (☎ 800/
455–0123). **Funjet Va-
cations,** based in Mil-
waukee, Wisconsin, and
Gogo Tours, based in
Ramsey, New Jersey, sell
packages to Washing-
ton, D.C., only through
travel agents. For rail
packages that combine
air, hotel, and tour
options, contact **Am-
trak's Great American
Vacations** (☎ 800/321–
8684).

Also contact **Amtrak**'s
Great American Vaca-
tions (☎ 800/321–
8684).

THEME TRIPS

LEARNING➤ **Smithso-
nian Study Tours and
Seminars** (✉ 1100
Jefferson Dr. SW, Room
3045, MRC 702, Wash-
ington, DC 20560,
☎ 202/357–4700, FAX
202/633–9250) offers

art, culture, and history seminars.

PERFORMING ARTS➤
Dailey-Thorp Travel (✉ 330 W. 58th St., #610, New York, NY 10019-1817, ☎ 212/307-1555 or 800/998-4677, FAX 212/974-1420) specializes in classical music and opera programs.

ORGANIZATIONS

The **National Tour Association** (✉ NTA, 546 E. Main St., Lexington, KY 40508, ☎ 606/226-4444 or 800/755-8687) and the **United States Tour Operators Association** (✉ USTOA, 211 E. 51st St., Suite 12B, New York, NY 10022, ☎ 212/750-7371) can provide lists of members and information on booking tours.

PUBLICATIONS

Contact the USTOA (☞ Organizations, *above*) for its **"Smart Traveler's Planning Kit."** Pamphlets in the kit include the "Worldwide Tour and Vacation Package Finder," "How to Select a Tour or Vacation Package," and information on the organization's consumer protection plan. Also get copy of the Better Business Bureau's **"Tips on Travel Packages"** (✉ Publication 24-195, 4200 Wilson Blvd., Arlington, VA 22203; $2). The National Tour Association will send you **"On Tour,"** a listing of its member operators, and a personalized package of information on group travel in North America.

TRAIN TRAVEL

More than 80 trains a day arrive at Washing-ton, D.C.'s **Union Station** on Capitol Hill (50 Massachusetts Ave. NE, ☎ 202/484-7540 or 800/872-7245). Also *see* Airport Transfers, *above*.

TRAVEL GEAR

For travel apparel, appliances, personal-care items, and other travel necessities, get a free catalog from **Magellan's** (☎ 800/962-4943, FAX 805/568-5406), **Orvis Travel** (☎ 800/541-3541, FAX 703/343-7053), or **TravelSmith** (☎ 800/950-1600, FAX 415/455-0554).

TRAVEL AGENCIES

For names of reputable agencies in your area, contact the **American Society of Travel Agents** (✉ ASTA, 1101 King St., Suite 200, Alexandria, VA 22314, ☎ 703/739-2782), the **Association of Canadian Travel Agents** (✉ Suite 201, 1729 Bank St., Ottawa, Ontario K1V 7Z5, ☎ 613/521-0474, FAX 613/521-0805) or the **Association of British Travel Agents** (✉ 55-57 Newman St., London W1P 4AH, ☎ 0171/637-2444, FAX 0171/637-0713).

V

VISITOR

INFORMATION

Contact the **Washington, D.C., Convention and Visitors Association** (1212 New York Ave. NW, 6th floor, Washington, DC 20005, ☎ 202/789-7000, FAX 202/789-7037), the **D.C. Committee to Promote Washington** (1212 New York Ave. NW, 2nd Floor, Washington, DC 20005, ☎ 800/422-8644), and the **National Park Service** (Office of Public Affairs, National Capital Region, 1100 Ohio Dr. SW, Washington, DC 20242, ☎ 202/619-7222, FAX 202/619-7302).

The **White House Visitor Center,** in Baldridge Hall in the Dept. of Commerce at 1450 Pennsylvania Ave. NW, has information on White House tours and special events. **National Park Service information kiosks** on the Mall, near the White House, next to the Vietnam Veterans Memorial, and at several other locations throughout the city can provide helpful information. **Dial-A-Park** (☎ 202/619-7275) is a recording of events at Park Service attractions in and around Washington. **Dial-A-Museum** (☎ 202/357-2020) is a recording of exhibits and special offerings at Smithsonian Institution museums.

If you're planning to visit sites in the surrounding areas, contact the **Maryland Department of Economic and Employment/Tourism Development** (✉ Office of Tourist Development, 217 E. Redwood St., 9th floor, Baltimore, MD 21202, ☎ 410/767-3400, FAX 410/333-6643) and the **Virginia Division of Tourism** (✉ 901 East Byrd St., Richmond, VA 23219, ☎ 804/786-4484 or 804/847-4882, FAX 804/786-1919). The **Virginia-Maryland Travel Center** (✉ 1629 K St. NW, ☎ 202/659-5523, FAX 202/659-8646) can book accommodations at

Virginia B&Bs (☎ 800/ 934–9184).

In the United Kingdom, also contact (☎ 0181/ 392–9187, FAX 0181/ 392–1318).

WEATHER

For current conditions and forecasts, plus the local time and helpful travel tips, call the **Weather Channel Connection** (☎ 900/932– 8437; 95¢ per minute) from a Touch-Tone phone.

The *International Traveler's Weather Guide* (✉ Weather Press, Box 660606, Sacramento, CA 95866, ☎ 916/ 974–0201 or 800/972– 0201; $10.95 includes shipping), written by two meteorologists, provides month-by-month information on temperature, humidity, and precipitation in more than 175 cities worldwide.

SMART TRAVEL TIPS A TO Z

Basic Information on Traveling in Washington and Savvy Tips to Make Your Trip a Breeze

THE GOLD GUIDE / SMART TRAVEL TIPS

A

AIR TRAVEL

If time is an issue, **always look for nonstop flights,** which require no change of plane. If possible, **avoid connecting flights,** which stop at least once and can involve a change of plane, even though the flight number remains the same; if the first leg is late, the second waits.

For better service, **fly smaller or regional carriers,** which often have higher passenger satisfaction ratings. Sometimes they have such in-flight amenities as leather seats or greater legroom and they often have better food.

CUTTING COSTS

The Sunday travel section of most newspapers is a good place to look for deals.

MAJOR AIRLINES➤ The least-expensive airfares from the major airlines are priced for round-trip travel and are subject to restrictions. Usually, you must **book in advance and buy the ticket within 24 hours** to get cheaper fares, and you may have to **stay over a Saturday night.** The lowest fare is subject to availability, and only a small percentage of the plane's total seats is sold at that price. It's smart to **call a number of airlines, and when you are quoted a good price, book it on**

the spot—the same fare may not be available on the same flight the next day. Airlines generally allow you to change your return date for a $25 to $50 fee. If you don't use your ticket, you can apply the cost toward the purchase of a new ticket, again for a small charge. However, most low-fare tickets are nonrefundable. To get the lowest airfare, **check different routings.** If your destination has more than one gateway, **compare prices to different airports.**

FROM THE U.K.➤ To save money on flights, **look into an APEX or Super-PEX ticket.** APEX tickets must be booked in advance and have certain restrictions. Super-PEX tickets can be purchased right at the airport.

ALOFT

AIRLINE FOOD➤ If you hate airline food, **ask for special meals when booking.** These can be vegetarian, low-cholesterol, or kosher, for example; commonly prepared to order in smaller quantities than standard fare, they can be tastier.

SMOKING➤ Smoking is not allowed on flights of six hours or less within the continental United States. Smoking is also prohibited on flights within Canada. For U.S. flights longer than six hours or international flights, **contact your carrier regarding**

their smoking policy. Some carriers have prohibited smoking throughout their system; others allow smoking only on certain routes or even certain departures of that route.

B

BUS TRAVEL

WMATA's red, white, and blue Metrobuses crisscross the city and nearby suburbs, with some routes running 24 hours a day. All bus rides within the District are $1.10. Free transfers, good for 1½ to 2 hours, are available on buses and in Metro stations. Bus-to-bus transfers are accepted at designated Metrobus transfer points. Rail-to-bus transfers must be picked up before boarding the train. There may be a transfer charge when boarding the bus. There are no bus-to-rail transfers.

BUSINESS HOURS

Banks are generally open weekdays 9–3. On Friday many stay open until 5 or close at 2 and open again from 4 to 6. Very few banks have lobby hours on Saturday.

Museums are usually open daily 10–5:30; some have extended hours on Thursday. Many private museums are closed Monday or Tuesday, and some museums in government office buildings are closed weekends. The Smithsonian often sets extended spring and summer hours for some of its museums (☎ 202/357–2700 for details).

Stores are generally open Monday–Saturday 10–7 (or 8). Some have extended hours on Thursday and many—especially those in shopping or tourist areas such as Georgetown—open Sunday anywhere from 10 to noon and close at 5 or 6.

C

CAMERAS, CAMCORDERS, & COMPUTERS

IN TRANSIT

Always **keep your film, tape, or disks out of the sun;** never put these on the dashboard of a car. Carry an extra supply of batteries, and **be prepared to turn on your camera, camcorder, or laptop computer for security personnel** to prove that it's real.

X-RAYS

Always **ask for hand inspection at security.** Such requests are virtually always honored at U.S. airports. Photographic film becomes clouded after successive exposure to airport x-ray machines. Videotape and computer disks are not damaged by X-rays, but **keep your tapes and disks away from metal detectors.**

CAR RENTAL

CUTTING COSTS

To get the best deal, **book through a travel agent who is willing to shop around.** When pricing cars, **ask where**

the rental lot is located. Some off-airport locations offer lower rates—even though their lots are only minutes away from the terminal via complimentary shuttle. You also may want to **price local car-rental companies,** whose rates may be lower still, although service and maintenance standards may not be as high as those of a national firm. Ask your agent to **look for fly-drive packages,** which also save you money, and **ask if local taxes are included** in the rental or fly-drive price. These can be as high as 20% in some destinations. Don't forget to find out about required deposits, cancellation penalties, drop-off charges, and the cost of any required insurance coverage.

Also **ask your travel agent about a company's customer-service record.** How has it responded to late plane arrivals and vehicle mishaps? Are there often lines at the rental counter, and—if you're traveling during a holiday period—does a confirmed reservation guarantee you a car?

INSURANCE

When driving a rented car, you are generally responsible for any damage to or loss of the rental vehicle, as well as any property damage or personal injury that you cause. Before you rent, **see what coverage you already have** under the terms of your personal auto insurance policy and credit cards.

For about $14 a day, rental companies sell protection, known as a

collision- or loss- damage waiver (CDW or LDW), that eliminates your liability for damage to the car; it's always optional and should never be automatically added to your bill.

In most states, the renter's personal auto insurance or other liability insurance covers damage to third parties. Only when the damage exceeds the renter's own insurance coverage does the car-rental company pay. If you do not have auto insurance or an umbrella insurance policy that covers damage to third parties, purchasing CDW or LDW is highly recommended.

U.K. CITIZENS

In the United States you must be 21 to rent a car; rates may be higher if you're under 25. You'll pay extra for child seats (about $3 per day), compulsory for children under five, and for additional drivers (about $2 per day). To pick up your reserved car you will need the reservation voucher, a passport, a U.K. driver's license, and a travel policy that covers each driver.

SURCHARGES

Before you pick up a car in one city and leave it in another, **ask about drop-off charges or one-way service fees,** which can be substantial. Note, too, that some rental agencies charge extra if you return the car before the time specified on your contract. To avoid a hefty refueling fee, **fill the tank just before you turn in the car—**but be aware that gas stations near the rental outlet may overcharge.

CHILDREN & TRAVEL

When traveling with children, **plan ahead** and **involve your youngsters** as you outline your trip. When packing, **include a supply of things to keep them busy** en route (☞ Children & Travel *in* Important Contacts A to Z). On sightseeing days, try to **schedule activities of special interest to your children,** like a trip to a zoo or a playground. If you **plan your itinerary around seasonal festivals,** you'll never lack for things to do. In addition, **check local newspapers for special events** mounted by public libraries, museums, and parks.

BABY-SITTING

For recommended local sitters, **check with your hotel desk.**

DRIVING

If you are renting a car, don't forget to **arrange for a car seat when you reserve.** Sometimes they're free.

FLYING

As a general rule, infants under two not occupying a seat fly for free. If your children are two or older **ask about special children's fares.** Age limits for these fares vary among carriers. Rules also vary regarding unaccompanied minors, so again, check with your airline.

BAGGAGE➤ In general, the adult baggage allowance applies to children paying half or more of the adult fare.

SAFETY SEATS➤ According to the FAA, it's a good idea to **use safety seats aloft** for children weighing less than 40 pounds. Airline policies vary. U.S. carriers allow FAA-approved models but usually require that you buy a ticket, even if your child would otherwise ride free, since the seats must be strapped into regular seats. However, some airlines may require you to hold your baby during takeoff and landing—defeating the seat's purpose.

FACILITIES➤ When making your reservation, **request for children's meals or freestanding bassinets** if you need them; the latter are available only to those seated at the bulkhead, where there's enough legroom. If you don't need a bassinet, **think twice before requesting bulkhead seats**—the only storage space for in-flight necessities is in inconveniently distant overhead bins.

GAMES

Milton Bradley and Parker Brothers have travel versions of some of their most popular games, including Yahtzee, Trouble, Sorry, and Monopoly. Prices run $5 to $8. Look for them in the travel section of your local toy store.

LODGING

Most hotels allow children under a certain age to stay in their parents' room at no extra charge; others charge them as extra adults. Be sure to **ask about the cutoff age.**

CUSTOMS & DUTIES

To speed your clearance through customs, **keep receipts for all your purchases abroad** and **be ready to show the inspector what you've bought.** If you feel that you've been incorrectly or unfairly charged a duty, you can **appeal assessments in dispute.** First ask to see a supervisor. If you are still unsatisfied, **write to the port director** your point of entry, sending your customs receipt and any other appropriate documentation. The address will be listed on your receipt. If you still don't get satisfaction, you can take your case to customs headquarters in Washington.

IN WASHINGTON

British visitors age 21 or over may import the following into the United States: 200 cigarettes or 50 cigars or 2 kilograms of tobacco; 1 U.S. liter of alcohol; gifts with a total value of $100. Restricted items include meat products, seeds, plants, and fruits. Never carry illegal drugs.

IN CANADA

If you've been out of Canada for at least seven days, you may bring in C$500 worth of goods duty-free. If you've been away for fewer than seven days but for more than 48 hours, the duty-free allowance drops to C$200; if your trip lasts between 24 and 48 hours, the allowance is C$50. You cannot pool allowances with family members. Goods claimed under the

C\$500 exemption may follow you by mail; those claimed under the lesser exemptions must accompany you.

Alcohol and tobacco products may be included in the seven-day and 48-hour exemptions but not in the 24-hour exemption. If you meet the age requirements of the province or territory through which you reenter Canada, you may bring in, duty-free, 1.14 liters (40 imperial ounces) of wine or liquor *or* 24 12-ounce cans or bottles of beer or ale. If you are 16 or older, you may bring in, duty-free, 200 cigarettes, 50 cigars or cigarillos, and 400 tobacco sticks or 400 grams of manufactured tobacco. Alcohol and tobacco must accompany you on your return.

An unlimited number of gifts with a value of up to C\$60 each may be mailed to Canada duty-free. These do not affect your duty-free allowance on your return. Label the package "Unsolicited Gift—Value Under \$60." Alcohol and tobacco are excluded.

IN THE U.K.

From countries outside the EU, including the United States, you may import, duty-free, 200 cigarettes, 100 cigarillos, 50 cigars, or 250 grams of tobacco; 1 liter of spirits or 2 liters of fortified or sparkling wine or liqueurs; 2 liters of still table wine; 60 milliliters of perfume; 250 milliliters of toilet water; plus £136 worth of other goods, including gifts and souvenirs.

D

DISABILITIES & ACCESSIBILITY

Every day Washington becomes more and more every American's city as accessibility continues to improve. The Metro has excellent facilities for visitors with vision and hearing impairments or mobility problems. Virtually all **streets have wide, level sidewalks with curb cuts,** though in Georgetown the brick-paved terrain can be bumpy. Most museums and monuments are accessible to visitors using wheelchairs.

When discussing accessibility with an operator or reservationist, **ask hard questions.** Are there any stairs, inside *or* out? Are there grab bars next to the toilet *and* in the shower/tub? How wide is the doorway to the room? To the bathroom? For the most extensive facilities, meeting the latest legal specifications, **opt for newer accommodations,** which more often have been designed with access in mind. Older properties or ships must usually be retrofitted and may offer more limited facilities as a result. Be sure to **discuss your needs before booking.**

DISCOUNTS & DEALS

You shouldn't have to pay for a discount. In fact, you may already be eligible for all kinds of savings. Here are some time-honored strategies for getting the best deal.

LOOK IN YOUR WALLET

When you **use your credit card to make travel purchases,** you may get free travel-accident insurance, collision damage insurance, medical or legal assistance, depending on the card and bank that issued it. Visa and MasterCard provide one or more of these services, so **get a copy of your card's travel benefits.** If you are a member of the AAA or an oil-company-sponsored road-assistance plan, always **ask hotel or car-rental reservationists for auto-club discounts.** Some clubs offer additional discounts on tours, cruises, or admission to attractions. And don't forget that auto-club membership entitles you to free maps and trip-planning services.

SENIORS CITIZENS & STUDENTS

As a senior-citizen traveler, you may be eligible for special rates, but you should mention your senior-citizen status up front. If you're a students or under 26 can also get discounts, especially if you have an official ID card (☞ Senior-Citizen Discounts *and* Students on the Road, *below*).

DIAL FOR DOLLARS

To save money, **look into "1-800" discount reservations services,** which often have lower rates. These services use their buying power to get a better price on hotels, airline tickets, and sometimes even car rentals. When booking a room, always **call the hotel's local toll-free**

number (if one is available) rather than the central reservations number—you'll often get a better price. Ask the reservationist about special packages or corporate rates, which are usually available even if you're not traveling on business.

JOIN A CLUB?

Discount clubs can be a legitimate source of savings, but you must use the participating hotels and visit the participating attractions in order to realize any benefits. Remember, too, that you have to pay a fee to join, so **determine if you'll save enough to warrant your membership fee.** Before booking with a club, **make sure the hotel or other supplier isn't offering a better deal.**

DRIVING

A car can be a drawback in Washington. Traffic is horrendous, especially at rush hours, and **driving is often confusing,** with many lanes and some entire streets changing direction suddenly at certain times of day.

The traffic lights in Washington sometimes stymie visitors. Most of the lights don't hang down over the middle of the streets but stand at the sides of intersections. Radar detectors are illegal in Virginia and the District.

LAY OF THE LAND

I–95 skirts Washington as part of the Beltway, the six- to eight-lane highway that encircles the city. The eastern half of the Beltway is labeled both I–95 and

I–495; the western half is just I–495. If you are coming from the south, take I–95 to I–395 and cross the 14th Street Bridge to 14th Street in the District. From the north, stay on I–95 south before heading west on Route 50, the John Hanson Highway, which turns into New York Avenue.

I–66 approaches the city from the southwest, but you may not be able to use it during weekday rush hours, when high-occupancy vehicle (HOV) restrictions apply: Cars must carry at least two people from 6:30 AM to 9 AM traveling eastbound inside the Beltway (I–495) and 4 PM to 6:30 PM traveling westbound. If you're traveling at off-peak hours or have enough people in your car to satisfy the rules, you can get downtown by taking I–66 across the Theodore Roosevelt Bridge to Constitution Avenue.

I–270 approaches Washington from the northwest before hitting I–495. To get downtown, take I–495 east to Connecticut Avenue south, toward Chevy Chase.

PARKING

Parking in Washington is an adventure; the **police are quick to tow** away or immobilize with a "boot" any vehicle parked illegally. (If you find you've been towed from a city street, call 202/727–5000.) Since the city's most popular sights are within a short walk of a Metro station anyway, **it's best to leave your car at the hotel.** Touring

by car is a good idea only if you're considering visiting sights in suburban Maryland or Virginia.

Most of the outlying, suburban Metro stations have parking lots, though these fill quickly with city-bound commuters. If you plan to park in one of these lots, arrive early, armed with lots of quarters. Private **parking lots downtown are expensive,** charging as much as $4 an hour and $13 a day. There is free, two-hour parking around the Mall on Jefferson Drive and Madison Drive, though these spots always seem to be filled. You can park free—in some spots all day—in parking areas off of Ohio Drive near the Jefferson Memorial and south of the Lincoln Memorial on Ohio Drive and West Basin Drive in West Potomac Park.

I

INSURANCE

Travel insurance can protect your monetary investment, replace your luggage and its contents, or provide for medical coverage should you fall ill during your trip. Most tour operators, travel agents, and insurance agents sell specialized health-and-accident, flight, trip-cancellation, and luggage insurance as well as comprehensive policies with some or all of these coverages. Comprehensive policies may also reimburse you for delays due to weather—an important consideration if you're traveling during the winter months. Some health-insurance policies do not cover preexisting conditions, but waivers may be available in specific cases. Coverage is sold by the companies listed in Important Contacts A to Z; these companies act as the policy's administrators. The actual insurance is usually underwritten by a well-known name, such as The Travelers or Continental Insurance.

Before you make any purchase, **review your existing health and homeowner's policies** to find out whether they cover expenses incurred while traveling.

BAGGAGE

Airline liability for baggage is limited to $1,250 per person on domestic flights. On international flights, it amounts to $9.07 per pound or $20 per kilogram for checked baggage (roughly $640 per 70-pound bag) and $400 per passenger for unchecked baggage. Insurance for losses exceeding the terms of your airline ticket can be bought directly from the airline at check-in for about $10 per $1,000 of coverage; note that it excludes a rather extensive list of items, shown on your airline ticket.

COMPREHENSIVE

Comprehensive insurance policies include all the coverages described above plus some that may not be available in more specific policies. If you have purchased an expensive vacation, especially one that involves travel abroad, comprehensive insurance is a must; **look for policies that include trip delay insurance,** which will protect you in the event that weather problems cause you to miss your flight, tour, or cruise. A few insurers will also sell you a waiver for preexisting medical conditions. Some of the companies that offer both these features are Access America, Carefree Travel, Travel Insured International, and TravelGuard (☞ Important Contacts A to Z).

FLIGHT

You should **think twice before buying flight insurance.** Often purchased as a last-minute impulse at the airport, it pays a lump sum when a plane crashes, either to a beneficiary if the insured dies or sometimes to a surviving passenger who loses his or her eyesight or a limb. Supplementing the airlines' coverage described in the limits-of-liability paragraphs on your ticket, it's expensive and basically unnecessary. Charging an airline ticket to a major credit card often automatically provides you with coverage that may also extend to travel by bus, train, and ship.

U.K. TRAVELERS

According to the Association of British Insurers, a trade association representing 450 insurance companies, it's wise to **buy extra medical coverage when you visit the United States.** You can buy an annual travel insurance policy valid for most vacations during the year in which it's purchased. If you are pregnant or have a preexisting medical condition make sure you're covered before buying such a policy.

TRIP

Without insurance, you will lose all or most of your money if you cancel your trip regardless of the reason. Especially if your airline ticket, cruise, or package tour is nonrefundable and cannot be changed, it's essential that you **buy trip-cancellation-and-interruption insurance.** When considering how much coverage you need, look for a policy that will cover the cost of your trip plus the nondiscounted price of a one-way airline ticket should you need to return home early. Read the fine print carefully, especially sections that define "family member" and "preexisting medical conditions." Also **consider default or bankruptcy insurance,** which protects you against a supplier's failure to deliver. Be aware, however, that if you buy such a policy from a travel agency, tour operator, airline, or cruise line, it may not cover default by the firm in question.

L

LODGING

APARTMENT & VILLA RENTAL

If you want a home base that's roomy enough for a family and comes with cooking facilities, **consider taking a furnished rental.** This can also save you money, but not always—some rentals are luxury properties (economical only when your party is large). Home-exchange directories list rentals—often second homes owned by prospective house swappers—and some services search for a house or apartment for you (even a castle if that's your fancy) and handle the paperwork. Some send an illustrated catalog; others send photographs only of specific properties, sometimes at a charge; up-front registration fees may apply.

HOME EXCHANGE

If you would like to find a house, an apartment, or some other type of vacation property to exchange for your own while on holiday, **become a member of a home-exchange organization,** which will send you its updated listings of available exchanges for a year, and will include your own listing in at least one of them. Arrangements for the actual exchange are made by the two parties involved, not by the organization.

M
MONEY

ATMS

CASH ADVANCES➤ Before leaving home, **make sure that your credit cards have been programmed for ATM use.**

N
NATIONAL MONUMENTS AND BATTLEFIELDS

If you are a frequent visitor, senior citizen, or traveler with a disability, you can **save money on**

entrance fees to national monuments and battlefields by getting a discount pass. The Golden Eagle Pass can be a good deal if you plan to visit several National Park Service–administered sites during your travels. Priced at $25, it entitles you and your companions to free admission to *all* national parks (although there are none nearby), monuments, and battlefields for a year. It does not cover additional fees such as those for camping or parking. Both the Golden Age Passport, for U.S. citizens or permanent residents 62 or older, and the Golden Access Passport, for travelers with disabilities, entitle holders to free entry to all national parks, monuments, and battlefields plus 50% off fees for the use of all facilities and services except those run by private concessionaires. Both passports are free; you must show proof of age and U.S. citizenship or permanent residency (such as a U.S. passport, driver's license, or birth certificate) or proof of disability. All three passes are available at all national park, monument, and battlefield entrances.

P
PACKING FOR WASHINGTON

Washington is basically informal, although **many restaurants require a jacket and tie.** Area theaters and nightclubs range from the slightly dressy (John F. Kennedy Center) to extremely casual (Wolf Trap Farm Park). For

sightseeing and casual dining, jeans and sneakers are acceptable just about anywhere. In summer, you'll want shorts and light shirts. Even in August, though, you might still want to have a shawl or light jacket for air-conditioned restaurants. Good walking shoes are a must. In January and February, you'll need a heavy coat and snow boots.

Bring an extra pair of eyeglasses or contact lenses in your carry-on luggage, and if you have a health problem, **pack enough medication** to last the trip. It's important that you **don't put prescription drugs or valuables in luggage to be checked,** for it could go astray.

LUGGAGE

Airline baggage allowances depend on the airline, the route, and the class of your ticket; ask in advance. In general, on domestic flights you are entitled to check two bags. A third piece may be brought on board, but it must fit easily under the seat in front of you or in the overhead compartment. In the United States, the FAA gives airlines broad latitude regarding carry-on allowances, and they tend to tailor them to different aircraft and operational conditions. Charges for excess, oversize, or overweight pieces vary.

SAFEGUARDING YOUR LUGGAGE➤ Before leaving home, **itemize your bags' contents** and their worth, and label them with your name, address, and phone number. (If you use your home address, cover it so that potential thieves can't see it readily.) Inside each bag, **pack a copy of your itinerary.** At check-in, **make sure that each bag is correctly tagged** with the destination airport's three-letter code. If your bags arrive damaged— or fail to arrive at all— file a written report with the airline before leaving the airport.

CANADIANS

No passport is necessary to enter the United States.

U.K. CITIZENS

British citizens need a valid passport to enter the United States. If you are staying for fewer than 90 days and traveling on a vacation, with a return or onward ticket, you probably will not need a visa. However, you will need to fill out the Visa Waiver Form, 1-94W, supplied by the airline.

It is advisable that you **leave one photocopy of your passport's data page** with someone at home and keep another with you, separated from your passport, while traveling. If you lose your passport, promptly call the nearest embassy or consulate and the local police; having the data page information can speed replacement.

S

SENIOR-CITIZEN DISCOUNTS

To qualify for age-related discounts,

mention your senior-citizen status up front when booking hotel reservations, not when checking out, and before you're seated in restaurants, not when paying the bill. Note that discounts may be limited to certain menus, days, or hours. When renting a car, **ask about promotional car-rental discounts**—they can net even lower costs than your senior-citizen discount.

STUDENTS ON THE ROAD

To save money, **look into deals available through student-oriented travel agencies.** To qualify, you'll need to have a bona fide student ID card. Members of international student groups are also eligible (☞ Students *in* Important Contacts A to Z).

SUBWAY TRAVEL

The WMATA provides bus and subway service in the District and in the Maryland and Virginia suburbs. The Metro, opened in 1976, is one of the country's cleanest and safest subway systems. Trains run weekdays 5:30 AM–midnight, weekends 8 AM–midnight. During the weekday rush hours (5:30–9:30 AM and 3–8 PM), trains come along every six minutes. At other times and on weekends and holidays, trains run about every 12–15 minutes. The base fare is $1.10; the actual price you pay depends on the time of day and the distance traveled. Children under age five ride free when accompanied by a

paying passenger, but there is a maximum of two children per paying adult.

Buy your ticket at the Farecard machines; they accept coins and crisp $1, $5, $10, or $20 bills. If the machine spits your bill back out at you, try folding and unfolding it before asking a native for help. The Farecard should be inserted into the turnstile to enter the platform. **Make sure you hang onto the card— you'll need it to exit at your destination.**

Some Washingtonians report that the Farecard's magnetic strip interferes with the strips on ATM cards and credit cards, so **keep the cards separated in your pocket or wallet.**

DISCOUNT PASSES

For $5 you can **buy a pass that allows unlimited trips for one day.** It's good all day on weekends, on holidays, and after 9:30 AM on weekdays. Passes are available at Metro Sales Outlets (including the Metro Center station) and at many hotels, banks, and Safeway and Giant grocery stores.

T

TAXIS

Taxis in the District are not metered; they operate instead on a curious zone system. **Before you set off, ask your cab driver how much the fare will be.** The basic single rate for traveling within one zone is $3.20. There is an extra $1.25 charge for each additional passenger and a $1 surcharge during the 4–6:30 PM rush hour. Bulky suitcases are charged at a higher rate, and a $1.50 surcharge is tacked on when you phone for a cab. Maryland and Virginia taxis are metered but are not allowed to take passengers between points in Washington.

Also *see* Airport Transfers *and* Taxis *in* Important Contacts A to Z, *above.*

TELEPHONES

LONG-DISTANCE

The long-distance services of AT&T, MCI, and Sprint make calling home relatively convenient and let you avoid hotel surcharges; typically, you dial an 800 number in the United States.

TOUR OPERATORS

A package or tour to Washington can make your vacation less expensive and more hassle-free. Firms that sell tours and packages reserve airline seats, hotel rooms, and rental cars in bulk and pass some of the savings on to you. In addition, the best operators have local representatives available to help you at your destination.

A GOOD DEAL?

The more your package or tour includes, the better you can predict the ultimate cost of your vacation. Make sure you know exactly what is covered, and **beware of hidden costs.** Are taxes, tips, and service charges included? Transfers and baggage handling? Entertainment and excursions? These can add up.

Most packages and tours are rated deluxe, first-class superior, first class, tourist, or budget. The key difference is usually accommodations. If the package or tour you are considering is priced lower than in your wildest dreams, **be skeptical.** Also, **make sure your travel agent knows the accommodations** and other services. Ask about the hotel's location, room size, beds, and whether it has a pool, room service, or programs for children, if you care about these. Has your agent been there in person or sent others you can contact?

BUYER BEWARE

Each year a number of consumers are stranded or lose their money when operators—even very large ones with excellent reputations—go out of business. To avoid becoming one of them, take the time to **check out the operator**—find out how long the company has been in business and ask several agents about its reputation. Next, **don't book unless the firm has a consumer-protection program.** Members of the USTOA and the NTA are required to set aside funds for the sole purpose of covering your payments and travel arrangements in case of default. Nonmember operators may instead carry insurance; look for the details in the operator's brochure—and for the name of an underwriter with a solid reputation. Note: When it comes to tour operators, **don't trust escrow accounts.** Although there are laws governing those of charter-flight operators, no governmental body prevents tour operators from raiding the till.

Next, **contact your local Better Business Bureau and the attorney general's offices** in both your own state and the operator's; have any complaints been filed? Finally, **pay with a major credit card.** Then you can cancel payment, provided that you can document your complaint. Always **consider trip-cancellation insurance** (☞ Insurance, *above*).

BIG VS. SMALL➤ Operators that handle several hundred thousand travelers per year can use their purchasing power to give you a good price. Their high volume may also indicate financial stability. But some small companies provide more personalized service; because they tend to specialize, they may also be more knowledgeable about a given area.

USING AN AGENT

Travel agents are excellent resources. In fact, large operators accept bookings made only through travel agents. But it's good to **collect brochures from several agencies** because some agents' suggestions may be skewed by promotional relationships with tour and package firms that reward them for volume sales. If you have a special interest, **find an agent with** expertise in that area; ASTA can provide leads in the United States. (Don't rely solely on your agent, though; agents may be unaware of small-niche operators, and some special-interest travel companies only sell direct.)

SINGLE TRAVELERS

Prices are usually quoted per person, based on two sharing a room. If traveling solo, you may be required to pay the full double-occupancy rate. Some operators eliminate this surcharge if you agree to be matched up with a roommate of the same sex, even if one is not found by departure time.

TRAVEL GEAR

Travel catalogs specialize in useful items that can **save space when packing** and make life on the road more convenient. Compact alarm clocks, travel irons, travel wallets, and personal-care kits are among the most common items you'll find.

U

U.S.

GOVERNMENT

The U.S. government can be an excellent source of travel information. Some of this is free and some is available for a nominal charge. When planning your trip, **find out what government materials are available.** For just a couple of dollars, you can get a variety of publications from the Consumer Information Center in Pueblo, Colorado. Free consumer information also is available from individual government agencies, such as the Department of Transportation or the U.S. Customs Service. For specific titles, see the appropriate publications entry in Important Contacts A to Z, *above*.

W

WHEN TO GO

Washington has **two delightful seasons: spring and autumn.** In spring, the city's ornamental fruit trees are budding, and its many gardens are in bloom. By autumn, most of the summer crowds have left and visitors can enjoy the museums, galleries, and timeless monuments in peace. Summers can be uncomfortably hot and humid (local legend has it that Washington was considered a "tropical hardship post" by some European diplomats). Winter witnesses the lighting of the National Christmas Tree and countless historic-house tours, but the weather is often bitter, with a handful of modest snowstorms that somehow bring this Southern city to a standstill. If you're interested in government, visit when Congress is in session. When lawmakers break for recess (at Christmas, Easter, July 4, and other holiday periods), the city seems a little less vibrant.

CLIMATE

What follows are the average daily maximum and minimum temperatures for Washington.

Jan.	47F	8C	May	76F	24C	Sept.	79F	26C
	34	− 1		58	14		61	16
Feb.	47F	8C	June	85F	29C	Oct.	70F	21C
	31	− 1		65	18		52	11
Mar.	56F	13C	July	88F	31C	Nov.	56F	13C
	38	3		70	21		41	5
Apr.	67F	19C	Aug.	86F	30C	Dec.	47F	8C
	47	8		68	20		32	0

1 Destination: Washington, D.C.

AMERICA'S HOMETOWN

To A SURPRISING DEGREE, life in Washington is not that different from life elsewhere in the country. People are born here, grow up here, get jobs here—by no means invariably with the federal government—and go on to have children, who repeat the cycle. Very often, they live out their lives without ever testifying before Congress, being indicted for influence peddling, or attending a state dinner at the White House.

Which is not to say that the federal government does not cast a long shadow over the city. Among Washington's 570,000 inhabitants are an awful lot of lawyers, journalists, and people who include the word "policy" in their job titles. It's just that D.C. is much more of a hometown than most tourists realize.

Just a few blocks away from the monuments and museums on the Mall are residential and business districts whose scale is very human. The houses are a crazy quilt of architectural styles, kept in linear formation by rows of lush trees. On the commercial streets, bookstores and ethnic groceries abound.

Redevelopment has left its mark. Fourteenth Street was once the capital's red-light district. The city was determined to clean up the strip, and to everyone's surprise it succeeded. Nor is much left of the tacky commercial district around Ninth and F streets. Washington's original downtown, it deteriorated when the city's center shifted to the west, to the "new" downtown of Connecticut Avenue and K Street. But the "old" downtown is being rejuvenated. The department stores that once drew crowds with their window displays have been renovated; there are new hotels and office buildings; and as the construction dust clears, the area is looking pretty good.

Many people who come here are worried about crime. Crime is certainly a major problem, as it is in other big cities, but Washington is not nearly as dangerous as its well-publicized homicide rate might lead you to believe. Most visitors have relatively little to fear. The drug-related shootings that have in the past made Washington a murder capital generally take place in remote sections of the city. Unless you go seeking out the drug markets, there isn't much chance you'll get caught in the cross fire of rival drug gangs. Crimes against property are more widespread, but still far from ubiquitous. Unlike New York, Washington is not full of expert pickpockets; nor is it plagued by gold-chain snatchers.

The city's Metro is generally safe, even at night. However, if you have to walk from your stop in a neighborhood that isn't well lit and trafficked, you probably should invest in a taxi. Of course, even exercising normal prudence, it is still possible that you will have an encounter with someone who believes that what's yours ought to be his. If that happens, don't argue.

Your attachment to the contents of your wallet is certain to be tested in another way, however. Panhandlers are now a fixture of the cityscape, and there is no avoiding their importunities. How you respond to them is a matter only your conscience can advise you on. Wealth and poverty have always coexisted in America's hometown; but poverty is now omnipresent, wearing a very human face.

—By Deborah Papier

A native of Washington, Deborah Papier has worked as an editor and writer for numerous local newspapers and magazines.

WHAT'S WHERE

It is often said that Washington does not have any "real" neighborhoods, the way nearby Baltimore does. Although it's true that Washingtonians are not given to huddling together on their front stoops, each area of the city does have a clearly defined personality.

The Mall

With nearly a dozen diverse museums ringing an expanse of green, **the Mall** is the closest thing the capital has to a theme park—but here, almost everything is free. Lindbergh's *Spirit of St. Louis,* the Hope Diamond, the Fonz's leather jacket, dinosaurs galore, and myriad modern and classical masterpieces await you. Of course, the Mall is more than just a front yard for all these museums: It's a picnicking park and a jogging path, an outdoor stage for festivals and fireworks, and America's town green.

The Monuments

Punctuating the capital like a huge exclamation point is the **Washington Monument**—at 555 feet 5 inches the world's tallest masonry structure. The **Jefferson Memorial's** rotunda rises alongside the Tidal Basin, where you can rent paddleboats and admire over 200 cherry trees, gifts from Japan and focus of a festival each spring. The **Lincoln Memorial** has a somber statue of the seated president gazing out over the Reflecting Pool. The **Vietnam Veterans Memorial** is one of the most visited sights in Washington, its black granite panels reflecting the sky, the trees, and the faces of those looking for the names of loved ones.

The White House Area

In a city full of immediately recognizable images, perhaps none is more familiar than the **White House.** In the neighborhood are some of the oldest houses in the city and two important art galleries: the Renwick Gallery—the Smithsonian's museum of American decorative arts—and the Corcoran Gallery of Art, known for its collections of photography, European Impressionist paintings, and portraits by American artists.

Capitol Hill

Anchoring the neighborhood is the Capitol Building, where the Senate and the House have met since 1800. But **Capitol Hill** is more than just the center of government. There are charming residential blocks here, lined with Victorian row houses and a fine assortment of restaurants, bars, and shops. Union Station, Washington's train depot, has vaulted, gilded ceilings, arched colonnades, statues of Roman legionnaires, and a modern mall-movie complex with food for every palate and pocketbook. Also in this area are the Supreme Court, the Library of Congress, and the Folger Shakespeare Library.

Old Downtown and Federal Triangle

In **Old Downtown**—the area within the diamond formed by Massachusetts, Louisiana, Pennsylvania, and New York avenues—are Chinatown, Ford's Theatre, and several important museums. The Pension Building, which has the largest columns in the world, houses the National Building Museum, devoted to architecture. Other museums include the National Museum of Women in the Arts, the National Portrait Gallery, and the National Museum of American Art. The National Aquarium is in the **Federal Triangle,** a mass of government buildings. And the Old Post Office Pavilion has shops, restaurants, and an indoor miniature golf course. You can tour the J. Edgar Hoover Federal Bureau of Investigation Building, with its exhibits illustrating famous past FBI cases. And at the National Archives, the original Declaration of Independence, Constitution, and Bill of Rights are on display.

Georgetown

Georgetown, the capital's wealthiest neighborhood (and a haven for architecture buffs) is also its most hopping: Restaurants, bars, nightclubs, and trendy boutiques line the narrow, crowded streets. Originally used for shipping, the C&O Canal today is a part of the National Park system: Walkers follow the towpath and canoeists paddle the calm waters; you can also go on a leisurely, mule-drawn trip aboard a canal barge. Washington Harbour is a postmodern riverfront development that includes restaurants, offices, apartments, and upscale shops; Georgetown Park is a multilevel shopping extravaganza; and Georgetown University is the oldest Jesuit school in the country. Dumbarton Oaks's 10 acres of formal gardens make it one of the loveliest spots in all of Washington.

Dupont Circle

One of the most fashionable and vibrant neighborhoods in Washington, **Dupont Circle** has a cosmopolitan air with its many restaurants, offbeat shops, and specialty bookstores; it is also home to the most visible segment of Washington's gay community. The exclusive Kalorama neighborhood (Greek for "beautiful view") is a peaceful, tree-lined enclave filled with embassies and luxurious homes. For a taste of the beautiful view, look down over Rock Creek Park, 1,800 acres of green, which has a planetarium, an 18-hole golf course, and equestrian and bicycle trails. The Phillips Collection is also here; its best known paintings include Renoir's *Luncheon of the Boating Party,* Degas's *Dancers at the Bar,* and a Cézanne self-portrait. At the National Geographic Society's Explorer's Hall, you can learn about the world in an interactive way.

Foggy Bottom

Foggy Bottom—an appellation earned years ago when smoke from factories combined with swampy air to produce a permanent fog along the waterfront—has three main claims to fame: the State Department, the Kennedy Center, and George Washington University. Watergate, one of the world's most legendary apartment-office complexes, is notorious for the events that took place here on June 17, 1972. As Nixon aides sat in a motel across the street, five men were caught trying to bug the headquarters of the Democratic National Committee.

Cleveland Park and the National Zoo

Tree-shaded **Cleveland Park,** in northwest Washington, has attractive houses and a suburban character, and is popular with professionals. Its Cineplex Odeon Uptown is a marvelous vintage-1936 Art Deco movie house. **The National Zoological Park,** part of the Smithsonian Institution, is one of the foremost zoos in the world. Star denizens include Komodo dragons and a giant panda.

Adams-Morgan

Close to Greenwich Village in spirit, **Adams-Morgan** is one of Washington's most ethnically diverse and interesting neighborhoods, home to a veritable United Nations of cuisines, offbeat shops, and funky bars and clubs. The neighborhood's grand 19th-century apartment buildings and row houses and its bohemian atmosphere have attracted young urban professionals, the businesses that cater to them, and the attendant parking and crowd problems.

Arlington, Virginia

The three attractions here—each linked to the military and accessible by Metro—make **Arlington** a part of any complete visit to the nation's capital: John F. Kennedy, Jacqueline Kennedy Onassis, and Robert Kennedy are buried in Arlington National Cemetery along with 200,000 veterans; the U.S. Marine Corps War Memorial is a 78-foot-high statue based on the Pulitzer-prize-winning photograph of five marines and a Navy corpsman raising a flag atop Mt. Suribachi on Iwo Jima; and the **Pentagon,** the headquarters of the Department of Defense, is an immense five-sided building where 23,000 people work.

Alexandria, Virginia

Alexandria's history is linked to the most significant events and personages of the Colonial, Revolutionary, and Civil War periods. This colorful past is still alive on the cobbled streets; on the revitalized waterfront, where clipper ships dock and artisans display their wares; and in restored 18th- and 19th-century homes, churches, and taverns. The history of African Americans in Alexandria and Virginia from 1749, when the city was founded, to the present is recounted at the Alexandria Black History Resource Center, near Robert E. Lee's boyhood home.

C&O Canal and Great Falls

The **C&O Canal** (☞ Georgetown, *above*) and the twin parks of **Great Falls**—on either side of the Potomac River 13 miles northwest of Georgetown—are part of the National Park system. The steep, jagged falls roar into a narrow gorge, providing one of the most spectacular scenic attractions in the East. Canoeing, bicycling, and fishing are popular. Glen Echo is a charming village of Victorian houses; Glen Echo Park is noted for its whimsical architecture and its splendid 1921 Dentzel carousel.

Annapolis, Maryland

Annapolis, Maryland's capital, is a popular destination for oyster catchers and yachting aficionados, and on warm sunny days at the City Dock, white sails billow against a redbrick background of waterfront shops and restaurants. Annapolis's enduring nautical reputation derives largely from the presence of the United States Naval Academy, whose handsomely uniformed students can often be seen on the city streets. One of the country's largest assemblages of 18th-century architecture, with no fewer than 50 pre-Revolutionary buildings, recalls the city's days as a major port.

Potomac Plantations

Three splendid examples of plantation architecture remain on the Virginia side of the Potomac just 15 miles or so south of the District. Easily visited in a day, these riverfront mansions offer a look into a way of life long gone. **Mount Vernon,** one of the most popular sights in the area, was the home of George Washington; **Woodlawn** was the estate of Washington's granddaughter; and **Gunston Hall** was the residence of George Mason—patriot and author of the document on which the Bill of Rights was based.

Fredericksburg, Virginia

This compact city 50 miles south of Washington near the falls of the Rappahannock River figured prominently at crucial points in the nation's history, particularly during the Revolutionary and Civil wars. Fredericksburg, a popular day-trip destination for history buffs and antiques collectors, has a 40-block National Historic District containing more than 350 18th- and 19th-century buildings.

PLEASURES AND PASTIMES

Government and Politics in Action

C-SPAN buffs will want to visit **Capitol Hill,** where they can observe the House and the Senate in action. The **Supreme Court's** hearings are also open to visitors. Washington also has many government buildings that can be toured without watching its denizens at work: These include the **Pentagon,** the **FBI Building,** the **Treasury,** and the **Federal Reserve.** And let's not forget the **White House.**

Military Memorials, Pageants, and Museums

Washington is a fitting spot to honor those who served and fell in defense of our country. More than 200,000 veterans are buried in **Arlington National Cemetery,** a place where visitors can trace America's history through the aftermath of its battles. The guard at the **Tomb of the Unknowns** is changed frequently with a precise ceremony. Near the cemetery is the **United States Marine Corps War Memorial** where there is a sunset parade in summer. The **Vietnam Veteran's Memorial** has more than 58,000 names etched in black granite; The **Korean War Veteran's Memorial** consists of a statue and a reflecting pool. Next to the statue that serves as the **Navy Memorial** is a visitor center and a theater that continuously shows the 30-minute, 70-millimeter film *At Sea,* a visually stunning look at life aboard a modern aircraft carrier. Moored in the Anacostia River nearby and on permanent display is the **Barry,** a decommissioned U.S. Navy destroyer open for tours.

The **Firearms Museum** has hundreds of guns, from those used in the Revolutionary War to high-tech pistols used by Olympic shooting teams. The **National Museum of American Jewish Military History** displays weapons, uniforms, medals, recruitment posters, and other memorabilia from every war in which this country has fought. Inscribed granite slabs in **Pershing Park** recount battles of World War I. The **National Cryptologic Museum** tells the story of military intelligence from 1526 to the present.

The **Marine Corps Museum** follows the corps from its inception in 1775 to its role in Desert Storm. The **Washington Navy Yard** has two military museums and a destroyer you can tour. The **Navy Museum** chronicles the U.S. Navy's history from the Revolution to the present. Exhibits include the foremast of the U.S.S. *Constitution* and a fighter plane that dangles from the ceiling. Children especially enjoy peering through the operating periscopes and pretending to launch torpedoes. In front of the museum is a collection of guns, cannons, and missiles. An annex is full of unusual submarines.

From June through August the Navy and the Marine Corps put on a multimedia **Summer Pageant** at an amphitheater across from the Navy Museum.

In Annapolis, you can tour the **United States Naval Academy** and visit the **museum in Preble Hall,** which tells the story of the U.S. Navy with displays of miniature ships and flags from the original vessels. Periodic **full-dress parades** and (in warmer months) daily noontime midshipmen's musters take place at various spots around campus.

When the Civil War broke out in 1861, **Fredericksburg, Virginia,** became the linchpin of the Confederate defense of Richmond and, as such, the inevitable target of Union assaults. In December 1862, Union forces attacked Fredericksburg in what was to be the first of four major battles fought in and around the town; you can tour its **battlefields and cemeteries.**

Architecture and the Decorative Arts

Washington National Cathedral, the sixthlargest cathedral in the world, will impress even the most hardened cathedral viewer with its Gothic arches, flying buttresses, and imaginative stonework.

Washington has many buildings of architectural interest and filled with exquisite period furniture, draperies, and china. The **White House**—with its watered silk–covered walls, its Empire settees, and personalized china—is the most obvious example of such a building. The **DAR Museum,** with its 33 period rooms decorated in styles representative of various U.S. states and its 50,000-item collection of Colonial and Federal silver, china, porcelain, and glass; and the **Hillwood Museum,** a Georgian mansion that contains a large collection of 18th- and 19th-century French and Russian decorative art such as gold and silver work, icons, lace, tapestries, china, and Fabergé eggs.

The **Renwick Gallery,** the Smithsonian's museum of American decorative arts, has exquisitely designed and crafted utilitarian items, as well as objects created out of such traditional craft materials as fiber and glass. Displays include Shaker furniture, enamel jewelry, and the opulently furnished Victorian-style Grand Salon.

The open interior of the massive redbrick **Pension Building,** one of the city's great spaces, has been the site of inaugural balls for more than 100 years. The eight central Corinthian columns are the largest in the world, rising to a height of 75 feet. This enormous edifice houses the **National Building Museum,** devoted to architecture and the building arts. It outlines the capital's architectural history, from its

monuments to its residential neighborhoods.

Many neighborhoods explored in our walking tours cover historic homes and other—formerly commercial—edifices that are open for tours. See especially **Georgetown, Dupont Circle, Annapolis, and Fredericksburg.**

Gardens

The paths of the **Constitution Gardens** wind through groves of trees, around a lake—a memorial to signers of the Declaration of Independence, and past the sobering Vietnam Veterans Memorial. **Dumbarton Oaks'** 10 acres of formal gardens, in a variety of styles, are some of the loveliest in the city. The grounds of Marjorie Merriweather Post's Georgian-style **Hillwood House** have a French-style parterre, a rose garden, a Japanese garden, paths through azaleas and rhododendrons, and a greenhouse containing 5,000 orchids. Exotic water lilies, lotuses, hyacinths, and other water-loving plants thrive at the **Kenilworth Aquatic Gardens,** a sanctuary of quiet pools and marshy flats. The gardens are home to a variety of wetland animals, including turtles, frogs, muskrats, and some 40 species of birds. The **United States Botanic Gardens** house all manner of plants, from cacti to orchids. In spring, the **United States National Arboretum** is a blaze of color. Summer at this 444-acre oasis brings blooms of clematis, peonies, rhododendrons, and roses. Also popular are the National Herb Garden and the National Bonsai Collection.

Parks

C&O Canal National Historical Park has one end in Georgetown and the other in Cumberland, Maryland. Canoeists paddle the canal's "watered" sections, while hikers and bikers use the 12-foot-wide towpath that runs alongside it. In warmer months you can hop a mule-drawn canal boat for a brief trip. You can also walk over a series of bridges to Olmsted Island in the middle of the Potomac for a spectacular view of the falls.

There are playgrounds and picnic tables at the 328-acre **East Potomac Park** as well as opportunities for tennis, swimming, golf, and miniature golf. Double-blossoming cherry trees line Ohio Drive; they bloom about two weeks after the single-blossoming variety that attracts throngs to the Tidal Basin each spring.

The waters of the Potomac River cascade dramatically over a steep, jagged gorge, creating the spectacle that gives the 800-acre **Great Falls Park** its name. Hikers follow trails, climbers scale the rock faces leading down to the water, and experienced kayakers shoot the rapids. There are also mule-drawn boat rides.

Huntley Meadows, a 1,200-acre refuge in Alexandria, Virginia, is known as a birder's delight. More than 200 species of fowl—from ospreys to owls, egrets to ibis—can be spotted here. Since much of the park is wetlands, it is a favorite of aquatic species.

The 1,800 acres of **Rock Creek Park** have bicycle routes and hiking and equestrian trails, a planetarium, and an 18-hole golf course.

New and Noteworthy

1996 is the 150th anniversary of the **Smithsonian Institution** and on August 10 there will be a birthday party on the National Mall. Smithsonian museums are trying to outdo one another: the **National Museum of African Art** and the **Arthur M. Sackler Gallery** team to present "Dar-Al-Islam: Art, Life and Cultures of the Islamic World" (late Apr.–late Oct.); "Cosmic Voyage," a new IMAX film, can be seen at the **National Air and Space Museum;** the newly refurbished gem hall has reopened at the **National Museum of Natural History;** and the **National Portrait Gallery** will have two rebel-themed exhibits: "East Coast/West Coast: Poet Rebels of the 1950s" (late Jan.–early May) and "Rebel Painters: The New York School, 1945–1960" (late Jan.–early Jun.).

The **Phillips Collection** celebrates its most famous painting, Renoir's *Luncheon of the Boating Party,* with an exhibit of Impressionist artists such as Monet, Manet, and Pissaro (late Sept.–early Feb. 1997).

The highlight of Washington's bustling restaurant scene continues to be the **Pennsylvania Quarter,** roughly the area from 6th to 13th Streets NW between Pennsylvania Avenue and H Street. This slowly gentrifying neighborhood offers a growing number of fine dining establishments in an area that for years was only inhabited during the day. Southern cooking and South American and Spanish cuisines, with bite-size portions, continue to be popular, although steaks are coming back in vogue.

Clubs and restaurants—catering to punk, jazz, and hiphop aficionados—continue to pop up on U Street NW between 12th and 16th streets. The popular **Bar Nun** on U Street gets weekend crowds who want a club atmosphere without pressure to dance (although dancing is possible). Pop music icons might go to Bar Nun after their concerts. For something unusual elsewhere in town, try the Elvis happy hour at **Las Cruces** or the weekly drag bingo night at **Planet Fred.** Jean-Louis Palladin, whose small restaurant, **Jean-Louis at the Watergate Hotel,** was often cited as one of the best in the country, closed in June. The renowned chef will open a new eatery at a future date, as yet unspecified.

As for politics, last year was a year of big change on both the national and the local levels. The national electorate threw out the Democratic rascals in favor of Republican rascals. Former mayor Marion S. Barry Jr., voted out of office four years ago after a widely publicized drug sting landed him in jail, made an amazing comeback and was re-elected mayor of Washington. It happened just as the city's financial troubles were prompting talk in Congress of returning control of the city to the federal government. Ah, Washington . . .

FODOR'S CHOICE

Buildings and Monuments

★ **The Capitol.** Home of the Senate and the House of Representatives, reminiscent of the Roman Pantheon in design, the marble Capitol is a fresco-and-statue-filled architectural marvel set on 68 acres of landscaped grounds as beautiful as the building itself.

★ **East Building of the National Gallery of Art.** The atrium of this angular marble I. M. Pei–designed wing is dominated by an Alexander Calder mobile and a huge wall-hanging by Joan Miró. The galleries here generally display modern art.

⭐ **Fredericksburg Battlefield Visitor Center.** At this informative tourist facility you can learn about Fredericksburg's role in the Civil War. Maps show how to reach hiking trails at the nearby Wilderness, Chancellorsville, and Spotsylvania Court House battlefields (all within 15 miles of Fredericksburg).

⭐ **Jefferson Memorial.** Jefferson had always admired the Pantheon in Rome—the rotundas he designed for the University of Virginia and his own Monticello were inspired by its dome—so architect John Russell Pope drew from the same source when he designed a graceful memorial facing the Tidal Basin, where cherry trees blossom in spring.

⭐ **Kenmore.** Kenmore was the home of Fielding Lewis, a patriot, plantation owner, and brother-in-law of George Washington. The lavish interior is said to contain some of the most beautiful rooms in America.

⭐ **Lincoln Memorial.** Many people consider the Lincoln Memorial to be the most inspiring monument in the city. Daniel Chester French's somber statue of the seated president, in the center of the memorial, gazes out over the Reflecting Pool.

⭐ **Mount Vernon.** Mount Vernon and the surrounding lands had been in the Washington family for nearly 90 years by the time George inherited it all in 1761. Visit plantation workshops, the kitchen, the carriage house, the gardens, reconstructions of the slave quarters, and the tomb of George and Martha Washington. There are sweeping Potomac views as well.

⭐ **United States Naval Academy.** The academy, established in 1845 on the site of a U.S. Army fort, occupies 329 scenic riverside acres and contains the crypt of the Revolutionary War hero John Paul Jones, the naval officer who, in an engagement with a British ship, uttered the famous declaration, "I have not yet begun to fight!"

⭐ **Vietnam Veterans Memorial.** It's a moving tribute to those who died in this war.

⭐ **Washington National Cathedral.** Although built in modern times, it's soaring medieval Gothic in style.

⭐ **White House.** If you think about it, it really is rather extraordinary that our president opens his house most mornings to throngs of visitors who peer past ropes at his family's dining and living rooms.

Activities

⭐ **Exploring the city with Scandal Tours** (☞ Important Contacts A to Z). This outrageous tour bypasses the monuments and takes you straight into the gutter. Costumed look-alikes dramatize scandals as you tour such sights as Gary Hart's town house and Watergate.

⭐ **Strolling the streets of Georgetown early on a weekend morning** before the narrow sidewalks fill with shoppers, brunchers, and browsers.

⭐ **Taking a boat ride to Mount Vernon.** The leisurely 4½-hour ride on the Potomac is a cool respite on sweltering days.

⭐ **Visiting the aviary at the National Zoo.** At this top-ranked zoo, innovative compounds show many animals in naturalistic settings: The Great Flight Cage is a walk-in aviary in which birds fly unrestricted.

Museums

⭐ **Corcoran Gallery of Art.** On exhibit are paintings by French Impressionists and the first great American portraitists as well as photography by modern American artists.

⭐ **National Air and Space Museum** is the most visited museum in the world. It displays the actual air- and spacecraft that have made history; the flight-simulating IMAX movies are not to be missed.

⭐ **National Gallery of Art.** The two buildings of the National Gallery hold one of the world's foremost collections of paintings, sculptures, and graphics.

⭐ **National Museum of American History.** Exploring America's cultural, political, technical, and scientific past, it shows off a steam locomotive, Muhammad Ali's boxing glove, and Nancy Reagan's inaugural gown.

⭐ **National Museum of Natural History.** Filled with bones, fossils, stuffed animals, a live insect zoo, and other natural delights, the National Museum of Natural History is one of the great natural history museums of the world.

⭐ **Phillips Collection.** It is as beloved for its well-known paintings as for its relaxed atmosphere and knowledgeable, art-student guards.

★ **United States Holocaust Memorial Museum.** In a clear and often graphic fashion, the museum tells the stories of the 11 million Jews, Gypsies, Jehovah's Witnesses, homosexuals, political prisoners, and others killed by the Nazis between 1933 and 1945.

Restaurants

★ **Galileo.** A spacious, popular Italian restaurant, Galileo makes everything in-house, from bread sticks to mozzarella. And everything tastes like it: terrific. $$$$

★ **Inn at Little Washington.** Though it's a 90-minute drive from Washington, this place is well worth the trip. Leave in the afternoon to enjoy views of rolling hills and small farms in the Virginia countryside. Once inside, the luxurious English country manor decor transports guests back in time. The fixed price menu changes daily and adjusts to the seasons, but you won't soon forget the multicourse gourmet feast. $$$$

★ **Le Lion D'Or.** Other French restaurants may flirt with fads, but this one sticks to the classics—or at any rate the neoclassics—and does them so well that its popularity remains undiminished year after year. $$$$

★ **Bombay Club.** An elegant Indian restaurant, the Bombay Club creates unusual seafood and vegetarian dishes, but the real standouts are the breads and the piscine appetizers. $$$

★ **Citronelle.** The essence of California chic, Citronelle's glass-front kitchen allows diners to see all the action as chefs scurry to and fro creating such culinary masterpieces as leek-encrusted salmon steak topped by a crisp fried-potato lattice. $$$

★ **Gerard's Place.** The focus is on such fresh, intriguingly prepared cuisine nouvelle entrées as poached lobster with a ginger, lime, and Sauternes sauce; venison served with dried fruits and pumpkin and beet-root purees; and seared tuna with black olives and roasted red peppers. Desserts are exquisite. $$$

★ **i Ricchi.** A favorite of critics and upscale crowds for its earthy cuisine from the Northern Italian province of Tuscany, I Ricchi has two menus, one for spring and summer, one for fall and winter. A sampling from the spring list, rolled pork and rabbit roasted in wine and fresh herbs, tastes as good as it sounds. $$$

★ **La Colline.** La Colline is one of the city's best French restaurants—in fact, one of the best restaurants of any type on Capitol Hill. The menu, which changes daily, places an emphasis on seafood. The dessert selection is plentiful, as is the wine list. $$$

★ **Red Sage.** The barbed-wire-and-lizard decor sets the stage for tasty Southwestern cuisine chock-full of chilis. $$$

★ **Vincenzo al Sole.** Here's a rarity: a restaurant lowering its prices while continuing to offer excellent food, with an emphasis on such simply prepared seafood dishes as *merluzzo alla calabrese* (roasted cod with capers and olives) and *branzino al salmoriglio* (grilled rockfish with oregano). $$$

★ **Café Atlántico.** Standouts in gourmet South American fare include conch fritters with tomato mango sauce, crepes with cuitlacoche (a rare truffle-like mushroom), and Argentine grilled beef with garlicky *chimichurri* sauce. $$

★ **City Lights of China.** One of the best Chinese eateries in Washington, City Lights of China consistently makes the top restaurant critics' lists every year. The traditional Chinese fare is excellent. Less common specialties are deftly cooked as well. $$

★ **Hibiscus Café.** African masks and multicolored neon accents hang from the ceiling of a modish restaurant with vibrant tableware and eclectic seating. Weekend crowds are drawn by spicy jerk chicken, blackened fish (such as grouper), shrimp curry, and flavorful soups (try the butternut-ginger bisque). $$

★ **Jaleo.** A lively Spanish bistro, Jaleo encourages you to make a meal out of its long list of hot and cold tapas snacks, although such entrées as grilled fish, seafood stew and paella—which comes in three different versions—are just as tasty (and equally filling). $$

★ **Sarinah Satay House.** With carved monkeys, parrots, and puppets, batik-clad waiters, and a lush, enclosed garden with real trees growing through the ceiling, Sarinah Satay House makes you feel like you're in exotic Indonesia, and the food is exquisite. $$

☆**Burma.** That the country is bordered by India, Thailand and China gives some indication of Burma's cuisine–curry and tamarind share pride of place with lemon, cilantro and soy seasonings. The menu has as many intriguing appetizers and salads as it does entrées. Your best bet is to bring a group and explore several options. $

☆**The Islander.** A Trinidadian eatery turns out some of Washington's most exciting and satisfying food. The Islander's tangy fish and vegetable soup, *accra* cod fritters, and herb-and-spice-marinated calypso chicken served with rice and a thick tomato-and-onion sauce will leave your tastebuds delirious with pleasure. $

☆**Meskerem.** Spicy Ethiopian food is served in a bright dining room or on a balcony where you can sit on the floor on leather cushions, with large woven baskets for tables. $

Hotels

Hay-Adams Hotel, part Italian Renaissance, part English Tudor, has some brightly decorated rooms with picture-postcard views of the White House; the afternoon tea is renowned, and the staff is dignified and friendly. $$$$

Willard Inter-Continental, an opulent beaux-arts hotel with a fascinating history, has hosted innumerable U.S. presidents and foreign heads of state. $$$$

Hotel Washington is Edwardian in character: Rooms have antique reproductions and windows festooned with swags, heavy draperies, and lace. Washingtonians bring visitors to the rooftop bar for cocktails and a view of the White House grounds and the Washington Monument. $$

Morrison-Clark Inn Hotel. Victorian with an airy, modern twist, this small and unusual historic inn has marble fireplaces and antiques-filled rooms. $$

Kalorama Guest House. Housed in five separate turn-of-the-century town houses, the Kalorama is eminently comfortable, with its dark wood walls, calico curtains, and antique oak furniture with traditional, slightly worn upholstery. The coffeepot is always on, and the staff is knowledgeable and friendly. $

FESTIVALS AND SEASONAL EVENTS

Washington has a lively calendar of special events; listed below are some of the most important or unusual.

WINTER

DEC.➤ **Christmas celebrations** start early in the month. Major events are listed below.

EARLY DEC.➤ The **Washington National Cathedral's Open House** celebrates the season's holidays with bagpipers, choral sing-alongs, and seasonal decorations in the Gothic-style cathedral (☎ 202/537–6200).

DEC. 6➤ The **25th Annual Scottish Christmas Walk** salutes Alexandria's Scottish heritage with a parade, bagpipers, house tours, crafts, and children's events (☎ 703/838–4200).

DEC. 13–14➤ **Old Town Christmas Candlelight Tours** visit historic Ramsay House, Gadsby's Tavern Museum, the Lee-Fendall House, and the Carlyle House in Old Town Alexandria. Included in the tour are music, colonial dancing, and light refreshments (☎ 703/838–4200).

MID-DEC.–MID-JAN.➤ **U.S. Botanic Gardens' Annual Winter Flower Show** bursts forth with more than 1,000 of the traditional holiday red, white, and pink poinsettias as well as a display of Christmas wreaths and trees (☎ 202/225–7099).

MID-DEC.➤ The **People's Christmas Tree Lighting** on the west side of the U.S. Capitol celebrates its 34rd anniversary this year. Military bands perform (☎ 202/224–6645).

MID-DEC.–JAN. 1➤ The **National Christmas Tree Lighting/Pageant of Peace** is accompanied by seasonal music and caroling. In mid-December (usually the second Thursday) the president lights the National Christmas Tree (on the Ellipse just south of the White House) at dusk. For the next few weeks the Ellipse grounds are the site of nightly choral performances, a Nativity scene, a burning Yule log, and a display of lighted Christmas trees representing each of the country's states and territories (☎ 202/619–7222).

MID–LATE DEC.➤ The **Nutcracker** is performed by the Washington Ballet at Warner Theatre (☎ 202/362–3606).

DEC. 24–25➤ The **Washington National Cathedral Christmas Celebration and Services** include Christmas carols, pageants, and seasonal choral performances (☎ 202/537–6200).

EARLY JAN.➤ **Washington Antiques Show** at the Omni Shoreham Hotel is an established, high-quality presentation for buyers and browsers (☎ 202/234–0700).

MID-JAN.➤ **Martin Luther King, Jr.'s birthday** is celebrated with speeches, dance, choral performances, and special readings. For more information, contact the Martin Luther King, Jr. Memorial Library (☎ 202/727–1186); the National Park Service (☎ 202/619–7222); or the Smithsonian (☎ 202/357–2700).

MID-JAN.➤ The **Chinese New Year Festival** explodes in Chinatown, amid a cacophony of firecrackers and a dragon-led parade (☎ 202/638–1041 or 202/724–4091).

MID-JAN.➤ **Robert E. Lee's birthday** is marked with 19th-century music and period food at Arlington House, the Custis-Lee mansion in Arlington Cemetery (☎ 703/557–0613).

FEB.➤ **African-American History Month** features special events, museum exhibits, and cultural programs (☎ 202/789–2403 or 202/727–1186).

EARLY FEB.➤ **Lincoln's birthday** celebrations include a wreath-laying ceremony and a reading of the Gettysburg Address at the Lincoln Memorial (☎ 202/619–7222).

MID-FEB.➤ **Frederick Douglass's birthday** is celebrated with a wreath-laying ceremony at the Frederick Douglass National Historic Site in Anacostia (☎ 202/619–7222 or 202/426–5961).

FEB. 17➤ **George Washington's birthday** is celebrated with a parade down Washington Street in Old Town Alexandria, a historic-homes tour, and Revolutionary War reenactments (☎ 703/838–4200 or 703/838–5005).

SPRING

MAR. 7–9➤ The **Spring Antiques Show,** at the Armory (☎ 301/738–1966; during show, 202/547–9215) hosts more than 185 dealers from 20 states, Canada, and Europe.

MID-MAR.➤ **St. Patrick's Day and Festival** begins with a parade down Constitution Avenue at 1 PM on March 17. The following days feature theater, folk music, and dance concerts (☎ 202/637–2474). For information on Old Town Alexandria's March 16 parade festivities, call ☎ 703/838–4200. Arlington House in Arlington National Cemetery goes green as well (☎ 703/557–0613).

MID-MAR.➤ The **Annual Bach Marathon** honors Johann Sebastian's birthday. Ten organists each play the massive pipe organ at Chevy Chase Presbyterian Church (⊠ 1 Chevy Chase Circle NW, ☎ 202/363–2202) from 1 to 6.

MAR. 29➤ The **Smithsonian Kite Festival,** for kite makers and kite fliers of all ages, is held on the Washington Monument grounds (☎ 202/357–3030).

MAR. 29–APR. 12➤ The **National Cherry Blossom Festival** opens with the traditional Japanese Lantern Lighting ceremony on the 29th (☎ 202/728–1137, 202/646–0366, or 202/619–7222).

APR.➤ **Imagination Celebration,** an annual month-

long festival for young people at the John F. Kennedy Center for the Performing Arts, draws some of the nation's best children's theater companies (☎ 202/467–4600).

EARLY APR.➤ The **White House Easter Egg Roll** brings children ages eight and under, with an accompanying adult, to the White House lawn (☎ 202/456–7041).

MID-APR.➤ The anniversary of **Thomas Jefferson's birthday** is marked by military drills and a wreath-laying at his memorial (☎ 202/619–7222).

MID-APR.➤ The **White House Spring Garden Tours** are walks around the Jacqueline Kennedy Rose Garden and the West Lawn; public rooms within the White House can also be visited (☎ 202/456–7041).

APR. 19–20➤ The **Georgetown House Tour,** now in its 70th year, offers the opportunity to view private homes. Admission includes high tea at historic St. John's Georgetown Parish Church (☎ 202/338–1796).

LATE APR.➤ The **Smithsonian's Washington Craft Show** exhibits one-of-a-kind, handcrafted objects by 100 of the country's best artisans (☎ 202/357–2700).

APR. 26➤ The **Alexandria Garden Tour** finds six private gardens and another half-dozen historical sights open to the public, with afternoon tea at the historic Athenaeum (☎ 703/838–4200).

APR. 29–MAY 11➤ The **D.C. International Film Festival** is where dozens of foreign and American

films premiere. Tickets are required (☎ 202/274–6810).

MAY 2–3➤ The **Washington National Cathedral Flower Mart** salutes a different country each year, with flower booths, crafts, and demonstrations (☎ 202/537–6200).

MID-MAY➤ The **Georgetown Garden Tour** shows off more than a dozen private gardens in one of the city's loveliest and most historic neighborhoods (☎ 202/333–6896).

MID-MAY➤ The **Joint Services Open House** at Andrews Air Force Base in suburban Maryland features two days' worth of static aircraft and weapons displays, precision parachute jumps, and either the Navy's Blue Angels or Air Force Thunderbirds aerobatic team (☎ 301/568–5995).

MID-MAY➤ **Malcolm X Day** pays tribute to the slain civil-rights leader. A week of workshops and films culminates in a commemoration on May 18, when concerts and speeches are held in Anacostia Park (☎ 202/396–1021 or 202/678–8352).

MAY 25➤ The **Memorial Day Weekend Concert,** performed by the National Symphony Orchestra at 7:30 PM on the West Lawn of the U.S. Capitol, officially welcomes the summer to Washington (☎ 202/619–7222).

MAY 26➤ **Memorial Day at Arlington National Cemetery** includes a wreath-laying ceremony at the Kennedy gravesite, a presidential wreath-laying at the Tomb of the Unknowns, and services at the Memorial Amphitheatre featuring military bands and a presidential keynote address (☎ 202/475–0856).

MAY 26➤ **Memorial Day at the U.S. Navy Memorial** has wreath-laying ceremonies at 10 AM and 1 PM, as well as an outdoor evening concert by the U.S. Navy Band.

MAY 26➤ **Memorial Day at the Vietnam Veterans Memorial** is celebrated with a wreath-laying ceremony and a concert by the National Symphony (☎ 202/619–7222).

MAY 26➤ This is the 17th annual **Memorial Day Jazz Festival** in Old Town Alexandria, with big-band music performed by local artists (☎ 703/883–4686).

LATE MAY–EARLY SEPT.➤ The **Military Band Summer Concert Series**, featuring the bands of the different branches of the armed forces, runs from Memorial Day to Labor Day. Every August the Army Band performs the *1812 Overture*, complete with real cannons (☎ 202/433–2525, 703/696–3718, 202/433–4011, or 202/767–5658).

SUMMER

JUNE–SEPTEMBER➤ The summer-long **Jazz Arts Festival** showcases some of the world's most accomplished and innovative musicians in free concerts at different venues in the D.C. area, many of them outdoors (☎ 202/783–0360).

JUNE➤ **Shakespeare Free for All** is a series of free, nightly performances at the open-air Carter Barron Amphitheater by the Washington Shakespeare Theatre (☎ 202/628–5770 or 202/619–7222).

JUNE 7–9➤ The family-oriented **Alexandria Waterfront Festival** promotes the American Red Cross and recognizes Alexandria's rich maritime heritage. Tall ships are open for visits, and there are arts and crafts displays, a 10K run, and a blessing of the fleet (☎ 703/549–8300).

MID-JUNE–MID-JULY➤ **Washington National Cathedral's Summer Festival of Music** features everything from Renaissance choral music to contemporary instrumental fare (☎ 202/537–6200).

JUNE 25–29 AND JULY 2–6➤ The **Festival of American Folklife**, sponsored by the Smithsonian and held on the Mall, celebrates the music, arts, crafts, and foods of various nations' cultures (☎ 202/357–2700).

JULY 4➤ The **Independence Day Celebration** includes a grand parade that marches past many of the capital's historic monuments. In the evening, the National Symphony Orchestra performs for free on the steps of the Capitol; this is followed by a fireworks display over the Washington Monument (☎ 202/619–7222).

MID-JULY–LATE AUG.➤ During the **Twilight Tattoo Series**, the 3rd U.S. Infantry, the U.S. Army Band, the Drill Team, and the Old Guard Fife and Drum Corps play on the

Ellipse grounds, between the White House and the Washington Monument, every Wednesday evening at 7 (☎ 703/696–3718).

LATE JULY➤ The **Hispanic Festival**, which takes place on the Mall, celebrates Latin American culture, food, music, dance, and theater.

LATE JULY➤ The **Virginia Scottish Games,** one of the largest Scottish festivals in the United States, includes traditional Highland dance, bagpipes, a national professional heptathlon, animal events, and fiddling competitions on the Episcopal High School grounds (✉ 3901 W. Braddock Rd., Alexandria, VA, ☎ 703/838–4200).

AUG. 30➤ The **National Frisbee Festival** (✉ National Mall, near Smithsonian's National Air and Space Museum, ☎ 301/645–5043) is the nation's largest noncompetitive assembly of Frisbee lovers. The disc-catching canines almost steal the show from the two-legged pros.

AUTUMN

SEPT. 7➤ The **Labor Day Weekend Concert** features the National Symphony Orchestra on the West Lawn of the U.S. Capitol (☎ 202/467–4600).

EARLY SEPT.➤ At the **John F. Kennedy Center's Open House** there are jugglers, musicians, dancers, and other performers on all five stages. Thousands throng to this free event every year (☎ 202/467–4600).

EARLY SEPT.➤ **Adams-Morgan Day** celebrates the African American and Latin American character of this unique neighborhood with live music, crafts, and cuisine (☎ 202/332–3292 or 202/789–7000).

MID-SEPT.➤ The **Constitution Day Commemoration** observes the anniversary of the signing of the U.S. Constitution. Events include a naturalization ceremony, speakers, and band concerts (✉ National Archives, ☎ 202/501–5000).

LATE SEPT.➤ The **Washington National Cathedral Open House** is a chance to share in cathedral-related crafts, music, and activities, including a climb up the central tower (☎ 202/537–6200).

LATE SEPT.➤ **Rock Creek Park Day** celebrates the park's 107th birthday, with music, children's activities, foods, and arts and crafts. The party runs from noon to dusk (☎ 202/426–6829).

OCT. 12–14➤ The **"Taste of DC" Festival** presents dishes from a variety of D.C. eateries. Food-tasting tickets are sold on site (☎ 202/789–7000).

MID-OCT.➤ The **White House Fall Garden Tours** provide an opportunity to see the splendid gardens of the White House, including the famous Rose Gardens and the South Lawn (☎ 202/456–7041).

MID-OCT.➤ The **Washington International Horse Show** is D.C.'s major equestrian event (☎ 301/840–0281).

OCT. 25➤ The **Marine Corps Marathon** attracts thousands of world-class runners. It begins at the Iwo Jima Marine Corps Memorial in Arlington, Virginia (☎ 703/690–3431).

LATE OCT.➤ **Theodore Roosevelt's birthday** is celebrated on Roosevelt Island in the Potomac, with tours of the island, exhibits, and family activities (☎ 202/619–7222).

MID-NOV.➤ **Veteran's Day** activities include services at Arlington National Cemetery, the Vietnam Veterans Memorial, and the U.S. Navy Memorial, as well as an 11 AM wreath-laying ceremony at the Tomb of the Unknowns, led by the president or another ranking official (☎ 202/475–0843).

MID-NOV.–LATE DEC.➤ *A Christmas Carol* returns year after year to historic Ford's Theatre (☎ 202/347–4833).

LATE DEC.➤ **White House Christmas Candlelight Tours** conducts evening tours (5–7 PM) of the White House lavishly adorned with traditional Christmas decorations. Tours are free but highly popular and admission is on a first-come, first-served basis; arrive early (☎ 202/456-2200 or 202/619–7222).

2 Exploring Washington

By John F. Kelly

Updated by
Bruce Walker

THE BYZANTINE WORKINGS of the federal government; the nonsensical, sound-bite-ready oratory of the
well-groomed politician; murky foreign policy pro-
nouncements issued from Foggy Bottom; and $600 toilet seats or-
dered by the Pentagon cause many Americans to cast a skeptical eye
on anything that happens "inside the Beltway." Washingtonians take
it all in stride, though, reminding themselves that, after all, those responsible for political hijinks don't come *from* Washington, they come
to Washington. Besides, such ribbing is a small price to pay for living
in a city whose charms extend far beyond the bureaucratic. World-class
museums and art galleries (nearly all of them free), tree-shaded and
flower-filled parks and gardens, bars and restaurants that benefit from
a large and creative immigrant community, and nightlife that seems to
get better with every passing year are as much a part of Washington
as floor debates or filibusters.

The location of the city that calls to mind politicking, back scratching, and delicate diplomacy is itself the result of a compromise. Tired
of its nomadic existence after having set up shop in eight different locations, Congress voted in 1785 to establish a permanent "Federal town."
Northern lawmakers wanted the capital on the Delaware River, in the
north, southerners wanted it on the Potomac, in the south. A deal was
struck when Virginia's Thomas Jefferson agreed to support the proposal that the federal government assume the war debts of the colonies
if New York's Alexander Hamilton and other northern legislators
would agree to locate the capital on the banks of the Potomac. George
Washington himself selected the exact site of the capital, a diamond-
shape, 100-square-mile plot that encompassed the confluence of the
Potomac and Anacostia rivers, not far from the president's estate at
Mount Vernon. To give the young city a bit of a head start, Washington included the already thriving tobacco ports of Alexandria, Virginia,
and Georgetown, Maryland, in the District of Columbia.

Pierre-Charles L'Enfant, a young French engineer who had fought in
the Revolution, offered his services in creating a capital "magnificent
enough to grace a great nation." His 1791 plan owes much to Ver-
sailles, with ceremonial circles and squares, a grid pattern of streets,
and broad, diagonal avenues. It was these grand streets that sparked
the first debates over L'Enfant's design and its execution. The families
that owned the estates and tobacco farms that would be transformed
into Washington had agreed to sell the sites needed for public buildings at $66.66 an acre, with the understanding that profits could be
made by selling the remaining land to those who wanted to be near
the federal government. They also agreed to turn over for free the land
to be used for streets and highways. When they discovered that L'Enfant's streets were 100 feet wide and that one thoroughfare—the
Mall—would be 400 feet across, they were horrified. Half the land on
the site would be turned over to the government for free for roads.

L'Enfant won the battle of the roads but he couldn't control his ob-
stinate ways and fought often with the three city commissioners Washington had appointed. When the nephew of one of the commissioners
started to build a manor house where L'Enfant had planned a street,
the Frenchman ordered it torn down. The overzealous L'Enfant was
fired and offered $2,500 and a lot near the White House in pay. He
refused, thinking it poor compensation for the services he had performed.
(A visionary who was a little too headstrong for his own good, L'En-

fant spent his later years petitioning Congress with long, rambling missives demanding satisfaction. He died penniless in 1825.)

L'Enfant had written that his plan would "leave room for that aggrandizement and embellishment which the increase in the wealth of the nation will permit it to pursue at any period, however remote." At times it must have seemed remote indeed, for the town grew so slowly that when Charles Dickens visited Washington in 1842 what he saw were "spacious avenues that begin in nothing and lead nowhere; streets a mile long that only want houses, roads, and inhabitants; public buildings that need but a public to be complete and ornaments of great thoroughfares which need only great thoroughfares to ornament."

It took the Civil War—and every war thereafter—to energize the city, by attracting thousands of new residents and spurring building booms that extended the capital in all directions. Streets in the once-backward town were paved in the 1870s and the first streetcars ran in the 1880s. Memorials to famous Americans like Lincoln and Jefferson were built in the first decades of the 20th century, along with the massive Federal Triangle, a monument to thousands of less-famous government workers.

Despite the growth and despite the fact that blacks have always played an important role in the city's history (black mathematician Benjamin Banneker surveyed the land with Pierre L'Enfant in the 18th century), Washington today remains essentially segregated. Whites—who account for about 30% of the population—reside mostly in northwest Washington. Blacks live largely east of Rock Creek Park and south of the Anacostia River.

It's a city of other unfortunate contrasts: Citizens of the capital of the free world couldn't vote in a presidential election until 1964, weren't granted limited home rule until 1974, and are represented in Congress by a single nonvoting delegate (though in 1990 residents elected two "shadow" senators, one of whom is political gadfly Jesse Jackson). Homeless people sleep on steam grates next to multimillion-dollar government buildings, and a flourishing drug trade has earned Washington the dubious distinction of murder capital of the United States. Though it's little consolation to those affected, most crime is restricted to neighborhoods far from the areas visited by tourists.

Still, there's no denying that Washington, the world's first planned capital city, is also one of its most beautiful. And though the federal government dominates the city psychologically as much as the Washington Monument dominates it physically, there are parts of the capital where you can leave politics behind. The walks that follow will take you through the monumental city, the governmental city, and the residential city. As you walk, look for evidence of L'Enfant's hand, still present despite growing pains and frequent deviations from his plan. His Washington was to be a city of vistas—pleasant views that would shift and change from block to block, a marriage of geometry and art. It remains this way today. Like its main industry, politics, Washington's design is a constantly changing kaleidoscope that invites contemplation from all angles.

THE MALL

The Mall is the heart of nearly every visitor's trip to Washington. With nearly a dozen diverse museums ringing the expanse of green, it's the closest thing the capital has to a theme park (unless you count the federal government itself, which has uncharitably been called "Disney-

Exploring Washington, D.C. *(Boxes Refer to Detail Maps)*

Cleveland Park and the National Zoo

Adams-Morg

Dupont Circle

Georgetown

California St.

S St.

R St.

Decatur Pl.

Sheridan Circle

Massachusetts Ave.

T St.

S St.

R

Corcoran

Q St.

Dupont Circle

Church St.

P St.

N St.

S St.

R St.

32nd St.

31st St.

Wisconsin Ave.

31st St.

30th St.

29th St.

28th St.

27th St.

Rock Creek

22nd St.

21st St.

20th St.

19th St.

Connecticut Ave.

New Hampshire Ave.

18th St.

17th St.

Florida Ave.

Columbia Rd.

P St.

O St.

N St.

M St.

C&O Canal

Whitehurst Fwy.

Francis Scott Key Bridge

L St.

29th St.

25th St.

29

Washington Circle

24th St.

23rd St.

22nd St.

M St.

L St.

K St.

Pennsylvania Ave.

The White House Area

I-66

Theodore Roosevelt Island

Virginia Ave.

G St.

F St.

E St.

D St.

C St.

17th St.

Constitution Ave.

50

Foggy Bottom

George Washington Memorial Pkwy.

Arlington Memorial Bridge

Columbia Island

Ladybird Johnson Park

Memorial Dr.

Lincoln Memorial

Reflecting Pool

Independence Ave.

Ohio Dr.

West Potomac Park

W. Basin Dr.

Kutz Bridge

Tidal Bas

Potomac River

ARLINGTON NATIONAL CEMETERY

Arlington

VIRGINIA

To Old Town Alexandria

The Monuments

NW ◄► NE

Florida Ave.

U St.

16th St.
15th St.
14th St.

T St.
S St.
R St.
Q St.

Vermont Ave.

Rhode Island Ave.
Florida Ave.

S St.

Lincoln Rd.

R St.
Q St.

New Jersey Ave.

3rd St.
1st St.

O St.

Church St.
Logan
Circle

P St.

O St.

New York Ave.

Scott
Circle

Rhode Island Ave.

Thomas
Circle

9th St.
8th St.
7th St.
6th St.
5th St.
4th St.
N St.

N St.
M St.
L St.

3rd St.
1st St.

North Capitol St.

M St.

16th St.
15th St.
13th St.
12th St.
11th St.
10th St.

Massachusetts Ave.

Mt. Vernon
Square

I St.
H St.

**Old Downtown and
Federal Triangle**

**Capitol
Hill**

3rd St.

New York Ave.

G St.
F St.
E St.

2nd St.

Union
Station

Columbus
Memorial
Fountain

The White
House

14th St.
15th St.

Pennsylvania
Ave.

D St.

Louisiana Ave.

Stanton
Park

NE

The
Ellipse

Constitution Ave.

US
Capitol

SE

Washington
Monument

Madison Dr.

National Gallery
of Art

THE MALL

Smithsonian
Institution

Jefferson Dr.

National
Air and Space
Museum

E. Capitol St.

Independence Ave.

Maryland Ave.

Folger
Park

C St.

Canal St.

The Mall

D St.

New Jersey Ave.

E St.

Outlet Bridge

Southwest Fwy.

G St.

Virginia Ave.

Jefferson
Memorial

Francis Case
Memorial
Bridge

Water St.

Maine Ave.

I St.

| 0 | | 500 yards |
| 0 | | 500 meters |

N

Washington Canal

SW ◄► SE

land on the Potomac"). As at a theme park, you may have to stand in an occasional line, but unlike the amusements at Disneyland almost everything you'll see here is free. (You may, however, need free, timed-entry tickets to some of the more popular traveling exhibitions. These are usually available at the museum information desk or by phone, for a service charge, from TicketMaster, at 202/432–7328.)

Of course, the Mall is more than just a front yard for all these museums. Bounded on the north and south by Constitution and Independence avenues, and on the east and west by 3rd and 14th streets, it's a picnicking park and a jogging path, an outdoor stage for festivals and fireworks, and America's town green. Nine of the Smithsonian Institution's fourteen museums in the Capitol lie within these boundaries. (The nearest Metro stops are Smithsonian, Archives/Navy Memorial, and L'Enfant Plaza).

In this space west of the "Congress House," Pierre L'Enfant had envisioned a "Grand Avenue, 400 feet in breadth, and about a mile in length, bordered with gardens, ending in a slope from the houses on each side." In the middle of the 19th century, horticulturalist Andrew Jackson Downing took a stab at converting the Mall into a large, English-style garden, with carriageways curving through groves of trees and bushes. This was far from the "vast esplanade" L'Enfant had in mind, and by the dawn of the 20th century the Mall had become an eyesore. It was dotted with sheds and bisected by railroad tracks. There was even a railroad station at its eastern end.

In 1900 Senator James McMillan, chairman of the Committee on the District of Columbia, asked a distinguished group of architects and artists to study ways of improving Washington's park system. The McMillan Commission, which included architects Daniel Burnham and Charles McKim, landscape architect Frederick Law Olmsted, Jr., and sculptor Augustus Saint-Gaudens, didn't confine its recommendations just to parks; its 1902 report would shape the way the capital looked for decades. The Mall received much of the group's attention and is its most stunning accomplishment. L'Enfant's plan was rediscovered, the sheds, railroad tracks, and carriageways were removed, and Washington finally had the monumental core it had been denied for so long.

Numbers in the text correspond to numbers in the margin and on the Mall map.

A Good Walk

Start your tour of the museums on the Mall in the **Smithsonian Institution Building** ① (also known as the Castle), home to the **Smithsonian Information Center.** To the right of the Castle is the **S. Dillon Ripley Center,** mostly classrooms and offices but occasionally featuring artworks from around the world. Entry to all Smithsonian museums and federal attractions is free, as are most guided tours of them. Prices for films, special events, etc., are noted in Sights to See, as are phone numbers for each museum. For general information on all Smithsonian museums call: 202/357–2700, TTY 202/357–1729.

Walk east on Jefferson Drive to the **Arts and Industries Building** ② and its collection of American Victoriana. The **Hirshhorn Museum and Sculpture Garden** ③ is the next building to the east on Jefferson Drive, featuring modern art and an outdoor sculpture garden. Cross 7th Street to get to the **National Air and Space Museum** ④, the most visited museum in the world. Continue east on Jefferson Drive to 4th Street and look at the large open space bounded by 3rd and 4th streets and Independence Avenue and Jefferson Drive SW, where the Smithsonian's **National Museum of the American Indian** is scheduled to open

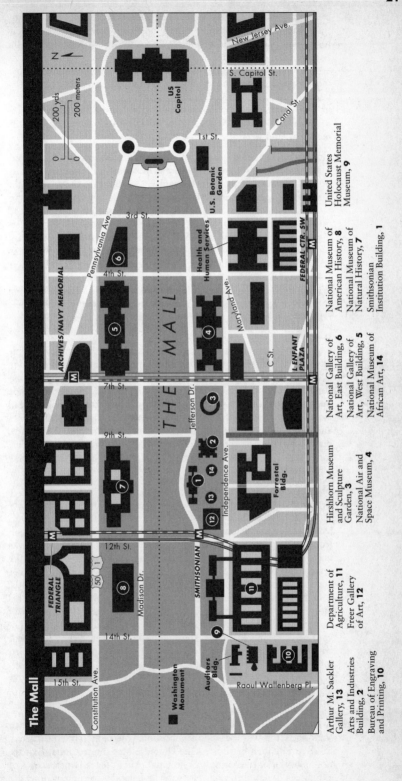

The Mall

Arthur M. Sackler Gallery, **13**
Arts and Industries Building, **2**
Bureau of Engraving and Printing, **10**

Department of Agriculture, **11**
Freer Gallery of Art, **12**

Hirshhorn Museum and Sculpture Garden, **3**
National Air and Space Museum, **4**

National Gallery of Art, East Building, **6**
National Gallery of Art, West Building, **5**
National Museum of African Art, **14**

National Museum of American History, **8**
National Museum of Natural History, **7**
Smithsonian Institution Building, **1**

United States Holocaust Memorial Museum, **9**

in 2002. Turn left on 4th Street and head across the Mall, and enjoy the view of the Capitol to your right and the Washington Monument to your left. Cross Madison Drive to get to the two buildings of the **National Gallery of Art.** The **West Building** ⑤ features works from the 13th to the 20th century, while the **East Building** ⑥ generally displays more contemporary works. Walk west on Madison Drive to the **National Museum of Natural History** ⑦, with some 120 million objects in its collection. The next building to the west is the **National Museum of American History** ⑧, which explores America's cultural, political, technical, and scientific past.

Go south on 14th Street, crossing the Mall and Independence Avenue, to the **United States Holocaust Memorial Museum** ⑨, a powerful reminder of the human capacity for inhumanity. One block to the south is the **Bureau of Engraving and Printing** ⑩, the source of all U.S. paper currency, stamps, military certificates, and presidential invitations. Head north up 14th Street, cross Independence Avenue and turn right, passing between the two buildings of the **Department of Agriculture** ⑪. Just across 12th Street is the **Freer Gallery of Art** ⑫ and its collection of Asian treasures. Just east of the Freer, off Independence Avenue, is the 4-acre **Enid Haupt Memorial Garden.** The garden sits mostly on top of two underground museums, the **Arthur M. Sackler Gallery** ⑬, sister museum to the Freer, and the **National Museum of African Art** ⑭, with objects representing hundreds of African cultures.

TIMING

Don't try to see all the Mall's attractions in a single day. Few people have the stamina for more than a half-day of museum or gallery going at a time. Children definitely won't. To avoid mental and physical exhaustion, try to devote at least two days to the Mall. Do the north side one day and the south the next. Or split your sightseeing on the Mall into museums the first day, art galleries the second. Check museum guides and maps for appealing exhibits that are not too far apart. Afterward, plan to do something relaxing that doesn't require more walking, as, for example, shopping tends to do. A picnic or afternoon tea may make more sense.

Sights to See

❸ **Arthur M. Sackler Gallery.** When Charles Freer endowed the gallery that bears his name, he insisted on a few conditions: Objects in the collection could not be loaned out, nor could objects from outside the collections be put on display. Because of the latter restriction it was necessary to build a second, complementary museum to house the Oriental art collection of Arthur M. Sackler, a wealthy medical researcher and publisher who began collecting Asian art as a student in the 1940s. Sackler allowed Smithsonian curators to select 1,000 items from his ample collection and pledged $4 million toward the construction of the museum. The collection includes works from China, the Indian subcontinent, Persia, Thailand, and Indonesia. Articles in the permanent collection include Chinese ritual bronzes, jade ornaments from the 3rd millennium BC, Persian manuscripts, and Indian paintings in gold, silver, lapis lazuli, and malachite. ⊠ *1050 Independence Ave. SW,* ☎ *202/357–2700, TTY 202/357–1729.* ⊇ *Free.* ☉ *Daily 10–5:30. Metro: Smithsonian.*

❷ **Arts and Industries Building.** Exhibiting a rich collection of American Victoriana, this was the second Smithsonian museum to be constructed. In 1876 Philadelphia hosted the United States International Exposition in honor of the nation's Centennial. After the festivities, scores of exhibitors donated their displays to the federal government. In order to house the objects that had suddenly come its way, the Smithsonian commissioned this redbrick and sandstone building. Designed by Adolph Cluss, the building was originally called the United States National Museum, the name that is still engraved in stone above the doorway. It was finished in 1881, just in time to host President James Garfield's inaugural ball.

The Arts and Industries Building housed a variety of artifacts that were eventually moved to other museums as the Smithsonian grew. It was restored to its original appearance and reopened during Bicentennial celebrations in 1976. Many of the objects on display—which include carriages, tools, furnishings, printing presses, even a steam locomotive—are from the original Philadelphia Centennial. The Smithsonian hopes to open the National African American Museum here in 2002. ⊠ *900 Jefferson Dr. SW,* ☎ *202/357–2700, TTY 202/357–1729.* ⌨ *Free.* ⊙ *Daily 10–5:30. Metro: Smithsonian.*

Auditor's Building. Built in 1879, the Auditor's Building is of passing interest as the first building dedicated exclusively to the work of printing America's money. Renovated in 1991, it's now home to the United States Forest Service. ⊠ *14th St. and Independence Ave. SW. Metro: Smithsonian.*

🖑 ⑩ **Bureau of Engraving and Printing.** Paper money has been printed in this huge building since 1914, when they stopped printing it in the Auditor's Building. Despite the fact that there are no free samples, the 30-minute guided tour of the bureau—which takes visitors past presses that turn out some $450 million a day—is one of the city's most popular. In addition to all the paper currency in the United States, stamps, military certificates, and presidential invitations are printed here too. ⊠ *14th and C Sts. SW,* ☎ *202/874–3019.* ⌨ *Free; Apr. 3–Sept., same-day timed-entry passes issued starting at 7:45 AM at Raoul Wallenberg Pl. SW entrance.* ⊙ *Weekdays 9–2. Metro: Smithsonian.*

⑪ **Department of Agriculture.** While there's nothing of interest to tourists inside, this sprawling complex is too gargantuan to ignore. The home of a major governmental agency responsible for setting and carrying out the nation's agricultural policies, it comprises two buildings. The older building, on the north side of Independence Avenue, was started in 1905 and was the first to be constructed by order of the McMillan Commission on the south side of the Mall. The cornices on the north side of this white-marble building feature depictions of forests and of grains, flowers, and fruits—some of the plants the department keeps an eye on. The newer building south of Independence Avenue covers two city blocks (an example, perhaps, of big government). ⊠ *Independence Ave. between 12th and 14th Sts. SW. Metro: Smithsonian.*

⑫ **Freer Gallery of Art.** One of the world's finest collections of masterpieces from Asia, the Smithsonian's Freer Gallery of Art was made possible by an endowment from Detroit industrialist Charles L. Freer, who retired in 1900 and devoted the rest of his life to collecting art. Opened in 1923, four years after its benefactor's death, its collection includes more than 26,000 works of art from the Far and Near East, including Asian porcelains, Japanese screens, Chinese paintings and bronzes, Korean stoneware, and examples of Islamic art.

Freer's friend James McNeill Whistler introduced him to Asian art, and the American painter is represented in the vast collection. On display in Gallery 12 is the "Peacock Room," a blue-and-gold dining room decorated with painted leather, wood, and canvas and designed by Whistler for a British shipping magnate. Freer paid $30,000 for the entire room and moved it from London to the United States in 1904. The works of other American artists Freer felt were influenced by the

Orient also are on display. The Freer reopened in 1993 after a $26-million renovation. Additions include three floors of underground space, more storage space, a gift shop, and an auditorium. The original splendor of the spectacular Peacock Room was restored as well. ⊠ *12th St. and Jefferson Dr. SW,* ☎ *202/357–2700, TTY 202/357–1729.* ▨ *Free.* ⊘ *Daily 10–5:30. Metro: Smithsonian.*

❸ Hirshhorn Museum and Sculpture Garden. An architecturally striking but aesthetically controversial building that opened in 1974, the Hirschhorn manages a collection that includes 4,000 paintings and drawings and 2,000 sculptures donated by Joseph H. Hirshhorn, a Latvian-born immigrant who made his fortune in this country running uranium mines. American artists such as Eakins, Pollock, Rothko, and Stella are represented, as are modern European and Latin masters, including Francis Bacon, Fernando Botero, Magritte, Miró, and Victor Vasarely.

The Hirshhorn's impressive sculpture collection is arranged in the open spaces between the museum's concrete piers and across Jefferson Drive in the sunken **Sculpture Garden.** The display in the Sculpture Garden includes one of the largest public American collections of works by Henry Moore (58 sculptures), as well as works by Honoré Daumier, Max Ernst, Alberto Giacometti, Pablo Picasso, and Man Ray. Auguste Rodin's *Burghers of Calais* is a highlight.

Dubbed by its detractors "the Doughnut on the Mall," the cylinder-shaped, reinforced-concrete building designed by Gordon Bunshaft is a fitting home for contemporary art. The severe exterior lines of the museum were softened a bit in 1992 when its plaza was relandscaped by James Urban. Grass and trees provide a counterpoint to the concrete, and a granite walkway rings the museum and its outside sculpture. The museum's gift shop is known for its contemporary jewelry. ⊠ *Independence Ave. and 7th St. SW,* ☎ *202/357–2700, TTY 202/357–1729.* ▨ *Free.* ⊘ *Daily 10–5:30, sculpture garden open daily 7:30–dusk. Metro: Smithsonian.*

★ ☙ **❹ National Air and Space Museum.** Opened in 1976, Air and Space is the most visited museum in the world, attracting some 12 million people each year. (It's thought to be the most-visited building on earth.) Twenty-three galleries tell the story of aviation from the earliest human attempts at flight. Suspended from the ceiling like plastic models in a child's room are dozens of aircraft, including the actual "Wright Flyer" that Wilbur Wright piloted over the sands of Kitty Hawk, North Carolina; Charles Lindbergh's "Spirit of St. Louis"; the X-1 rocket plane in which Chuck Yeager broke the sound barrier; and the X-15, the fastest plane ever built.

Other highlights include a backup model of the Skylab orbital workshop that visitors can walk through; the Voyager airplane that Dick Rutan and Jeana Yeager flew nonstop around the world; the Lockheed Vega piloted by Amelia Earhart in 1932 in the first solo transatlantic flight by a woman; and the U.S.S. *Enterprise* model used in the "Star Trek" TV show, which is currently unviewable due to repairs. Visitors can also touch a piece of the moon: a 4-billion-year-old slice of rock collected by Apollo 17 astronauts. (Moon rock is one of the rarest substances on earth and, soon after the museum opened, a few zealous tourists tried to add the rock to their collections. The display is now wired with a motion alarm and watched by a uniformed guard.)

Don't let long lines deter you from seeing a show in the museum's **Samuel P. Langley Theater.** IMAX films shown on the five-story-high screen—including *The Dream Is Alive, To Fly!* and *The Blue Planet*—usually feature swooping aerial scenes that will convince you you've left the ground. Purchase tickets up to two weeks in advance or as soon as you arrive (prices vary but are inexpensive), then tour the museum. Upstairs, the **Albert Einstein Planetarium,** which charges a small fee, projects images of celestial bodies on a domed ceiling. Double features are often shown in Langley Theater after the museum has closed; for information, call 202/357–1686. ⊠ *Jefferson Dr. and 6th St. SW,* ☎ *202/357–2700, TTY 202/357–1729.* 🎟 *Free.* ◷ *Daily 10–5:30, extended summer hrs determined annually. Metro: Smithsonian.*

NEED A
BREAK?

Two restaurants are at the eastern end of the National Air and Space Museum: **The Wright Place** is a table-service restaurant that takes reservations (☎ 202/371–8777); the **Flight Line** is a self-service cafeteria. They each have a large selection of foods, but at peak times lines can be long.

★ **National Gallery of Art.** The two buildings of the National Gallery hold one of the world's foremost collections of paintings, sculptures, and graphics. If you want to view the museum's holdings in (more or less) chronological order, it's best to start your exploration of this magnif-

❺ icent gallery in the **West Building.** Opened in 1941, the domed building was a gift to the nation from financier Andrew Mellon. (The dome was one of architect John Russell Pope's favorite devices. He designed the domed Jefferson Memorial and the National Archives, with its domed rotunda.)

A wealthy banker and oil company executive, Andrew Mellon served as secretary of the treasury under three presidents and as ambassador to the United Kingdom. He first came to Washington in 1921, and lived for many years in a luxurious apartment near Dupont Circle, in a building that today houses the National Trust for Historic Preservation (☞ Dupont Circle, *below*). Mellon had long collected great works of art, acquiring some on his frequent trips to Europe. In 1931, when the Soviet government was short on cash and selling off many of its art treasures, Mellon stepped in and bought more than $6 million worth of old masters, including *The Alba Madonna* by Raphael and Botticelli's *Adoration of the Magi.* Mellon promised his collection to America in 1936, the year before his death. He also donated the funds for the construction of the huge gallery and resisted suggestions it be named after him.

The West Building's **Great Rotunda,** with its 24 marble columns surrounding a fountain topped with a statue of Mercury, sets the stage for the masterpieces on display in the more than 100 separate galleries. You'll probably want to wander the rooms at your own pace, taking in the wealth of art. A tape-recorded tour of the building's better-known holdings is available for a $4 rental fee at the ground floor sales area adjacent to the Rotunda. If you'd rather explore on your own, get a map at one of the two information desks; one is just inside the Mall entrance (off Madison Drive), the other is near the Constitution Avenue entrance on the ground floor.

The National Gallery's permanent collection includes works from the 13th to the 20th century. A comprehensive survey of Italian paintings and sculpture includes *The Adoration of the Magi* by Fra Angelico and Fra Filippo Lippi and *Ginevra de'Benci,* the only painting by da Vinci in the western hemisphere. Flemish and Dutch works, displayed in a series of attractive paneled rooms, include *Daniel in the Lions' Den,* by Rubens, and a self-portrait by Rembrandt. The Chester Dale Collection comprises works by Impressionist painters such as Degas, Monet, Renoir, and Mary Cassatt.

⑥ To get to the **National Gallery of Art's East Building** you can take a moving walkway that travels below ground between the two buildings. But to appreciate architect I. M. Pei's impressive, angular East Building, enter it from outside rather than from underground. Exit the West Building through its eastern doors, and cross 4th Street. (As you cross, look to the north: Seeming to float above the Doric columns and pediment of the D.C. Superior Court is the green roof and redbrick pediment of the Pension Building, four blocks away.)

The East Building opened in 1978 in response to the changing needs of the National Gallery. The awkward trapezoidal shape of the building site, which had been taken up by tennis courts and rose bushes planted during Lady Bird Johnson's spruce-up campaign, prompted Pei's dramatic approach: Two interlocking spaces shaped like triangles provide room for galleries, auditoriums, and administrative offices. While the East Building's triangles contrast sharply with the symmetrical classical facade and gentle dome of the West Building, both buildings are constructed of pink marble from the same Tennessee quarries. Despite its severe angularity, Pei's building is inviting. The axe-blade-like southwest corner has been darkened and polished smooth by thousands of hands irresistibly drawn to it.

The atrium of the East Building is dominated by two massive works of art: Alexander Calder's mobile *Untitled* and *Woman*, a huge wall-hanging by Joan Miró. The galleries here generally display modern art, though the East Building serves as a home for major temporary exhibitions that span years and artistic styles. ⊠ *Constitution Ave. between 3rd and 7th Sts. NW*, ☎ *202/737–4215, TTY 202/842–6176.* ⌷ *Free.* ☉ *Mon.–Sat. 10–5, Sun. 11–6. Metro: Archives/Navy Memorial.*

NEED A BREAK?	Two restaurants on the concourse level between the East and West buildings of the National Gallery offer bleary-eyed and foot-sore museum goers the chance to recharge. The **Buffet** serves a wide variety of soups, sandwiches, salads, hot entrées, and desserts. The **Cascade Café** has a smaller selection, but customers enjoy the soothing effect of the gentle waterfall that splashes against the glass-covered wall. If you're in the East Building, try the Terrace Café; in the West Building, dine in the Garden Café.

⑭ **National Museum of African Art.** With a permanent collection of more than 7,000 objects representing hundreds of African cultures, the National Museum of African Art is one of the Smithsonian's two underground museums (the other is the Freer Gallery of Art). It was founded in 1964 as a private educational institution dedicated to the collection, exhibition, and study of the traditional arts of Africa. On display are masks, carvings, textiles, and jewelry, all made from materials such as wood, fiber, bronze, ivory, and fired clay. A new permanent exhibit explores the personal objects—chairs, pipes, cups, snuff containers—that were a part of daily life in 19th- and early 20th-century Africa. These items show how aesthetics are integrated with utility to create works of peculiar beauty. Because many pieces of African art are made of organic materials, the museum also runs a conservation laboratory, where curators work to arrest the decay of the valuable collection. ⊠ *950 Independence Ave. SW*, ☎ *202/357–4600, TTY 202/357–4814.* ⌷ *Free.* ☉ *Daily 10–5:30. Metro: Smithsonian.*

☁ **⑧** **National Museum of American History.** Opened in 1964 as the National Museum of History and Technology and renamed in 1980, the exhibits here explore America's cultural, political, technical, and scientific past. The incredible diversity of artifacts helps the Smithsonian live up to its nickname as "the Nation's attic." This is the museum that displayed Muhammad Ali's boxing gloves, the Fonz's leather jacket, and the Bunkers' living room furniture from "All in the Family." Visitors can wander for hours on the museum's three floors. The exhibits on the first floor emphasize the history of science and technology and include such items as farm machines, antique automobiles, early phonographs, and a 280-ton steam locomotive. The permanent "Science in American Life" exhibit—opened in 1994 and covering a whopping 12,000 square feet—shows how science has shaped American life through such breakthroughs as the mass production of penicillin, the development of plastics, and the birth of the environmental movement. The second floor is devoted to U.S. social and political history and features an exhibit on everyday American life just after the Revolution. A permanent exhibit, "First Ladies: Political Role and Public Image," displays the gowns worn by various presidential wives, but it goes beyond fashion to explore the women behind the satin, lace, and brocade. The third floor has installations on ceramics, money, graphic arts, musical instruments, photography, and news reporting.

Be sure to check out Horatio Greenough's statue of the first president (by the west-wing escalators on the second floor). Commissioned by Congress in 1832, the statue was intended to grace the Capitol Rotunda. It was there for only a short while, however, since the toga-clad likeness proved shocking to legislators who grumbled that it looked as if the father of our country had just emerged from a bath. The statue was first banished to the east grounds of the Capitol, then given to the Smithsonian in 1908. Those who want a more interactive visit should stop at two places: In the **Hands On History Room** visitors can ride a high-wheeler bike, harness a mule, or sort mail as it was done on the railroads in the 1870s. In the **Hands On Science Room** you can do one of 25 experiments, including testing a water sample and exploring DNA fingerprinting. ⊠ *Constitution Ave. and 14th St. NW,* ☎ *202/357–2700, TTY 202/357–1729.* ▣ *Free.* ☉ *Daily 10–5:30, Hands On History room Tues.–Sun. noon–3, Hands On Science room daily 10–5:30, extended spring and summer hrs determined annually. Metro: Smithsonian.*

★ ☾ **❼** **National Museum of Natural History.** Most of the Smithsonian's collection of objects—some 120 million specimens—are stored in the National Museum of Natural History. It was constructed in 1910, and two wings were added in the '60s. The result is one of the great natural history museums of the world, filled with bones, fossils, stuffed animals, and other natural delights. Exhibits also explore the many ingenious ways that humans adapt to their environment.

The first-floor rotunda is dominated by a stuffed, 8-ton, 13-foot African bull elephant, one of the largest specimens ever found. (The tusks are fiberglass; the original ivory ones were apparently far too heavy for the stuffed elephant to support.) Off to the right is the popular **Dinosaur Hall.** Fossilized skeletons on display range from a 90-foot-long diplodocus to a tiny thesalosaurus neglectus (a small dinosaur so named because its disconnected bones sat forgotten for years in a college drawer before being reassembled).

In the west wing are displays on birds, mammals, and sea life. Many of the preserved specimens are from the collection of animals bagged by Teddy Roosevelt on his trips to Africa. Not everything in the museum is dead, though. The sea-life display features a living coral reef, complete with fish, plants, and simulated waves. The halls north of the rotunda contain tools, clothing, and other artifacts from many cultures, including those of Native America and of Asia, the Pacific, and Africa.

The highlight of the second floor is the **mineral and gem collection.** Objects include the largest sapphire on public display in the country (the Logan Sapphire, 423 carats), the largest uncut diamond (the Oppenheimer Diamond, 253.7 carats), and, of course, the Hope Diamond, a blue gem found in India and reputed to carry a curse (though Smithsonian guides are quick to pooh-pooh this notion). The amazing gem collection is second in value only to the crown jewels of Great Britain. (The Hall of Gems was closed for renovations at press time and is expected to reopen in fall 1997; however, its more spectacular objects will remain on display.)

Also on the second floor is the renovated **O. Orkin Insect Zoo,** named for the pest control magnate who donated the money to modernize the exhibits. Visitors can view 68 species of live insects, from bees to tarantulas. You can even go on hands and knees through a termite mound.

If you've always wished you could get your hands on the objects behind the glass, stop by the **Discovery Room,** in the northwest corner of the first floor. Here elephant tusks, petrified wood, seashells, rocks, feathers, and other items from the natural world can be handled by children and their parents. ✉ *Constitution Ave. and 10th Sts. NW,* ☎ *202/357–2700, TTY 202/357–1729.* ✆ *Free.* ☉ *Daily 10–5:30; Discovery Room Tues.–Fri. noon–2:30, weekends 10:30–3:30; in spring and summer free passes distributed starting at 11:45 weekdays, 10:15 weekends; Naturalist Center Mon.–Sat. 10:30–4; extended spring and summer hrs determined annually. Metro: Smithsonian.*

National Sculpture Garden Ice Rink. In winter, you can rent skates at this circular iceskating rink, which is located across the Mall directly opposite the National Gallery of Art. Ice cream and other refreshments are available at the green building during the summer. ✉ *7th St. and Constitution Ave. NW,* ☎ *202/371–5340. Metro: Archives/Navy Memorial.*

❶ Smithsonian Institution Building. The first Smithsonian museum constructed, it is better known as the Castle. Although British scientist and founder James Smithson had never visited America, his will stipulated that, should his nephew, Henry James Hungerford, die without an heir, Smithson's entire fortune would go to the United States, "to found at Washington, under the name of the Smithsonian Institution, an establishment for the increase and diffusion of knowledge among men."

Smithson died in 1829, Hungerford in 1835, and in 1838 the United States received $515,169 worth of gold sovereigns. After eight years of congressional debate over the propriety of accepting funds from a private citizen, the Smithsonian Institution was finally established in 1846. The red sandstone, Norman-style headquarters building on Jefferson Drive was completed in 1855 and originally housed all of the Smithsonian's operations, including the science and art collections, research laboratories, and living quarters for the institution's secretary and his family. Known as "the Castle," the building was designed by James Renwick, the architect of St. Patrick's Cathedral in New York City. The statue in front of the Castle's entrance is not of Smithson but of Joseph Henry, the scientist who served as the institution's first secretary. Smithson's body was brought to America in 1904 and is entombed in a small room to the left of the Castle's Mall entrance.

The museums on the Mall are the Smithsonian's most visible presence, but the organization also sponsors traveling exhibitions and maintains research posts in such places as the Chesapeake Bay and the tropics of Panama.

Today the Castle houses Smithsonian administrative offices and is home to the Woodrow Wilson International School for Scholars. To get your bearings or help in deciding which Mall attractions you want to visit, drop by the **Smithsonian Information Center** in the Castle. A 20-minute video provides an overview of the various Smithsonian museums, and monitors display information on the day's events. Interactive videos provide more detailed information on the museums as well as other attractions in the Capitol. The Information Center opens at 9 AM, an hour before the other museums open, so you can plan your day on the Mall without wasting valuable sightseeing time. ⊠ *1000 Jefferson Dr. SW,* ☎ *202/357–2700, TTY 202/357–1729.* ⌸ *Free.* ☉ *Daily 9–5:30; closed Dec. 25. Metro: Smithsonian.*

To the right of the Castle is the pagodalike entrance to the **S. Dillon Ripley Center,** an underground collection of classrooms and offices named after a past Smithsonian secretary. Works from around the world are periodically shown in the center's International Gallery.

★ ❾ **United States Holocaust Memorial Museum.** Museums usually celebrate the best that humanity can achieve. This James Ingo Freed-designed museum instead illustrates the worst. The museum tells the story of the 11 million Jews, Gypsies, Jehovah's Witnesses, homosexuals, political prisoners, and others killed by the Nazis between 1933 and 1945. Striving to give a you-are-there experience, the graphic presentation is as extraordinary as the subject matter: Upon arrival, each visitor is issued an "identity card" containing biographical information on a real person from the Holocaust. As visitors move through the museum, they read sequential updates on their cards. The museum recounts the Holocaust in almost cinematic fashion, with documentary films, videotaped oral histories, and a collection that includes such items as a German freight car, used to transport Jews from Warsaw to the Treblinka death camp, and the Star of David patches that Jewish prisoners were made to wear. Like the history it covers, the museum can be profoundly disturbing; it is not recommended for visitors under 11. Plan to spend at least four hours here. After this powerful—even wrenching—experience, the adjacent **Hall of Remembrance** provides a space for quiet reflection. ⊠ *100 Raoul Wallenberg Pl. SW (enter from Raoul Wallenberg Pl. or 14th St. SW),* ☎ *202/488–0400; tickets also available through Ticketmaster,* ☎ *202/432–7328.* ⌸ *Free, although same-day timed-entry passes necessary (often not available after 11 AM).* ☉ *Daily 10–5:30. Metro: Smithsonian.*

THE MONUMENTS

Washington is a city of monuments. In the middle of traffic circles, on tiny slivers of park, and at street corners and intersections, statues, plaques, and simple blocks of marble honor the generals, politicians, poets, and statesmen who helped shape the nation. The monuments dedicated to the most famous Americans are west of the Mall on ground reclaimed from the marshy flats of the Potomac. This is also the location of Washington's cherry trees, gifts from Japan and focus of a festival each spring.

Numbers in the text correspond to numbers in the margin and on the Monuments map.

A Good Walk

Start with the tallest of them all, the 555-foot **Washington Monument** ① (Metro: Smithsonian) at the western end of the Mall. Then follow 15th Street southward past Independence Avenue to the **Tidal Basin** ②. The path that skirts the Tidal Basin leads to the Outlet Bridge and the **Jefferson Memorial** ③, designed by John Russell Pope and inspired by the Pantheon in Rome. Continue along the sidewalk that hugs the Tidal Basin and cross **Inlet Bridge** and enter **West Potomac Park.** Follow West Basin Drive to Ohio Drive, then cross Independence Avenue to the **Lincoln Memorial** ④. Walk down the steps of the Lincoln Memorial and to the left to the **Vietnam Veterans Memorial** ⑤, one of the most popular sites in Washington, and **Constitution Gardens** ⑥. Walk north to Constitution Avenue and head east to the stone **Lockkeeper's House** ⑦ at the corner of Constitution Avenue and 17th Street, the last remaining monument to Washington's unsuccessful experiment with a canal.

TIMING

Allow four or five hours to tour the monuments. This includes time to relax on a park bench and to grab a snack from either a vendor or one of the snack bars east of the Washington Monument and near the Lincoln Memorial. If you are visiting during the first two weeks in April, take some extra time around the Washington Monument and the Tidal Basin to marvel at the cherry blossoms, one of Washington's most famous—albeit short-lived–attractions. From mid-April through November, you might want to set aside an hour for a relaxing paddleboat ride in the Tidal Basin. During the summer, if it's an extremely hot day you may want to hop a Tourmobile bus and travel between the monuments in air-conditioned comfort.

Sights to See

❻ **Constitution Gardens.** Many ideas were proposed to develop a 50-acre site that was once home to "temporary" buildings erected by the Navy before World War I and not removed until after World War II. President Nixon is said to have favored something resembling Copenhagen's Tivoli Gardens. The final design was a little plainer, with paths winding through groves of trees and, on the lake, a tiny island paying tribute to the signers of the Declaration of Independence, their signatures carved into a low stone wall. ⊠ *Constitution Ave. between 17th and 23rd Sts. NW. Metro: Foggy Bottom.*

NEED A
BREAK?

At the circular **snack bar** just west of the Constitution Gardens lake you can get hot dogs, potato chips, candy bars, soft drinks, and beer at prices lower than those charged by most street vendors.

❸ **Jefferson Memorial.** The monument honoring the third president of the U.S. is the southernmost of the major monuments in the District. Congress decided that Jefferson deserved a monument positioned as prominently as those in honor of Washington and Lincoln, and this spot directly south of the White House seemed ideal. Jefferson had always admired the Pantheon in Rome—the rotundas he designed for the University of Virginia and his own Monticello were inspired by its dome—so architect John Russell Pope drew from the same source when he designed this memorial to our third president. Dedicated in 1943, it houses a statue of Jefferson. Its walls are lined with inscriptions based on his writings. One of the best views of the White House can be seen from the memorial's top steps. ⊠ *Tidal Basin, south bank,* ☎ *202/426–6821.* ▣ *Free.* ☉ *Daily 8 AM–midnight. Metro: Archives/Navy Memorial.*

★ ☜ ❹ **Lincoln Memorial.** Many people consider the Lincoln Memorial to be the most inspiring monument in the city. This was not always the case. While today it would be hard to imagine Washington without the Lincoln and Jefferson memorials, both were criticized when first built. The Jefferson Memorial was dubbed "Jefferson's muffin"; critics lam-

The Monuments

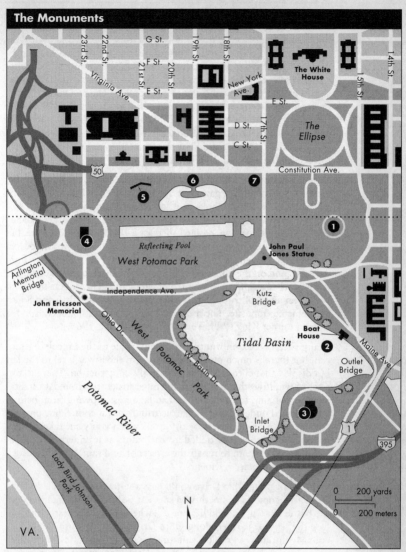

Constitution Gardens, **6**
Jefferson Memorial, **3**
Lincoln Memorial, **4**
Lockkeeper's house, **7**
Tidal Basin, **2**
Vietnam Veterans Memorial, **5**
Washington Monument, **1**

basted the design as outdated and too similar to that of the Lincoln Memorial. Some also complained that the Jefferson Memorial blocked the view of the Potomac from the White House. Detractors of the Lincoln Memorial thought it inappropriate that the humble Lincoln be honored with what amounts to a modified but nonetheless rather grandiose Greek temple. The white Colorado-marble memorial was designed by Henry Bacon and completed in 1922. The 36 Doric columns represent the 36 states in the Union at the time of Lincoln's death; the names of the states appear on the frieze above the columns. Above the frieze are the names of the 48 states in the Union when the memorial was dedicated. (Alaska and Hawaii are noted by an inscription on the terrace leading up to the memorial.)

Daniel Chester French's somber statue of the seated president, in the center of the memorial, gazes out over the Reflecting Pool. Though the 19-foot-high sculpture looks as if it were cut from one huge block of stone, it actually comprises 28 interlocking pieces of Georgia marble. (The memorial's original design called for a 10-foot-high sculpture, but experiments with models revealed that a statue that size would be lost in the cavernous space.) Inscribed on the south wall is the Gettysburg Address, and on the north wall is Lincoln's second inaugural address. Above each inscription is a mural painted by Jules Guerin: On the south wall is an angel of truth freeing a slave; the unity of North and South are depicted opposite. The memorial served as a fitting backdrop for Martin Luther King's "I have a dream" speech in 1963.

Many visitors look only at the front and inside of the Lincoln Memorial, but there is much more to explore. On the lower level to the left is a display that chronicles the memorial's construction. There is also a set of windows that look onto the huge structure's foundation. Stalactites (hanging from above) and stalagmites (growing from below) have formed underneath the marble tribute to Lincoln. Some parts of the Lincoln Memorial may be off-limits when you visit. Like the Jefferson, the Lincoln is shrouded in scaffolding as it undergoes a three- to five-year program to repair the effects of acid rain, insects, jet fuel, and other destructive elements.

If you walk along Ohio Drive you'll pass a series of playing fields. Softball has become as competitive a sport as politics in Washington, and the battle to secure a field here or elsewhere in the city starts long before the season. Farther along Ohio Drive, directly south of the Lincoln Memorial, is a granite sculpture honoring **John Ericsson,** builder of the ironclad *Monitor,* which took on the Confederate *Merrimac* at Hampton Roads off the coast of Virginia during the Civil War.

A memorial to veterans of the Korean War, between Independence Avenue and the Lincoln Memorial, in a grove of trees called Ash Woods, was dedicated on July 27, 1995—the 42nd anniversary of the Korean War armistice. **The Korean War Veterans Memorial** consists of a column of soldiers marching toward an American flag, along with a reflecting pool and a granite wall etched with war scenes.

Although visiting the area around the Lincoln Memorial during the day allows you to take in an impressive view of the Mall to the east, the best time to see the memorial itself is at night. Spotlights illuminate the outside while inside, light and shadows play across Lincoln's gentle face. ✉ *West end of Mall,* ☎ *202/426–6895.* ⊠ *Free.* ⊘ *24 hrs; staffed daily 8 AM–midnight. Metro: Foggy Bottom.*

❼ **Lockkeeper's House.** The stone Lockkeeper's House is the only remaining monument to Washington's unsuccessful experiment with a canal. L'Enfant's design called for a canal to be dug from the Tiber—a branch of the Potomac that extended from where the Lincoln Memorial is now—across the city to the Capitol and then south to the Anacostia River. (L'Enfant even envisioned the president riding in a ceremonial barge from the White House to the Capitol.) The City Canal became more nuisance than convenience, and by the Civil War it was a foul-smelling cesspool that often overran its banks. The stone building at this corner was the home of the canal's lockkeeper until the 1870s, when the waterway was covered over with B Street, which was renamed Constitution Avenue in 1932. ⊠ *Constitution Ave. and 17th St. Metro: Federal Triangle, 5 blocks east on 12th St.*

② Tidal Basin. This placid pond was part of the Potomac until 1882, when portions of the river were filled in to improve navigation and create additional parkland, including that upon which the Jefferson Memorial was later built. Paddleboats have been a fixture on the Tidal Basin for years. You can rent one at the boathouse on the east side of the basin, southwest of the Bureau of Engraving.

Walking along the sidewalk that hugs the Tidal Basin, you'll see two grotesque sculpted heads on the sides of the **Inlet Bridge.** The inside walls of the bridge also sport two other interesting sculptures: bronze, human-headed fish that spout water from their mouths. The bridge was refurbished in the 1980s at the same time the chief of the park—a Mr. Jack Fish—was retiring. Sculptor Constantine Sephralis played a little joke: These fish heads are actually Fish's head.

Once you cross the bridge, you have a choice: You can walk to the left, along the Potomac, or continue along the Tidal Basin to the right. The latter route is somewhat more scenic, especially when the cherry trees are in bloom. The first batch of these trees arrived from Japan in 1909. The trees were infected with insects and fungus, however, and the Department of Agriculture ordered them destroyed. A diplomatic crisis was averted when the United States politely asked the Japanese for another batch, and in 1912 Mrs. William Howard Taft planted the first tree. The second was planted by the wife of the Japanese ambassador. About 200 of the original trees still grow near the Tidal Basin. (The Tidal Basin's cherry trees are the single-flowering Akebeno and Yoshino variety. Double-blossom Fugenzo and Kwanzan trees grow in East Potomac Park and flower about two weeks after their more famous cousins.)

The trees are now the centerpiece of Washington's Cherry Blossom Festival, held each spring. The festivities are kicked off by the lighting of a ceremonial Japanese lantern that rests on the north shore of the Tidal Basin, not far from where the first tree was planted. The once-simple celebration has grown over the years to include concerts, fashion shows, and a parade. Park Service experts try their best to predict exactly when the buds will pop. The trees are usually in bloom for about 10–12 days at the beginning of April. When winter refuses to release its grip, the parade and festival are held anyway, without the presence of blossoms, no matter how inclement the weather. And when the weather complies, and the blossoms are at their peak at the time of the festivities, Washington rejoices. ⊠ *Northeast bank of Tidal Basin,* ☎ *202/484–0206.* 🎫 *Paddleboat rental $8 per hr, $1.75 each additional 15 mins.* ☉ *Mid-Apr.–late Nov., daily 10–6, weather permitting. Metro: Archives/Navy Memorial.*

West Potomac Park, the green expanse to the west of the Tidal Basin, is a pleasant place to sit and rest for a while, to watch the rented paddleboats skim the surface of the Tidal Basin, and to feed the squirrels that usually approach looking for handouts. The character of West Potomac Park will change over the next few years as the $47.2 million Franklin Delano Roosevelt Memorial is constructed. FDR asked for a simple memorial (in fact, one already sits on a wedge of grass in front of the National Archives) but boosters have for years been pushing for something more grandiose. When it's completed (tentatively in 1996) the memorial will comprise a long sequence of walkways and shaded, exterior "rooms" containing sculptures and inscriptions about the 32nd president.

⑤ Vietnam Veterans Memorial. Renowned for its power to evoke deep and poignant reflection, the Vietnam Veterans Memorial was conceived by Jan Scruggs, a former infantry corporal who had served in Vietnam. The stark design by Maya Ying Lin, a 21-year-old Yale architecture student, was selected in a 1981 competition. Upon its completion in 1982, the memorial was decried by some veterans as a "black gash of shame." With the addition of Frederick Hart's statue of three soldiers and a flagpole just south of the wall, most critics were won over.

The wall is one of the most visited sites in Washington, its black granite panels reflecting the sky, the trees, and the faces of those looking for the names of friends or relatives who died in the war. The names of more than 58,000 Americans are etched on the face of the memorial in the order of their deaths. Directories at the entrance and exit to the wall list the names in alphabetical order. (It was recently discovered that because of a clerical error the names of some two dozen living vets are carved into the stone as well.) For help in finding a specific name, ask a ranger at the blue-and-white hut near the entrance. Thousands of offerings are left at the wall each year: letters, flowers, medals, uniforms, snapshots. The National Park Service collects these and stores them in a warehouse in Lanham, Maryland, where they are fast becoming another memorial. Tents are often set up near the wall by veterans groups; some provide information on soldiers who remain missing in action, and others are on call to help fellow vets deal with the sometimes overwhelming emotions that grip them when visiting the wall for the first time. ⊠ *Constitution Gardens, 23rd St. and Constitution Ave. NW,* ☎ *202/634–1568.* ⊠ *Free.* ☉ *24 hrs; staffed daily 8 AM–midnight. Metro: Foggy Bottom.*

Vietnam Women's Memorial. After years of debate over its design and necessity, the Vietnam Women's Memorial, honoring the women who served in that conflict, was finally dedicated on Veterans Day 1993. The FDR, Korean War, and Vietnam Women's memorials—as well as proposed memorials to military women, black patriots, and George Mason—have troubled some Washingtonians. They feel the city is entering an unnecessary monument-building boom in the 1990s. Each veterans' and special-interest group seems to want its own separate memorial and there's concern that too many grandiose designs (each group, of course, wants its memorial to be the biggest) are clogging Washington's monumental core. Be this as it may, the Vietnam Women's Memorial is a stirring sculpture group consisting of two uniformed women caring for a wounded male soldier while a third woman kneels nearby. ⊠ *Constitution Gardens, southeast of Vietnam Veterans Memorial. Metro: Foggy Bottom.*

① Washington Monument. At the western end of the Mall, the 555-foot, 5-inch Washington Monument punctuates the capital like a huge exclamation point. Visible from nearly everywhere in the city, it serves as a landmark for visiting tourists and lost motorists alike.

Congress first authorized a monument to General Washington in 1783. In his 1791 plan for the city, Pierre L'Enfant selected a site (the point where a line drawn west from the Capitol crossed one drawn south from the White House), but it wasn't until 1833, after years of quibbling in Congress, that a private National Monument Society was formed to select a designer and to search for funds. Robert Mills's winning design called for a 600-foot-tall decorated obelisk rising from a circular colonnaded building. The building at the base was to be an American pantheon, adorned with statues of national heroes and a massive statue of Washington riding in a chariot pulled by snorting horses.

Because of the marshy conditions of L'Enfant's original site, the position of the monument was shifted to firmer ground 100 yards southeast. (If you walk a few steps north of the monument you can see the stone marker that denotes L'Enfant's original axis.) The cornerstone was laid in 1848 with the same Masonic trowel Washington himself had used to lay the Capitol's cornerstone 55 years earlier. The Monument Society continued to raise funds after construction was begun, soliciting subscriptions of one dollar from citizens across America. It also urged states, organizations, and foreign governments to contribute memorial stones for the construction. Problems arose in 1854, when members of the anti-Papist "Know Nothing" party stole a block donated by Pope Pius IX, smashed it, and dumped its shards into the Potomac. This action, a lack of funds, and the onset of the Civil War kept the monument at a fraction of its final height, open at the top, and vulnerable to the rain. A clearly visible ring about a third of the way up the obelisk testifies to this unfortunate stage of the monument's history: Although all of the marble in the obelisk came from the same Maryland quarry, that used for the second phase of construction came from a different stratum and is of a slightly different shade.

In 1876 Congress finally appropriated $200,000 to finish the monument, and the Army Corps of Engineers took over construction, thankfully simplifying Mills's original design. Work was finally completed in December 1884, when the monument was topped with a 7½-pound piece of aluminum, then one of the most expensive metals in the world. Four years later the monument was opened to visitors, who rode to the top in a steam-operated elevator. (Only men were allowed to take the 20-minute ride; it was thought too dangerous for women, who as a result had to walk up the stairs if they wanted to see the view.)

The Washington Monument is the world's tallest masonry structure. The view from the top takes in most of the District and parts of Maryland and Virginia. Visitors are no longer permitted to climb the 898 steps leading to the top. (Incidents of vandalism and a disturbing number of heart attacks on the steps convinced the Park Service that letting people walk up on their own wasn't such a good idea.) Most weekends during the spring and summer there are walk-down tours at 10 and 2, with a volunteer guide describing the monument's construction and showing the 193 stone and metal plaques that adorn the inside. (The tours are sometimes canceled due to lack of staff. Call the day of your visit to confirm.)

There is usually a wait to take the minute-long elevator ride up the monument's shaft; Park Service rangers standing at the head of the line are good at estimating how long, generally 10 to 15 minutes for each side of the monument that is lined with people. If the line goes all the way around the monument, you'll wait anywhere from 40 minutes to an hour. In an effort to do away with the long lines, the Park Service has started using a free timed-ticket system from April through Labor Day. A limited number of tickets are available at the kiosk on 15th St. daily beginning at 7:30 AM, with a limit of six tickets per person. Tickets are good during a specified half-hour period. No tickets are required after 8 PM. Advance tickets are available from Ticketmaster (☎ 202/432–7328) or from the kiosk on 15th St. There is a $1.50 per ticket service charge when using Ticketmaster. ⊠ *Constitution Ave. and 15th St. NW,* ☎ *202/426–6840.* 🖅 *Free.* ☉ *Apr.–Labor Day, daily 8 AM–midnight; Sept.–Mar., daily 9–5. Metro: Smithsonian.*

After your ascent and descent, walk on the path that leads south from the monument. On your right you'll pass the open-air **Sylvan Theater,** scene of a variety of musical performances during the warmer months.

THE WHITE HOUSE AREA

In a world full of immediately recognizable images, few are better known—not just in the U.S. but from Chile to China—than the white-washed, 32-room, Irish country house-like mansion at 1600 Pennsylvania Avenue, the country's most famous address, known as the White House. The residence of arguably the single most powerful person on the planet, it has an awesome majesty, having been the home of every U.S. president but, ironically, the father of our country, George Washington. This is where the buck stops in America and where the nation turns in times of crisis. After joining the more than 1.5 million people who visit the White House each year, strike out into the surrounding streets to explore the president's neighborhood, which includes some of the oldest houses in the city.

Numbers in the text correspond to numbers in the margin and on the White House Area map.

A Good Walk

Your first stop should be the **White House Visitor Center** ① at 14th and E Streets. Go north one block on 15th Street, then turn left to the ★**White House** ②. Across Pennsylvania Avenue is **Lafayette Square** ③, with its statues, trees, and flowers. Opposite the park, on H Street, is the golden-domed **St. John's Episcopal Church** ④, the so-called "Church of the Presidents." Head west on H Street to Jackson Place and the Federal-style **Decatur House** ⑤, built for naval hero Stephen Decatur and his wife Susan in 1819. Walk down Jackson Place to Pennsylvania Avenue and turn right to the **Renwick Gallery** ⑥, another member of the Smithsonian family of museums, and its neighbor **Blair House,** used as a residence by visiting heads of state. Go south on 17th Street past the **Old Executive Office Building** ⑦, once home to the War, Navy, and State departments. At the corner of 17th Street and New York Avenue is the **Corcoran Gallery of Art** ⑧, one of the few large non-Smithsonian museums in Washington. Proceed one block west on New York Avenue to the unusually shaped **Octagon** ⑨, with exhibits on the architecture and history of Washington. A block south on 18th Street is the **Department of the Interior** building ⑩, decorated with 1930s murals illustrating the department's work as overseer of most of the country's federally owned land and natural resources. Walk back east on E Street to 17th Street to the three buildings of the **American Red Cross** ⑪, one of which features three Tiffany stained glass windows. A block south is **Memorial Continental Hall** ⑫, headquarters of the Daughters of the American Revolution, with thirty-three period rooms decorated in a variety of styles. Just across C Street to the south of Continental Hall is the **House of the Americas** ⑬, the headquarters of the Organization of American States. Behind the House of the Americas is the **Art Museum of the Americas** ⑭, a small gallery that features works by 20th-century Latin American artists. Head east on Constitution Avenue and take the first left after 17th Street, following the curving drive that encircles the **Ellipse** ⑮. Take E Street east to 15th Street, then turn left and pass between the mammoth **William Tecumseh Sherman Monument** ⑯ on the left, and **Pershing Park** ⑰ on the right, a quiet, sunken garden honoring General "Blackjack" Pershing, commander in chief of the American Expeditionary Force in World War I. Continue north up 15th Street to admire the impressive **Treasury Building** ⑱, the largest Greek Revival edifice in Washington, where this walk concludes.

TIMING

Touring the area around the White House could easily take you an entire day, depending on how long you visit each of the several museums along the way. Unlike many other tourist-intensive sights, you actually might get into the White House with less of a wait during the busy spring and summer season, thanks to the timed-ticket system used from March through September. If your interests lean toward history, you'll probably be more interested in Decatur House, the DAR Museum and the Octagon. If art is your passion, you'll want spend extra time at the Corcoran and Renwick galleries.

Sights to See

⑪ **American Red Cross.** Although it hosts occasional art exhibits, the American Red Cross national headquarters is mainly of passing interest. It's composed of three buildings. The primary building, a neoclassical structure of blinding white marble built in 1917, commemorates the service and devotion of the women who cared for the wounded on both sides during the Civil War. The building's Georgian-style board of governors hall has three stained-glass windows designed by Louis Tiffany. ⊠ *430 17th St. NW,* ☎ *202/737–8300.* 🎫 *Free.* ☉ *Weekdays 9–4. Metro: Farragut West.*

⑭ **Art Museum of the Americas.** With changing exhibits highlighting 20th-century Latin American artists, this small gallery is in a building that formerly served as the residence for the secretary general of the OAS. ⊠ *201 18th St. NW,* ☎ *202/458–6016.* 🎫 *Free.* ☉ *Tues.–Sat. 10–5. Metro: Farragut West.*

Blair House. A green canopy marks the entrance to Blair House, the residence used by heads of state visiting Washington. Harry S. Truman lived here from 1948 to 1952 while the White House was undergoing its much-needed renovation. A plaque on the fence honors White House policeman Leslie Coffelt, who died in 1950 when Puerto Rican separatists attempted to assassinate President Truman at this site. ⊠ *1651 Pennsylvania Ave. Metro: McPherson Square.*

Boy Scouts Memorial. Near the Ellipse stands this group of heroic statuary: a uniformed Boy Scout flanked by a male figure representing patriotism and a female figure who holds the light of faith. *East of Ellipse, near 15th St. NW. Metro: McPherson Square.*

⑧ **Corcoran Gallery of Art.** The Corcoran is one of the few large museums in Washington outside the Smithsonian family. The beaux arts–style building, its copper roof green with age, was designed by Ernest Flagg and completed in 1897. The gallery's permanent collection numbers more than 11,000 works, including paintings by the first great American portraitists John Copley, Gilbert Stuart, and Rembrandt Peale. The Hudson River School is represented by such works as *Mount Corcoran* by Albert Bierstadt and Frederic Church's *Niagara.* There are also portraits by John Singer Sargent, Thomas Eakins, and Mary Cassatt. European art is seen in the Walker Collection (late-19th- and early 20th-century paintings, including works by Courbet, Monet, Pissarro, and Renoir) and the Clark Collection (Dutch, Flemish, and French Romantic paintings, and the restored entire 18th-century Grand Salon of the Hotel d'Orsay in Paris). Be sure to see Samuel Morse's *Old House of Rep-*

38

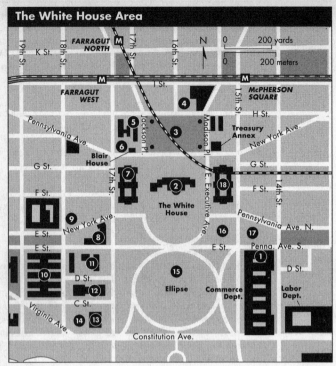

resentatives and Hiram Powers's *Greek Slave,* which scandalized Victorian society. (The latter, a statue of a nude woman with her wrists chained, was considered so shocking by Victorian audiences that separate viewing hours were established for men and women, and children under 16 were not allowed to see it at all.) Photography and works by contemporary American artists are also among the Corcoran's strengths. The adjacent Corcoran School is the only four-year art college in the Washington area. The **Winder Building** (⌧ 604 17th St.), one block north on 17th Street, was erected in 1848 as one of the first office blocks in the capital and was used during the Civil War as the headquarters of the Union Army. ⌧ *17th St. and New York Ave. NW,* ☏ *202/638–1439 or 202/638–3211.* ⌧ *Suggested donation: $3.* ☉ *Mon., Wed., and Fri.–Sun. 10–5; Thurs. 10–9; tours of permanent collection Fri.–Wed. at noon, Thurs. at 7:30 PM. Metro: Farragut West.*

NEED A BREAK?	In the Corcoran Gallery the **Café des Artistes** has a lunch menu that includes a selection of salads, light entrées, desserts, and a refreshing assortment of fruit and vegetable shakes. The café also serves a Continental breakfast, an English tea complete with scones and clotted cream, and dinner on Thursday, when the museum is open late. The Sunday brunch, where gospel singers and a jazz band perform live, is very popular.

⑤ Decatur House. Designed by Benjamin Latrobe, Decatur House was built for naval hero Stephen Decatur and his wife Susan in 1919. A redbrick, Federal-style building on the corner of H Street and Jackson Place, it was the first private residence on President's Park (the White House doesn't really count as *private*). Decatur had earned the affection of the nation in battles against the British and the Barbary pirates. Planning to start a political career, he used the prize money Congress awarded him for his exploits to build this home near the White House. Tragically, only 14 months after he moved in, Decatur was killed in a duel with James Barron, a disgruntled former Navy officer who held Decatur responsible for his court-martial. Later occupants of the house included Henry Clay, Martin Van Buren, and the Beales, a prominent family from the West whose modifications of the building include a parquet floor showing the state seal of California. The house is now operated by the National Trust. The first floor is furnished as it was in Decatur's time. The second floor is furnished in the Victorian style favored by the Beale family, who owned it until 1956 (thus making Decatur House both the first and *last* private residence on Lafayette Square). The National Trust store around the corner (entrance on H Street) sells a variety of books, postcards, and gifts. ⊠ *748 Jackson Pl. NW,* ☎ *202/842–0920.* 🎫 *$4.* ⊘ *Tues.–Fri. 10–3, weekends noon–4; tours on the hr and ½ hr. Metro: Farragut West.*

Many of the row houses neighboring Decatur House along Jackson Place date from the pre–Civil War or Victorian periods; even the more modern additions, though—such as those at 718 and 726—are designed in a style that blends with their more historic neighbors. **Count Rochambeau,** aide to General Lafayette, is honored with a statue at the park's southwest corner.

🔟 **Department of the Interior.** Designed by Waddy B. Wood, the Department of the Interior building was the most modern government building in the city and the first with escalators and central air-conditioning at the time of its construction in 1937. The outside of the building is somewhat plain, but much of the interior is decorated with paintings that reflect the Interior Department's work. Hallways feature heroic oil paintings of dam construction, panning for gold, and cattle drives. You'll pass several of these if you visit the **Department of the Interior Museum** on the first floor. (You can enter the building at its E Street or C Street doors; adults must show photo ID.) The museum tour will take you past more of the three dozen murals located throughout the building. Soon after it opened in 1938, the museum became one of the most popular attractions in Washington; evening hours were maintained even during World War II. The small museum tells the story of the Department of the Interior, a huge agency dubbed the "Mother of Departments" because from it grew the Departments of Agriculture, Labor, Education, and Energy. Today Interior oversees most of the country's federally owned land and natural resources, and exhibits in the museum outline the work done by the Bureau of Land Management, the U.S. Geological Survey, the Bureau of Indian Affairs, the National Park Service, and other Interior branches. The museum retains much of its New Deal–era flavor—including meticulously created dioramas depicting various historic events and American locales—and is, depending on your tastes, either quaint or outdated. Still, it's a nice contrast to the high-tech video museums of today. It is in the process of getting a facelift that promises to modernize it. The Indian Craft Shop across the hall from the museum sells Native American pottery, dolls, carvings, jewelry, baskets, and books. Call at least two weeks ahead to schedule a tour of the building's architecture and murals. ⊠ *C and E Sts. between 18th and 19th Sts. NW,* ☎ *202/208–4743.* 🎫 *Free.* ⊘ *Weekdays 8–5; closed federal holidays. Metro: Farragut West.*

🔟 **Ellipse.** Once actually part of the backyard of the White House, the Ellipse offers a vantage point from which you can see the Washington Monument and the Jefferson Memorial to the south and the red-tile roof of the Department of Commerce to the east, with the tower of the Old Post Office Building sticking up above it. To the north you have a good view of the back of the White House; the rounded portico and Harry Truman's second-story porch are clearly visible. The south lawn of the White House serves as a heliport for *Marine One,* the president's helicopter. On Easter Monday the south lawn is also the scene of the White House Easter Egg Roll. The **National Christmas Tree** grows on the northern edge of the Ellipse. Each year in mid-December it is lighted by the president during a festive ceremony that marks the beginning of the holiday season. ⊠ *Bounded by Constitution Ave. and E, 15th, and 17th Sts. Metro: Farragut West or McPherson Square.*

The Ellipse's rather weather-beaten **gate house** at the corner of Constitution Avenue and 17th Street once stood on Capitol Hill. It was designed in 1828 by Charles Bulfinch, the first native-born American to serve as architect of the Capitol, and was moved here in 1874 after the Capitol grounds were redesigned by Frederick Law Olmsted. A twin of the gate house stands at Constitution Avenue and 15th Street.

⑬ House of the Americas. Headquarters of the Organization of American States, House of the Americas contains a cool patio adorned with a pre-Columbian–style fountain and lush tropical plants. This tiny rain forest is a good place to rest when Washington's summer heat is at its most oppressive. The upstairs Hall of Flags and Heroes contains, as the name implies, busts of generals and statesmen from the various OAS member countries as well as each country's flag. ⊠ *17th St. and Constitution Ave. NW,* ☎ *202/458–3000.* ◻ *Free.* ☼ *Weekdays 9–5:30. Metro: Farragut West.*

❸ Lafayette Square. A lovely park bounded by Pennsylvania Avenue, Madison Place, H Street, and Jackson Place, Layfayette Square is an intimate oasis amid downtown Washington. With such an important resident living across the street, National Capital Park Service gardeners lavish extra attention on the square's trees and flower beds.

When Pierre L'Enfant proposed the location for the Executive Mansion, the only building north of what is today Pennsylvania Avenue was the Pierce family farmhouse, which stood at the northeast corner of the present square. An apple orchard and a family burial ground were the area's two other main features. During the construction of the White House, workers' huts and a brick kiln were set up, and soon private residences began popping up around the square (though sheep would continue to graze on it for years). L'Enfant's original plan for the city designated this area as part of "President's Park"; in essence it was the president's front yard, just as what is now the Ellipse was once the president's backyard. The egalitarian Thomas Jefferson, concerned that large, landscaped White House grounds would give the wrong impression in a democratic country, ordered that the area be turned into a public park. Soldiers camped in the square during the War of 1812 and the Civil War, turning it at both times into a muddy pit. Today, protesters set their placards up in Lafayette Square, jockeying for positions that face the White House. Although the National Park Service can't restrict the protesters' freedom of speech, it does try to restrict the size of their signs.

Standing in the center of the park—and dominating the square—is a large **statue of Andrew Jackson.** Erected in 1853 and cast from bronze cannon that Jackson had captured during the War of 1812, this was the first equestrian statue made in America. (An exact duplicate faces St. Louis Cathedral in New Orleans's Jackson Square.)

Jackson's is the only statue of an American in the park. The other statues are of foreign-born soldiers who helped in America's fight for independence. In the southeast corner is the park's namesake, the **Marquis de Lafayette,** the young French nobleman who came to America to fight in the Revolution. When Lafayette returned to the United States in 1824 he was given a rousing welcome: He was wined and dined in the finest homes and showered with gifts of cash and land.

The colonnaded building across Madison Place at the corner of Pennsylvania Avenue is an annex to the Treasury Department. The modern redbrick building farther on, at 717 Madison Place, houses a variety of judicial offices. Its design—with the squared-off bay windows—is echoed in the taller building that rises behind it and is mirrored in the **New Executive Office Building** on the other side of Lafayette Square. Planners in the '20s recommended that the private houses on Lafayette Square, many built in the Federal period, be torn down and replaced with a collection of uniform neoclassical-style government buildings. A lack of funds providentially kept the neighborhood intact, and in the early '60s John and Jacqueline Kennedy worked to save the historic town houses.

The next house down, yellow with a second-story ironwork balcony, was built in 1828 by Benjamin Ogle Tayloe. During the McKinley administration, Ohio Senator Marcus Hanna lived here, and the president's frequent visits earned it the nickname the "Little White House." Dolley Madison lived in the next-door Cutts-Madison House after her husband died. Both the Tayloe and Madison houses are now part of the Federal Judicial Center.

Continue down Madison Place. The next statue is that of **Thaddeus Kosciuszko,** the Polish general who fought alongside American colonists against the British. If you head east on H Street for half a block, you'll come to the **United States Government Bookstore** (✉ 1510 H St. NW, ☎ 202/653–5075), the place to visit if you'd like to buy a few pounds of the millions of tons of paper the government churns out each year. Here is where you'll find a copy of the latest federal budget or *The Surgeon General's Report on Nutrition and Health. Metro: McPherson Square.*

NEED A BREAK?	Adviser to Woodrow Wilson and other presidents, Bernard Baruch used to eat his lunch in Lafayette Park; you can, too. Nearby, **Loeb's Restaurant** (✉ 15th and I Sts. NW) is a New York–style deli that serves up salads and sandwiches to eat there or to go.

⑫ **Memorial Continental Hall.** A beaux arts building serving as headquarters of the Daughters of the American Revolution, Memorial Continental Hall was the site each year of the DAR's congress until the larger Constitution Hall was built around the corner. An entrance on D Street leads to the **DAR Museum.** Its 50,000-item collection includes fine examples of Colonial and Federal silver, china, porcelain, stoneware, earthenware, and glass. Thirty-three period rooms are decorated in styles representative of various U.S. states, ranging from an 1850 California adobe parlor to a New Hampshire attic filled with toys from the 18th and 19th centuries. Docents are available for tours weekdays 10–2:30. ✉ 1776 D St. NW, ☎ 202/879–3240. 🎟 *Free.* ☉ *Weekdays 8:30–4, Sun. 1–5. Metro: Farragut West.*

⑨ **Octagon.** This octagon actually has six, rather than eight, sides. Designed by William Thornton (the Capitol's architect), it was built for John Tayloe III, a wealthy Virginia plantation owner and was completed in 1801. Thornton chose the unusual shape to conform to the acute angle formed by L'Enfant's intersection of New York Avenue and 18th Street.

After the White House was burned in 1814 the Tayloes invited James and Dolley Madison to stay in the Octagon. It was in a second-floor study that the Treaty of Ghent, ending the War of 1812, was signed. By the late 1800s the building was used as a rooming house. In this century the house served as the headquarters of the American Institute of Architects before the construction of AIA's rather unexceptional building behind it.

A renovation in the 1960s revealed the Octagon's intricate plaster molding and the original 1799 Coade stone mantels (named for the man who invented a now-lost method of casting crushed stone). A far more thorough restoration, completed in 1996, returned the Octagon to its 1815 appearance, topped off by a new, and historically accurate, cypress-shingle roof, complete with balustrade. The galleries inside host changing exhibits on architecture, city planning, and Washington history and design. ⊠ *1799 New York Ave. NW,* ☎ *202/638–3105, TTY 202/638–1538.* ▱ *$3.* ⊙ *Tues.–Fri. 10–4, weekends noon–4. Metro: Farragut West.*

❼ Old Executive Office Building. Once one of the most detested buildings in the city, it now is one of the most beloved. It was built between 1871 and 1888 and originally housed the War, Navy, and State departments. Its architect, Alfred B. Mullett, patterned it after the Louvre, but detractors quickly criticized the busy French Empire design—with its mansard roof, tall chimneys, and 900 freestanding columns—as an inappropriate counterpoint to the Greek Revival Treasury Building that sits on the other side of the White House. Numerous plans to alter the facade foundered due to lack of money. The granite edifice may look like a wedding cake, but its high ceilings and spacious offices make it popular with occupants, who include members of the executive branch. Dan Quayle had his office in here; Albert Gore, Jr., is a little closer to the action, in the West Wing of the White House, just down the hall from the president. The Old Executive Office Building has played host to numerous historic events. It was here that Secretary of State Cordell Hull met with Japanese diplomats after the bombing of Pearl Harbor, and it was here that Oliver North and Fawn Hall shredded Iran-Contra documents. ⊠ *Across Pennsylvania Ave. west of White House. Metro: Farragut West.*

⑰ Pershing Park. A quiet sunken garden honors General "Blackjack" Pershing, famed for his failed attempt to capture the Mexican revolutionary Pancho Villa in 1916-1917 and then for commanding the American expeditionary force in World War I, among other military exploits. Engravings on the stone walls recount pivotal campaigns from that war. Ice-skaters glide on the square pool in the winter. ⊠ *15th St. and Pennsylvania Ave. Metro: McPherson Square.*

One block to the north of Pershing Park is the venerable **Hotel Washington** (☞ Chapter 5). Its lobby is narrow and unassuming, but the view from the rooftop Sky Top Lounge—open May to October—is one of the best in the city. ⊠ *515 15th St.,* ☎ *202/638–5900. Metro: McPherson Square.*

❻ Renwick Gallery. The Renwick has been at the forefront of the crafts movement, and its collection includes exquisitely designed and made utilitarian items, as well as objects created out of such traditional craft media as fiber and glass. The words "Dedicated to Art" are engraved above the entrance to the French Second Empire–style building, designed by Smithsonian Castle architect James Renwick in 1859 to house the art collection of Washington merchant and banker William Wilson Corcoran. Corcoran was a Southern sympathizer who spent the duration of the Civil War in Europe. While he was away his unfinished building was pressed into service by the government as a quartermaster general's post.

In 1874 the Corcoran, as it was then called, opened as the first private art museum in the city. Corcoran's collection quickly outgrew the building and in 1897 it was moved to a new gallery a few blocks south on 17th Street (described below). After a stint as the U.S. Court of Claims, this building was restored, renamed after its architect, and opened in 1972 as the Smithsonian's museum of American decorative arts. Although crafts were once the poor relations of the art world—handwoven rugs and delicately carved tables were considered somehow less "artistic" than, say, oil paintings and sculptures—they have recently come into their own.

Not everything in the museum is Shaker furniture and enamel jewelry, though. The second-floor Grand Salon is still furnished in the opulent Victorian style Corcoran favored when his collection adorned its walls. Paintings are hung in tiers, one above the other, and in Corcoran's portrait the Renwick itself is visible in the background. ⊠ *Pennsylvania Ave. and 17th St. NW,* ☎ *202/357–2700, TTY 202/357–1729.* ☜ *Free.* ☉ *Daily 10–5:30. Metro: McPherson Square.*

④ St. John's Episcopal Church. The golden-domed, so-called "Church of the Presidents" sits directly across Lafeyette Park from the White House. Every president since Madison has visited the church, and many worshiped here on a regular basis. Built in 1816, the church was the second building on the square. Benjamin Latrobe, who worked on both the Capitol and the White House, designed it in the form of a Greek cross, with a flat dome and a lantern cupola. The church has been altered somewhat since then; later additions include the Doric portico and the cupola tower. You can best sense the intent of Latrobe's design while standing inside under the saucer-shape dome of the original building. Not far from the center of the church is pew 54, where visiting presidents are seated. The kneelers of many of the pews are embroidered with the presidential seal and the names of several chief executives. Brochures are available inside for those who would like to take a self-guided tour. ⊠ *16th and H Sts. NW,* ☎ *202/347–8766.* ☜ *Free.* ☉ *Mon.–Sat. 8–3, tours after 11 AM Sun. service and by appointment. Metro: McPherson Square.*

Just east of the church is the four-story **St. John's Parish House,** built in 1836 by Matthew St. Clair Clark, clerk of the House of Representatives. The house's most famous resident was Lord Alexander Baring Ashburton, the British Minister who lived here in 1842 while negotiating a dispute over the position of the U.S.-Canadian border. The house later served as the British legation.

Across 16th Street stands the **Hay-Adams Hotel,** one of the most opulent hostelries in the city and a favorite with Washington insiders and visiting celebrities. It takes its name from a double house, owned by Lincoln biographer John Hay and historian Henry Adams, that stood on this spot. Next to it is the **Chamber of Commerce of the United States,** its neoclassical facade typical of the type of building that might have surrounded Lafayette Park had JFK not intervened. The statue at the northwest corner of Lafayette Square is of **Baron von Steuben,** the Prussian general who drilled Colonial troops during the Revolution.

⑱ Treasury Building. Once used as a repository for currency, this is the largest Greek Revival edifice in Washington. Pierre L'Enfant had intended for Pennsylvania Avenue to stretch in a straight, unbroken line from the White House to the Capitol. The plan was ruined by the construction of the Treasury Building on this site just east of the White House. Robert Mills, the architect responsible for the Washington Monument and the Patent Office (now the National Museum of American Art), designed the grand colonnade that stretches down 15th Street. Construction of the Treasury Building started in 1836 and, after several additions, was finally completed in 1869. Guided 90-minute tours are given every Saturday, except holiday weekends, at 10, 10:20, 10:40 and 11, and take visitors past the Andrew Johnson suite, used by Johnson as the executive office while Mrs. Lincoln moved out of the White House; the two-story marble Cash Room; and a 19th-century burglarproof vault lining that saw duty when the Treasury stored currency. Register at least one week ahead for the tour; visitors must provide name, date of birth, and Social Security number and must show a photo ID at the start of the tour. ⊠ *15th St. and Pennsylvania Ave. NW,* ☎ *202/622–0896, TTY 202/622–0692.* 🎟 *Free. Metro: McPherson Square.*

NEED A
BREAK?

About one block from the TreasuryBuilding is a glittering urban mall, **The Shops** (⊠ National Press Bldg., F and G Sts. between 13th and 14th Sts. NW), which houses table-service restaurants such as the **Boston Seafood Company**, as well as faster and cheaper fare in its top-floor Food Hall. The luxurious **Old Ebbitt Grill** (⊠ 675 15th St. NW, ☎ 202/347–4800) is a popular watering spot for journalists and television news correspondents. On Mondays, Benkay (⊠ 727 15th St. NW, lower level) has an $8 sushi buffet.

★ ☺ ❷ **White House.** This "house" surely has the best known address in the U.S.: 1600 Pennsylvania Avenue. Pierre L'Enfant called it the President's House; it was known formally as the Executive Mansion; and in 1902 Congress officially proclaimed it the White House, though, contrary to popular belief, it had been given that nickname even before its white sandstone exterior was painted to cover the fire damage it suffered during the War of 1812. Irishman James Hoban's plan, based on the Georgian design of Leinster Hall near Dublin and of other Irish country houses, was selected in a contest, in 1792. The building wasn't ready for its first occupant, John Adams, the second U.S president, until 1800, and so, in a colossal irony, George Washington, who seems to have slept everyplace else, never slept here. Completed in 1829, it has undergone many structural changes since then: Thomas Jefferson, who had entered his own design in the contest under an assumed name, added terraces to the east and west wings. Andrew Jackson installed running water. James Garfield put in the first elevator. Between 1948 and 1952, Harry Truman had the entire structure gutted and restored, adding a second-story porch to the south portico. Each family that has called the White House home has left its imprint on the 132-room mansion. George Bush installed a horseshoe pit. Most recently, Bill Clinton had a customized jogging track put in.

Tuesday through Saturday mornings (except holidays), from 10 AM to noon, selected public rooms on the ground floor and first floor of the White House are open to visitors. The White House Visitor Center disburses tickets March through September; in other months, go directly to the Southeast gate (before 10 AM) or the East gate (after 10 AM), both on East Executive Avenue, between the White House and the Treasury Building. The lines can be long, but the wait is worthwhile if you're interested in a firsthand look at what is perhaps the most important building in the city. There is seating on the Ellipse for those waiting to see the White House, and volunteer marching bands, drill teams, and other musical groups entertain those who are stuck in line. You can write to your representative or senator's office 8–10 weeks in advance of your trip to request special VIP passes for tours between 8 and 10 AM, but these tickets are extremely limited. On selected week-

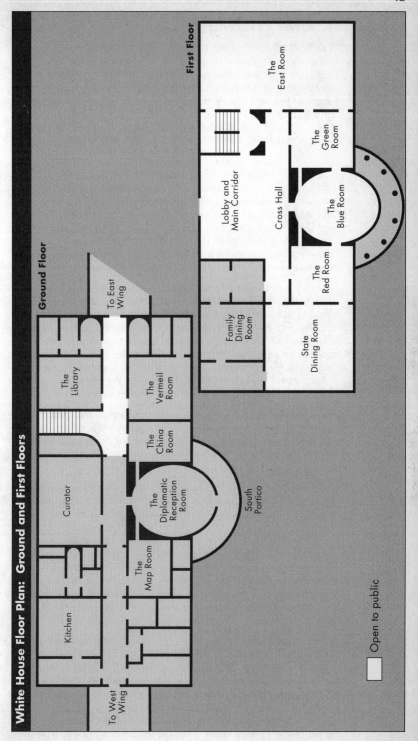

White House Floor Plan: Ground and First Floors

Ground Floor

Kitchen

Curator

The Library

To East Wing

The Map Room

The China Room

The Vermeil Room

The Diplomatic Reception Room

South Portico

To West Wing

First Floor

Lobby and Main Corridor

Cross Hall

Family Dining Room

State Dining Room

The Red Room

The Blue Room

The Green Room

The East Room

Open to public

ends in April and October, the White House is open for garden tours. In December it's decorated for the holidays.

You'll enter the White House through the East Wing lobby on the ground floor, walking past the Jacqueline Kennedy Rose Garden. Your first stop is the large white-and-gold **East Room,** the site of presidential news conferences. In 1814 Dolley Madison saved the room's full-length portrait of George Washington from torch-carrying British soldiers by cutting it from its frame, rolling it up, and spiriting it out of the White House. (No fool she, Dolley also rescued her own portrait.) A later occupant, Teddy Roosevelt, allowed his children to ride their pet pony in the East Room.

The Federal-style **Green Room,** named for the moss-green watered silk that covers its walls, is used for informal receptions and "photo opportunities" with foreign heads of state. Notable furnishings in this room include a New England sofa that once belonged to Daniel Webster and portraits of Benjamin Franklin, John Quincy Adams, and Abigail Adams. The president and his guests are often shown on TV sitting in front of the Green Room's English Empire mantel, engaging in what are invariably described as "frank and cordial" discussions.

The elliptical **Blue Room,** the most formal space in the White House, is furnished with a gilded Empire-style settee and chairs that were ordered by James Monroe. (Monroe asked for plain wooden chairs, but the furniture manufacturer thought such unadorned furnishings too simple for the White House and took it upon himself to supply chairs more in keeping with their surroundings.) The White House Christmas tree is placed in this room each year. Another well-known elliptical room, the president's **Oval Office,** is in the semidetached West Wing of the White House, along with other executive offices.

The **Red Room** is decorated as an American Empire–style parlor of the early 19th century, with furniture by the New York cabinetmaker Charles-Honoré Lannuier. You'll recognize the marble mantel as the twin of the mantel in the Green Room.

The **State Dining Room,** second in size only to the East Room, can seat 140 guests. The room is dominated by G. P. A. Healy's portrait of Abraham Lincoln, painted after the president's death. The stone mantel is inscribed with a quotation from one of John Adams's letters: "I pray heaven to bestow the best of blessings on this house and all that shall hereafter inhabit it. May none but honest and wise men ever rule under this roof." In Teddy Roosevelt's day a stuffed moose head hung over the mantel. Keep in mind that the White House is occasionally closed without notice for official functions. Baby strollers are not allowed on the tour. ✉ *1600 Pennsylvania Ave. NW,* ☎ *202/456–7041 or 202/619–7222.* ✍ *Free.* ⊘ *Tues.–Sat. 10–noon. Metro: McPherson Square.*

❶ **White House Visitor Center.** If you're visiting the White House during the months of March through September, you need to stop by the visitor center for free tickets. Tickets are dispensed on a first-come, first-served basis. (They are often gone by 9 AM.) Your ticket will show the approximate time of your tour. In other months, simply join the line that forms along East Executive Avenue, between the White House and the Treasury Building. Also at the center are exhibits pertaining to the White House's construction, its decor, and the families who have lived there. Photographs, artifacts, and videos relate the house's history to those who don't have the opportunity to tour the building personally. The official address is ✉ *1450 Pennsylvania Avenue NW, in Commerce*

Department's Baldrige Hall, E St. between 14th and 15th streets, ☎ *202/208–1631.* ⌨ *Free.* ⊙ *Daily 7:30–4. Metro: McPherson Square.*

⑯ William Tecumseh Sherman Monument. Sherman, whose Atlanta Campaign in 1864 cut a bloody swath of destruction through the Confederacy, was said to be the greatest Civil War general, as the sheer size of this massive monument, set in a small park, would seem to attest. ⊠ *Bounded by E and 15th Sts., East Executive Ave., and Alexander Hamilton Pl. Metro: Federal Triangle.*

Just north of this memorial is the southern facade of the Treasury Building, its entrance guarded by a **statue of Alexander Hamilton,** the department's first secretary.

CAPITOL HILL

The people who live and work on "the Hill" do so in the shadow of the edifice that lends the neighborhood its name: the gleaming white Capitol building. More than just the center of government, however, the Hill also includes charming residential blocks lined with Victorian row houses and a fine assortment of restaurants, bars, and shops. Capitol Hill's boundaries are disputed: It's bordered to the west, north, and south by the Capitol, Union Station, and I Street, respectively. Some argue that Capitol Hill extends east to the Anacostia River, others that it ends at 11th Street near Lincoln Park. The neighborhood does in fact seem to grow as members of Capitol Hill's active historic-preservation movement restore more and more 19th-century houses.

Numbers in the text correspond to numbers in the margin and on the Capitol Hill map.

A Good Walk

Start your exploration of the Hill at **Union Station** ①, beautifully restored in 1988. Next door is the **City Post Office,** also home to the **National Postal Museum** ②, the newest member of the Smithsonian family. Just east of Union Station is the **Thurgood Marshall Federal Judiciary Building** ③, with its spectacular atrium. Follow Delaware Avenue from the fountain at Union Station. On the left you'll pass the **Russell Senate Office Building** ④; to the right is the **memorial to Robert A. Taft** ⑤. Cross Constitution Avenue to the **Capitol** ⑥, where Congress helps decide how to spend your federal tax dollars. Walk down the northernmost to Pennsylvania Avenue and the white-marble **Peace Monument** ⑦. Walking south on First Street you'll pass the **Capitol Reflecting Pool,** the **Grant Memorial** ⑧, and the **James Garfield Memorial** ⑨. Across Maryland Avenue is the **United States Botanic Gardens** ⑩, an indoor museum of orchids, cacti, and other kinds of plant life. The ornate **Bartholdi Fountain** ⑪ is in a park across Independence Avenue. Continue east on Independence Avenue, past the **Rayburn, Longworth,** and **Cannon House office buildings,** to the **Jefferson Building** of the **Library of Congress** ⑫.

Behind the Jefferson Building stands the **Folger Shakespeare Library** ⑬, the world's foremost collection of works by and about Shakespeare and his times. The **Supreme Court Building** ⑭ is down the street on First Street, near East Capitol Street. One block north, at the corner of Constitution Avenue and 2nd Street, is the redbrick **Sewall-Belmont House** ⑮, the oldest house on Capitol Hill. For a taste of the residential side of the Hill, follow Maryland Avenue to Stanton Park, then walk two blocks south on 4th Street NE to A Street. The **Frederick Douglass Townhouse** ⑯ (not open to the public) is at 316 A Street. The houses on the **south side of East Capitol Street** ⑰, one block south on 4th Street, offer a sample of the different architectural styles on the Hill. Crossing East Capitol Street brings you to the southeast quadrant of the city. Artist Constantino Brumidi lived in the stucco house at **326 A Street** ⑱ while he was working on the Capitol.

TIMING

Touring the Capitol and the sites around it should take you about six hours, allowing for about an hour each at Union Station, the Capitol, and the Botanic Gardens, with plenty of time left for the Library of Congress and the Folger Shakespeare Library. If you want to see Congress in action, bear in mind that the House and Senate are usually not in session the month of August. Supreme Court cases usually are heard October through June, Monday through Thursday of two weeks in each month.

Sights to See

❶ **Bartholdi Fountain.** Frédéric-Auguste Bartholdi, sculptor of the more famous—and much larger—Statue of Liberty, created this delightful fountain, some 25 feet tall, for the Philadelphia Centennial Exhibition of 1876. With its aquatic monsters, sea nymphs, tritons, and lighted globes (once gas, now electric), the fountain represents the elements of water and light. The U.S. Government purchased the fountain after the exhibition and placed it on the grounds of the old Botanic Garden on the Mall. It was moved to its present location in 1932. ✉ *1st St. and Independence Ave. SW. Metro: Federal Center.*

★ ☙ ❻ **Capitol.** As beautiful as the building itself are the Capitol grounds, landscaped in the late-19th century by Frederick Law Olmsted, Sr., who, along with Calvert Vaux, created New York City's Central Park. On these 68 acres you will find both the tamest squirrels in the city and the highest concentration of television news correspondents, jockeying for a good position in front of the Capitol for their "stand-ups." A few hundred feet northeast of the Capitol are two cast-iron car shelters, left over from the days when horse-drawn trolleys served the Hill. Olmsted's six pinkish, bronze-topped lamps directly east from the Capitol are a treat, too.

When planning the city, Pierre L'Enfant described the gentle rise on which the Capitol sits, known then as Jenkins Hill, as "a pedestal waiting for a monument." The design of this monument was the result of a competition held in 1792; the winner was William Thornton, a physician and amateur architect from the West Indies. With its central rotunda and dome, Thornton's Capitol is reminiscent of Rome's Pantheon, a similarity that must have delighted the nation's founders, who felt the American government was based on the principles of the Republic of Rome.

The cornerstone was laid by George Washington in a Masonic ceremony on September 18, 1793, and in November 1800, both the Senate and the House of Representatives moved down from Philadelphia to occupy the first completed section of the Capitol: the boxlike portion between the central rotunda and today's north wing. (Subsequent efforts to find the cornerstone Washington laid have been unsuccessful, though when the east front was extended in the 1950s, workmen found a knee joint thought to be from a 500-pound ox that was roasted at the 1793 celebration.) By 1806 the House wing had been completed, just to the south of what is now the domed center, and a covered wooden walkway joined the two wings.

The Congress House grew slowly and suffered a grave setback on August 24, 1814, when British troops led by Sir George Cockburn marched on Washington and set fire to the Capitol, the White House, and nu-

Capitol Hill

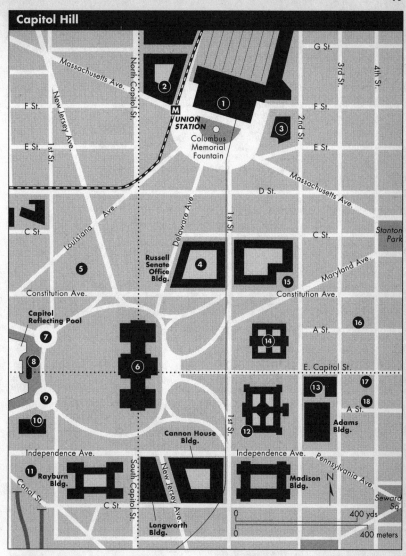

Bartholdi Fountain, **11**

Capitol, **6**

Folger Shakespeare Library, **13**

Frederick Douglass Townhouse, **16**

Grant Memorial, **8**

James Garfield Memorial, **9**

Library of Congress/Jefferson Building, **12**

National Postal Museum, **2**

Peace Monument, **7**

Robert A. Taft Memorial, **5**

Russell Senate Office Building, **4**

Sewall-Belmont House, **15**

South side of East Capitol Street, **17**

Supreme Court Building, **14**

326 A Street, **18**

Thurgood Marshall Federal Judiciary Building, **3**

Union Station, **1**

United States Botanic Gardens, **10**

50

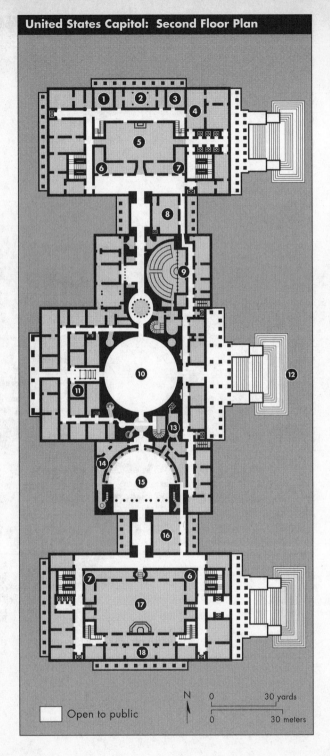

United States Capitol: Second Floor Plan

Open to public

N

0   30 yards

0   30 meters

merous other government buildings. (Cockburn reportedly stood on the House Speaker's chair and asked his men, "Shall this harbor of Yankee democracy be burned?" The question was rhetorical; the building was torched.) The wooden walkway was destroyed and the two wings gutted, but the walls were left standing after a violent rainstorm doused the flames. Fearful that Congress might leave Washington, residents raised money for a hastily built "Brick Capitol" that stood where the Supreme Court is today. Architect Benjamin Henry Latrobe supervised the rebuilding of the Capitol, adding such American touches as the corn-cob-and-tobacco-leaf capitals to columns in the east entrance to the Senate wing. He was followed by Boston-born Charles Bulfinch, and in 1826 the Capitol, its low wooden dome sheathed in copper, was finally finished.

North and south wings were added in the 1850s and '60s to accommodate a growing government trying to keep pace with a growing country. The elongated edifice extended farther north and south than Thornton had planned, and in 1855, to keep the scale correct, work began on a tall cast-iron dome. President Lincoln was criticized for continuing this expensive project while the country was in the throes of the bloody Civil War, but he called the construction "a sign we intend the Union shall go on." This twin-shelled dome, a marvel of 19th-century engineering, rises 285 feet above the ground and weighs 9 million pounds. It expands and contracts up to 4 inches a day, depending on the outside temperature. The figure on top of the dome, often mistaken for Pocahontas, is called *Freedom*. Sculptor Thomas Crawford had first planned for the 19-foot-tall bronze statue to wear the cloth liberty cap of a freed Roman slave, but southern lawmakers, led by Jefferson Davis, objected. An "American" headdress composed of a star-encircled helmet surmounted with an eagle's head and feathers was substituted. After being plucked from the dome by helicopter, *Freedom* received a much needed sprucing up in 1993.

The Capitol has continued to grow. In 1962 the east front was extended 34 feet, creating 100 additional offices. Preservationists have fought to keep the west front from being extended, since it is the last remaining section of the Capitol's original facade. A compromise was reached in 1983, when it was agreed that the facade's crumbling sandstone blocks would simply be replaced with stronger limestone.

Guided tours of the Capitol usually start beneath the dome in the Rotunda, but if there's a crowd you may have to wait in a line that forms at the top of the center steps on the east side. If you want to forgo the tour, which is brief but informative, you may look around on your own. Enter through one of the lower doors to the right or left of the main steps. Start your exploration under Constantino Brumidi's *Apotheosis of Washington*, the fresco in the center of the dome. Working as Michelangelo did in the Sistine Chapel, applying paint to wet plaster, Brumidi completed this fresco in 1865. The figures in the inner circle represent the 13 original states of the Union; those in the outer ring symbolize arts, sciences, and industry. The flat, sculpture-style frieze around the rim of the Rotunda depicting 400 years of American history was started by Brumidi. While painting Penn's treaty with the Indians, the 74-year-old artist slipped on the 58-foot-high scaffold and almost fell off. Brumidi managed to hang on until help arrived, but he died a few months later from shock brought on by the incident. The work was continued by another Italian, Filippo Costaggini, but the frieze wasn't finished until American Allyn Cox added the final touches in 1953.

Notice the Rotunda's eight immense oil paintings of scenes from American history. The four scenes from the Revolutionary War are by John

Trumbull, who served alongside George Washington and painted the first president from life. Twenty-six people have lain in state in the Rotunda, including nine presidents, from Abraham Lincoln to Lyndon Baines Johnson. Underneath the Rotunda, above an empty crypt that was designed to hold the remains of George and Martha Washington, is an exhibit chronicling the construction of the Capitol.

South of the Rotunda is Statuary Hall, once the legislative chamber of the House of Representatives. The room has an interesting architectural feature that maddened early legislators: A slight whisper uttered on one side of the hall can be heard on the other. (Don't be disappointed if this parlor trick doesn't work when you're visiting the Capitol; sometimes the hall is just too noisy.) When the House moved out, Congress invited each state to send statues of two great deceased citizens for placement in the former chamber. Because the weight of the accumulated statues threatened to cave the floor in, some of the sculptures were dispersed to various other spots throughout the Capitol.

To the north, on the Senate side, you can look into the chamber once used by the Supreme Court and into the splendid Old Senate Chamber above it, both of which have been restored. Also be sure to see the Brumidi Corridor on the ground floor of the Senate wing. Frescoes and oil paintings of birds, plants, and American inventions adorn the walls and ceilings, and an intricate, Brumidi-designed bronze stairway leads to the second floor. The Italian artist also memorialized several American heroes, painting them inside trompe l'oeil frames. Trusting that America would continue to produce heroes long after he was gone, Brumidi left some frames empty. The most recent one to be filled, in 1987, honors the crew of the space shuttle *Challenger*.

If you want to watch some of the legislative action in the **House or Senate chambers** while you're on the Hill you'll have to get a gallery pass from the office of your representative or senator. (To find out where those offices are, ask any Capitol police officer, or call 202/224–3121.) In the chambers you'll notice that Democrats sit to the right of the presiding officer, Republicans to the left—the opposite, it's often noted, of their political leanings. You may be disappointed by watching from the gallery. Most of the day-to-day business is conducted in the various legislative committees, many of which meet in the congressional office buildings. The Washington Post's daily "Today in Congress" lists when and where the committees are meeting. To get to a House or Senate office building, go to the Capitol's basement and ride the miniature subway used by legislators.

When you're finished exploring the inside of the Capitol, make your way to the **west side.** In 1981, Ronald Reagan broke with tradition and moved the presidential swearing-in ceremony to this side of the Capitol, which offers a dramatic view of the Mall and monuments below and can accommodate more guests than the east side, where all previous presidents took the oath of office. ✉ *East end of Mall,* ☎ *202/224–3121 or 202/225–6827 (guide service).* 🎟 *Free.* ☉ *Daily 9– 4:30; summer hrs determined annually, but Rotunda and Statuary Hall usually open daily 9–8. Metro: Capitol South or Union Station.*

NEED A
BREAK?

A meal at a **Capitol cafeteria** may give you a glimpse of a well-known politician or two. A public dining room on the first floor, Senate-side, is open 7:30 AM–3:30 PM. A favorite with legislators is the Senate bean soup, made and served every day since 1901 (no one is sure exactly why, though the menu, which you can take with you, outlines a few popular theories).

⑬ Folger Shakespeare Library. The Folger Library's collection of works by and about Shakespeare and his times is second to none. The white-marble Art Deco building, designed by architect Paul Philippe Cret, is decorated with scenes from the Bard's plays. Inside is a reproduction of an inn-yard theater, which is the setting for performances of chamber music, baroque opera, and other events appropriate to the surroundings, and a gallery, designed in the manner of an Elizabethan Great Hall, which hosts rotating exhibits from the library's collection. ⊠ *201 E. Capitol St. SE,* ☎ *202/544–4600.* ▣ *Free.* ☽ *Mon.–Sat. 10–4. Metro: Capitol South.*

⑯ Frederick Douglass Townhouse. No longer open to the public, a gray house with the mansard roof was the first Washington home of the fiery abolitionist and writer. The building once housed the National Museum of African Art, but when the museum moved to new quarters on the Mall (☞ The Mall, *above*) in 1987, the Douglass townhouse was closed. Even though you can't go inside it's worth knowing if you should pass by (it's not far from the Supreme Court building) that here is where one of the seminal figures of the Civil War era once lived. ⊠ *316 A St. Metro: Capitol South.*

⑧ Grant Memorial. The 252-foot-long memorial to the 16th American president and commander in chief of the Union forces during the Civil War is the largest sculpture group in the city. The statue of Ulysses S. Grant on horseback is flanked by Union artillery and cavalry. ⊠ *Near 1st St. and Maryland Ave. SW. Metro: Federal Center.*

⑨ James Garfield Memorial. Near the Grant Memorial and the United States Botanic Gardens is a memorial to the 20th president of the United States. James Garfield was assassinated in 1881 after only a few months in office. His bronze statue stands on a pedestal with three other bronze figures seated around it; one bears a tablet inscribed with the words "Law," "Justice" and "Prosperity," which the figures presumably represent. Grand though this may seem, Garfield's two primary claims to fame were that he was the last log cabin president, and that his was the second presidential assassination (Lincoln's was first) ending the second-shortest presidency. ⊠ *1st St. and Maryland Ave. SW. Metro: Federal Center.*

⑫ Library of Congress. One of the world's largest libraries, the Library of Congress contains some 108 million items, of which only a quarter are books. The remainder includes manuscripts, prints, films, photographs, sheet music, and the largest collection of maps in the world. Also part of the library is the Congressional Research Service, which, as the name implies, works on special projects for senators and representatives.

The green-domed **Jefferson Building,** the oldest of the three buildings that make up the library, is at Independence Avenue and 1st Street SE. Like many buildings in Washington that seem a bit overwrought (the Old Executive Office Building is another example), the library was criticized when it was completed, in 1897. Some detractors felt its Italian Renaissance design was a bit too florid. Congressmen were even heard to grumble that its dome—topped with the gilt "Flame of Knowledge"—competed with that of their Capitol. It is certainly decorative, with busts of Dante, Goethe, Hawthorne, and other great writers perched above its entryway. *The Court of Neptune,* Roland Hinton Perry's fountain at the base of the front steps, rivals some of Rome's best fountains.

Provisions for a library to serve members of Congress were originally made in 1800, when the government set aside $5,000 to purchase and house books that legislators might need to consult. This small collection was housed in the Capitol but was destroyed in 1814, when the British burned the city. Thomas Jefferson, then in retirement at Monticello, offered his personal library as a replacement, noting that "there is, in fact, no subject to which a Member of Congress may not have occasion to refer." Jefferson's collection of 6,487 books, for which Congress eventually paid him $23,950, laid the foundation for the great national library. (Sadly, another fire in 1851 wiped out two-thirds of Jefferson's books.) By the late 1800s it was clear the Capitol building could no longer contain the growing library, and the Jefferson Building was constructed. The **Adams Building,** on 2nd Street behind the Jefferson, was added in 1939. A third structure, the **James Madison Building,** opened in 1980; it is just south of the Jefferson Building, between Independence Avenue and C Street.

In 1996, the Jefferson and Adams buildings, which had been closed for renovations, were reopened to the public. The gem of the Jefferson Building is the richly decorated Great Hall, adorned with mosaics, paintings, and curving marble stairways. The grand, octagonal Main Reading Room, its central desk surrounded by mahogany readers' tables, is either inspiring or overwhelming to researchers. Computer terminals have replaced the wooden card catalogues, but books are still retrieved and dispersed the same way: Readers (18 years or older) hand request slips to librarians and wait patiently for their materials to be delivered. Researchers aren't allowed in the stacks and only members of Congress can check books out.

But books are only part of the story. Family trees are explored in the Local History and Genealogy Reading Room. In the Folklife Reading Room, patrons can listen to LP recordings of American Indian music or hear the story of B'rer Rabbit read in the Gullah dialect of Georgia and South Carolina. Items from the library's collection—which includes a Gutenberg Bible—are often on display in the Jefferson and Madison buildings. Classic films are shown for free in the 64-seat Mary Pickford Theater (call 202/707–5677 for information). Groups of 10 or more should call ahead for reservations. ⊠ *Jefferson Bldg., 1st St. and Independence Ave. SE,* ☎ *202/707–8000 or 202/707–6400 (taped schedule of general and special reading room hours).* 🎟 *Free.* ☽ *Call for hours open, which change daily. Tours weekdays at 11:30, 1, 2:30, and 4 from Great Hall. Metro: Capitol South.*

NEED A BREAK?	It's easy to grab a bite in the Library of Congress vicinity. The sixth floor dining halls of the **Madison Building** of the library itself offer great views and inexpensive fare. Or head for the library's **Adams Building,** where the south side of Pennsylvania Avenue SE, between Second and Fourth Streets, is lined with restaurants and bars frequented by those who live and work on the Hill. Another option is **Le Bon Cafe** (⊠ 210 2nd St. SE), a cozy French bistro serving excellent coffees, pastries, and light lunches.

⑤ Memorial to Robert A. Taft. Rising up above the trees in the triangle formed by Louisiana, New Jersey, and Constitution Avenues, a monolithic carillon pays tribute to the longtime Republican senator and son of the 27th president and longtime Republican senator. ⊠ *Constitution and New Jersey Aves. Metro: Union Station.*

② National Postal Museum. In the newest member of the Smithsonian family of museums, exhibits underscore the important part the mail played in the development of America and include horse-drawn mail coaches, railway mail cars, actual airmail planes, every U.S. stamp issued, many foreign stamps, and a collection of philatelic rarities. The National Museum of Natural History may have the Hope Diamond, but the National Postal Museum has in its collection the container used to mail the priceless gem to the Smithsonian. The museum takes up only a portion of what is the Washington **City Post Office,** designed by Daniel Burnham and completed in 1914. Nostalgic odes to the noble mail carrier are inscribed on the exterior of the marble building; one of them eulogizes the "Messenger of sympathy and love, servant of parted friends, consoler of the lonely, bond of the scattered family, enlarger of the common life." After extensive renovation, the building reopened as the National Postal Museum in 1993. ⊠ *2 Massachusetts Ave. NE,* ☎ *202/357–2700.* ▭ *Free.* ⊘ *Daily 10–5:30. Metro: Union Station.*

❼ Peace Monument. A white-marble memorial depicts America in the form of a woman grief-stricken over sailors lost at sea during the Civil War; she is weeping on the shoulder of a second female figure representing History. The plaque inscription refers movingly to navy personnel who "fell in defence of the union and liberty of their country 1861-1865." ⊠ *Traffic circle at 1st St. and Pennsylvania Ave. Metro: Union Station.*

❹ Russell Senate Office Building. Many buildings in Washington don't offer much to see, yet it still enriches a stroll through the city to know what they are as you pass by. The Russell Senate Office Building is one of them. Completed in 1909, this was the first of the Senate office buildings, and it's where many senators work when the they aren't convened in their grand meeting room: the U.S. Senate. Note the delicate treatment below the second-story windows that resembles twisted lengths of fringed cloth. Beyond it are the Dirksen and Hart Senate Office Buildings, which serve the same purpose. ⊠ *1st St. and Constitution Ave. NE. Metro: Union Station.*

❶❺ Sewall-Belmont House. This house, the oldest home on Capitol Hill, is now the headquarters of the National Woman's Party. It has a museum that chronicles the early days of the women's movement and is filled with period furniture and portraits and busts of such suffrage-movement leaders as Lucretia Mott, Elizabeth Cady Stanton, and Alice Paul. The redbrick house was built in 1800 by Robert Sewall. Part of the structure dates from the early 1700s, a record for the neighborhood. From 1801 to 1813 Secretary of the Treasury Albert Gallatin lived here. He finalized the details of the Louisiana Purchase in his front-parlor office. The house became the only private residence burned in Washington during the British invasion of 1814, after a resident fired on advancing British troops from an upper-story window. (It was, in fact, the only resistance the British met. The rest of the country was disgusted at Washington's inability to defend itself.) ⊠ *144 Constitution Ave. NE,* ☎ *202/546–3989.* ▭ *Free.* ⊘ *Tues.–Fri. 10–3, Sat. noon–4. Metro: Union Station.*

On Maryland Avenue, one block east of the Sewall-Belmont House, is the headquarters of the **Veterans of Foreign Wars.** The building is of less interest than the organization itself. Created in 1899 by veterans of the Spanish-American War, its focus is now on the rehabilitation of disabled veterans of subsequent wars and military engagements, as well as on the promotion of patriotism and community service. With more than 2.1 million members, the Veterans of Foreign Wars rivals the American Legion in size and influence.

❶❼ South side of East Capitol Street. While here, you can get a sample of the residential area of the Hill. Walk along East Capitol Street, the border between the northeast and southeast quadrants of the city, and you'll notice the orange and yellow trash cans emblazoned with the silhouette of a Native American, reminders that East Capitol street is a main thoroughfare to RFK Stadium, home turf of the Washington Redskins. In the '50s there was a plan to construct government office buildings on both sides of East Capitol Street as far as Lincoln Park, seven blocks to the east. The neighborhood's active historic-preservation supporters successfully fought the proposal. The houses on the south side of East Capitol Street are a representative sampling of homes on the Hill. The corner house, Number 329, has a striking tower with a bay window and stained glass. Next door are two Victorian houses with iron trim below the second floor. A pre–Civil War Greek-Revival frame house sits behind a trim garden at Number 317. ⊠ *E. Capitol St. between 3rd and 4th Sts. Metro: Capitol South.*

⑭ Supreme Court Building. It wasn't until 1935 that the Supreme Court got its own building: a white-marble temple with twin rows of Corinthian columns designed by Cass Gilbert. In 1800, the justices arrived in Washington along with the rest of the government but were for years shunted around various rooms in the Capitol; for a while they even met in a tavern. William Howard Taft, the only man to serve as both president and chief justice, was instrumental in getting the court a home of its own, though he died before it was completed.

The Supreme Court convenes on the first Monday in October and remains in session until it has heard all of its cases and handed down all its decisions (usually the end of June). On Monday through Wednesday of two weeks in each month, the justices hear oral arguments in the velvet-swathed court chamber. Visitors who want to listen can choose to wait in either of two lines. One, the "three-to-five-minute" line, shuttles visitors through, giving them a quick impression of the court at work. If you choose the other, for those who'd like to stay for the whole show, it's best to be in line by 8:30 AM. The main hall of the Supreme Court is lined with busts of former chief justices; the courtroom itself is decorated with allegorical friezes. Perhaps the most interesting appurtenance in the imposing building, however, is a basketball court on one of the upper floors (it's been called the highest court in the land). ⊠ *1st and E. Capitol Sts. NE,* ☎ *202/479–3000.* ⌨ *Free.* ☉ *Weekdays 9–4:30. Metro: Capitol South.*

⑱ 326 A Street. A now-private home in a quiet neighborhood behind the Library of Congress's Adams Building, number 326 was the stucco abode of artist Constantino Brumidi when creating works of art for the Capitol building, most famously the fresco *Apotheosis of Washington* which adorns the center of the great dome (☞ Capitol Hill, *above*). *Metro: Capitol South.*

❸ Thurgood Marshall Federal Judiciary Building. If you're in the Union Station neighborhood, the signature work of architect Edward Larabee Barnes is worth taking a moment to pop inside for a look at its spectacular atrium featuring a garden of bamboo five stories tall. ⊠ *Massachusetts Ave. opposite Union Station. Metro: Union Station.*

❶ Union Station. With its 96-foot-high coffered ceiling gilded with eight pounds of gold leaf, the city's train station is one of the Capitol's great spaces and is used for inaugural balls and other festive events. In 1902 the McMillan Commission—charged with suggesting ways to improve the appearance of the city—recommended that the many train lines that sliced through the capital share one main depot. Union Station was opened in 1908 and was the first building completed under the commission's plan. Chicago architect and commission member Daniel H. Burnham patterned the station after the Roman Baths of Diocletian.

For many visitors to Washington, the capital city is first seen framed through the grand station's arched doorways. In its heyday, during World War II, more than 200,000 people swarmed through the station daily. By the '60s, however, the decline in train travel had turned the station into an expensive white-marble elephant. It was briefly, and unsuccessfully, transformed into a visitor center for the Bicentennial; but by 1981 rain was pouring in through the neglected station's roof, and passengers boarded trains at a ramshackle depot behind the station.

The Union Station you see today is the result of a restoration completed in 1988, an effort intended to be the beginning of a revival of Washington's east end. It's hoped that the shops, restaurants, and nine-screen movie theater in Union Station will draw more than just train travelers to the beaux arts building. The jewel of the structure remains its meticulously restored main waiting room. Forty-six statues of Roman legionnaires, one for each state in the Union when the station was completed, ring the grand room. The statues were the subject of controversy when the building was first opened. Pennsylvania Railroad president Alexander Cassatt (brother of artist Mary) ordered sculptor Louis Saint-Gaudens to alter the statues, convinced that the legionnaires' skimpy outfits would scandalize female passengers. The sculptor obligingly added a shield to each figure, obscuring any offending body parts.

The east hall, now filled with vendors, was once an expensive restaurant. It is decorated with Pompeiian tracery and plaster walls and columns painted to look like marble. At one time the station also featured a secure presidential waiting room, now restored. The private waiting room was by no means a frivolous addition: Twenty years before Union Station was built, President Garfield was assassinated in the public waiting room of the old Baltimore and Potomac terminal on 6th Street. Call ahead to arrange a group tour. ⊠ *Massachusetts Ave. north of Capitol,* ☎ *202/289–1908. Metro: Union Station.*

The **Columbus Memorial Fountain,** designed by Lorado Taft, sits in the plaza in front of Union Station. A caped, steely-eyed Christopher Columbus stares into the distance, flanked by a hoary, bearded figure (the Old World) and an Indian brave (the New).

NEED A BREAK? On Union Station's lower level you'll find more than 20 food stalls offering everything from pizza to sushi. There are several restaurants throughout the station, one of the best being **America,** with a menu of regional foods that lives up to its expansive name.

👋 ⑩ **United States Botanic Gardens.** The rather cold exterior belies the peaceful, plant-filled oasis within. The conservatory includes a cactus house, a fern house, and a subtropical house filled with orchids. Seasonal displays include blooming plants at Easter, chrysanthemums in the fall, and Christmas greens and poinsettias in December and January. Brochures just inside the doorway offer helpful gardening tips. ⊠ *1st St. and Maryland Ave. SW,* ☎ *202/225–8333.* ☞ *Free.* ☉ *Daily 9–5. Metro: Federal Center SW.*

OLD DOWNTOWN AND FEDERAL TRIANGLE

Just because Washington is a planned city doesn't mean the plan was executed flawlessly. Pierre L'Enfant's design has been alternately shelved and rediscovered several times in the last 200 years. Nowhere have the city's imperfections been more visible than on L'Enfant's grand thoroughfare, Pennsylvania Avenue. By the early '60s it had become a national disgrace, the dilapidated buildings that lined it home to pawn shops and cheap souvenir stores. While riding up Pennsylvania Avenue in his inaugural parade, a disgusted John F. Kennedy is said to have turned to an aide and said, "Fix it!" Washington's downtown—once within the diamond formed by Massachusetts, Louisiana, Pennsylvania, and New York avenues—had its problems, too, many as a result of the riots that rocked the capital in 1968 after the assassination of Martin Luther King, Jr. In their wake, many downtown businesses left the area and moved north of the White House.

In recent years developers have rediscovered "old downtown," and buildings are now being torn down or remodeled at an amazing pace. After several false starts Pennsylvania Avenue is shining once again. This walk explores the old downtown section of the city, then swings around to check the progress on the monumental street that links the Congress House—the Capitol—with the President's House.

Numbers in the text correspond to numbers in the margin and on the Old Downtown and Federal Triangle map.

A Good Walk

Start at the redbrick **Pension Building** ①, at 4th and F streets (Metro: Judiciary Square), now home to the National Building Museum. The **Old Adas Israel Synagogue,** at 3rd and G streets, is the oldest synagogue in Washington. Across F Street from the Pension Building is **Judiciary Square** ②, where you'll find city and federal courthouses and the **National Law Enforcement Officers Memorial,** dedicated to police officers killed in the line of duty. Continue over to 6th Street and up to H Street to Washington's tiny Chinatown. The **Surratt Boarding House** ③, a meeting place for the assassins of Abraham Lincoln, is there as well (✉ 604 H St. NW). The **Friendship Arch** ④ spans H Street at 7th Street. To the west, at 9th and H streets, is the **Washington Convention Center** ⑤.

Continue west on H Street and right on 13th Street to the **National Museum of Women in the Arts** ⑥, with exhibits dating from the Renaissance to the present. Across the street (✉ 1300 New York Ave. NW) is the **InterAmerican Development Bank Cultural Center,** which features changing exhibits by artists from member countries in Latin America and the Caribbean. Walking south to 12th and G streets, you'll pass Hecht's, the downtown area's remaining major department store. The city's largest public library, the **Martin Luther King Memorial Library** ⑦, is at 9th and G streets. Two of the Smithsonian's non-Mall museums, the **National Portrait Gallery** on the south and the **National Museum of American Art** on the north, are in the **Old Patent Office Building** ⑧, bounded by F, G, 7th, and 9th streets. Just across the F Street pedestrian mall and to the left is the **Tariff Commission Building** ⑨. Sadly, the stretch of F Street west of here, once a main shopping area, now is dotted with cut-rate electronics stores, vacant stores and offices, and street vendors.

Turn left off F Street onto 10th Street to **Ford's Theatre** ⑩, where Abraham Lincoln was shot. The place where he died, the **Petersen House** ⑪, is across the street. Follow Pennsylvania Avenue three blocks west to **Freedom Plaza** ⑫, with its statue of Revolutionary War hero General Casimir Pulaski. Across E Street from the plaza is Washington's oldest stage, the **National Theatre.**

The cluster of government buildings south of Freedom Plaza between 15th Street, Pennsylvania Avenue, and Constitution Avenue is **Federal Triangle.** The triangle includes, from west to east, the **Department of**

Commerce ⑬ building (home of the **National Aquarium**), the **District Building** ⑭, the **Old Post Office Building** ⑮, the **Internal Revenue Service** building (worth noting mainly as mission control for the collection of your federal tax dollars), the **Department of Justice** (the **J. Edgar Hoover Federal Bureau of Investigation Building** ⑯ is across Pennsylvania Avenue and not actually part of the Federal Triangle), the **National Archives** ⑰, and the **Apex Building** ⑱, home of the **Federal Trade Commission.** The three-tier fountain across 6th Street is a memorial to Andrew Mellon, the former secretary of the treasury who oversaw construction of the Federal Triangle. The stunning white-stone-and-glass building across Pennsylvania Avenue is the **Canadian Embassy** ⑲. The intersection of 7th Street and Pennsylvania and Indiana avenues has numerous statues and memorials and a fountain. Across 7th Street, near the **General Winfield Scott** memorial, is the **Navy Memorial** ⑳, consisting of a huge map carved into the plaza and a statue of a lone sailor.

TIMING

While many of the attractions on this walk are places you look at rather than go inside, it is still an all-day affair, especially if you plan to tour the FBI headquarters, where there is usually a three- to four-hour wait. If the popularity of the FBI tour is any indication, most people are glad they stuck it out. You may or may not think the best time to visit the National Aquarium is for the shark feedings (Monday, Wednesday, and Saturday at 2) or pirhana feedings (Tuesday, Thursday, and Sunday at 2), when the frenzy inside the tanks often seems well-matched by that of the crowds jockeying to see the action.

Sights to See

⑱ **Apex Building.** The triangular Apex Building, completed in 1938, is the home of the **Federal Trade Commission.** Adorning the building is a carving that depicts various aspects of trade. Note the relief decorations representing *Agriculture* (the harvesting of grain, by Concetta Scaravaglione) and *Trade* (two men bartering over an ivory tusk, by Carl Schmitz) over the doorways on the Constitution Avenue side. Two heroic statues by Michael Lantz on either side of the rounded eastern portico, each depicting a muscular, shirtless workman wrestling with a wild horse, represent *Man Controlling Trade.* Just across 6th Street is a three-tier fountain decorated with the signs of the zodiac; it is a memorial to Andrew Mellon, who as secretary of the treasury oversaw construction of the $125 million Federal Triangle (and who, as a deep-pocketed philanthropist, was the driving force behind the National Gallery of Art, just across Constitution Avenue). ⊠ *Eastern tip of Federal Triangle. Metro: Archives/Navy Memorial.*

⑲ **Canadian Embassy.** A spectacular edifice constructed of stone and glass, the Canadian Embassy was designed by Arthur Erickson and completed in 1988. Inside, a gallery periodically displays exhibits on Canadian culture and history. ⊠ *501 Pennsylvania Ave. NW,* ☎ *202/682–1740.* 🎟 *Free.* ☉ *Weekdays 10–5 when an exhibition is mounted; otherwise, the gallery is closed. Metro: Archives/Navy Memorial.*

Chinatown. You know you're entering Washington's compact Chinatown when you notice the Chinese characters on the street signs. The area is somewhat down-at-the-heels—you'll find boarded-up buildings and graffiti-covered walls—but this is the place to go for Chinese food in the District. Cantonese, Sichuan, Hunan, and Mongolian are among the delectable culinary styles you can sample. Nearly every restaurant has a roast duck hanging in the window, and the shops here sell a wide variety of Chinese goods. Most interesting are traditional pharmacies purveying folk medicines such as dried eels, powdered bones, and a

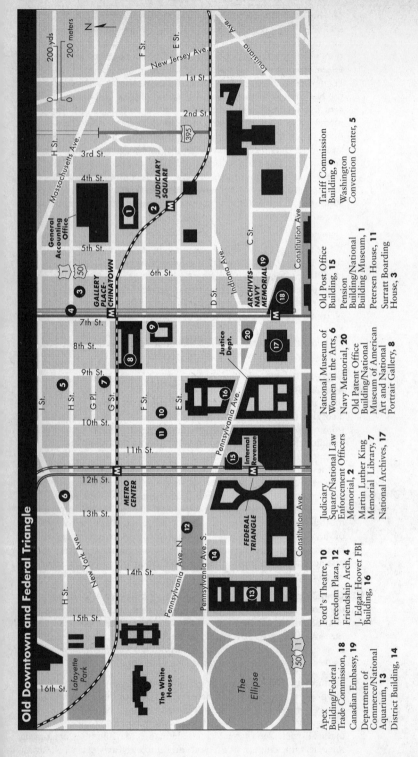

Old Downtown and Federal Triangle

N

0   200 yds
0   200 meters

Apex
Building/Federal
Trade Commission, **18**
Canadian Embassy, **19**
Department of
Commerce/National
Aquarium, **13**
District Building, **14**

Ford's Theatre, **10**
Freedom Plaza, **12**
Friendship Arch, **4**
J. Edgar Hoover FBI
Building, **16**

Judiciary
Square/National Law
Enforcement Officers
Memorial, **2**
Martin Luther King
Memorial Library, **7**
National Archives, **17**

National Museum of
Women in the Arts, **6**
Navy Memorial, **20**
Old Patent Office
Building/National
Museum of American
Art and National
Portrait Gallery, **8**

Old Post Office
Building, **15**
Pension
Building/National
Building Museum, **1**
Petersen House, **11**
Surratt Boarding
House, **3**

Tariff Commission
Building, **9**
Washington
Convention Center, **5**

Cherry blossoms, Jefferson Memorial at Tidal Basin,
Washington, D.C.
Photo © 1992 Peter Guttman,
author of Fodor's *Nights to Imagine*

variety of unusual herbs for teas and broths believed to promote health, longevity, and sexual potency. ⊠ *Bounded by G, H, 5th, and 8th Sts. Metro: Gallery Place/Chinatown.*

NEED A
BREAK?
If the smells of Chinese cooking have activated your taste buds, try the highly rated **Mr. Yung's** (⊠ 740 6th St. NW). It specializes in Cantonese cuisine, and if you're lucky enough to be in the neighborhood between 11 and 3, be sure to sample the addictively delicious bite-size appetizers known as dim sum, a traditional Chinese breakfast or lunch.

⑬ Department of Commerce. The western base of Federal Triangle between 14th and 15th streets is the home of the Department of Commerce, charged with promoting U.S. economic development and technological advancement. When it opened in 1932 the Commerce building was the world's largest government office building. It's a good thing there's plenty of space; incongruously, the **National Aquarium** is housed inside. Established in 1873, it's the country's oldest public aquarium, with more than 1,200 fish and other creatures representing 250 species of fresh- and saltwater life on display. Its tanks are alive with brilliantly colored tropical fish from every corner of the globe, firehose-thick moray eels, curious frogs and turtles, silvery schools of flesh-chomping piranhas, and even more fearsome sharks. A "touch tank" lets you handle more hospitable sea creatures such as crabs and oysters. ⊠ *14th St. and Pennsylvania Ave. NW,* ☏ *202/482–2825.* ⊡ *$2.* ☉ *Daily 9–5; sharks fed Mon., Wed., and Sat. at 2; piranhas fed Tues., Thurs., and Sun. at 2. Metro: Federal Triangle.*

⑭ District Building. Home to Washington's City Council, the beaux arts District Building is of scant sightseeing interest, but if you're visiting Federal Triangle it's part of the view. That's because it's a survivor. Erected in 1908, it hardly fit in with the grand plan in 1929 to turn Federal Triangle into an oasis of classically uniform architecture with a European flavor. When the plan was scrapped, the building lingered. It's in poor shape, however, and in 1992, Mayor Sharon Pratt Kelly moved several city agencies to tony digs near Judiciary Square. (The inclusion in Pratt's own office of such amenities as a gas fireplace and granite countertops did not endear her to taxpayers.) ⊠ *Federal Triangle, 14th St. and Pennsylvania Ave. S. Metro: Federal Triangle.*

Federal Triangle. To the south of Freedom Plaza, Federal Triangle consists of a mass of government buildings constructed from 1929 to 1938. Notable are the Department of Commerce Building (with the National Aquarium inside), the District Building, the Old Post Office Building, the Internal Revenue Service Building, the Department of Justice, the National Archives, and the Apex Building, which houses the Federal Trade Commission.

Before Federal Triangle was developed, government workers were scattered throughout the city, largely in rented offices. Looking for a place to consolidate this work force, city planners hit on the area south of Pennsylvania Avenue known, at the time, as "Murder Bay," a notorious collection of rooming houses, taverns, tattoo parlors, and brothels. A uniform classical architectural style, with Italianate red-tile roofs and interior plazas reminiscent of the Louvre, was chosen for the building project.

Federal Triangle's planners envisioned interior courts filled with plazas and parks, but the needs of the motor car foiled any such grand plans. A park was planned for the spot of land between 13th and 14th streets across from the Commerce Building, but for many years it was an immense parking lot; now a federal office building containing an international cultural and trade center is being built there. ⊠ *15th St. and Pennsylvania and Constitution Aves. Metro: Federal Triangle.*

❿ Ford's Theatre. In 1861, Baltimore theater impresario John T. Ford leased the First Baptist Church building that stood on this site and turned it into a successful music hall. The building burned down late in 1862, and Ford rebuilt it. The events of April 14, 1865, would shock the nation and close the theater. On that night, during a production of *Our American Cousin,* John Wilkes Booth entered the presidential box and assassinated Abraham Lincoln. The stricken president was carried across the street to the house of tailor William Petersen. Charles Augustus Leale, a 23-year-old doctor, attended to the president, whose injuries would have left him blind had he ever regained consciousness. To let Lincoln know that someone was nearby, Leale held his hand throughout the night. Lincoln died the next morning.

The federal government bought Ford's Theatre in 1866 for $100,000 and converted it into office space. It was remodeled as a Lincoln museum in 1932 and was restored to its 1865 appearance in 1968. The basement museum—with artifacts such as Booth's pistol and the clothes Lincoln was wearing when he was shot—reopened in 1990 after a complete renovation. The theater itself continues to present a complete schedule of plays. *A Christmas Carol* is an annual holiday favorite. ⊠ *511 10th St. NW,* ☎ *202/426–6924.* ☞ *Free.* ☉ *Daily 9–5; theater closed when rehearsals or matinees are in progress (generally Thurs. and weekends); Lincoln Museum in basement remains open at these times. Metro: Metro Center.*

⓬ Freedom Plaza. In 1988, Western Plaza was renamed Freedom Plaza to honor Dr. Martin Luther King, to avoid confusion with similarly named projects by the same developer—Western Development, and to be geographically consistent; its location, bounded by 13th, 14th, and E streets and Pennsylvania Avenue, is eastern, not western. Freedom Plaza's east end is dominated by a **statue of General Casimir Pulaski,** the Polish nobleman who led an American cavalry corps during the Revolutionary War and was mortally wounded in 1779 at the Siege of Savannah. He gazes over a plaza that is inlaid in bronze with a detail from L'Enfant's original 1791 plan for the Federal City. Bronze outlines the President's Palace and the Congress House; the Mall is represented by a green lawn. Cut into the edges are quotations about the capital city, not all of them complimentary. To compare L'Enfant's vision with today's reality, stand in the middle of the map's Pennsylvania Avenue and look west. L'Enfant had planned an unbroken vista from the Capitol to the White House, but the Treasury Building, begun in 1836, ruined the view. Turning to the east you'll see the U.S. Capitol sitting on Jenkins Hill like an American Taj Mahal.

There's a lot to see and explore in the blocks near Freedom Plaza. The beaux arts **Willard Hotel** is on the corner of 14th Street and Pennsylvania Avenue. There was a Willard Hotel on this spot long before this ornate structure was built in 1901. The original Willard was the place to stay in Washington if you were rich or influential (or wanted to give that impression). Abraham Lincoln stayed there while waiting to move into the nearby White House. Julia Ward Howe stayed there during the Civil War and wrote "The Battle Hymn of the Republic" after gazing down from her window to see Union troops drilling on Pennsylvania Avenue. It's said the term "lobbyist" was coined to describe the favor seekers who would buttonhole President Ulysses S. Grant in the hotel's public rooms. The second Willard, its mansard roof dotted with circular windows, was designed by Henry Hardenbergh, architect of New York's Plaza Hotel. Although it was just as opulent as the hotel it replaced, it fell on hard times after World War II. In 1968 it closed, standing empty until 1986, when it reopened, amid much fanfare, after an ambitious restoration. The Willard's rebirth is one of the most visible successes of the Pennsylvania Avenue Development Corporation, the organization charged with reversing the decay of America's Main Street.

Just north of Freedom Plaza, on F Street between 13th and 14th streets, are **The Shops,** a collection of stores in the National Press Building, itself home to dozens of domestic and foreign media organizations. The Shops has sit-down restaurants and fast food in its upstairs Food Hall. Washington's oldest stage, the **National Theatre,** also overlooks the plaza. This National has been here since 1922, though there has been a theater on this spot since 1835. After seeing her first play here at the age of six, Helen Hayes vowed to become an actress. If you plan ahead you can take a free tour of the historic theater that includes the house, stage, backstage, wardrobe room, dressing rooms, the area under the stage, the Helen Hayes Lounge, and the memorabilia-filled archives. Tours are given for a minimum of 10 people; make reservations at least one week in advance. ⊠ *1321 Pennsylvania Ave. NW,* ☎ *202/783– 3370.* ☒ *Free. Metro: Federal Triangle.*

❹ **Friendship Arch.** A colorful and ornate 75-foot-wide arch spanning H Street at 7th Street is a reminder of Washington's sister-city relationship with Beijing. *Metro: Gallery Place/Chinatown.*

InterAmerican Development Bank Cultural Center. Founded in 1959, the IADB is an international bank that finances economic and social development in Latin America and the Caribbean. Its small cultural center hosts changing exhibits of paintings, sculptures, and artifacts from member countries. Since it's located across the street from the National Museum of Women in the Arts, which is also worth a visit, you can kill two birds with one stone. ⊠ *1300 New York Ave. NW,* ☎ *202/942– 8287.* ☒ *Free.* ⊙ *Weekdays 11–6. Metro: Metro Center.*

☜ ⑯ **J. Edgar Hoover Federal Bureau of Investigation Building.** The one-hour tour of the FBI building remains one of the most popular tourist activities in the city. A brief film outlines the Bureau's work, while exhibits describe famous past cases and illustrate the FBI's fight against organized crime, terrorism, bank robbery, espionage, extortion, and other criminal activities. There's everything from gangster John Dillinger's death mask to a poster display of the 10 Most Wanted criminals. (Look carefully: Two bad guys were apprehended as a result of tips from tour takers!) You'll also see the laboratories where the FBI painstakingly studies evidence. The high point of the tour comes right at the end: A special agent gives a live-ammo firearms demonstration in the building's indoor shooting range.

Although it overlooks Federal Triangle, the FBI building is actually on the wrong side of Pennsylvania Avenue to be part of the triangle. (The main **Department of Justice** building, however, is part of Federal Triangle; like the rest of Federal Triangle, it's sprinkled with Art Deco details, including the cylindrical aluminum torches outside the doorways, adorned with bas-relief figures of bison, dolphins, and birds.) A hulking presence on the avenue, the FBI building was decried from birth as hideous. Even Hoover himself is said to have called it the "ugliest building I've ever seen." Opened in 1974, it hangs over 9th Street like a poured-concrete Big Brother. One thing is certain, it is secure. At peak times there may be a three- to four-hour wait for a tour. ⊠ *10th St. and Pennsylvania Ave. NW (tour entrance on E St. NW),* ☎ *202/324–*

3447. ✉ *Free.* ☉ *Tours weekdays 8:45–4:15; closed federal holidays.*
Metro: Federal Triangle.

❷ Judiciary Square. As the name implies, this is the District's judicial core,
with both city and federal courthouses arranged around it. The **National Law Enforcement Officers Memorial** was dedicated here in October 1991. A 3-foot-high wall bears the names of more than 15,000
American police officers killed in the line of duty since 1794. On the
third line of panel 13W are the names of six officers killed by William
Bonney, better known as Billy the Kid. J. D. Tippit, the Dallas policeman killed by Lee Harvey Oswald, is honored on the ninth line of panel
63E. Given the dangerous nature of police work, it will be one of the
few memorials to which names will continue to be added. Two blocks
away is a visitor center with exhibits on the history of the memorial
and computers that allow you to look up officers by name, date of death,
state, and department. A small shop sells souvenirs. Call to arrange
for a free tour. ✉ *605 E St. NW,* ☎ *202/737–3400.* ✉ *Free.* ☉ *Weekdays 9–5, Sat. 10–5, Sun. noon–5. Metro: Judiciary Square.*

❼ Martin Luther King Memorial Library. Designed by Ludwig Miës van
der Rohe, one of the founders of modern architecture, this squat black
building at 9th and G streets is the largest public library in the city. A
mural on the first floor depicts events in the life of the Nobel Prize–winning civil rights activist. Used books are almost always on sale at bargain prices in the library's gift shop. ✉ *901 G St. NW,* ☎ *202/727–1111.*
✉ *Free.* ☉ *Mon., Wed., and Thurs. 10–7; Tues. 10–9; Fri. and Sat.
10–5:30; Sun. 1–5. Metro: Gallery Place.*

⓱ National Archives. If the Smithsonian Institution is the nation's attic,
the Archives is the nation's basement, and it bears responsibility for
the cataloguing and safekeeping of important government documents
and other items. The Declaration of Independence, the Constitution,
and the Bill of Rights are on display in the Rotunda of the Archives
building, in a case made of bulletproof glass, illuminated with green
light, and filled with helium gas (to protect the irreplaceable documents).
At night and on Christmas—the only day the Archives are closed—
they are lowered into a vault. Other objects in the Archives' vast collection include bureaucratic correspondence, veterans and immigration
records, treaties, even Richard Nixon's resignation letter and the rifle
Lee Harvey Oswald used to assassinate John F. Kennedy.

The Archives building fills the area between 7th and 9th streets and
Pennsylvania and Constitution avenues on Federal Triangle. Beside it
is a small park with a modest **memorial to Franklin Roosevelt.** The
desk-size piece of marble on the sliver of grass is exactly what the president asked for (though this hasn't stopped fans of the 32nd president
in their successful efforts to secure a grander memorial to FDR in West
Potomac Park, due to be completed in 1996). Designed by John Russell Pope, the Archives building was erected in 1935 on the site of the
old Center Market. This large block had been a center of commerce
since the early 1800s, when barges plying the City Canal (which flowed
where Constitution Avenue is now) were loaded and unloaded here.
A vestige of this mercantile past lives on in the name given to the two
semicircular developments across Pennsylvania Avenue from the
Archives—**Market Square.** City planners hope that the residential development will enliven this stretch of Pennsylvania Avenue.

Turn right onto 9th Street and head to the Constitution Avenue side
of the Archives. All the sculpture that adorns the building was carved
on the site, including the two statues that flank the flight of steps facing the Mall, *Heritage* and *Guardianship*, by James Earle Fraser. Fraser

also carved the scene on the pediment, which represents the transfer of historic documents to the recorder of the Archives. (Like nearly all pediment decorations in Washington, the scene is bristling with electric wires designed to thwart the advances of destructive pigeons.) Call at least three weeks in advance to arrange a behind-the-scenes tour (☎ 202/501–5205). ✉ *Constitution Ave. between 7th and 9th Sts. NW,* ☎ *202/501–5000.* 🎫 *Free.* ☉ *Apr.–Labor Day, daily 10–9:30; Sept.–Mar., daily 10–5:30; tour weekdays at 10:15 and 1:15. Metro: Archives/Navy Memorial.*

❻ National Museum of Women in the Arts. Works by prominent female artists from the Renaissance to the present are showcased in this beautifully restored 1907 Renaissance Revival building, one of the larger non-Smithsonian museums, designed by Waddy Wood. Ironically, it was once a men-only Masonic temple. When the museum opened in 1987 some questioned the wisdom of segregating artists by sex. Since then its acclaimed exhibitions have won over most naysayers. In addition to displaying traveling shows, the museum houses a permanent collection that includes paintings, drawings, sculpture, prints, and photographs by such artists as Georgia O'Keeffe, Mary Cassatt, Élisabeth Vigée-Lebrun, Frida Kahlo, and Judy Chicago. ✉ *1250 New York Ave. NW,* ☎ *202/783–5000.* 🎫 *Suggested donation $3.* ☉ *Mon.–Sat. 10–5, Sun. noon–5. Metro: Metro Center.*

....

NEED A BREAK?   For a casual lunch in an elegant setting, the café in the **National Museum of Women in the Arts** is just the place.

....

⓴ Navy Memorial. A huge outdoor plaza, the Navy Memorial includes a granite map of the world and a seven-foot statue, *The Lone Sailor.* In the summer, the memorial's concert stage is the site of military band performances. To the northeast, in the Market Square Development, is the memorial's visitor center, complete with gift shop and "Navy Memorial Log Room," where visitors can use computers to look up the service records of Navy veterans entered into the log. There's also the 250-seat, wide-screen Arleigh & Roberta Burke Theater, home of continuous screenings of the 30-minute, 70-millimeter film *At Sea.* Produced by the same company that made the IMAX hit *To Fly, At Sea* is a visually stunning look at life aboard a modern aircraft carrier. A memorial to **General Winfield Scott** is in the park adjacent to the Navy Memorial. ✉ *701 Pennsylvania Ave. NW,* ☎ *202/737–2300; tickets also available from Ticketmaster,* ☎ *202/628–3557 or 800/723–3557; group tickets, 202/432–7328.* 🎫 *At Sea $3.75.* ☉ *Visitor center Mar.–Nov., Mon.–Sat. 9:30–5, Sun. noon–5; Dec.–Feb., Mon.–Sat. 10–4, Sun. noon–4. Metro: Archives/Navy Memorial.*

❽ Old Patent Office Building. Two Smithsonian museums now share the Old Patent Office Building. The **National Portrait Gallery,** with its Civil War photographs, paintings, and prints, presidential portraits, and Time magazine covers, is on the south. The **National Museum of American Art,** with displays on early American and western art, is on the north. Construction on the south wing, which was designed by Washington Monument architect Robert Mills, started in 1836. When the huge Greek-Revival quadrangle was completed in 1867 it was the largest building in the country. Many of its rooms housed glass display cabinets filled with the models that inventors were required to submit with their patent applications.

During the Civil War, the Patent Office, like many other buildings in the city, was turned into a hospital. Among those caring for the wounded here were Clara Barton and Walt Whitman. In the 1950s the building was threatened with demolition to make way for a parking lot, but the efforts of preservationists saved it. The Smithsonian opened it to the public in 1968.

The first floor of the National Museum of American Art holds displays of early American art and art of the West, as well as a gallery of painted miniatures. Be sure to see *The Throne of the Third Heaven of the Nations' Millennium General Assembly,* by James Hampton. Discarded materials, such as chairs, bottles, and light bulbs, are sheathed in aluminum and gold foil in this strange and moving work of religious art. On the second floor are works by the American Impressionists, including John Henry Twachtman and Childe Hassam. There are also plaster models and marble sculptures by Hiram Powers, including the plaster cast of his famous work *The Greek Slave,* the original of which is housed in the Corcoran Gallery (☞ the White House Area, *above*). Just outside the room containing Powers's work is a copy of a sculpture Augustus Saint-Gaudens created for Henry Adams. Adams's wife had committed suicide and the original of this moving, shroud-draped figure sits above her grave in Rock Creek Cemetery. Also on this floor are massive landscapes by Albert Bierstadt and Thomas Moran. The third floor is filled with modern art, including works by Leon Kroll and Edward Hopper that were commissioned during the '30s by the federal government. The Lincoln Gallery—site of the receiving line at Abraham Lincoln's 1865 inaugural ball—has been restored to its original appearance and contains modern art by Jasper Johns, Robert Rauschenberg, Milton Avery, Kenneth Noland, and others. ⊠ *8th and G Sts. NW,* ☎ *202/357–2700, TTY 202/357–1729.* ⊟ *Free.* ☉ *Daily 10–5:30. Metro: Gallery Place.*

You can enter the National Portrait Gallery from any floor of the National Museum of American Art or walk through the courtyard between the two wings. The best place to start a circuit of the Portrait Gallery is on the restored third floor. The mezzanine level of the wonderfully busy room features a **Civil War exhibition,** with portraits, photographs, and lithographs of such wartime personalities as Julia Ward Howe, Frederick Douglass, Ulysses S. Grant, and Robert E. Lee. There are also life casts of Abraham Lincoln's hands and face. The Renaissance-style gallery has been restored to its original splendor, complete with colorful tile flooring and a stained-glass skylight. Highlights of the Portrait Gallery's second floor include the **Hall of Presidents** (featuring a portrait or sculpture of each chief executive) and the George Washington "Lansdowne" portrait. The first floor features portraits of well-known American athletes and performers. *Time* magazine gave the museum its collection of Person of the Year covers and many other photos and paintings that the magazine has commissioned over the years. Parts of this collection are periodically on display. ⊠ *8th and F Sts. NW,* ☎ *202/357–2700, TTY 202/357–1729.* ⊟ *Free.* ☉ *Daily 10–5:30. Metro: Gallery Place.*

If you leave the pair of museums in the Patent Office Building by way of the National Portrait Gallery's F Street doors, you'll come upon another of Washington's beautiful views. Directly ahead, four blocks away in the Federal Triangle, is the **National Archives** building. To the east is the green barrel-roof of **Union Station,** and to the west you can see the **Treasury Department Building.**

NEED A BREAK?

The **Patent Pending** restaurant, between the two museums, serves an ample selection of salads, sandwiches, hot entrées, and other treats. Tables and chairs in the large museum courtyard make sitting outside enjoyable when the weather is pleasant.

⑮ Old Post Office Building. When it was completed in 1899, this Romanesque building on Federal Triangle was the largest government building in the District, the first with a clock tower, and the first with an electric power plant. Despite these innovations, it earned the sobriquet "old" after only 18 years, when a new District post office was constructed near Union Station. When urban planners in the '20s decided to impose a uniform design on Federal Triangle, the Old Post Office was slated for demolition (some critics said it stood out like an "old tooth"). First a lack of money during the Depression, then the intercession of preservationists, headed by Nancy Hanks of the National Endowment for the Arts, saved the fanciful granite building. Major renovation was begun in 1978, and in 1984 the public areas in the Old Post Office Pavilion—an assortment of shops and restaurants inside the airy central courtyard—were opened. Other shops and restaurants were added to the pavilion's three-story, glass-enclosed East Atrium in 1992, along with Juggling Capitol, where you can get the juggling lesson (using balls, clubs, scarves, or sticks) you know you've always wanted. A sign clearly states store policy: "You drop it, you buy it ... just kidding."

Park Service rangers who work at the Old Post Office consider a trip to the observation deck in the **clock tower** to be one of Washington's best-kept secrets. Although not as tall as the Washington Monument, it offers nearly as impressive a view. Even better, it's usually not as crowded, the windows are bigger, and—unlike the monument's windows—they're open, allowing cool breezes to waft through. (The tour is about 15 minutes long.) On the way down be sure to look at the Congress Bells, cast at the same British foundry that made the bells in London's Westminster Abbey. The bells are rung to honor the opening and closing of Congress and on other important occasions, such as when the Redskins win the Super Bowl. ⊠ *Pennsylvania Ave. and 12th St. NW; tower,* ☎ *202/606–8691; pavilion, 202/289–4224.* ▩ *Free.* ☉ *Tower Easter–Labor Day, daily 7:30 AM–11 PM (last tour 10:45); Sept.–Mar., daily 10–6 (last tour 5:45). Metro: Federal Triangle.*

Cross 10th Street from the Old Post Office Pavilion. Look to your left at the delightful trompe l'oeil mural on the side of the **Lincoln Building** two blocks up. It appears as if there's a hole in the building. There's also a portrait of the building's namesake. Closer to Pennsylvania Avenue on 10th Street is an example of one of Washington's strangest and most popular architectural conceits: a "façademy." In this, an old building—usually a three- or four-story row house—is demolished except for its picturesque facade, which is preserved as a decorative exterior and integrated with the new office building rising up behind it. In this case the façademy is a multi-arched, redbrick facade of a 1909 building that serves as the pretty face of a massive shop-and-office block.

NEED A
BREAK?

A variety of international fast foods are available on the lower level of the Post Office Pavilion, including Indian (Indian Delight), Greek (Greek Taverna), Japanese (Sushi Shogun), and an American favorite for dessert: Ben & Jerry's.

Pennsylvania Avenue. The Capitol's most historically important thoroughfare will repeatedly thread through your sightseeing walks. Newly inaugurated presidents travel west on Pennsylvania Avenue on their way to the White House. Thomas Jefferson started the parade tradition in 1805 after taking the oath of office for his second term. He was accompanied by a few friends and a handful of congressmen. Four years later James Madison made things official by instituting a proper inaugural celebration. The flag holders on the lamp posts are clues that

Pennsylvania Avenue remains the city's foremost parade route. With the Capitol at one end and the White House at the other, the avenue symbolizes both the distance and the connection between these two branches of government.

When Pennsylvania Avenue first opened in 1796, it was an ugly and dangerous bog. Attempts by Jefferson to beautify the road by planting poplar trees were only partially successful: Many were chopped down for firewood. In the mid-19th century, crossing the rutted thoroughfare was a dangerous proposition, and rainstorms often turned the street into a river. The avenue was finally paved with wooden blocks in 1871.

At the confluence of 7th Street and Pennsylvania and Indiana avenues is a multitude of statues and monuments. The **Grand Army of the Republic** memorial pays tribute to the men who won the Civil War. Less conventional is the nearby stork-surmounted **Temperance Fountain.** It was erected in the 19th century by a teetotaling physician named Cogswell who hoped the fountain, which once dispensed ice-cold water, would lure people from the evils of drink.

Redevelopment has rejuvenated Pennsylvania Avenue and the neighboring **Pennsylvania Quarter,** the name given to the mix of condominiums, apartments, retail spaces, and restaurants in the blocks bounded by Pennsylvania Avenue and 6th, 9th, and G streets. The area includes the Lansburgh complex, at the corner of 8th and E streets. Built around three existing buildings (including the defunct Lansburgh department store), the complex includes the Shakespeare Theatre, which in 1992 moved from its former home in the Folger Library to this state-of-the-art, 447-seat space. *Metro: Archives/Navy Memorial.*

NEED A
BREAK?

At **Planet Hollywood** (⌂ 1101 Pennsylvania Ave. NW, ☎ 202/783-7827) you can eat and drink surrounded by such Hollywood set pieces and costumes as Darth Vader's shiny black mask, and a Klingon battle cruiser from the *Star Trek* movies. Meanwhile, film clips run on drop-down movie screens; the works of chain co-owners Bruce Willis and Arnold Schwarzenegger are, naturally, well represented.

❶ Pension Building. The open interior of this mammoth redbrick edifice is one of the city's great spaces and has been the site of inaugural balls for more than 100 years. (The first ball was for Grover Cleveland in 1885; because the building wasn't finished at the time, a temporary wooden roof and floor were erected.) The eight central Corinthian columns are the largest in the world, rising to a height of 75 feet. Though they look like marble, each is made of 75,000 bricks, covered with plaster and painted to resemble Siena marble. Each year NBC tapes its "Christmas in Washington" TV special in the breathtaking hall.

The building was erected between 1882 and 1887 to house workers who processed the pension claims of veterans and their survivors, an activity that intensified after the Civil War. The architect was U.S. Army Corps of Engineers General Montgomery C. Meigs, who took as his inspiration the Italian Renaissance–style Palazzo Farnese in Rome. The Pension Building now houses the **National Building Museum,** devoted to architecture and the building arts. "Washington: Symbol and City" is a permanent exhibit that outlines the capital's architectural history, from monumental core to residential neighborhoods. Recent temporary exhibits have explored the rebuilding of Oklahoma City and the dome as a symbol of American democracy.

Before entering the building, walk down its F Street side. The terra-cotta frieze by Caspar Buberl between the first and second floors depicts soldiers marching and sailing in an endless procession around the building. Architect Meigs lost his oldest son in the Civil War, and, though the frieze depicts Union troops, he intended it as a memorial to all who were killed in the bloody war. Meigs designed the Pension Building with workers' comfort in mind long before anyone knew that cramped, stuffy offices could cause "sick building syndrome." Note the three "missing" bricks under each window that helped keep the building cool by allowing air to circulate.

For a nice view of the building head west on F Street, cross 5th Street, and look back. The prison block–like structure north of the Pension Building houses the General Accounting Office. ⊠ *F St. between 4th and 5th Sts. NW,* ☎ *202/272–2448.* ▣ *Free.* ◷ *Mon.–Sat. 10–4, Sun. noon–4; tour weekdays at 12:30, weekends at 12:30 and 1:30. Metro: Judiciary Square.*

The nearby **Old Adas Israel Synagogue** is the oldest synagogue in Washington. Built in 1876 at 6th and G streets NW, the redbrick, Federal Revival–style building was moved to its present location in 1969 to make way for an office building. Exhibits in the Lillian and Albert Small Jewish Museum inside explore Jewish life in Washington. ⊠ *3rd and G Sts. NW,* ☎ *202/789–0900.* ▣ *Suggested donation $2.* ◷ *Sun.–Thurs. 10–4. Metro: Judiciary Square.*

⑪ **Petersen House.** Lincoln died in the house of William Petersen, a tailor, on the morning after being shot. You can see the restored front and back parlors of the house, as well as the bedroom where the president died. Most of the furnishings are not original, but the pillow and bloodstained pillowcases are those used on that fateful night. ⊠ *516 10th St. NW,* ☎ *202/426–6830.* ▣ *Free.* ◷ *Daily 9–5. Metro: Metro Center.*

NEED A BREAK?	Right around the corner and across the street from Petersen House is the **Hard Rock Cafe** (⊠ 999 E St. NW, ☎ 202/737-7625), which opened its Washington branch in 1989, bringing hearty American food, a modest selection of beers, and lots of those famous T-shirts. (The Hard Rock's gift shop opened a full year before the restaurant did.) This is a popular spot for tourists, so if you're not up to waiting in line, try to arrive early for lunch or dinner.

③ **Surratt Boarding House.** A plaque by the front door attests that it was here John Wilkes Booth and his co-conspirators plotted the assassination of Abraham Lincoln. The current occupant of the building is a Chinese restaurant. ⊠ *604 H Street NW. Metro: Gallery Place/Chinatown.*

⑨ **Tariff Commission Building.** The Tariff Commission Building, designed by Robert Mills and finished in 1866, is one of three historic buildings to occupy the same site. When the Capitol was burned by the British in 1814, Congress met temporarily in a hotel that stood in this spot. Another earlier building housed the nation's first public telegraph office, operated by Samuel F. B. Morse. ⊠ *Diagonally opposite F St. mall. Metro: Gallery Place/Chinatown.*

The block of F Street between 9th and 10th streets, a block or two from the Tariff Commission Building, has long been a center of shopping in the District. It's dotted with cut-rate electronics stores, pawn shops, and lingerie stores, and the sidewalks are usually crowded with shoppers looking over the wares of street vendors, who hawk everything from sweatshirts and sunglasses to perfumes and panty hose. Many residents fear that developers' new-found interest in old downtown may threaten this lively part of the city.

GEORGETOWN

Long before the District of Columbia was formed, Georgetown, Washington's oldest neighborhood, was a separate city that boasted a harbor full of ships and warehouses filled with tobacco. Washington has filled in around Georgetown over the years, but the former tobacco port retains an air of aloofness. Its narrow streets, which refuse to conform to Pierre L'Enfant's plan for the Federal City, make up the capital's wealthiest neighborhood and are the nucleus of its nightlife.

The area that would come to be known as George (after George II), then George Towne and, finally, Georgetown, was part of Maryland when it was settled in the early 1700s by Scottish immigrants, many of whom were attracted to the region's tolerant religious climate. Georgetown's position at the farthest point up the Potomac one could reach by boat made it an ideal transit-and-inspection point for farmers who grew tobacco in Maryland's interior. In 1789 the state granted the town a charter, but two years later Georgetown—along with Alexandria, its counterpart in Virginia—was included by George Washington in the Territory of Columbia, site of the new capital.

While Washington struggled, Georgetown thrived. Wealthy traders built their mansions on the hills overlooking the river; merchants and the working class lived in more modest homes closer to the water's edge. In 1810 a third of Georgetown's population was black—both free people and slaves. The **Mt. Zion United Methodist Church** on 29th Street is the oldest black church in the city and was a stop on the Underground Railroad. Georgetown's rich history and success instilled in citizens of both colors feelings of superiority that many feel linger today. (When Georgetowners thought the dismal capital was dragging them down, they asked to be given back to Maryland, the way Alexandria was given back to Virginia in 1845). Tobacco eventually became a less important commodity, and Georgetown became a milling center, using water power from the Potomac. When the Chesapeake & Ohio (C&O) Canal was completed in 1850, the city intensified its milling operations and became the eastern end of a waterway that stretched 184 miles to the west. The canal took up some of the slack when Georgetown's harbor began to fill with silt and the port lost business to Alexandria and Baltimore, but the canal never became the success it was meant to be.

In the years that followed, Georgetown was a far cry from the fashionable spot it is today. Clustered near the water were a foundry, a fish market, paper and cotton mills, and a power station for the city's streetcar system, all of which made Georgetown a smelly industrial district. It still had its Georgian, Federal, and Victorian homes, though, and when the New Deal and World War II brought a flood of newcomers to Washington, Georgetown's tree-shaded streets and handsome brick houses were rediscovered. Pushed out in the process were Georgetown's blacks, most of whom rented the houses they lived in.

Today some of Washington's most famous citizens call Georgetown home, including *Washington Post* matriarch Katherine Graham, former *Post* editor Ben Bradlee, celebrity biographer Kitty Kelley, and political insider Pamela Churchill Harriman. Georgetown's historic preservationists are among the most vocal in the city. Part of what the activists want protection from is the crush of people who descend on their community every night. This is Washington's center for restaurants, bars, nightclubs, and trendy boutiques. On M Street and Wisconsin Avenue, visitors can indulge just about any taste and take home almost any upmarket souvenir. Harder to find is a parking place.

Georgetown owes some of its charm and separate growth to geography. This town-unto-itself is separated from Washington to the east by Rock Creek. On the south it's bordered by the Potomac, on the west by Georgetown University. How far north does Georgetown reach? Probably not much farther than the large estates and parks above R Street, though developers and real estate agents would be happy to take Georgetown right up to the Canadian border if it increased the value of property along the way.

The lack of a Metro station in Georgetown means you'll have to take a bus or walk to this part of Washington. It's about a 15-minute walk from the Dupont Circle or Foggy Bottom Metro station. (If you'd rather take a bus, the G2 Georgetown University bus goes from Dupont Circle west along P Street. The 34 and 36 Friendship Heights buses leave from 22nd and Pennsylvania and deposit you at 31st and M.)

Numbers in the text correspond to numbers in the margin and on the Georgetown map.

A Good Walk

Start your exploration of Georgetown at 31st and M streets, in front of the **Old Stone House** ①, possibly Washington's only pre-Revolutionary building. Around the corner, at 1221 31st Street, is the 1858 **Customs House** ②. Cross over M Street to Thomas Jefferson Street (between 30th and 31st streets). The 200-year-old two-story brick structure at Number 1058 was built as a **Masonic lodge** ③. Follow Thomas Jefferson Street as it passes over the **C&O Canal** ④, now used by joggers, bikers, and canoeists. During spring and summer, you can take a mule-drawn canal boat ride. Cross K Street to **Washington Harbour** ⑥, a development that includes restaurants, offices, apartments, and upscale shops. A **plaque** at 31st and K streets commemorates **Suter's Tavern** ⑦, where George Washington made the land deal that became the District of Columbia. Three **warehouses** ⑧ at the foot of Wisconsin Avenue were built around 1830 by trader **Francis Dodge.** Up Wisconsin Avenue, across the street, stands the Gothic Revival **Grace Episcopal Church** ⑨.

Cross the canal again at Wisconsin Avenue. On one side of the street is a memorial to the builders of the canal; on the other side, at the **Vigilant Firehouse** ⑩, is a plaque dedicated to a former fire dog. At the intersection of Wisconsin Avenue and M Street—the heart of Georgetown—turn left to the upscale Victorian-style **Georgetown Park** ⑪, that rarest of rarities: an archtecturally attractive shopping mall (⊠ 3222 M St. NW). Both M Street and Wisconsin Avenue are lined with restaurants and boutiques selling just about anything you could want, from the latest fashions to antiques furniture and jewelry—but don't expect any bargains. Continue along M Street to the **Markethouse** ⑫, an 1865 brick building currently occupied by Dean & Deluca, the trendy specialty grocer. M Street west leads to the **Key Bridge** into Rosslyn, Virginia. A house owned by Francis Scott Key, author of the national anthem, was demolished in 1947 to make way for the bridge that would bear his name. How's that for irony. The **Francis Scott Key Memorial Park** ⑬ lies at the foot of the D.C. side of Key Bridge.

To head to the residential area, continue on M Street past the old brick streetcar barn at Number 3600 (now a block of offices), turn right, and climb the **75 steps** ⑭ from the film *The Exorcist.* You'll see that it is indeed a truly terrifying fall, especially when being hurled by a demon. If you're not up to the climb, walk up 34th Street instead. **Halcyon House** ⑮, built by the first secretary of the Navy is at 34th and Prospect streets. It's a hodge-podge of architectural styles. The beautiful campus of **Georgetown University** ⑯, the oldest Jesuit school in the coun-

Georgetown

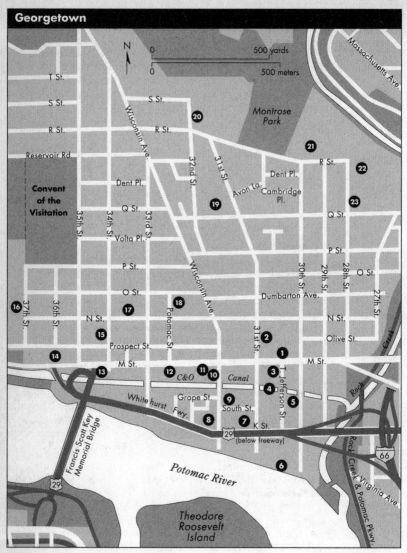

C & O Canal, **4**

Cox's Row, **17**

Customs House, **2**

Dumbarton House, **23**

Dumbarton Oaks, **20**

Evermay, **22**

Exorcist steps, **14**

Foundry Mall, **5**

Francis Dodge
Warehouses, **8**

Francis Scott Key
Memorial Park, **13**

Georgetown Park, **11**

Georgetown
University, **16**

Grace Episcopal
Church, **9**

Halcyon House, **15**

Markethouse, **12**

Masonic Lodge, **3**

Oak Hill Cemetery, **21**

Old Stone House, **1**

St. John's
Church, **18**

Suter's Tavern
plaque, **7**

Tudor Place, **19**

Vigilant Firehouse, **10**

Washington
Harbour, **6**

try, is a few blocks to the west. **Cox's Row** ⑰, a group of five Federal houses between 3339 and 3327 N Street, was built in 1817 by a former mayor of Georgetown. The redbrick house at **3307 N Street** was the home of then-Senator John F. Kennedy and his family before they moved downtown to 1600 Pennsylvania Avenue.

Turn left onto Potomac Street and walk a block up to O Street, several blocks of which still have cobblestones and trolley tracks. **St. John's Church** ⑱ (✉ 3240 O St. NW) was built in 1809 and has been a popular house of worship among U.S. presidents ever since. Go up 31st Street to Q Street, where through the trees you can see **Tudor Place** ⑲, built in 1816, a neoclassical mansion with a dramatic domed portico. **Dumbarton Oaks** ⑳, on 32nd Street, north of R Street, contains two world-class art collections and 10 acres of formal gardens. Three other sylvan retreats lie north of R Street. **Dumbarton Oaks Park** sprawls to the north and west of the estate, **Montrose Park** lies to the east, and further east is **Oak Hill Cemetery** ㉑, overlooking Rock Creek, where many historical figures are interred. Walk south on 28th Street past the 200-year-old Georgian manor house **Evermay** ㉒ (✉ 1623 28th St. NW), now a private home with lovely strollable grounds. Around the corner on Q Street is **Dumbarton House** ㉓, headquarters of the National Society of the Colonial Dames of America. It's filled with magnificent period antiques.

TIMING

You can easily spend a pleasant day in Georgetown, partly because some of the sites (Tudor Place, Dumbarton Oaks, Oak Hill Cemetery, Evermay, and Dumbarton House) are somewhat removed from the others and partly because there are so many intriguing shops and colorful people to look at that the street scene invites lingering. Georgetown is almost always crowded and, especially at night, not very automobile-friendly; driving and parking are usually difficult. The wise take the Metro—although the nearest station is a 15-minute walk away—the bus or a taxi (☞ Georgetown introduction, *above*).

Sights to See

⟡ ❹ **C&O Canal.** This waterway kept Georgetown open to shipping after its harbor had filled with silt. George Washington was one of the first to advance the idea of a canal linking the Potomac with the Ohio River across the Appalachians. Work started on the C&O Canal in 1828, and when it opened in 1850, its 74 locks linked Georgetown with Cumberland, Maryland, 184 miles to the northwest (still short of its intended destination). Lumber, coal, iron, wheat, and flour moved up and down the canal, but it was never as successful as its planners had hoped it would be. Many of the bridges spanning the canal in Georgetown were too low to allow anything other than fully loaded barges to pass underneath, and competition from the Baltimore & Ohio Railroad eventually spelled an end to profitability. Today the canal is a part of the National Park system, and walkers follow the towpath once used by mules while canoeists paddle the canal's calm waters. Between April and October you can go on a leisurely, mule-drawn trip aboard the *Georgetown* canal barge. Tickets are available across the canal, in the Foundry Mall. ✉ *1057 Thomas Jefferson St. NW,* ☎ *202/653–5190, 301/299–2026; group reservations and rates, 301/299–3613.* 💲 *$5.* ☾ *90-min barge trip mid-Apr.–early Nov., Wed.–Sun. at 11, 1, and 3.*

❶⑰ **Cox's Row.** Architecture buffs, especially those interested in Federal and Victorian houses, enjoy wandering along the redbrick sidewalks of upper Georgetown. The average house here has two signs on it: a brass plaque notifying passersby of the building's historic interest and a window decal that warns burglars of its state-of-the-art alarm system.

To get a representative taste of the houses in the area, walk along the 3300 block of N Street. The group of five Federal houses between 3339 and 3327 N Street is known collectively as Cox's Row, after John Cox, a former mayor of Georgetown, who built them in 1817. The flat-front, redbrick Federal house at **3307 N Street** was the home of then-Senator John F. Kennedy and his family before the White House beckoned.

2 **Customs House.** The old Renaissance Revival–style Customs House was built in 1858 to serve the port of Georgetown. It's been transformed into the Georgetown branch of the U.S. Postal Service, and there's really no reason to go inside unless you want to buy stamps or mail postcards. ⊠ *1221 31st St.*

23 **Dumbarton House.** Its symmetry and the two curved wings on the north side make Dumbarton, built around 1800, a distinctive example of Georgian architecture. The man who built the house, Joseph Nourse, was registrar of the U.S. Treasury. Other well-known Americans have spent time at the house, including Dolley Madison, who is said to have stopped here when fleeing Washington in 1814. One hundred years later, the house was moved 50 feet up the hill, when Q Street was cut through to the Dumbarton Bridge. Today it serves as the headquarters of the National Society of the Colonial Dames of America.

Eight rooms inside Dumbarton House have been restored to Colonial splendor, with period furnishings such as mahogany American Chippendale chairs, hallmark silver, Persian rugs, and a breakfront cabinet filled with rare books. Other notable items include a 1789 Charles Willson Peale portrait of Benjamin Stoddert's children (with an early view of Georgetown harbor in the background), Martha Washington's traveling cloak, and a British redcoat's red coat. Group tours may be arranged by appointment. ⊠ *2715 Q St. NW,* ☎ *202/337–2288.* ✉ *Suggested donation $3.* ⊙ *Tues.–Sat. 10–12:15.*

20 **Dumbarton Oaks.** Don't confuse Dumbarton Oaks with the nearby Dumbarton House. In 1944 one of the most important events of the 20th century took place in Dumbarton Oaks, when representatives of the United States, Great Britain, China, and the Soviet Union met in the music room here to lay the groundwork for the United Nations.

Career diplomat Robert Woods Bliss and his wife Mildred bought the property in 1920 and set about taming the sprawling grounds and removing 19th-century additions that had marred the Federal lines of the 1801 mansion. In 1940 the Blisses conveyed the estate to Harvard University, which maintains world-renowned collections of Byzantine and pre-Columbian art there. Both are small but choice, reflecting the enormous skill and creativity going on at roughly the same time on two sides of the Atlantic. The Byzantine collection includes beautiful examples of both religious and secular items executed in mosaic, metal, enamel, and ivory. Pre-Columbian works—artifacts and textiles from Mexico and Central and South America by such peoples as the Aztec, Maya, and Olmec—are arranged in an enclosed glass pavilion designed by Philip Johnson. Also on view to the public are the lavishly decorated music room and selections from Mrs. Bliss's collection of rare illustrated garden books.

If you have even a mild interest in flowers, shrubs, trees, and magnificent natural beauty, you'll enjoy a visit to Dumbarton Oaks's 10 acres of formal gardens, one of the loveliest spots in all of Washington (enter via R Street). Designed by noted landscape architect Beatrix Farrand, the gardens incorporate elements of traditional English, Italian, and French styles. A full-time crew of a dozen gardeners toils to maintain the stunning collection of terraces, geometric gardens, tree-shaded brick walks, fountains, arbors, and pools. Plenty of well-positioned benches make this a good place for resting weary feet, too. ⊠ *Art collections, 1703 32nd St. NW,* ☎ *202/339–6401 or 202/342–3200; gardens,* ⊠ *31st and R Sts. NW.* 🎟 *Art collections, suggested donation $1; gardens Apr.–Oct. $3, Nov.–Mar. free.* 🕐 *Art collections Tues.–Sun. 2–5; gardens Apr.–Oct., daily 2–6; Nov.–Mar., daily 2–5; both closed national holidays and Dec. 24.*

㉒ Evermay. A Georgian manor house built around 1800 by real estate speculator Samuel Davidson, Evermay is almost hidden by its black-and-gold gates and high brick wall. Davidson wanted it that way. He sometimes took out advertisements in newspapers warning sightseers to avoid his estate "as they would a den of devils or rattlesnakes." The mansion is in private hands, but its grounds are often opened for garden tours. ⊠ *1623 28th St. NW.*

⑭ The Exorcist Steps. The heights of Georgetown to the north above N Street contrast with the busy jumble of the old waterfront. To reach the higher ground you can walk up M Street past the old brick streetcar barn at Number 3600 (now a block of offices), turn right, and climb the 75 steps that figured prominently in the eerie movie *The Exorcist.* If you prefer a less demanding climb, walk up 34th Street instead.

❺ Foundry Mall. The mall gets its name from an old foundry that overlooked the canal at 30th Street. Around the turn of the century it was turned into a veterinary hospital that cared for mules working on the canal. Today it's a restaurant. ⊠ *1057 Thomas Jefferson St. NW.*

❽ Francis Dodge Warehouses. The last three buildings at the foot of the west side of Wisconsin Avenue are reminders of Georgetown' mercantile past. They were built around 1830 by trader and merchant Francis Dodge. Note the heavy stone foundation of the southernmost warehouse, its star-end braces, and the broken hoist in the gable end. According to an 1838 newspaper ad, Georgetown shoppers could visit Dodge's grocery to buy such items as "Porto Rico Sugar, Marseilles soft-shelled Almonds and Havanna Segars." While the dry goods of yesteryear have been replaced by small nonprofit organizations, the buildings don't look they house modern offices and their facades make an interesting snapshot.

⑬ Francis Scott Key Memorial Park. A small noisy park situated the Key Bridge honors the Washington attorney who "by the dawn's early light" penned the national anthem, upon seeing that the flag had survived the night's British bombardment of Ft. McHenry in Baltimore harbor during the War of 1812. A replica of the 15-star, 15-stripe flag that inspired Key flies over the park 24 hours a day. Here Georgetown's quaint demeanor contrasts with the silvery skyscrapers of Rosslyn, Virginia, across the Potomac. ⊠ *M St. between 34th St. and Key Bridge.*

Georgetown Estates. Georgetown's largest and grandest estates occupy the northern part of the neighborhood, commanding fine views of Rock Creek to the east and of the Potamac River below. Once you're in Georgetown, the best way to get to the estates is to walk north either on Wisconsin Avenue (the bustling commercial route) or a block east, on 31st Street (a quieter residential street), depending on your mood. Strolling 31st Street will give you a chance to admire more of the city's finest houses.

⑪ Georgetown Park. A multilevel shopping extravaganza answers the question, If the Victorians had invented shopping malls, what would they look like? Such high-ticket stores as F.A.O. Schwarz, Williams-Sonoma, Polo/Ralph Lauren, and Godiva Chocolates can be found within this artful, skylit mass of polished brass, tile flooring, and potted plants. If you've always looked down your nose at mall architecture, Georgetown Park might win you over. ⊠ *3222 M St. NW,* ☎ *202/298–5577.*

NEED A
BREAK?
Across the street from Georgetown Park, **Pizzeria Uno** (⊠ 3211 M St. NW) has brought Chicago-style pizza to the heart of Georgetown. The deep-dish pies take a while to cook, but the wait is worth it. Those in a hurry may want to order the "personal-size" pizza: It's ready in five minutes and costs less than $6.

⑯ Georgetown University. Founded in 1789 by John Carroll, first American bishop and first archbishop of Baltimore, Georgetown is the oldest Jesuit school in the country. About 12,000 students attend Georgetown, known now as much for its perennially successful basketball team as for its fine programs in law, medicine, and the liberal arts. When seen from the Potomac or from Washington's high ground, the Gothic spires of Georgetown's older buildings give the university an almost medieval look. ⊠ *37th and O Sts.*

⑨ Grace Episcopal Church. In the mid- to late-19th century the Gothic Revival Grace Episcopal Church served the boatmen and workers from the nearby C&O Canal. At the time the area was one of the poorest Georgetown. Today Georgetown real estate values are so stratospheric that the idea any parcel of it could ever have been had for a song seems almost incredible. Grace Episcopal now sits in a thriving commercial district. While there are some pricy condos, residential Georgetown is mainly north of M Street. ⊠ *Wisconsin Ave. near C&O Canal.*

⑮ Halcyon House. Built in 1783 by Benjamin Stoddert, the first secretary of the Navy, Halcyon House has been the object of many subsequent additions and renovations. It's now a motley assortment of architectural styles. Prospect Street, where the house is set, gets its name from the fine views it affords of the waterfront and the river below. ⊠ *34th and Prospect Sts.*

Key Bridge. Heading west on M Street leads to the into Rosslyn, Virginia, via Key Bridge. A house owned by Francis Scott Key, author of the national anthem, was demolished in 1947 to make way for the bridge that would bear his name.

⑫ Markethouse. A stroll up either M Street or Wisconsin Avenue will take you past a dizzying array of merchandise: expensive bicycling accessories, gold chains and necklaces, antique jewelry, furniture, the latest fashions, music tapes and CDs, you name it. Also part of the scene is the Markethouse, an 1865 brick building that once housed a market filled with food stalls. There has been some sort of market on this spot since 1795, and in 1993 Dean & Deluca, the trendy Manhattan specialty grocer, moved in, a welcome addition, as gourmet shops in Washington are few and far between. Inside, expensive meats, cheeses, and exotic coffees beckon, along with tempting sandwiches and pastries that make delicious snacks during a Georgetown stroll. Nowhere else in the Capitol can you find more than a dozen types olives—or food, cookbooks, and cookware—in one place. ⊠ *M and Potomac Sts.*

③ Masonic Lodge. A two-story brick structure, Georgetown's Masonic Lodge was built around 1810. Freemasonry, the world's largest secret society, was started by British stonemasons and cathedral builders as early as the 14th century; the fraternal order now has a much broader international membership that has included U.S. presidents—among them George Washington—as well as members of Congress. It's no accident that the Freemasons chose Georgetown to be the site of a lodge. Although Georgetown today is synonymous with affluence, for most of its history it was a working–class city, and the original names of its streets—Water Street, The Keys, Fishing Lane—attest to the past importance of traditional trades like fishing to the region's economy. The area south of M Street (originally called Bridge Street because of the bridge that spanned Rock Creek to the east) was inhabited by tradesmen, laborers, and merchants who were good candidates for expanding the Masons' ranks. Among the lodge's interesting details are a pointed facade and recessed central arch, features that suggest the society's traditional attachment to the building arts. ⊠ *1058 Thomas Jefferson St.*

㉑ **Oak Hill Cemetery.** In addition to Dumbarton Oaks, three other sylvan retreats lie north of R Street in upper Georgetown. Originally part of the estate of diplomat Robert Woods Bliss (☞ Dumbarton Oaks, *above*), **Dumbarton Oaks Park** sprawls to the north and west. **Montrose Park** lies to the east of the estate. Further east is Oak Hill Cemetery, its funerary obelisks, crosses, and gravestones spread out like an amphitheater of the dead on a hill overlooking Rock Creek. Near the entrance is an 1850 Gothic-style chapel designed by Smithsonian Castle architect James Renwick. Across from the chapel is the resting place of actor, playwright, and diplomat John H. Payne, who is remembered today primarily for his song "Home Sweet Home." A few hundred feet to the north is the circular tomb of William Corcoran, founder of the Corcoran Gallery of Art. ⊠ *30th and R Sts. NW,* ☎ *202/337–2835.* ▣ *Free.* ☉ *Weekdays 10–4; closed major holidays.*

❶ **Old Stone House.** What was early American life like? Here's the Capitol's oldest window into the past. Work on this fieldstone house, thought to be Washington's only surviving pre-Revolutionary building, was begun in 1764 by a cabinetmaker named Christopher Layman. The house, now a museum, was used as both a residence and a place of business by a succession of occupants. Five of the house's rooms are furnished with the simple sturdy artifacts—plain tables, spinning wheels, etc.—of 18th century middle–class life. The National Park Service maintains the house and its lovely gardens in the rear, which are planted with fruit trees and perennials. ⊠ *3051 M St. NW,* ☎ *202/426–6851.* ▣ *Free.* ☉ *Memorial Day–Labor Day, daily 9–5; Labor Day–Memorial Day, Wed.–Sun. 9–5; closed major holidays.*

1083 Thomas Jefferson Street. The two-story brick building was built around 1865 as a stable for the horses and hearses of a nearby undertaker and cabinetmaker. The wide doors on the right let the horses in; the hoist beam above the right-most window was used to lift hay and wood to the second floor. Three fine brick Federal houses are grouped south of the Georgetown Dutch Inn (☞ Chapter 5) at **1069, 1067,** and **1063 Thomas Jefferson Street.** Number 1063 has attractive flat lintels with keystones and a rounded keystone arch above the door.

⑱ **St. John's Church.** West of Wisconsin Avenue, a several-blocks-long stretch of O Street still has remnants from an earlier age: cobblestones and streetcar tracks. Residents are so proud of the cobblestones that even concrete patches have been scored to resemble them. Prominent in this section of Georgetown is St. John's Church, built in 1809 and attributed to Dr. William Thornton, architect of the Capitol. Later alterations have left it looking more Victorian than Federal. Known as the "Church of the Presidents" owing to the large number of White House occupants who have worshipped there, St. John's is also noted for its stained glass windows. At the corner of the churchyard is a memorial to Colonel Ninian Beall, the Scotsman who received the original patent for the land that would become Georgetown. ⊠ *3240 O St. NW,* ☎ *202/338–1796.*

❼ Suter's Tavern. Peer through a vine-covered fence at a vacant lot to see a **plaque** commemorating Suter's Tavern. In March 1791, in the one-story hostelry that stood on this spot, George Washington met with the men who owned the tobacco farms and swampy marshes to the east of Georgetown and persuaded them to sell their land to the government so construction of the District of Columbia could begin. The tradesmen, laborers, and merchants of the neighborhood today are architects, ad executives, and public relations people. Their offices still line **K Street.** In many of these offices you can hear the rumble of cars on the Whitehurst Freeway, the elevated road above K Street that leads to the Francis Scott Key Memorial Bridge. ⊠ *31st and K Sts.*

❶❾ Tudor Place. Stop at Q Street between 31st and 32nd streets, look through the trees to the north, at the top of a sloping lawn, and you'll see the neoclassical Tudor Place, designed by Capitol architect William Thornton and completed in 1816. On a house tour you'll see chairs that belonged to George Washington, Francis Scott Key's desk, and spurs of members of the Peter family who were killed in the Civil War (although the house was in Washington, the family was true to its Virginia roots and fought for Dixie). The grounds contain many specimens planted in the early 19th century. The house was built for Thomas Peter, son of Georgetown's first mayor, and his wife, Martha Custis, Martha Washington's granddaughter. It was because of this connection to the president's family that Tudor Place came to house many items from Mount Vernon. The yellow stucco house is interesting for its architecture—especially the dramatic, two-story domed portico on the south side—but its familial heritage is even more remarkable: Tudor Place stayed in the same family for 178 years, until 1983, when Armistead Peter III died. Before his death, Peter established a foundation to restore the house and open it to the public. Tour reservations are advised. ⊠ *1644 31st St. NW,* ☎ *202/965–0400.* 🎫 *Suggested donation $6.* ☉ *Tour Tues.–Fri. at 10, 11:30, 1, and 2:30; Sat. hourly 10–4 (last tour at 3); garden spring and fall, Sun. noon–4.*

❶⓿ Vigilant Firehouse. Built in 1840, the Vigilant Firehouse bears a memorial plaque that reads, "Bush, the Old Fire Dog, died of Poison, July 5th, 1869, R.I.P." Across the street, just north of the C&O Canal, is a simple granite **obelisk** honoring the men who built the waterway. ⊠ *1066 Wisconsin Ave.*

❻ Washington Harbour. Stately columns and the liberal use of glass as a construction material are hallmarks of Washington Harbour, a glittering postmodern riverfront development designed by Arthur Cotton Moore. Included are such restaurants as the two-story Sequoia, China Regency, Tony & Joe's Seafood Place, and the Riverside Grille, as well as offices, apartments, and upscale shops. Highlights of the central plaza are a large fountain and a futuristic, lighthouse-like structure made up of four towering white columns. Several restaurants offer outdoor dining. From the edge of Washington Harbour you can see the Watergate complex and Kennedy Center to the east while the waters of the Potomac gently lap at the edge of the dock. Those who prefer the water to the streets often arrive by boat, docking just yards from outdoor diners. At night, the entire area sparkles like a Christmas scene with hundreds of twinkling white lights.

DUPONT CIRCLE

Three of Washington's main thoroughfares intersect at Dupont Circle: Connecticut, New Hampshire, and Massachusetts avenues. With a handsome small park and a splashing fountain in the center, Dupont Circle is more than a deserted island around which traffic flows, making it an exception among Washington circles. The activity on the circle spills over into the surrounding streets, one of the liveliest, most vibrant neighborhoods in Washington.

Development near Dupont Circle started during the post–Civil War boom of the 1870s. As the city increased in stature, the nation's wealthy and influential citizens began building their mansions near the circle. The area underwent a different kind of transformation in the middle of this century, when the middle and upper classes deserted Washington for the suburbs, and in the '60s the circle became the starting point for rowdy, litter-strewn marches sponsored by various counterculture groups. Today the neighborhood is once again fashionable, and its many restaurants, offbeat shops, and specialty bookstores lend it a distinctive, cosmopolitan air. Stores and clubs catering to the neighborhood's large gay community are abundant.

Numbers in the text correspond to numbers in the margin and on the Dupont Circle map.

A Good Walk

Start your exploration in **Dupont Circle** ① itself (Metro: Dupont Circle), with its large central fountain. Carefully cross the circle traffic and head down New Hampshire Avenue to the **Heurich Mansion** ②, home of the **Historical Society of Washington, D.C.** Cross New Hampshire Avenue and go left on O Street. Not all the homes here are mansions, but the typical brick Victorian row houses on this block tend to be large and spacious. Turn right on 21st Street to the opulent **Walsh-McLean House** ③ at Massachusetts Avenue, built by an Irishman who struck gold in Colorado. Head west on Massachusetts Avenue to Number 2118, **Anderson House** ④, where you'll find the art and treasures a former diplomat collected during his travels. It also serves as the headquarters of the patriotic organization, the Society of the Cincinnati.

Head west on Q Street to the **Bison Bridge** ⑤ (officially the Dumbarton Bridge), so-called because of its four bronze statues of the shaggy horned beasts. The bridge goes over Rock Creek to Georgetown. Walk north on 23rd Street and pass between two more embassies, those of Turkey and Romania, both on **Sheridan Circle.** This area of Massachusetts Avenue, going either direction from the circle, is known as Embassy Row, with the various nations' flags flying in front of their respective embassies. Turn left on Massachusetts Avenue and you are on Embassy Row, where the **Cameroon Embassy** is housed in the mansion (⊠ 2349 Massachusetts Ave.). Turn right on S Street and go past the statue of Irish patriot **Robert Emmet,** dedicated in 1966 to celebrate the 50th anniversary of Irish independence. The former home of the 28th president, the **Woodrow Wilson House** ⑥, is a few hundred feet down S Street. Right next door is the **Textile Museum** ⑦, founded by Bristol-Myers heir George Hewitt Myers to house and show some of his 12,000 textiles and 1,500 carpets.

Walk north on 23rd Street until it dead-ends at the Tudor mansion at **2221 Kalorama Road** ⑧, currently the residence of the French ambassador. Walking down Kalorama toward Connecticut, the large beige building on the left near Connecticut Avenue is the Chinese Embassy. Turn right, down Connecticut Avenue. On the left, at 1919

Dupont Circle

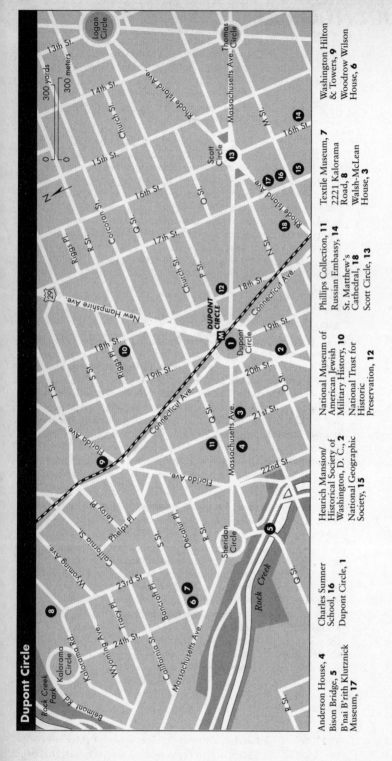

Anderson House, **4**
Bison Bridge, **5**
B'nai B'rith Klutznick
Museum, **17**

Charles Sumner
School, **16**
Dupont Circle, **1**

Heurich Mansion/
Historical Society of
Washington, D. C., **2**
National Geographic
Society, **15**

National Museum of
American Jewish
Military History, **10**
National Trust for
Historic
Preservation, **12**

Phillips Collection, **11**
Russian Embassy, **14**
St. Matthew's
Cathedral, **18**
Scott Circle, **13**

Textile Museum, **7**
2221 Kalorama
Road, **8**
Walsh-McLean
House, **3**

Washington Hilton
& Towers, **9**
Woodrow Wilson
House, **6**

Connecticut, is the **Washington Hilton & Towers** ⑨, the site of John Hinckley's 1981 failed assassination attempt on Ronald Reagan. Go left on R Street for two blocks to the **National Museum of American Jewish Military History** ⑩, which chronicles Jews' military service in every war this country has fought. Follow R Street back across Connecticut to the **Fondo Del Sol Visual Art and Media Center,** a nonprofit center featuring art, poetry, and music of the Americas. Walk south on 21st Street and discover some of the many private art galleries in the area.

Another of Washington's great art museums is the **Phillips Collection** ⑪ at 21st and Q streets, the country's first permanent museum of modern art. Continue east on Q Street, then turn right at Connecticut to the circle. Follow Massachusetts Avenue east to the **National Trust for Historic Preservation** ⑫, formerly a luxury apartment building, at 18th Street and Massachusetts Avenue. Further east on Massachusetts Avenue is the **Brookings Institution,** Washington's best-known liberal think tank. At the corner at 16th Street you'll find the **Australian Embassy,** which has occasional art exhibits. And now you've arrived at yet another circle. **Scott Circle** ⑬, with its equestrian statue of **General Winfield Scott,** is at the intersections of Massachusetts and Rhode Island avenues and 16th Street. On the west side of Scott Circle there is a statue of fiery orator **Daniel Webster.** If you walk to the south side of the circle and look down 16th Street you'll get a familiar view of the columns of the White House six blocks away. Across the circle is an unusual memorial to **S. C. F. Hahnemann,** the founder of the homeopathic system of medicine.)

Continue down 16th Street to the **Jefferson Hotel,** a former apartment building now noted for its luxury rooms and service. Still farther down 16th Street, the **Russian Embassy** ⑭ (✉ 1125 16th St. NW) occupies the mansion built for the widow of George Pullman of railroad-car renown. Turn right onto M Street. On the southwest corner of 16th and M streets sits the headquarters of the **National Geographic Society** ⑮, where you can explore the new interactive video touch-screens in **Explorers Hall.** The **Charles Sumner School** ⑯, across M Street from National Geographic, was built in 1872 as a school for black children. It's now used mainly for conferences, but it also has a permanent exhibit on the history of the city's public school system and hosts occasional art exhibits. Now head up 17th Street to Rhode Island Avenue, where you'll find the **B'nai B'rith Klutznick Museum** ⑰, which follows the history of Jewish people for the past 20 centuries. Half a block west on Rhode Island Avenue is **St. Matthew's Cathedral** ⑱, the seat of Washington's Catholic archbishop. John F. Kennedy frequently attended the church, which also was the site of his funeral mass.

TIMING

Visiting the Dupont Circle area should take about half a day, although you can find things to keep you busy all day. The most time-consuming sites will probably be the National Geographic Society's Explorer Hall, the Phillips Gallery, and Anderson House—there is so much to see—although the treasures inside the Textile, B'nai B'rith Klutznik, and American Jewish Military History museums will captivate and hold you as well.

Sights to See

❹ **Anderson House.** A palatial home that's a mystery even to many longtime Washingtonians, who assume it's just another embassy, Anderson House is not an embassy, though it does have a link to the diplomatic world. Larz Anderson was a diplomat whose career included postings to Japan and Belgium. Anderson and his heiress wife, Isabel, toured the world, picking up objects that struck their fancy. They filled their residence, which was constructed in 1905, with the booty of their travels, including choir stalls from an Italian Renaissance church, Flemish tapestries, and a large—if spotty—collection of Asian art. All this remains in the house for visitors to see.

In accordance with Anderson's wishes, the building also serves as the headquarters of a group to which he belonged: the **Society of the Cincinnati.** The oldest patriotic organization in the country, the society was formed in 1783 by a group of officers who had served with George Washington during the Revolutionary War. The group took the name Cincinnati from Cincinnatus, a distinguished Roman who, circa 500 BC, led an army against Rome's enemies and later quelled civil disturbances in the city. After each success, rather than seek political power that could have easily been his, he returned to the idealistic purity of a simple life on his farm. The story impressed the American officers, who saw in it a mirror of their own situation: They too would leave the battlefields behind to get on with the business of forging a new nation. (One such member went on to name the city in Ohio.) Today's members are direct descendants of those American revolutionaries.

Many of the displays in the society's museum focus on the Colonial period and the Revolutionary War. One room—painted in a marvelous trompe l'oeil style that deceives visitors into thinking the walls are covered with sculpture—is filled with military miniatures from the United States and France. (Because of the important role France played in defeating the British, French officers were invited to join the society. Pierre L'Enfant, "Artist of the Revolution" and planner of Washington, designed the society's eagle medallion.)

The house is often used by the federal government to entertain visiting dignitaries. Amid the glitz, glamour, beauty, and patriotic spectacle of the mansion are two delightful painted panels in the solarium that depict the Andersons' favorite motor-car sightseeing routes around Washington. ✉ *2118 Massachusetts Ave. NW,* ☎ *202/785–2040.* ✆ *Free.* ◷ *Tues.–Sat. 1–4. Metro: Dupont Circle.*

Australian Embassy. Many foreign embassies in Washington host art exhibits or cultural programs open to the public. One of the best galleries is at the Australian Embassy, which periodically displays masterpieces from Down Under. If you're lucky, you'll see aboriginal artifacts and dot paintings of striking originality and beauty, as well as contemporary landscapes and portraits with a uniquely Australian character. Renovations are planned, however; if you're making a special trip, call first. ✉ *1601 Massachusetts Ave. NW,* ☎ *202/797–3000.* ✆ *Free.* ◷ *Weekdays 8:30–4:30. Metro: Dupont Circle.*

❺ Bison Bridge. Tour guides at the Smithsonian's Museum of Natural History are quick to remind visitors that America never had buffalo; the big shaggy animals that roamed the plains were bison. (True buffalo are African and Asian animals of the same family.) Though many maps and guidebooks call this the Buffalo Bridge, the four bronze statues by A. Phimister Proctor are of bison. Officially called the **Dumbarton Bridge,** the structure stretches across Rock Creek Park into Georgetown. Its sides are decorated with busts of Native Americans, the work of architect Glenn Brown, who, along with his son Bedford, designed the bridge in 1914. The best way to see the busts is to walk the footpath along Rock Creek or to lean over the green railings beside the bison and peer through the trees. ✉ *23rd and Q Sts. NW. Metro: Dupont Circle.*

⓱ B'nai B'rith Klutznick Museum. Devoted to the history of the Jewish people, this museum's permanent exhibits span 20 centuries and highlight Jewish festivals and the rituals employed to mark the various stages of life. A wide variety of Jewish decorative art, adorning such items as spice boxes and Torah covers, is on display. Changing exhibits highlight the work of contemporary Jewish artists. ✉ *1640 Rhode Island Ave. NW,* ☎ *202/857–6583.* ✉ *Suggested donation $2.* ☉ *Sun.–Fri. 10–5; closed federal and Jewish holidays. Metro: Dupont Circle or Farragut North.*

Cameroon Embassy. The westernmost of the beaux arts–style mansions built along Massachusetts Avenue in the late-19th and early 20th centuries today houses the Cameroon Embassy. The building is a fanciful castle with a conical tower, bronze weather vane, and intricate detailing around the windows and balconies. ✉ *2349 Massachusetts Ave. Metro: Dupont Circle.*

16 Charles Sumner School. Built in 1872 for the education of black children in the Capitol, the Charles Sumner School takes its name from the Massachusetts senator who delivered a blistering attack against slavery in 1856 and was savagely caned as a result by a congressman from South Carolina. The building was designed by Adolph Cluss, who created the Arts and Industries Building on the Washington Mall. It is typical of the District's Victorian-era public schools. Beautifully restored in 1986, the school serves mainly as a conference center, though it hosts changing art exhibits and houses a permanent collection of memorabilia relating to the city's public school system. The school is often closed for conferences. Call ahead to arrange a group tour. ✉ *1201 17th St. NW,* ☎ *202/727–3419.* ✉ *Free.* ☉ *Tues.–Fri. 10–5. Metro: Farragut North.*

Cosmos Club. Founded in 1878, the Cosmos Club was and is perhaps the most exclusive private club in the city. Neither money nor influence will get you on the membership rolls. It takes brains. Different rooms in the club celebrate members who have won the Nobel Prize or appeared on postage stamps. The formerly men-only club started accepting women in 1988. Judith Martin (a.k.a. Miss Manners) was one of the first admitted. ✉ *2121 Massachusetts Ave. Metro: Dupont Circle.*

1 Dupont Circle. Originally known as Pacific Circle, this hub was the westernmost circle in Pierre L'Enfant's original design for the Federal City. The name was changed in 1884, when Congress authorized construction of a bronze statue honoring Civil War hero Admiral Samuel F. Dupont. The statue fell into disrepair, and Dupont's family—who had never liked it anyway—replaced it in 1921 with the fountain you see today. The marble fountain, with its allegorical figures Sea, Stars, and Wind, was created by Daniel Chester French, the sculptor of Lincoln's statue in the Lincoln Memorial.

As you look around the circumference of the circle, you'll be able to see the special constraints within which architects in Washington must work. Since a half-dozen streets converge on Dupont Circle, the buildings around it are, for the most part, wedge shaped and set on oddly shaped plots of land like massive slices of pie.

Only two of the great houses that stood on the circle in the early 20th century remain today. The Renaissance-style house at **15 Dupont Circle,** next to P Street, was built in 1903 for Robert W. Patterson, publisher of the *Washington Times-Herald.* Patterson's daughter, Cissy, who succeeded him as publisher of the paper, was known for hosting parties that attracted such notables as William Randolph Hearst, Douglas MacArthur, and J. Edgar Hoover. In 1927, while Cissy was living in New York City and the White House was being refurbished, Calvin Coolidge and his family stayed in this Dupont Circle home. The

Coolidges received American flier Charles Lindbergh here; some of the most famous photographs of Lindy were taken as he stood on the house's balcony and smiled down at the crowds below. Sissy willed it to the American Red Cross in 1948, and the Washington Club, a private club, bought it from them in 1951.

The **Sulgrave Club,** at the corner of Massachusetts Avenue, was also once a private home and is now likewise a club. Neither club is open to the public. *Metro: Dupont Circle.*

NEED A BREAK?

Connecticut Avenue near Dupont Circle is chockablock with restaurants. The **Chesapeake Bagel Bakery** (⊠ 1636 Connecticut Ave. NW) is a low-key lunchroom that serves a wide variety of bagel sandwiches. **Ferrara** (⊠ above Q St. entrance to Metro) and **Starbucks** (⊠ Connecticut Ave. NW above Dupont Circle) are part of the invasion of specialty coffee shops that also serve sweets. At **Kramerbooks** (⊠ 1517 Connecticut Ave. NW), relax over dinner or a drink after browsing the volumes on display. One of the best Chinese restaurants in the city, **City Lights of China** (⊠ 1731 Connecticut Ave. NW) serves Cantonese, Sichuan, and Mandarin dishes. Specialties include Peking duck, whole fish steamed with ginger, and eggplant in garlic sauce.

Fondo Del Sol Visual Art and Media Center. A nonprofit center devoted to the cultural heritage of the Americas, the Fondo Del Sol Visual Art and Media Center offers changing exhibitions covering contemporary, pre-Columbian, and folk art. The center also offers a program of lectures, concerts, poetry readings, exhibit tours, and an annual summer festival featuring salsa and reggae music. ⊠ *2112 R St. NW,* ☎ *202/483–2777.* ⊡ *About $3.* ☉ *Wed.–Sat. 12:30–5. Metro: Dupont Circle.*

❷ Heurich Mansion. Currently housing the **Historical Society of Washington, D.C.,** the Heurich Mansion is a severe Romanesque Revival building that was the home of Christian Heurich, a German orphan who made his fortune in this country in the beer business. Heurich's brewery was in the Foggy Bottom neighborhood, where the Kennedy Center stands today. Brewing was a dangerous business in the 19th century, and fires had more than once reduced Heurich's beer factory to ashes. Perhaps because of this he insisted that his home, completed in 1894, be fireproof. Although 17 fireplaces were installed—some with onyx facings, one with the bronze image of a lion staring out from the back—not a single one ever held a fire.

After Heurich's widow died, in 1955, the house was turned over to the Historical Society and today is its headquarters and houses its voluminous archives. All the furnishings in the house were owned and used by the Heurichs. The interior of the house is an eclectic Victorian treasure trove of plaster detailing, carved wooden doors, and painted ceilings. The downstairs breakfast room, where Heurich, his wife, and their three children ate most of their meals, is decorated like a rathskeller and is adorned with such German sayings as "A good drink makes old people young."

Heurich must have taken the German proverbs seriously. He drank his beer every day, had three wives (not all at once), and lived to be 102. (In 1986 Heurich's grandson Gary started brewing the family beer again. Though it's made in Utica, New York, he vows to someday build another Heurich brewery near Washington.) Docents who give tours of the house are adept at answering questions about other Washington landmarks, too. ⊠ *1307 New Hampshire Ave. NW,* ☎ *202/785–2068.* ⊡ *45-min house tour $3.* ☉ *Wed.–Sat. 10–4; tour Wed.–Sat. at noon, 1, 2, and 3. Metro: Dupont Circle.*

NEED A
BREAK? The Dupont Circle branch of **Pan Asian Noodles & Grill** (✉ 2020 P St.
NW, ☎ 202/872–8889) is one of three locations in Washington. All
offer reasonably priced noodle dishes from the Orient.

Jefferson Hotel (☞ Chapter 5). Designed by Jules H. de Sibour, the man
responsible for the ultra-lavish, 11,000-square-foot McCormick Apartments, the Jefferson Hotel also started out as apartments but was converted to a hotel in the '50s. It has a reputation for luxury and discretion
and is a favorite temporary home for White House cabinet members
awaiting confirmation. ✉ *16th and M Sts. Metro: Farragut North.*

☝ ⑮ **National Geographic Society.** Founded in 1888, the society is best
known for its yellow-border magazine, found in doctor's offices, family rooms, and attics across the country. The society has sponsored numerous expeditions throughout its 100-year history, including those
of Admirals Peary and Byrd and underwater explorer Jacques Cousteau.
Explorers Hall, entered from 17th Street, is the magazine come to life.
Recently renovated, Explorers Hall invites visitors to learn about the
world in a decidedly interactive way. You can experience everything
from a minitornado to video "touch-screens" that explain various geographic concepts and then quiz you on what you've learned. The most
dramatic events take place in Earth Station One, a 72-seat amphitheater that sends the audience on a journey around the world. The centerpiece is a hand-painted globe, 11 feet in diameter, that floats and
spins on a cushion of air, showing off different features of the planet.
✉ *17th and M Sts.,* ☎ *202/857–7588; group tours, 202/857–7689.*
🎫 *Free.* ☉ *Mon.–Sat. and holidays 9–5, Sun. 10–5. Metro: Farragut
North.*

⑩ **National Museum of American Jewish Military History.** The museum's
focus is on American Jews as being first and foremost American citizens who have served in every war the nation has fought. On display
are their weapons, uniforms, medals, recruitment posters, and other military memorabilia.The few specifically religious items—a camouflage
yarmulke, rabbinical supplies fashioned from shell casings and parachute
silk—underscore the strange demands placed on religion during war.
✉ *1811 R St. NW,* ☎ *202/265–6280.* 🎫 *Free.* ☉ *Weekdays 9–5, Sun.
1–5; closed federal and Jewish holidays. Metro: Dupont Circle.*

⑫ **National Trust for Historic Preservation.** Housed in this building were
some of the most luxurious apartments in the city. The beaux arts–style
McCormick Apartments, designed by Jules H. de Sibour, were built in
1917 and contained only six apartments, one on each floor, each with
11,000 square feet of space. Some of Washington's most prominent
citizens lived here, including hostess Perle Mesta and Andrew Mellon,
secretary of the treasury under three presidents, whose top-floor flat
contained many of the paintings that would later go to the National
Gallery of Art. During World War II the building was converted to office space, and in 1977 it was bought by the National Trust. The
building is closed to the public, but a quick peek at the circular lobby
will give you an idea of the lavish world its onetime residents inhabited. Naturally, given the work of its current occupant, the building
has been historically preserved. ✉ *18th St. and Massachusetts Ave.
Metro: Dupont Circle.*

⑪ **Phillips Collection.** The first permanent museum of modern art in the
country, the masterpiece-filled Phillips Collection is unique both in ori-
gin and content. In 1918 Duncan Phillips, grandson of a founder of
the Jones and Laughlin Steel Company, started to collect art for a museum that would stand as a memorial to his father and brother, who
had died within 13 months of each other. Three years later what was

first called the Phillips Memorial Gallery opened in two rooms of this Georgian-Revival home near Dupont Circle.

Not interested in a painting's market value or its faddishness, Phillips searched for works that impressed him as outstanding products of a particular artist's unique vision. Holdings include works by Georges Braque, Paul Cézanne, Paul Klee, Henri Matisse, John Henry Twachtman, and the largest museum collection in the country of the work of Pierre Bonnard. The exhibits change regularly. The collection's best-known paintings include Renoir's *Luncheon of the Boating Party, Repentant Peter* by both Goya and El Greco, *A Bowl of Plums* by 18th-century artist Jean-Baptiste Siméon Chardin, Degas's *Dancers at the Bar,* Van Gogh's *Entrance to the Public Garden at Arles,* and Cézanne's self-portrait, the painting Phillips said he would save first if his gallery caught fire. During the '20s, Phillips and his wife, Marjorie, started to support American Modernists such as John Marin, Georgia O'Keeffe, and Arthur Dove.

The Phillips is a comfortable museum. Works of a favorite artist are often grouped together in "exhibition units," and, unlike most other galleries (where uniformed guards appear uninterested in the masterpieces around them), the Phillips employs students of art, many of whom are artists themselves, to sit by the paintings and answer questions.

The Phillips family moved out of the house in 1930. An addition was built in 1960 and renovated and renamed the Goh Annex in 1989. It gave the Phillips 50% more exhibition space and is host to traveling exhibits and rotating selections from the museum's permanent collection. On Thursdays, the museum stays open late, enticing people with chamber music or jazz, and a café that serves light dinners. ⊠ *1600 21st St. NW,* ☎ *202/387–2151.* ▧ *$6.50, Thurs. night $5.* ☉ *Tues., Wed., Fri., and Sat. 10–5; Thurs. 10–8:30; Sun. noon–7; tour Wed. and Sat. at 2; gallery talks 1st and 3rd Thurs. of month at 12:30. Metro: Dupont Circle.*

⑭ Russian Embassy. The red, white, and blue flag of Russia flies before the Russian Embassy. Here's where some of the Cold War's most famous spies were based and where some of the most notorious American traitors sought sanctuary. For example, John A. Walker, Jr., the one-time Navy warrant officer who eventually enlisted the help of his son, his brother, and his best friend in his spying activities, walked into the embassy in October 1967 with a list of codes for U.S. military cipher machines. The ornate mansion was originally built for the widow of George Pullman of railroad-car fame. It first did diplomatic duty as the Imperial Russian Embassy, then became the Soviet Embassy, and now it's Russian once again. The rest of the ex-Soviet republics were left scrambling for their own embassies after the breakup of the USSR in 1991. ⊠ *1125 16th St. NW. Metro: Farragut North.*

⑱ St. Matthew's Cathedral. St. Matthew's is the seat of Washington's Catholic archbishop. John F. Kennedy frequently worshiped in this Renaissance-style church, and in 1963 his funeral mass was held within its richly decorated walls. Set in the floor, directly in front of the main altar, is a memorial to the slain president: "Here rested the remains of President Kennedy at the requiem mass November 25, 1963, before their removal to Arlington where they lie in expectation of a heavenly resurrection." A memorial to nuns who served as nurses during the Civil War is across Rhode Island Avenue. ⊠ *1725 Rhode Island Ave. NW,* ☎ *202/347–3215.* ▧ *Free.* ☉ *Weekdays and Sun. 6:30–6:30, Sat. 7:30–6:30; tour Sun. 2–4:15. Metro: Farragut North.*

13 **Scott Circle.** The equestrian statue of **General Winfield Scott** was cast from cannon captured in the Mexican War. On the west side of the traffic circle in which it sits there is a statue of fiery orator **Daniel Webster.** If you walk to the south side of the circle and look down 16th Street you'll get a familiar view of the columns of the White House, six blocks away. Across the circle is an interesting memorial to **S. C. F. Hahnemann,** his statue sitting in a recessed wall, his head surrounded by a mosaic of colorful tiles. (Who, you ask, was S. C. F. Hahnemann? He was the founder of the homeopathic system of medicine and the namesake of Hahnemann Medical School in Philadel-phia.) ✉ *Massachusetts and Rhode Island Aves. and 16th St. Metro: Archives/Navy Memorial.*

7 **Textile Museum.** In the 1890s, founder George Hewitt Myers pur-chased his first Oriental rug for his dorm room at Yale and subsequently collected more than 12,000 textiles and 1,500 carpets. An heir to the Bristol-Myers fortune, Myers and his wife lived two houses down from Woodrow Wilson, at 2310 S Street, in a home designed by John Russell Pope, architect of the National Archives and Jefferson Memo-rial. Myers bought the Waddy Wood-designed house next door, at Num-ber 2320, and opened his museum to the public in 1925. Rotating exhibits are taken from a permanent collection of historic and ethno-graphic items that include Coptic and pre-Columbian textiles, Kash-mir embroidery, and Turkman tribal rugs. At least one show of modern textiles—such as quilts or fiber art—is mounted each year. ✉ *2320 S St. NW,* ☎ *202/667–0441.* ✉ *Suggested donation $5.* ☉ *Mon.–Sat. 10–5, Sun. 1–5; closed major holidays; highlight tour Sept.–May, Wed. and weekends at 2. Metro: Dupont Circle.*

8 **2221 Kalorama Road.** S Street is an informal dividing line between the Dupont Circle area to the south and the exclusive **Kalorama** neigh-borhood to the north. The name for this peaceful, tree-filled enclave— Greek for "beautiful view"—was contributed by politician and writer Joel Barlow, who bought the large tract in 1807. Kalorama is filled with embassies and luxurious homes. The Tudor mansion at 2221 Kalorama Road, where 23rd Street runs into Kalorama Road, was built in 1911 for mining millionaire W. W. Lawrence, but since 1936 it has been the residence of the French ambassador. For a taste of the beautiful view that so captivated Barlow, walk west on Kalorama Road, then turn right on Kalorama Circle. At the bottom of the circle you can look down over Rock Creek Park, the finger of green that pokes into northwest Washington.

3 **Walsh-McLean House.** Tom McLean was an Irishman who made a for-tune with a Colorado gold mine and came to Washington to show his wealth. Washington was the perfect place to establish a presence for America's late-19th-century nouveau riche. It was easier to enter "so-ciety" in the nation's planned capital than in New York or Philadel-phia, and wealthy industrialists and lucky entrepreneurs flocked to the city on the Potomac. Walsh announced his arrival with this 60-room mansion. His daughter, Evalyn Walsh-McLean, the last private owner of the Hope Diamond (now in the Smithsonian's Museum of Natural History), was one of the city's leading hostesses. Today the house is used as an embassy by the Indonesian government. The **Jockey Club** restaurant in the redbrick Ritz-Carlton Hotel (☞ Chapter 5) across the street is a favorite lunching spot of Washington power brokers. ✉ *2020 Massachusetts Ave. NW. Metro: Dupont Circle.*

9 **Washington Hilton & Towers.** The Washington Hilton is the home of the largest ballroom on the East Coast, with an area of 35,000 square feet and seating 4,200 people. Its main interest is that it's also the site of John Hinckley's 1981 assassination attempt on Ronald Reagan at the entrance on T Street NW, off Connecticut Avenue. ⊠ *1919 Connecticut Ave. Metro: Dupont Circle.*

6 **Woodrow Wilson House.** Wilson is the only president who stayed in Washington after leaving the White House. (He's also the only president buried in the city, inside the Washington Cathedral.) He and his second wife, Edith Bolling Wilson, retired in 1920 to this Georgian Revival house designed by Washington architect Waddy B. Wood. (Wood also designed the Department of the Interior Building on C Street and the National Museum of Women in the Arts building.) The house had been built in 1915 for a carpet magnate, and on the first and third floors you can still see the half-snaps that run along the edges of the floors to hold down the long-gone wall-to-wall carpeting.

President Wilson suffered a stroke toward the end of his second term, in 1919, and he lived out the last few years of his life on this quiet street. Edith made sure he was comfortable; she had a bed constructed that was the same dimensions as the large Lincoln bed Wilson had slept in while in the White House. She also had the house's trunk lift electrified so the partially paralyzed president could move from floor to floor. When the streetcars stopped running in 1962 the elevator stopped working. It had received its electricity directly from the streetcar line.

Wilson died in 1924. Edith survived him by 37 years. After she died in 1961, the house and its contents were bequeathed to the National Trust for Historic Preservation. On view inside are such items as a Gobelins tapestry, a baseball signed by King George V, and the shell casing from the first shot fired by U.S. forces in World War I. The house also contains memorabilia related to the history of the short-lived League of Nations, including the colorful flag Wilson hoped would be adopted by that organization. ⊠ *2340 S St. NW,* ☎ *202/387–4062.* ▣ *$5.* ☉ *Tues.–Sun. 10–4; closed major holidays. Metro: Dupont Circle.*

FOGGY BOTTOM

The Foggy Bottom area of Washington—bordered roughly by the Potomac and Rock Creek to the west, 20th Street to the east, Pennsylvania Avenue to the north, and Constitution Avenue to the south—has three main claims to fame: the State Department, the Kennedy Center, and George Washington University. In 1763 a German immigrant named Jacob Funk purchased this land, and a community called Funkstown sprang up on the Potomac. This nickname is only slightly less amusing than the present one, an appellation that is derived from the wharves, breweries, lime kilns, and glassworks that were near the water. Smoke from these factories combined with the swampy air of the low-lying ground to produce a permanent fog along the waterfront.

The smoke-belching factories ensured work for the hundreds of German and Irish immigrants who settled in Foggy Bottom in the 19th century. By the 1930s, however, industry was on the way out, and Foggy Bottom had become a poor, predominantly black part of Washington. The opening of the State Department headquarters in 1947 reawakened middle-class interest in the neighborhood's modest row houses. Many of them are now gone, and Foggy Bottom today suffers from a split personality, and tiny, one-room-wide row houses sit next to large, mixed-use developments.

While the Foggy Bottom neighborhood has its own Metro stop, many attractions are a considerable distance away. If you don't relish long walks or time is limited, check the Foggy Bottom map to see if you need to make travel alternate arrangements to visit specific sights.

Numbers in the text correspond to numbers in the margin and on the Foggy Bottom map.

A Good Walk

Start your exploration near the Foggy Bottom Metro station at 23rd and I streets. The sprawling campus of **George Washington University** ① covers much of Foggy Bottom south of Pennsylvania Avenue between 19th and 24th streets. Walk west from the Metro station on the I Street pedestrian mall, then turn left on New Hampshire Avenue. At Virginia Avenue you'll run into the **Watergate** ②, possibly the world's most notorious apartment-office complex, forever a part of our language for the role it played in the downfall of a president. Walk south on New Hampshire Avenue, past the Saudi Arabian Embassy, to the **John F. Kennedy Center for the Performing Arts** ③, Washington's premiere cultural center. Walk back up New Hampshire Avenue; then turn right on G Street, right on Virginia Avenue (follow the outstretched arm of the statue of Benito Juárez, the 19th-century Mexican statesman) and right on 23rd Street. The Pan American Health Organization, American headquarters of the World Health Organization, is at 23rd Street and Virginia Avenue, in the circular building that looks like a huge car air filter. Two blocks down 23rd Street is the massive **Department of State building** ④, with its opulent **Diplomatic Reception Rooms,** filled with museum-quality furnishings. The **U.S. Naval Medical Command** sits on a hill across C Street, on a site of a former naval observatory.

Follow 23rd Street to Constitution Avenue and turn left. On the south side of Constitution are the Lincoln and Vietnam Veterans memorials (☞ The Monuments, *above*). The John Russell Pope–designed **American Pharmaceutical Association** ⑤ building sits at the corner of Constitution Avenue and 23rd Street. One block east is the **National Academy of Sciences** ⑥, where you often will find free art exhibits. Robert Berks's **sculpture of Albert Einstein** sits in front of the Academy. The white-marble **Federal Reserve Building** ⑦ (designed by Folger Library architect Paul Cret) is on Constitution Avenue between 21st and 20th streets. Turn left on 20th Street. The fountain one block up in Robert Owen Park is perfect for cooling hot and tired feet. Crossing Virginia Avenue and continuing north on 20th Street will take you back onto the campus of George Washington University. Foggy Bottom's immigrant past is apparent in the **United Church** at 20th and G streets. Built in 1891 for blue-collar Germans in the neighborhood, the church still conducts services in German the first and third Sunday of every month. Walk north to Pennsylvania Avenue. To the right—near Number 1901—are the only two survivors of a string of 18th-century row houses known as the **Seven Buildings** ⑧, both now dwarfed by the taller office block behind them. The modern glass office building at **2000 Pennsylvania** ⑨ incorporates a row of hollowed out and refurbished Victorian houses as part of its facade.

TIMING

Foggy Bottom is a half-day walk. Touring the State Department and the Federal Reserve Building should take about two hours. A good chunk of time will be spent walking between sites, since this area is not as densely packed with points of interest as are most others.

Sights to See

❺ American Pharmaceutical Association. You might think the American Pharmaceutical Association is a rather odd sightseeing recommendation, even just for a casual glance as you're passing by. But aside from the fact that the white-marble building was designed in 1934 by noted architect John Russell Pope, who also designed the Lincoln Memorial and the National Gallery of Art, the American Pharmaceutical Association is as much a symbol of modern Washington as any government edifice. It's the home of one of more than 3,000 trade and professional associations (as obscure as the Cast Iron Soil Pipe Institute and as well-known as the National Association of Broadcasters) that have chosen the Capitol for their headquarters, eager to represent their members' interests before the government. ⊠ *Constitution Ave. and 23rd St. Metro: Foggy Bottom.*

❹ Department of State building. The foreign policy of the United States is formulated and administered by battalions of brainy analysts in the huge State Department building, which also serves as the headquarters of the United States Diplomatic Corps. All is presided over by the Secretary of State, who is fourth in line for the presidency (after the Vice President, Speaker of the House, and president *pro tempore* of the Senate) should the president be unable to serve. On the top floor are the opulent **Diplomatic Reception Rooms,** decorated in the manner of great halls of Europe and the rooms of Colonial American plantations. The museum-quality furnishings include a Philadelphia highboy, a Paul Revere bowl, and the desk on which the Treaty of Paris was signed. The largest room boasts a specially loomed carpet so heavy and large it had to be airlifted in by helicopter. The rooms are used 15–20 times a week to entertain foreign diplomats and heads of state; you can see them, too, but you need to register for a tour well in advance of your visit. Summer tours must be booked up to three months in advance. ⊠ *23rd and C Sts. NW,* ☎ *202/647–3241, TTY 202/736–4474.* ⌑ *Free.* ☉ *Tour weekdays at 9:30, 10:30, and 2:45. Metro: Foggy Bottom.*

❼ Federal Reserve Building. Whether or not interest rates are raised or lowered in an attempt to control the economy gets decided in this imposing marble edifice, its bronze entryway topped by a massive eagle. Designed by Folger Library architect Paul Cret, the "the Fed" is on Constitution Avenue between 21st and 20th streets. It seems to say, "Your money's safe with us." Even so, there isn't any money here. Ft. Knox and New York's Federal Reserve Bank hold most of the Federal Reserve System's gold. The stolid building is a bit more human inside, with a varied collection of art and four special art exhibitions every year. A 45-minute tour includes a film that attempts to explain exactly what it is that "the Fed" does. Call 202/452–2526 to arrange a tour. ⊠ *Enter on C St. between 20th and 21st Sts.,* ☎ *202/452–3686.* ⌑ *Free.* ☉ *Weekdays 9:30–2, tour Thurs. at 2:30. Metro: Foggy Bottom.*

❶ George Washington University. George Washington had always hoped the capital would be home to a world-class university. He even left 50 shares of stock in the Patowmack Canal Co. to endow it. Congress never acted upon his wishes, however, and it wasn't until 1822 that the university that would eventually be named after the first president began to take shape. The private Columbian College in the District of Columbia opened that year with the aim of training students for the Baptist ministry. In 1904 the university shed its Baptist connections and changed its name to George Washington University. In 1912 it moved to its present location and since that time has become the second largest landholder in the District (after the federal government). Students have ranged from J. Edgar Hoover to Jacqueline Kennedy Onassis. In addition to modern university buildings GWU occupies many 19th-century houses. The downtown campus covers much of Foggy Bottom south of Pennsylvania Avenue between 19th and 24th streets. *Metro: Foggy Bottom.*

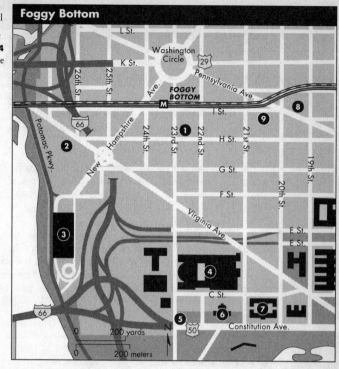

Foggy Bottom

❸ **John F. Kennedy Center for the Performing Arts.** Thanks to the Kennedy Center Washington regularly hosts such world-class performers as the Dance Theatre of Harlem, the Joffrey Ballet of Chicago, the monologuist Spalding Gray, the Juilliard String Quartet, jazz vocalist Nnenna Freelon, violinist Pichas Zukerman, and singing great Ray Charles. Luminaries like these did not always flock to the city. Prior to 1971, Washington after dark was primarily known for cocktail parties, not culture. The opening of the Kennedy Center in that year instantly established the Capitol as a cultural mecca on an international scale. Concerts, ballets, opera, musicals, and drama are presented in the center's five theaters, and movies are screened almost every night in the theater of the American Film Institute.

The idea for a national cultural center had been proposed by President Eisenhower in 1958. John F. Kennedy had also strongly supported the idea, and after his assassination it was decided to dedicate the center to him as a living memorial. Some critics have called the center's square design unimaginative—it's been dubbed the cake box that the more decorative Watergate came in—but no one has denied that the building is immense. The Grand Foyer, lighted by 18 1-ton Orrefors crystal chandeliers, is 630 feet long. (Even at this size it is mobbed at intermission.) Many of the center's furnishings were donated by foreign countries: The chandeliers came from Sweden, the Matisse tapestries outside the Opera House came from France, and the 3,700 tons of white Carrara marble for the interior and exterior of the building were a gift from Italy. Flags fly in the Hall of Nations and the Hall of States, and in the center of the foyer is a 7-foot-high bronze **bust of Kennedy** by sculptor Robert Berks.

The Friends of the Kennedy Center maintain a **Performing Arts Library** on the roof terrace level, mounting periodic theatrical and musical exhibits (original Mozart manuscripts were a recent offering). If you can tolerate the sound of jets screaming up the Potomac to National Airport, you can get one of the city's better views from the rooftop terrace: To the north are Georgetown and the National Cathedral; to the west Theodore Roosevelt Island and Rosslyn, Virginia; and to the south the Lincoln and Jefferson memorials. ⊠ *New Hampshire Ave. and Rock Creek Pkwy. NW,* ☎ *202/467–4600; tour information, 202/416–8341; Performing Arts Library, 202/707–8780.* ▧ *Free.* ☉ *Daily 10–9 (or until last show lets out); box office Mon.–Sat. 10–9, Sun. and holidays noon–9; tour daily 10–1; Performing Arts Library Tues.–Sat. noon–8. Metro: Foggy Bottom.*

NEED A BREAK?   There are two restaurants on the top floor of the Kennedy Center. The **Roof Terrace Restaurant** is the more expensive, with a lunch menu that offers open-face sandwiches and salads. The **Encore Café** has soups, chili, salads, and hot entrées starting at under $5.

❻ National Academy of Sciences. Inscribed in Greek under the cornice is a quotation from Aristotle on the value of science. Inside, there are often free art exhibits—not all of them relating to science. In front of the academy is Robert Berks's **sculpture of Albert Einstein,** done in the same lumpy, mashed-potato style as the artist's bust of JFK in the Kennedy Center. ⊠ *2101 Constitution Ave. NW,* ☎ *202/334–2000.* ▧ *Free.* ☉ *Weekdays 8:30–5. Metro: Foggy Bottom.*

❽ Seven Buildings. Only two buildings remain of the string of 18th-century row houses known as the Seven Buildings. One of the five that have been demolished had served as President Madison's executive mansion after the British burned the White House in 1814. The two survivors are now dwarfed by the taller office block behind them. ⊠ *Near 1901 Pennsylvania Ave. Metro: Foggy Bottom.*

❾ 2000 Pennsylvania Avenue. It's a shame that so many important historical buildings fail to survive as a city matures. The row of residences on Pennsylvania Avenue between 20th and 21st streets escaped the fate of the Seven Buildings (☞ *above*) by being incorporated—literally—into the present. The Victorian houses have been hollowed out and refurbished to serve as the entryway for a modern glass office building at 2000 Pennsylvania Avenue. The backs of the buildings are under the sloping roof of the new development, preserved as if in an urban terrarium. *Metro: Foggy Bottom.*

United Church. Foggy Bottom's immigrant past is apparent in the United Church. Built in 1891 for blue-collar Germans in the neighborhood, the church still conducts services in German the first and third Sunday of every month. ⊠ *20th and G Sts. Metro: Foggy Bottom.*

❷ Watergate. Thanks to the events that took place on the night of June 17, 1972, the Watergate is possibly the world's most notorious apartment-office complex. As Nixon aides E. Howard Hunt, Jr., and G. Gordon Liddy sat in the Howard Johnson Motor Lodge across the street, five of their men were caught trying to bug the Democratic National Committee, headquartered on the sixth floor of the building, in an attempt to subvert the democratic process on behalf of the then president of the United States. A marketing company occupies the space today.)

The suffix "-gate" is attached to any political scandal nowadays, but the Watergate itself was named after a monumental flight of steps that lead down to the Potomac behind the Lincoln Memorial. The original Watergate was the site of band concerts until airplane noise from nearby National Airport made the locale impractical.

Even before the break-in, the Watergate—which first opened in 1965—was well known in the Capitol. Within its distinctive curving lines and behind its "toothpick" balusters have lived some of Washington's most famous—and infamous—citizens, including attorney general John Mitchell and presidential secretary Rose Mary Woods of Nixon White House fame, and such power brokers as Jacob Javits, Alan Cranston, and Bob and Elizabeth Dole. The embassies of Qatar, the United Arab Emirates, Sweden, and Yemen are also in the Watergate. ⊠ *2600 Virginia Ave. Metro: Foggy Bottom.*

CLEVELAND PARK AND THE NATIONAL ZOO

Cleveland Park, a tree-shaded neighborhood in northwest Washington, owes its name to onetime summer resident Grover Cleveland and its development to the streetcar line that was laid along Connecticut Avenue in the 1890s. President Cleveland and his wife, Frances Folson, escaped the heat of downtown Washington in 1886 by establishing a summer White House on Newark Street between 35th and 36th streets. Many prominent Washingtonians followed suit. When the streetcar came through in 1892, construction in the area snowballed. Developer John Sherman hired local architects to design houses and provided amenities such as a fire station and a streetcar-waiting lodge to entice home buyers out of the city and into "rural" Cleveland Park. Today the neighborhood's attractive houses and suburban character are popular with Washington professionals.

Numbers in the text correspond to numbers in the margin and on the Cleveland Park and the National Zoo map.

A Good Walk

Start your exploration at the Cleveland Park Metro station at Connecticut Avenue and Ordway Street NW. The Colonial-style Park and Shop on the east side of Connecticut Avenue was Washington's first shopping center with off-street parking. The Art Deco style is well-represented by many of the buildings and apartments along some of the main thoroughfares in Northwest Washington, including Connecticut Avenue. The **Cineplex Odeon Uptown** ① (⊠ 3426 Connecticut Ave.), a marvelous vintage-1936 Art Deco movie house, is a reminder of the days when movie theaters were something other than boring little boxes. Continue south on Connecticut Avenue. You'll cross a sliver of Rock Creek Park, via a bridge decorated with eight Art Deco lights. Off to your left you'll see the city's finest Art Deco apartment house, the **Kennedy-Warren** ② (⊠ 3133 Connecticut Ave. NW), with stylized carved eagles flanking the driveways. Follow Connecticut Avenue two more blocks to the **National Zoological Park** ③, another member of the Smithsonian family. The zoo's most famous resident, Hsing-Hsing, is the only giant panda in the United States. Stately old apartment buildings line Connecticut Avenue south of the zoo. Cross Cathedral Avenue and enter the **Woodley Park** section of the city. The cross-shaped **Wardman Tower** ④, at the corner of Connecticut Avenue and Woodley Road, was built in 1928 as a luxury apartment building. Once famous for its famous residents, it is now part of the Sheraton Washington Hotel.

TIMING

Most of your time here will be spent at the zoo, and how long you stay will depend on how much you like zoos. Popular visiting times are when the giant panda Hsing-Hsing is fed at 11 and 3, and a sea lion training demonstration held at 11:30.

Sights to See

① **Cineplex Odeon Uptown.** If you're in the mood for a movie during your stay in the Capitol and want to see it in a grand entertainment palace of yesteryear, the Cineplex Odeon Uptown is the place to go. Unlike most old theaters across the nation, which have been chopped up and transformed into multiplexes, this marvelous vintage-1936 Art Deco movie house, the only one of its kind left in Washington, has remained true to its origins, with a single huge screen and an inviting balcony. ⊠ *3426 Connecticut Ave. NW,* ☎ *202/966–5400. Metro: Cleveland Park.*

② **Kennedy-Warren.** Art Deco lovers won't want to miss the Kennedy Warren. The apartment house is a superb example of the style, with such period detailing as decorative aluminum panels and a streamlined entryway, stone griffins under the pyramidal copper roof, and stylized carved eagles flanking the driveways. Perhaps in keeping with its elegant architecture, this is one of the last apartment buildings in town to still have a doorman. ⊠ *3133 Connecticut Ave. NW. Metro: Cleveland Park.*

③ **National Zoological Park.** Part of the Smithsonian Institution, the National Zoo is one of the foremost zoos in the world. Created by an Act of Congress in 1889, the 163-acre zoological park was designed by landscape architect Frederick Law Olmsted, the man who designed the U.S. Capitol grounds. (Before the zoo opened in 1890, live animals used as taxidermists' models had been kept on the Mall.) For years the zoo's most famous residents were giant pandas Hsing-Hsing and Ling-Ling, gifts from China in 1972. But female Ling-Ling died of heart failure in 1993 at age 23. Sympathy cards poured in from all over the country, the zoo tried in vain to fertilize some of Ling-Ling's extracted eggs, and her body was donated to the Smithsonian's Museum of Natural History. Hsing-Hsing is now the only giant panda in the United States.

The zoo has had breeding success with numerous other species, however, including red pandas, Pere David's deer, golden lion tamarins, and pygmy hippopotamuses. The only Komodo dragons in the country are at the National Zoo. Innovative compounds show many animals in naturalistic settings, including the Great Flight Cage—a walk-in aviary in which birds fly unrestricted. Giant crabs, octopuses, cuttlefish, and worms are displayed in an invertebrate exhibit. Zoolab, the Reptile Discovery Center, and the Bird Resource Center all offer activities that teach young visitors about biology. The most ambitious addition to the zoo is Amazonia, a reproduction of a South American rain forest ecosystem. Such fish as twig cats and arowanas swim behind glass walls, while overhead, monkeys and birds flit from tree to tree. The temperature is a constant 85 degrees, with 85% humidity. Also new to the zoo is the Cheetah Conservation Area, a grassy compound that's home to a family of the world's fastest cats. Amazonia and the Cheetah Conservation Area are the most visible attempts by the zoo to show animals in more naturalistic settings and heighten visitors' appreciation of those environments. ⊠ *3000 block of Connecticut Ave. NW,* ☎ *202/673–4800 or 202/673–4717.* ▣ *Free.* ☉ *Apr. 15–Oct. 15, grounds daily 8–8, animal buildings daily 9–6, Amazonia daily 10–4; Oct. 16–Apr. 14, grounds daily 8–6, animal buildings daily 9–4:30, Amazonia daily 10–4:30. Metro: Cleveland Park or Woodley Park/Zoo.*

Woodley Park. The stretch of Connecticut Avenue south of the National Zoological Park is bordered by venerable apartment buildings. Passing Cathedral Avenue (the first cross-street south of the zoo) you enter a part of town known as Woodley Park. Like Cleveland Park to the north, Woodley Park grew as the streetcar advanced into this part of Washington. In 1800 Philip Barton Key, uncle of Francis Scott Key,

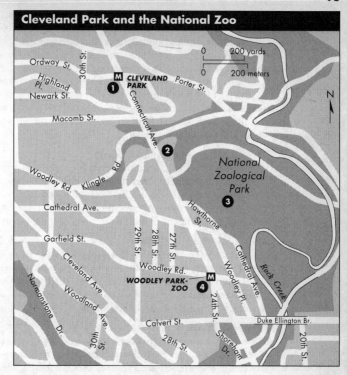

Cleveland Park and the National Zoo

built Woodley, a Georgian mansion on Cathedral Avenue between
29th and 31st streets. The white stucco mansion was the summer
home of four presidents: Van Buren, Tyler, Buchanan, and Cleveland.
It is now owned by the private Maret School. *Metro: Woodley Park/Zoo.*

❹ **Wardman Tower.** At the corner of Connecticut Avenue and Woodley
Road is the cross-shaped, Georgian-style tower built by developer Harry
Wardman in 1928 as a luxury apartment building. Washingtonians called
the project "Wardman's Folly," convinced no one would want to stay
in a hotel so far from the city—some 25 blocks from the White House;
most upscale residential buildings, especially older ones, are within a
few blocks. Contrary to early predictions, however, The Wardman
Tower was famous for its well-known residents, who included Dwight
D. Eisenhower, Herbert Hoover, Clare Booth Luce, Dean Rusk, Earl
Warren, and Caspar Weinberger. It is now part of the Sheraton Washington Hotel. ⊠ *2660 Woodley Rd. NW. Metro: Woodley Park/Zoo.*

ADAMS-MORGAN

To the young, the hip, the cool, and the postmodern, Washington has
the reputation of being a rather staid town, more interested in bu-
reaucracy than boogie, with all the vitality of a seersucker suit. It may
have the Hope Diamond, these detractors say, but that's about the only
thing that really sparkles. What they mean, of course, is that Washington isn't New York City. And thank goodness, say Washingtonians,
who wouldn't want to give up their clean subway, comfortable standard of living, or place in the political spotlight, even if it did mean
being able to get a decent corned beef sandwich or a double espresso
at three in the morning. Besides, Washington does have **Adams-Morgan.** It may not be Greenwich Village, but it's close enough in spirit
to satisfy all but the most hardened black-clad, shade-sporting cynics.

Adams-Morgan (roughly, the blocks north of Florida Avenue, between Connecticut Avenue and 16th Street NW) is Washington's most ethnically diverse neighborhood. And as is so often the case, that means it's one of Washington's most interesting areas, home to a veritable United Nations of cuisines, offbeat shops, and funky bars and clubs. The name itself, fashioned in the 1950s by neighborhood civic groups, serves as a symbol of the area's melting pot character: It's a conjunction of the names of two local schools, the predominantly white Adams School and the largely black Morgan School. Today Adams-Morgan is home to every shade in between, too, with large Latino and West African populations.

The neighborhood's grand 19th-century apartment buildings and row houses and its bohemian atmosphere have attracted young urban professionals, the businesses that cater to them, the attendant parking and crowd problems, and the inevitable climb in real estate values. It's all caused some longtime Adams-Morganites to wonder if their neighborhood is in danger of mutating into another Georgetown.

Adams-Morgan already has one thing in common with Georgetown: There's no Metro stop. It's a 15-minute walk from the Woodley Park/Zoo Metro station: Walk south on Connecticut, then turn left on Calvert Street, and cross over Rock Creek Park on the Duke Ellington Bridge. The heart of Adams-Morgan is at the crossroads of Adams Mill Road, Columbia Road, and 18th Street.

A Good Walk
Some walks are most enjoyable if followed in the suggested sequence. Not so here. Wander from the path described to make your own discoveries in the serendipitous spirit of this fascinating area.

Begin by turning left on **Columbia Road.** At tables stretched along the street, vendors hawk watches, leather goods, knockoff perfumes, cassette tapes (blank and prerecorded), sneakers, clothes, and handmade jewelry. The store signs—Casa Lebrato, Urgente Express (the latter the name of a business that specializes in shipping to and from Central America)—are a testament to the area's Latin flavor; on these blocks you'll hear as much Spanish as English.

Cross Columbia at Ontario Road and backtrack. If you'd rather see the neighborhood on two wheels than two feet, turn left onto Champlain Street and rent a bicycle at **City Bikes** (✉ 2501 Champlain St. NW, ☎ 202/265–1564); call ahead to reserve a bike on weekends.

Continue west on Columbia Road to its intersection with 18th Street. On Saturday mornings a **market** springs up on the plaza in front of the Crestar bank, at the southwest corner of 18th and Columbia, with vendors selling fruits, vegetables, flowers, and breads.

If Columbia Road east of 18th is Adams-Morgan's Latin Quarter, 18th Street south of Columbia is its restaurant corridor. In the next few blocks you'll pass—besides McDonald's—restaurants serving the cuisines of China, Mexico, India, El Salvador, Ethiopia, France, the Caribbean, Thailand, Argentina, Italy, Vietnam, and, believe it or not, America. If you can't make up your mind, there's even a palm reader who can help decide what your future has in store.

You can also feed your hunger for the outré or offbeat with the funky shops on 18th Street. Here you'll find the mission-style furniture, Russell Wright crockery and Fiestaware, aerodynamic Art Deco armchairs, Bakelite telephones, massive chromium toasters, kidney-shape Formica-top coffee tables, skinny neckties, and tacky salt-and-pepper shakers that, through time and television reruns, have been transformed from kitsch into collectibles. For a real trip down memory lane, **Retrospec-**

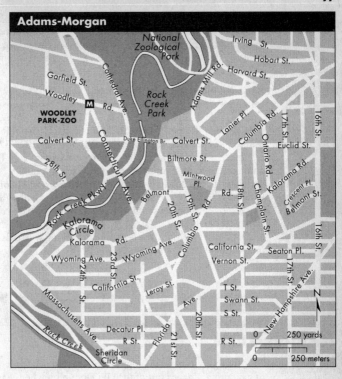

Adams-Morgan

tive (✉ 2324 18th St. NW, ☏ 202/483–8112) is among the stores worth checking out.

Once you've had your fill of Jetsons lunchboxes and mesmerizing lava lamps, proceed to the souklike **Bazaar Atlas** (✉ 2405 18th St. NW, ☏ 202/332–4911). It specializes in ethnic goods such as leather, carved wood, and rugs from various African countries, as well as hammered metal from Morocco. Across the street is **Kobos** (✉ 2444 18th St. NW, ☏ 202/332–9580), owned by a Ghanaian immigrant who sells African jewelry and clothes fashioned from colorful *kente* cloth.

Continue down 18th Street and you'll come **Idle Time Books** (✉ 2410 18th St. NW, ☏ 202/232–4774), which stocks used and out-of-print titles. In the same direction, about 2 blocks south of Kobos, the spirit of the neighborhood is alive in **1800 Belmont Arts** (✉ 1800 Belmont Rd., ☏ 202/234–5802), home to nearly a dozen Afrocentric artists and vendors. Inside are clothing stores, galleries, and a goldsmith.

The west side of 18th Street is home to a gamut of antiques shops, including **Chenonceau Antiques** (✉ 2314 18th St. NW, ☏ 202/667–1651) and its classic 19th- and 20th-century American pieces. Antiques shoppers should also keep an eye out for secondhand shops set up in alleys or warehouses here.

Nearby is the **District of Columbia Arts Center** (DCAC), a combination art gallery-performance space. DCAC exhibits the cutting-edge work of local artists and is the home of offbeat plays, including that uncategorizable category known as performance art. ✉ 2438 18th St. NW, ☏ 202/462–7833. ▤ *Gallery free, performance costs vary.* ☉ *Tues.–Fri. 2–6 and during performances (generally Thurs.–Sun. 7 PM–midnight).*

Of course, the measure of any neighborhood is the tone it takes when the sun goes down. In the spring and summer, restaurants open their windows or set out tables on the sidewalks. Those lucky enough to have rooftop seating find diners lining up to eat under the stars. (Washington can be notoriously hot in the summer, but one of Adams-Morgan's charms has always been that its slight elevation wraps it in cooling breezes.)

Although the neighborhood's bar and club scene isn't as varied as its restaurant scene, there are some standouts. Tap dancers use the bar as a stage Friday and Saturday evenings at the decidedly Gallic jazz club **Café Lautrec** (⊠ 2431 18th St. NW, ☎ 202/265–6436). **Chief Ike's Mambo Room** (⊠ 1725 Columbia Rd. NW, ☎ 202/332–2211) is as eclectic as its name, with DJs playing everything from R&B to disco and a mural of its namesake, Dwight Eisenhower, in a Native American headdress. Locals cue them up at **Bedrock Billiards** (⊠ 1841 Columbia Rd. NW, ☎ 202/667–7665), a pool hall with eight tables and a '50s fashion sense. **Club Heaven** is upstairs from a bar named **Hell** (⊠ 2327 18th St. NW, ☎ 202/667–4355) and has dancing to live and recorded synth-pop music. More in keeping with Adams-Morgan's international flavor is **Bukom Café** (⊠ 2442 18th St. NW, ☎ 202/265–4600), home on weekends to West African music.

Remember that the last trains leave the Woodley Park Metro station at around midnight, so if you can't tear yourself away, be prepared to take a cab.

ARLINGTON

The Virginia suburb of Arlington County was once part of the District of Columbia. Carved out of the Old Dominion when Washington was created, it was returned to Virginia along with the rest of the land west of the Potomac in 1845. Washington hasn't held a grudge, though, and there are three attractions in Arlington—each linked to the military—that should be a part of any complete visit to the nation's capital: Arlington National Cemetery, the U.S. Marine Corps War Memorial, and the Pentagon. All are accessible by Metro, and a trip across the Potomac makes an enjoyable half day of sightseeing.

Numbers in the text correspond to numbers in the margin and on the Arlington map.

A Good Walk

To begin your exploration, take the Metro to the Arlington Cemetery station (about a 10-minute ride from downtown), travel on a Tourmobile bus (☞ Sightseeing *in* Important Contacts A to Z), or walk across Memorial Bridge from the District (southwest of the Lincoln Memorial) to **Arlington National Cemetery** ①. The visitor center has detailed maps of the cemetery. They also can help you locate a specific grave. Just west of the visitor center you'll find the **Kennedy graves** ②, where John F. Kennedy, two of his children who died in infancy, and his wife Jacqueline Bouvier Kennedy Onassis are buried. Long before it was a cemetery, this land was part of the 1,100-acre estate of George Washington Parke Custis, a descendant of Martha and (by marriage) George Washington. Between 1802 and 1817 Custis built **Arlington House** ③ (also called the Custis-Lee Mansion). Walk south on Crook Walk past row upon row of simple white headstones, following the signs to the **Tomb of the Unknowns** ④, where the remains of unknown soldiers from both World Wars, Korea, and Vietnam are buried. Below the Tomb of the Unknowns is **Section 7A** ⑤, where many distinguished veterans are buried. To reach the sites at the northern end of the cemetery and to make your way into the city of Arlington, first walk north along Roosevelt Drive to Schley Drive (you'll pass the Memorial Gate), then turn right on Custis Walk to the Ord & Weitzel Gate. On your way you'll pass **Section 27** ⑥, where 3,800 former slaves are buried. They lived at Freedman's Village, established at Arlington in 1863 to provide housing, education, and employment training for ex-slaves who had traveled to the Capitol. Leaving the cemetery through the Ord & Weitzel Gate, cross Marshall Drive carefully, and walk to the 49-bell **Netherlands Carillon** ⑦, a gift from the Dutch people. To the north is the **United States Marine Corps War Memorial** ⑧, perhaps better known as the Iwo Jima Memorial, honoring all marines who lost their lives while serving their country. By executive order, a flag flies over the memorial 24 hours a day. Take the Metro to the **Pentagon** ⑨, which has its own station; its escalator surfaces right inside the huge office building. Somewhat of a construction marvel, the gargantuan building, headquarters of the Department of Defense, with 17½ miles of corridors, was built in just two years.

TIMING

Visiting the various sites at Arlington National Cemetery could take a half-day or longer, depending on your stamina and interest. Factor in an hour or so for the Pentagon tour.

Sights to See

❸ **Arlington House.** The somber plot of land composing Arlington Cemetery hasn't always been a cemetery. It was in Arlington that the two most famous names in Virginia history—Washington and Lee—became intertwined. George Washington Parke Custis—raised by Martha and George Washington, his grandmother and step-grandfather—built Arlington House (also known as the Custis-Lee Mansion) between 1802 and 1817 on his 1,100-acre estate overlooking the Potomac. After his death, the property went to his daughter, Mary Anna Randolph Custis. In 1831, Mary Custis married Robert E. Lee, a recent graduate of West Point. For the next 30 years the Custis-Lee family lived at Arlington House.

In 1861, Lee was offered command of the Union forces. He declined, insisting that he could never take up arms against his native Virginia. The Lees left Arlington House that spring, never to return. Union troops soon occupied the estate, making it the headquarters of the officers who were charged with defending Washington. When Mrs. Lee was unable to appear in person to pay a $92.07 property tax the government had assessed, the land was confiscated and a portion set aside as a military cemetery.

Its heavy Doric columns and severe pediment make Arlington House one of the area's best examples of Greek Revival architecture. The plantation home was designed by George Hadfield, a young English architect who for a while supervised construction of the Capitol. The view of Washington from the front of the house is superb. In 1955 Arlington House was designated a memorial to Robert E. Lee. It looks much as it did in the 19th century, and a quick tour will take you past objects once owned by the Custises and the Lees. ⊠ *Between Lee and Sherman Drs.,* ☎ *703/557–0613.* ⊡ *Free.* ☉ *Apr.–Sept., daily 9:30–6; Oct.–Mar., daily 9:30–4:30.*

❶ **Arlington National Cemetery.** Some 250,000 American war dead, as well as many notable Americans (among them Presidents William Howard Taft and John F. Kennedy, General John Pershing, and Admiral Robert E. Peary) are interred in these 612 acres across the Potomac River from Washington, established as the nation's cemetery in 1864. While you are at Arlington you will probably hear the clear, doleful sound of a trumpet playing taps or the sharp reports of a gun salute. Approximately 15 funerals are held here daily. It is projected the cemetery will be filled in 2020. Although not the largest cemetery in the country, Arlington is certainly the best known, a place where visitors can trace America's history through the aftermath of its battles.

To get there, you can take the Metro, travel on a Tourmobile bus or walk across Memorial Bridge from the District (southwest of the Lincoln Memorial). If you're driving, there's a large paid parking lot at the skylit **visitor center** on Memorial Drive. Stop at the center for a free brochure with a detailed map of the cemetery. (If you're looking for a specific grave, the staff will consult microfilm records and give you directions on how to find it. You should know the deceased's full name and, if possible, his or her branch of service and year of death.) ☎ *703/697–2131.* ▨ *Free.* ☉ *Apr.–Sept., daily 8–7; Oct.–Mar., daily 8–5.*

Tourmobile tour buses leave from just outside the visitor center Apr. 1–Sept. 30, daily 8:30–6:30; Oct. 1–Mar. 31, daily 8:30–4:30. You can buy tickets ($4) here for the 40-minute tour of the cemetery, which includes stops at the Kennedy grave sites, the Tomb of the Unknowns, and Arlington House. Touring the cemetery on foot means a fair bit of hiking, but it will give you a closer look at some of the thousands of graves spread over these rolling Virginia hills. If you decide to walk, head west from the visitor center on Roosevelt Drive and then turn right on Weeks Drive.

❷ **Kennedy graves.** A highlight of any visit to Arlington National Cemetary is a visit to the graves of John F. Kennedy and other members of his family. JFK is buried under an eternal flame near two of his children who died in infancy, and his wife Jacqueline Bouvier Kennedy Onassis. The graves are just west of the visitor center. Across from the graves is a low wall engraved with quotations from Kennedy's inaugural address. JFK's grave was opened to the public in 1967 and since that time has become the most-visited grave site in the country. Nearby, marked by a simple white cross, is the grave of his brother, Robert Kennedy.

❼ **Netherlands Carillon.** A visit to Arlington National Cemetery affords the opportunity for a lovely and unusual musical experience, thanks to a 49-bell carillon presented to the United States by the Dutch people in 1960 in gratitude for aid received during World War II. A performance season featuring guest carillonneurs usually runs through the spring and summer. For one of the most inclusive views of Washington, look to the east across the Potomac. From this vantage point, the Lincoln Memorial, the Washington Monument, and the Capitol are bunched together in a side-by-side formation. ⊠ *Mead and Marshall Drs.,* ☎ *703/285–3093.*

❾ **Pentagon.** To call the colossal edifice that serves as headquarters of the United States Department of Defense "mammoth" is an understatement. This is, quite simply, the largest office building in the world. Actually the Pentagon is not one but five concentric buildings, collectively as wide as three Washington Monuments laid end to end, that cover a vast 34 acres. The buildings are connected by 17½ miles of corridors through which 23,000 military and civilian personnel pass each day. There are 691 drinking fountains, 7,754 windows, and a blizzard of other eye-popping statistics. Astonishingly, all this was completed in 1943 after just two years of construction.

The escalator from the Pentagon Metro station surfaces right into the gargantuan office building. The 75-minute tour of the Pentagon takes you past only those areas that are meant to be seen by outside visitors.

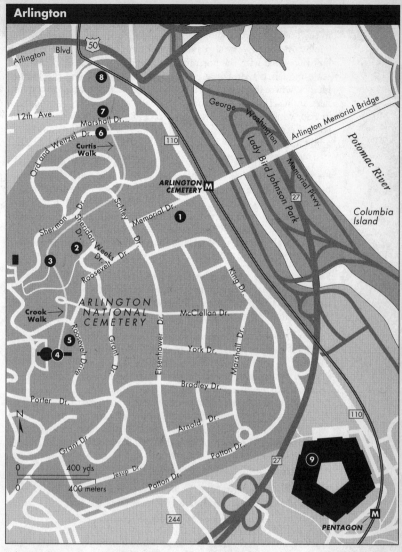

Arlington House, **3**

Arlington National
Cemetery, **1**

Kennedy graves, **2**

Netherlands
Carillon, **7**

Pentagon, **9**

Section 7A, **5**

Section 27, **6**

Tomb of the
Unknowns, **4**

United States Marine
Corps War
Memorial, **8**

In other words, you won't see situation rooms, communications centers, or gigantic maps outlining U.S. and foreign troop strengths. A uniformed serviceman or -woman (who conducts the entire tour walking backward, lest anyone slip away down a corridor) will take you past hallways lined with the portraits of past and present military leaders, scale models of Air Force planes and Navy ships, and the Hall of Heroes, where the names of all the Congressional Medal of Honor winners are inscribed. Occasionally you will catch a glimpse through an interior window of the Pentagon's 5-acre interior courtyard. In the center—at ground zero—is a hot dog stand. A photo ID is required for admission. ⊠ *Off I–395, Arlington, VA,* ☎ *703/695–1776.* ⌨ *Free.* ☉ *Tour weekdays every ½ hr 9:30–3:30; closed federal holidays.*

Pierre L'Enfant grave. In front of Arlington House in Arlington National Cemetery, next to a flag that flies at half staff whenever there is a funeral in the cemetery, is the flat-top grave of Pierre L'Enfant, designer of the Federal City. L'Enfant died in 1825, a penniless, bitter man who felt he hadn't been recognized for his planning genius. He was originally buried in Maryland, but his body was moved here with much ceremony in 1909.

⑤ Section 7A. Many distinguished veterans are buried in this area of Arlington National Cemetery below the Tomb of the Unknowns, including boxing champ Joe Louis, ABC newsman Frank Reynolds, actor Lee Marvin, and World War II fighter pilot Col. "Pappy" Boyington.

⑥ Section 27. Some 3,800 former slaves are buried in this part of Arlington National Cemetery, all former residents of Freedman's Village, established within Arlington in 1863 to provide housing, education, and employment training for ex-slaves who had traveled to the Capitol. In the cemetery, the headstones are marked with their names and the word "Civilian" or "Citizen." Buried at grave 19 in the first row of section 27 is William Christman, a Union private who died of peritonitis in Washington on May 13, 1864. He was the first soldier interred at Arlington National Cemetery during the Civil War. ⊠ *West end of Memorial Bridge, Arlington, VA,* ☎ *703/607–8052.* ⌨ *Free.* ☉ *Apr.–Sept., daily 8–7; Oct.–Mar., daily 8–5.*

④ Tomb of the Unknowns. Many countries established a memorial to their war dead after World War I. In the United States, the first burial at the Tomb of the Unknowns took place at Arlington National Cemetery on November 11, 1921, when the Unknown Soldier from "The Great War" was interred under the large white-marble sarcophagus. Unknown servicemen killed in World War II and Korea were buried in 1958. The unknown serviceman killed in Vietnam was laid to rest on the plaza on Memorial Day 1984. Soldiers from the Army's U.S. 3rd Infantry ("The Old Guard," portrayed in the movie *Gardens of Stone*) keep watch over the tomb 24 hours a day, regardless of weather conditions. Each sentinel marches exactly 21 steps, then faces the tomb for 21 seconds, symbolizing the 21-gun salute, America's highest military honor. The guard is changed with a precise ceremony during the day—every half-hour from April 1 to September 30 and every hour the rest of the year. At night the guard is changed every two hours.

The **Memorial Amphitheater** west of the tomb is the scene of special ceremonies on Veterans Day, Memorial Day, and Easter. Decorations awarded to the unknowns by foreign governments and U.S. and foreign organizations are displayed in an indoor trophy room. Across from the amphitheater are memorials to the astronauts killed in the *Challenger* shuttle explosion and to the servicemen killed in 1980 while trying to rescue American hostages in Iran. Rising beyond that is the mast from the USS *Maine,* the American ship that was sunk in Havana Harbor in 1898, killing 299 men and sparking the Spanish-American War.

⑧ United States Marine Corps War Memorial. Better known simply as "Iwo Jima," this memorial, despite its familiarity, has lost none of its power to stir the emotions. Honoring marines who have given their lives since the corps was formed in 1775, the statue, sculpted by Felix W. de Weldon, is based on Joe Rosenthal's Pulitzer Prize–winning photograph of five marines and a Navy corpsman raising a flag atop Mount Suribachi on the Japanese island of Iwo Jima on February 19, 1945. By executive order, a real flag flies 24 hours a day from the 78-foot-high memorial. On Tuesday evenings at 7 from late May to late August there is a Marine Corps sunset parade on the grounds of the memorial. On parade nights a free shuttle bus runs from the Arlington Cemetery visitor parking lot (☎ 202/433–6060). A few words of caution: It is dangerous to visit the memorial after dark.

North of the memorial is the Arlington neighborhood of Rosslyn. Like parts of downtown Washington and Crystal City farther to the south, Rosslyn is almost empty at night once the thousands of people who work there have gone home. Its tall buildings do provide the preternaturally horizontal Washington with a bit of a skyline, but this has come about not without some controversy: Some say the silvery, wing-shape Gannett Buildings are too close to the flight path followed by jets landing at National Airport.

ALEXANDRIA

Just a short Metro ride (or bike ride) away from Washington, Old Town Alexandria today attracts visitors seeking a break from the monuments and hustle-and-bustle of the District and interested in an encounter with America's Colonial heritage. Founded in 1749 by Scottish merchants eager to capitalize on the booming tobacco trade, Alexandria emerged as one of the most important ports in Colonial America. The city's history is linked to the most significant events and personages of the Colonial and Revolutionary periods. This colorful past is still alive in restored 18th- and 19th-century homes, churches, and taverns; on the cobbled streets; and on the revitalized waterfront, where clipper ships dock and artisans display their wares.

The quickest way to get to Old Town is to take the Metro to the King Street stop (about 25 minutes from Metro Center). If you're driving you can take either the George Washington Memorial Parkway or Jefferson Davis Highway (Route 1) south from Arlington.

Numbers in the text correspond to numbers in the margin and on the Old Town Alexandria map.

A Good Walk

Start your walk through Old Town at the **Alexandria Convention & Visitors Bureau,** in **Ramsay House** ①, the home of the town's first postmaster and lord mayor and the oldest house in Alexandria. Across the street, at the corner of Fairfax and King Street, is the **Stabler-Leadbeater Apothecary** ②, the second-oldest apothecary in the country. It was the equivalent of a corner drugstore to Alexandrians, including George Washington and the Lee family. Two blocks south on Fairfax Street, just beyond Duke Street, stands the **Old Presbyterian Meetinghouse** ③, where Scottish patriots met during the the Revolutionary War. The **Tomb of the Unknown Soldier of the American Revolution** is in a corner of the churchyard. Walk back up Fairfax Street one block and turn right on Prince Street to **Gentry Row,** the block between Fairfax and Lee streets. The striking, reddish-brown Greek Revival edifice at the corner of Prince and Lee streets is the **Athenaeum** ④, which was built as a bank in the 1850s. Many of the city's sea captains built their homes on the block of Prince Street between Lee and Union, which became known as **Captain's Row** ⑤. Continue east on Prince Street to the Alexandria waterfront, with its many shops and restaurants. One of Alexandria's most popular attractions is the **Torpedo Factory Arts Center** ⑥, a collection of art studios and galleries in a former munitions plant one block to the north up Union Street (at the foot of King Street). Here you also will find the **Alexandria Archaeology Program,** with exhibits of artifacts found during excavations dug in Alexandria are on display. Follow Cameron Street back toward town. **Carlyle House** ⑦, which was patterned after a Scottish country manor house, is at the corner or Cameron and North Fairfax streets.

One block west along Cameron, at the corner of Royal Street, is **Gadsby's Tavern Museum** ⑧, a political and social center in the late 18th century. Continue west on Cameron Street for three blocks and turn right on Washington Street. The corner of Washington and Oronoco streets (three blocks north) is known as **Lee Corner** ⑨ because at one time a Lee-owned house stood on each of the four corners. Two survive. One is the **Lee-Fendall House,** the home of (among others) Richard Henry Lee, signer of the Declaration of Independence, and cavalry commander Henry "Light Horse Harry" Lee. The other is the **boyhood home of Robert E. Lee** ⑩, directly across Oronoco Street. Although they were a tiny minority, there were in fact 52 free blacks living in Alexandria in 1790. The **Alexandria Black History Resource Center** ⑪, two blocks north and two blocks west of Lee's boyhood home, tells the history of African Americans in Alexandria and Virginia. Head back to Washington Street and go south to the corner of Queen Street. The **Lloyd House** ⑫, a fine example of Georgian architecture, it is now part of the Alexandria Library system. At the corner of Cameron and Washington streets, one block south, stands the English Georgian country-style **Christ Church** ⑬. Walk south two blocks to the **Lyceum** ⑭ at the corner of South Washington and Prince streets. It has served several purposes since it was built in 1839, but it now houses two art galleries and a museum focusing on local history. The **Confederate Statue** in the middle of Washington and Prince streets marks the point at which, after Union forces had occupied the city, the 800 soldiers of Alexandria's garrison assembled before marching out of town to join the Confederate Army. Two blocks to the west on South Alfred Street is the **Friendship Fire House** ⑮, now restored and outfitted like a typical 19th-century firehouse. It's a long walk (or a quick bus ride on Bus 2 or 5 west on King Street) but worth the trouble to visit the **George Washington Masonic National Memorial** ⑯ on Callahan Drive at King Street, a mile west of the center of the city. In good weather, the open 9th floor observation decks affords spectacular views of Alexandria and Washington in the distance.

TIMING
The Alexandria tour should take about four hours, not counting a trip to the George Washington Masonic National Memorial. Add another hour for a roundtrip visit to the memorial; add just a half hour if you plan to get on the Metro across the street at the King Street station); budget yet another hour to take the tour.

Sights to See

⑪ **Alexandria Black History Resource Center.** The history of African Americans in Alexandria and Virginia from 1749 to the present is recounted here. Alexandria's history is hardly limited to the families of

George Washington and Robert E. Lee. The federal census of 1790 recorded 52 free blacks living in the city, and the port town was one of the largest slave exportation points in the South, with at least two bustling slave markets. ⊠ *638 N. Alfred St.,* ☎ *703/838–4356.* ☞ *Free.* ⊙ *Tues.–Sat. 10–4.*

④ Athenaeum. One of the most noteworthy structures in Alexandria, the Athenaeum is a striking, reddish-brown Greek Revival edifice at the corner of Prince and Lee streets. It was built as a bank in the 1850s. ⊠ *201 Prince St.*

⑩ Boyhood home of Robert E. Lee. The childhood home in Alexandria of the commander in chief of the Confederate forces during the Civil War is a fine example of a 19th-century town house with Federal architecture and antique furnishings and paintings. ⊠ *607 Oronoco St.,* ☎ *703/548–8454.* ☞ *$3.* ⊙ *Mon.–Sat. 10–4, Sun. 1–4; closed Dec. 15–Feb. 1 except on Sun. closest to Jan. 19 for Lee's birthday celebration; occasionally closed weekends for private events.*

⑤ Captain's Row. Many of the Alexandria's sea captains built their homes on the block of Prince Street between Lee and Union, hence the name. The cobblestones in the street were allegedly laid by Hessian mercenaries who had fought for the British during the Revolution and were held in Alexandria as prisoners of war.

⑦ Carlyle House. The grandest of Alexandria's older houses, Carlyle House was patterned after a Scottish country manor house. The structure was completed in 1753 by Scottish merchant John Carlyle. This was General Braddock's headquarters and the place where he met with five royal governors in 1755 to plan the strategy and funding of the early campaigns of the French and Indian War. ⊠ *121 N. Fairfax St.,* ☎ *703/549–2997.* ☞ *$3.* ⊙ *Tues.–Sat. 10–4:30, Sun. noon–4:40; tour every ½ hr.*

⑬ Christ Church. Both Washington and Lee were pewholders in this Alexandria, Virginia, church. (Washington paid 36 pounds and 10 shillings—a lot of money in those days—for Pew 60.) Built in 1773, Christ Church is a fine example of an English Georgian country-style church. It has a fine Palladian window, an interior balcony, and a wrought-brass-and-crystal chandelier brought from England at Washington's expense. ⊠ *118 N. Washington St.,* ☎ *703/549–1450.* ☞ *Free.* ⊙ *Weekdays 9–4, Sat. 9–4, Sun. 2–4:30; occasionally closed weekends for private events.*

Confederate Statue. In 1861, when Alexandria was occupied by Union forces, the 800 soldiers of the city's garrison marched out of town to join the Confederate Army. In the middle of Washington and Prince streets stands the Confederate Statue marking the point at which they assembled. In 1885 Confederate veterans proposed a memorial to honor their fallen comrades. This statue, based on John A. Elder's painting *Appomattox,* is of a lone soldier glumly surveying the battlefields after General Robert E. Lee's surrender. The names of 100 Alexandria Confederate dead are carved on the base.

⑮ Friendship Fire House. Alexandria's showcase firehouse is outfitted like a typical 19th-century firehouse. ⊠ *107 S. Alfred St.,* ☎ *703/838–3891.* ☞ *Suggested donation $1.* ⊙ *Fri. and Sat. 10–4, Sun. 1–4.*

⑧ Gadsby's Tavern Museum. Gadsby's Tavern Museum is housed in the old City Tavern and Hotel, which was a center of political and social life in the late 18th century. George Washington attended birthday celebrations in the ballroom here. A tour of the facilities takes you through the taproom, game room, assembly room, ballroom, and com-

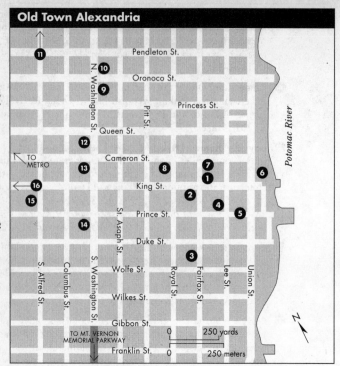

Old Town Alexandria

munal bedrooms. ⊠ *134 N. Royal St.,* ☎ *703/838–4242.* ⊠ *$3.* ⊗ *Oct.–Mar., Tues.–Sat. 11–4, Sun. 1–4 (last tour 3:15); Apr.–Sept., Tues.–Sat. 10–5, Sun. 1–5 (last tour 4:15); tour 15 mins before and 15 mins after the hr.*

16 George Washington Masonic National Memorial. Since Alexandria, like Washington, has no really tall buildings, the spire of the George Washington Masonic National Memorial dominates the surroundings and is visible for miles. The building fronts King Street, one of Alexandria's major east-west arteries; from the 9th floor observation deck visitors get a spectacular view of Alexandria, with Washington in the distance. The building contains furnishings from the first Masonic lodge in Alexandria, in which George Washington was a member; he became a Mason in 1852 and was a Worshipful Master, a high rank, at the same time he served as president. ⊠ *101 Callahan Dr.,* ☎ *703/683–2007.* ⊠ *Free.* ⊗ *Daily 9–5; 50-min guided tour of building and observation deck daily at 9:30, 10:30, 11:30, 1, 2, 3, and 4.*

9 Lee Corner. The corner of Alexandria's Washington and Oronoco streets is known as Lee Corner because at one time a Lee-owned house stood on each of the four corners. Two survive. One is the **Lee-Fendall House,** the home of several illustrious members of the Lee family, including Richard Henry Lee, signer of the Declaration of Independence, and cavalry commander Henry "Light Horse Harry" Lee. ⊠ *614 Oronoco St.,* ☎ *703/548–1789.* ⊠ *$3.* ⊗ *Tues.–Sat. 10–4, Sun. noon–4; occasionally closed weekends for private events.*

12 Lloyd House. A fine example of Georgian architecture, Lloyd House, built in 1797, is now operated as part of the Alexandria Library and houses a collection of rare books and documents relating to city and state history. ⊠ *220 N. Washington St.,* ☎ *703/838–4577.* ⊠ *Free.* ⊗ *Mon.–Sat. 9–5.*

⑭ **Lyceum.** Built in 1839, the Lyceum served alternately as the Alexandria Library, a Civil War hospital, a residence, and an office building. It was restored in the 1970s and now houses two art galleries, a gift shop, and a museum devoted to the area's history. A limited amount of travel information for the entire state is also available here. ⊠ *201 S. Washington St.,* ☎ *703/838–4994.* ☒ *Free.* ☉ *Mon.–Sat. 10–5, Sun. noon–5.*

❸ **Old Presbyterian Meetinghouse.** Built in 1774, the Old Presbyterian Meetinghouse was, as its name suggests, more than a church. It was a gathering place in Alexandria vital to Scottish patriots during the Revolution. Eulogies for George Washington were delivered here on December 29, 1799. In a corner of the churchyard you'll find the **Tomb of the Unknown Soldier of the American Revolution.** ⊠ *321 S. Fairfax St.,* ☎ *703/549–6670.* ☒ *Free.* ☉ *Sanctuary weekdays 9–5 (if locked, obtain key from church office at 316 S. Royal St.).*

❶ **Ramsay House.** The best place to start a tour of Alexandria's Old Town is at the **Alexandria Convention & Visitors Bureau,** in Ramsay House, the home of the town's first postmaster and lord mayor, William Ramsay. The structure is believed to be the oldest house in Alexandria. Ramsay was a Scotsman, as a swatch of his tartan on the door proclaims. Travel counselors here provide information, brochures, and self-guided walking tours of the town. Visitors are given a 24-hour permit that allows them to park free at any two-hour metered spot. ⊠ *221 King St., 22314,* ☎ *703/838–4200, TTY 703/838–6494.* ☉ *Daily 9–5.*

❷ **Stabler-Leadbeater Apothecary.** Once patronized by George Washington and the Lee family, Alexandria's Stabler-Leadbeater Apothecary is the second-oldest apothecary in the country. It was here, on October 17, 1859, that Lt. Col. Robert E. Lee received orders to move to Harper's Ferry to suppress John Brown's insurrection. The shop now houses a small museum of 18th-century apothecary memorabilia, including one of the finest collections of apothecary bottles in the country (some 800 bottles in all). ⊠ *105–107 S. Fairfax St.,* ☎ *703/836–3713.* ☒ *$2.* ☉ *Mon.–Sat. 10–4, Sun. 1–5.*

❻ **Torpedo Factory Arts Center.** A former munitions plant (naval torpedoes were actually manufactured here during World War I and World War II), now converted into studios and galleries for some 175 professional artists and artisans, the Torpedo Factory Arts Center is one of Alexandria's most popular attractions. Almost every imaginable medium is represented, from printmaking and sculpture to jewelry making, pottery, and stained glass. Visitors can view the workshops, and most of the art and crafts are for sale at reasonable prices. ⊠ *105 N. Union St.,* ☎ *703/838–4565.* ☒ *Free.* ☉ *Daily 10–5.*

The Torpedo Factory complex also houses the **Alexandria Archaeology Program,** a city-operated research facility devoted to urban archaeology and conservation. Artifacts from excavations dug in Alexandria are on display. ⊠ *105 N. Union St.,* ☎ *703/838–4399.* ☒ *Free.* ☉ *Tues.–Fri. 10–3, Sat. 10–5, Sun. 1–5.*

AROUND WASHINGTON

The city and environs of Washington (including parts of Maryland and Virginia) are dotted with worthwhile attractions that are outside the range of the walks presented in this chapter. You may find some intriguing enough to go a little out of your way to visit. The nearest Metro stop is noted only if it's within reasonable walking distance of a given sight.

All Souls' Unitarian Church. The design of All Souls', erected in 1924, is based on that of St. Martin-in-the-Fields in London. ⊠ *16th and Harvard Sts. NW,* ☎ *202/332–5266.*

Anacostia Museum. The richness of African-American culture is on display in the Anacostia museum, a Smithsonian museum in Southeast Washington's historic Anacostia neighborhood. Past exhibits have covered black inventors and aviators, the influential role of black churches, the history of the civil rights movement, African-American life in the antebellum South, and the beauty of African-American quilts. ⊠ *1901 Fort Pl. SE,* ☎ *202/287–3369.* ☒ *Free.* ☼ *Daily 10–5. Metro: Navy Yard.*

♻ **The Awakening.** A giant sculpture of a bearded man emerging from the ground near Hains Point, *The Awakening* is beloved by children. Adults are captivated, too. ⊠ *Hains Pt., East Potomac Park.*

Bethune Museum and Archives. Mary McLeod Bethune founded Florida's Bethune-Cookman College, established the National Council of Negro Women, and served as an adviser to President Franklin D. Roosevelt. Exhibits in the museum named after her focus on the achievements of black women. The museum also hosts concerts, lectures, and films throughout the year. ⊠ *1318 Vermont Ave. NW,* ☎ *202/332–1233.* ☒ *Free.* ☼ *Weekdays 10–4. Metro: McPherson Square.*

College Park Airport Museum. College Park, Maryland's claim to fame is the world's oldest operating airport. Opened in 1909, it has been the site of numerous aviation firsts. Orville and Wilbur Wright tested military planes here and their presence is evident in the museum's early aviation memorabilia. The airport's Air Fair every September features antique airplanes, hot-air balloons, and a Wright Brothers lookalike contest. ⊠ *1909 Corporal Frank Scott Dr., College Park, MD,* ☎ *301/864–6029.* ☒ *Free.* ☼ *Wed.–Fri. 11–3, weekends 11–5.*

Eastern Market (☞ Chapter 8). Eastern Market has always been a bustling center of activity on Capitol Hill since it was built in 1873. It was designed by Adolph Cluss, the architect of the Smithsonian Arts and Industries Museum. Inside are shops, restaurants, and galleries. There is a flea market outside on weekends. ⊠ *7th and C Sts. SE. Metro: Eastern Market.*

Firearms Museum. The National Rifle Association's museum was moved from downtown Washington to suburban Virginia in 1994. Exhibits examine the role firearms have played in the history of America. Hundreds of guns are on display. Exhibits change periodically, but the permanent collection includes muzzle-loading flintlocks used in the Revolutionary War, high-tech pistols used by Olympic shooting teams, and weapons that once belonged to American presidents, such as Teddy Roosevelt's .32-caliber Browning pistol and a Winchester rifle used by Dwight Eisenhower. In the next two to three years the museum will be expanded to several times its present size. ⊠ *National Rifle Association, 11250 Waples Mill Rd., Fairfax, VA,* ☎ *703/267–1600.* ☒ *Free.* ☼ *Weekdays 10–4; closed major holidays.*

Flying Circus Airshow. Stunt flying, wing walking, and open cockpit biplane rides for the public are among the attractions at the Flying Circus Airshow. Billing itself as the only remaining barnstorming show in the country, the Flying Circus operates out of a Virginia aerodrome about 90 minutes by car from Washington. ⊠ *Rte. 17, Bealeton, VA, between Fredericksburg and Warrenton,* ☎ *540/439–8661.* ☒ *$9.* ☼ *May–Oct, Sun.; gates open at 11; show 2:30.*

Franciscan Monastery and Gardens. Not far from the **National Shrine of the Immaculate Conception** (☞ *below*), the Byzantine-style Franciscan Monastery contains facsimiles of such Holy Land shrines as the Grotto of Bethlehem and the Holy Sepulcher. Underground are reproductions of the catacombs of Rome. The gardens are especially beautiful, planted with roses that bloom in the summer. ⊠ *14th and Quincy Sts. NE,* ☎ *202/526–6800.* ▦ *Donation requested.* ☉ *Daily 9–5; catacombs tour on the hr (except noon) Mon.–Sat. 9–4, Sun. 1–4. Metro: Brookland–Catholic University.*

Frederick Douglass National Historic Site. Cedar Hill, the Anacostia home of noted abolitionist Frederick Douglass, was the first place designated by Congress as a Black National Historic Site. Douglass, an ex-slave who delivered fiery abolitionist speeches at home and abroad, resided here from 1877 until his death in 1895. The house has a wonderful view of the Federal City across the Anacostia River and contains many of Douglass's personal belongings. A short film on Douglass's life is shown at a nearby visitor center. ⊠ *1411 W St. SE,* ☎ *202/426–5961.* ▦ *Free.* ☉ *Mid-Oct.–mid-Apr., daily 9–4 (last tour 3); mid-Apr.–mid-Oct., daily 9–5 (last tour 4); tour on the hr. Metro: Anacostia, then Bus B2.*

Freedmen's Memorial. A bronze statue of Abraham Lincoln standing above a newly freed slave who has just broken his chains, the Freedmen's Memorial was dedicated on April 14, 1876, the 11th anniversary of the president's assassination. Money for its construction was donated by hundreds of ex-slaves. ⊠ *Lincoln Park, Massachusetts Ave. between 11th and 13th Sts. NE.*

Goddard Space Flight Center. Space flight is brought down to earth at this NASA museum in a suburban Maryland complex, a 30-minute drive from Washington, where scientists and technicians monitor spaceships circling the Earth, the solar system, and beyond. Local model rocket clubs send their handiwork skyward the first and third Sundays of each month. ⊠ *Soil Conservation Rd. and Greenbelt Rd., Greenbelt, MD,* ☎ *301/286–8981.* ▦ *Free.* ☉ *Daily 10–4; tours weekdays at 11 and 2, Sat. 11:30 and 2:30, Sun. 11.*

Hillwood Museum. Hillwood House, cereal heiress Marjorie Merriweather Post's 40-room Georgian mansion in Washington, contains a large collection of 18th- and 19th-century French and Russian decorative art that includes gold and silver work, icons, lace, tapestries, china, and Fabergé eggs. Also on the estate are a dacha filled with Russian objects and an Adirondacks-style cabin that houses an assortment of Native American artifacts. The grounds are composed of lawns, formal French and Japanese gardens, and paths that wind through plantings of azaleas, laurels, and rhododendrons. Make reservations for the house tour well in advance. ⊠ *4155 Linnean Ave. NW,* ☎ *202/686–5807.* ▦ *House and grounds $10; grounds only $2.* ☉ *House tour Mar.–Jan., Tues.–Sat. 9:30–3; grounds Mar.–Jan., Tues.–Sat. 9–5. Metro: Van Ness/UDC.*

Intelsat. The Washington headquarters of Intelsat, an international satellite cooperative, are in a striking glass building that looks as though it, too, had come down from space. The 45-minute tour includes a brief film about the work of the organization and a look at rocket and satellite models in the high-tech visitor center. You can also look down upon control rooms where satellite traffic is monitored. Space buffs will enjoy the visit. Reservations are essential. ⊠ *3400 International Dr. NW, 1 block west of Connecticut Ave. and Van Ness St. NW,* ☎ *202/944–7500.* ▦ *Free. Metro: Van Ness/UDC.*

Islamic Mosque and Cultural Center. The Muslim faithful are called to prayer five times a day from atop the 162-foot-high minaret of the Islamic Mosque and Cultural Center. Each May, the Muslim Women's Association sponsors a bazaar, with crafts, clothing, and food for sale. Visitors wearing shorts will not be admitted; women must wear scarves to cover their heads. ⊠ *2551 Massachusetts Ave. NW,* ☎ *202/332–8343.* ⊘ *Center daily 10–5; mosque open for all 5 prayers, dawn–past sunset.*

Maine Avenue Seafood Market. Washington isn't far from the Chesapeake Bay, the Atlantic Ocean beyond that, and the bounty of both, as this market attests. It bustles with activity as more than a dozen vendors sell fresh crabs, fish, shrimp, squid, clams, and other types of seafood. If you work up an appetite there are seven restaurants stretched out along Maine Avenue, including local seafood powerhouse **Phillips Flagship**. All have terraces overlooking the Washington Channel and the motorboats, houseboats, and sailboats that are moored there. ⊠ *Maine Ave. SW. Metro: Waterfront.*

Marine Corps Barracks. A popular rite of spring and summer in the Capitol is the leathernecks performing at the Marine Corps Barracks. Each Friday evening at 8:45 from May to September the Marine Corps Drum and Bugle Corps, the Marine Band, and the Silent Drill Team present a dress parade filled with martial music and precision marching. Reservations are required; call three weeks in advance. ⊠ *8th and I Sts. SE,* ☎ *202/433–6060.* ▣ *Free. Metro: Eastern Market.*

Marine Corps Museum. The story of the corps from its inception in 1775 to its role in Desert Storm is recounted in Washington's Marine Corps Museum. A variety of artifacts—uniforms, weapons, documents, photographs—outline the growth of the corps, including its embrace of amphibious assault and the strategy of "vertical envelopment" (helicopters, to you and me). ⊠ *9th and M Sts. SE, Bldg. 58,* ☎ *202/433–3534.* ▣ *Free.* ⊘ *Fall–spring, Mon.–Sat. 10–4, Sun. noon–5; summer, Mon.–Thurs. and Sat. 10–4, Fri. 10–8, Sun. noon–5.*

Meridian House and the White-Meyer House. Meridian International Center, a nonprofit institution promoting international understanding, now owns two handsome mansions designed by John Russell Pope. The 30-room Meridian House was built in 1920 by Irwin Boyle Laughlin, scion of a Pittsburgh steel family and former ambassador to Spain. The Louis XVI–style home features parquet floors, ornamental iron grillwork, handsome moldings, period furniture, tapestries, and a garden planted with European linden trees. Next door is the Georgian-style house built for Henry White (former ambassador to France) that was later the home of the Meyer family, publishers of the *Washington Post*. The first floors of both houses are open to the public and are the scene of periodic art exhibits with an international flavor. ⊠ *1630 and 1624 Crescent Pl. NW,* ☎ *202/667–6670.* ▣ *Free.* ⊘ *Wed.–Sun. 2–5.*

Metropolitan African Methodist Episcopal Church. Completed in 1886, the Gothic-style Metropolitan African Methodist Episcopal Church became one of the most influential black churches in the city. Abolitionist orator Frederick Douglass worshiped here and Bill Clinton chose the church as the setting for his inaugural prayer service. ⊠ *1518 M St. NW,* ☎ *202/331–1426. Metro: Farragut North.*

Mexican Cultural Institute. In a glorious 1911 Italianate house that was once the Embassy of Mexico, the Mexican Cultural Institute has on display 19th- and 20th-century Mexican art, including the works of Diego Rivera, José Clemente Orozco, David Alfaro, Sigueiros, and Juan

O'Gorman. ✉ *2829 16th St. NW,* ☎ *202/728–1628.* 🎟 *Free.* ☉ *Tues.–Sat. 11–5.*

National Capitol Trolley Museum. A selection of the Capitol's historic trolleys has been rescued and restored and is now on display at a museum in suburban Maryland, along with streetcars from Europe and elsewhere in America. For a nominal fare you can go on a 2-mile ride through the country. ✉ *Bonifant Rd. between Layhill Rd. and New Hampshire Ave., Wheaton, MD,* ☎ *301/384–6088.* ☉ *Trolley-ride $2.50.* ☉ *Jan.–Nov., weekends and Memorial Day, July 4, and Labor Day noon–5; Dec., weekends 5–9 for "Holly Trolley Illuminations"; July and Aug., Wed. 11–3.*

National Cryptologic Museum. A 30-minute drive from Washington, Maryland's new National Cryptologic Museum is a surprise, telling in a public way the anything but public story of "sigint" (stands for "signals intelligence"), the government's gleaning of intelligence data from radio signals, messages, radar, and such by cracking other governments' secret codes. Connected to the super-secret National Security Agency, the museum recounts the history of intelligence from 1526 to the present. Displays include rare cryptographic books from the 16th century, items used in the Civil War, World War II cipher machines, and a Cray supercomputer of the sort that does the code work today. ✉ *Colony Seven Rd., near Fort Meade, MD (Baltimore–Washington Pkwy. north to Rte. 32E),* ☎ *301/688–5849.* 🎟 *Free.* ☉ *Weekdays 9–3, Sat. 10–2; closed federal holidays.*

National Museum of Health and Medicine. Opened in Washington more than 125 years ago, the medical museum features exhibits that illustrate medicine's fight against injury and disease. Included are displays on the Lincoln and Garfield assassinations and one of the world's largest collections of microscopes. Because some exhibits are fairly graphic (the wax surgical models and various organs floating in alcohol, for example), the museum may not be suitable for young children or the squeamish. ✉ *Walter Reed Army Medical Center, 6825 16th St. NW,* ☎ *202/782–2200.* 🎟 *Free.* ☉ *Daily 10–5:30.*

National Shrine of the Immaculate Conception. The largest Catholic church in the United States, the National Shrine of the Immaculate Conception was begun in 1920 and built with funds contributed by every parish in the country. Dedicated in 1959, the shrine is a blend of Romanesque and Byzantine styles, with a bell tower that reminds many of St. Mark's in Venice. ✉ *Michigan Ave. and 4th St. NE,* ☎ *202/526–8300.* ☉ *Apr.–Oct., daily 7–7; Nov.–Mar., daily 7–6; Sat. vigil mass at 5:15; Sun. mass at 7:30, 9, 10:30, noon, 1:30 (in Latin), and 4:30. Metro: Brookland–Catholic University.*

National Weather Service Science and History Center. A suburban Maryland museum displaying the tools of the National Oceanic and Atmospheric Administration, the National Weather Service Science and History Center opened in 1990. Among its fascinating objects are remote data collectors, weather satellites, and "TOTO," a robotlike Totable Tornado Observatory used to study twisters. There's also the actual 1891 Cairo, Illinois, U.S. Weather Bureau office, complete with the original furniture, record books, and meteorological instruments. ✉ *1325 East-West Hwy., Silver Spring, MD,* ☎ *301/713–0622.* 🎟 *Free.* ☉ *Weekdays 8:30–5.*

Navy Art Gallery. Rotating exhibits of Navy-related paintings, sketches, and drawings, many created during combat by Navy artists, enliven a one-room gallery in the Capitol. The bulk of the collection illustrates World War II. ✉ *9th and M Sts. SE, Bldg. 67,* ☎ *202/433–3815.* 🎟

Free. ⊘ Labor Day–Memorial Day, Wed.–Fri. 9–4, weekends 10–4; Memorial Day–Labor Day, Wed.–Fri. 9–5, weekends 10–4; closed federal holidays. Metro: Navy Yard.

↺ **Navy Museum.** A former Washington weapons factory is an appropriate and atmospheric setting for a museum chronicling the history of the U.S. Navy from the Revolution to the present. Exhibits range from the fully rigged foremast of the USS *Constitution* (better known as "Old Ironsides") to a U.S. Navy Corsair fighter plane dangling from the ceiling. All around are models of fighting ships, displays on battles, and portraits of the sailors who fought them. Children especially enjoy peering through the operating periscopes and pretending to launch torpedoes at the display ship *Barry* floating a few hundred yards away in the Anacostia River. In front of the museum is a collection of guns, cannons, and missiles. An annex is full of unusual submarines. Call ahead to schedule a free weekday highlights tour. ⊠ *9th and M Sts. SE, Bldg. 76,* ☎ *202/433–4882.* ⊠ *Free. ⊘ Weekdays 9–4 (Memorial Day–Labor Day 9–5), weekends and holidays 10–5. Metro: Navy Yard.*

Paul E. Garber Facility. A collection of Smithsonian warehouses in suburban Maryland, the Paul E. Garber Facility is where flight-related artifacts are stored and restored prior to their display at the National Air and Space Museum on the Mall. Among the 160 objects on view here are such historic craft as a Soviet MiG-15 from the Korean War and a Battle of Britain–era Hawker Hurricane IIC, as well as model satellites and assorted engines and propellers. A behind-the-scenes look at how the artifacts are preserved is included on the three-hour walking tour. Note: The tour is for ages 14 and up, and there is no heating or air-conditioning at the facility, so plan accordingly. Reservations for a tour must be made three to eight weeks in advance. ⊠ *Old Silver Hill Rd. and St. Barnabas Rd., Suitland, MD,* ☎ *202/357–1400.* ⊠ *Free. ⊘ Tour weekdays at 10, weekends at 10 and 1.*

St. Sophia Cathedral. The Greek Orthodox St. Sophia Cathedral is noted for the handsome mosaic work on the interior of its dome. Saint Sophia holds a festival of Greek food and crafts each May and October. ⊠ *Massachusetts Ave. and 36th St. NW,* ☎ *202/333–4730.*

Sasakawa Peace Foundation. An odd little art gallery in D.C.'s downtown business district, the Sasakawa Peace Foundation is bankrolled by a Japanese industrialist whose stated aim is to increase understanding between the United States and Japan. Contemporary Japanese and American artists show such work as ceramics, enamels, sculpture, and photographs. Visitors can also browse through a library of Japanese literature. Free videotapes on Japanese life are shown Thursday from noon to 2. ⊠ *1819 L St. NW,* ☎ *202/296–6694.* ⊠ *Free. ⊘ Weekdays 10–6. Metro: Farragut North.*

Scottish Rite Temple. A dramatic Masonic shrine, the Scottish rite Temple was patterned after the Mausoleum of Halicarnassus. Tours available weekdays 8–2. ⊠ *1733 16th St. NW,* ☎ *202/232–3579.*

Temple of the Church of Jesus Christ of Latter-Day Saints. A striking Mormon temple in suburban Maryland—one of its white towers is topped with a golden statue of the Mormon angel and prophet, Moroni—the Temple of the Church of Jesus Christ of the Latter-Day Saints has become a Washington landmark. It is closed to non-Mormons, but a visitor center offers a lovely view of the white-marble church and has a film about the temple and what takes place inside. Tulips, dogwoods, and azaleas bloom in the 57-acre grounds each spring. In December, Washingtonians enjoy the Festival of Lights—300,000 of them—and a live nativity. ⊠ *9900 Stoneybrook Dr., Kensington, MD,* ☏ *301/587–0144.* ⊙ *Grounds and visitor center daily 10–9.*

The Peace of God that Passeth Understanding. Also known by the title *Grief, The Peace of God that Passeth Understanding* is a figure of a shroud-draped woman. Henry Adams commissioned Augustus Saint-Gaudens to create a memorial to Adams's wife, who committed suicide in 1885. The result is thought by many to be the most moving sculpture in the city. ⊠ *Rock Creek Cemetery, Rock Creek Rd. and Webster St. NW.*

Washington Dolls' House and Toy Museum. A collection of American and imported dolls, dollhouses, toys, and games, most from the Victorian period, fills a compact museum, founded in 1975 by a dollhouse historian. Miniature accessories, dollhouse kits, and antique toys and games are on sale in the museum's shops. ⊠ *5236 44th St. NW,* ☏ *202/244–0024.* ⊡ *$3.* ⊙ *Tues.–Sat. 10–5, Sun. noon–5. Metro: Friendship Heights.*

Washington National Cathedral. Construction of Washington National Cathedral, a stunning Gothic church—the sixth-largest cathedral in the world—started in 1907 and was finished on September 30, 1990, when the building was consecrated. Like its 14th-century counterparts, the National Cathedral (officially **Washington's Cathedral Church of St. Peter and St. Paul**) has a nave, flying buttresses, transepts, and vaults that were built stone by stone. It is adorned with fanciful gargoyles created by skilled stone carvers. The tomb of Woodrow Wilson, the only president buried in Washington, is on the south side of the nave. The expansive view of the city from the Pilgrim Gallery is exceptional. The cathedral is under the governance of the Episcopal church but has played host to services of many denominations. ⊠ *Wisconsin and Massachusetts Aves. NW,* ☏ *202/537–6200; tour information, 202/537–6207.* ⊡ *Suggested donation for tour $2.* ⊙ *Fall, winter, and spring, daily 10–4:30; Memorial Day–Labor Day, weekdays 10–9, weekends 10–4:30; Sun. services at 8, 9, 10, 11, and 6:30; evensong at 4; tours Mon.–Sat. 10–3:15, Sun. 12:30–2:45.*

Washington Navy Yard. The Navy's oldest shore establishment, the Washington Navy Yard was authorized in 1799. The facility is now a supply and administrative center, but attractions you can tour, such as two military museums and a destroyer, make it a must-see for anyone interested in military history. ⊠ *901 M St. SE. Metro: Navy Yard.*

Moored in the Anacostia River nearby and on permanent display is the *Barry,* a decommissioned U.S. Navy destroyer open for tours. ☏ *202/433–3377.* ⊡ *Free.* ⊙ *Mar.–Aug., Tues.–Sun. 10–5; Sept.–Feb., Tues.–Sun. 10–4.*

From June through August the Navy and Marines put on a multimedia Summer Pageant at an amphitheater across from the Navy Museum. ☏ *202/433–2218.*

3 Washington for Children

By John F. Kelly

Updated by
Bruce Walker

WASHINGTON MAY SEEM mainly for grown-ups. After all, running the government of a superpower is serious stuff. But the home of the White House, Capitol, and Supreme Court also boasts the National Museum of Natural History, Capital Children's Museum, and National Zoo, beloved by kids. Not every child is wowed by the Jefferson Memorial but nearly all love an elevator ride to the top of the Washington Monument with its spectacular vistas. History that seems dry and dusty in the classroom comes alive for children in Washington as they visit landmarks seen in movies and on TV, meet a real FBI agent on a super-popular tour, and behold uncut sheets of dollar bills rolling off the presses at the Bureau of Printing and Engraving. In an age of belt-tightening, another big plus is that most attractions are free.

In the past, despite kid-friendly sights, Washington had few hotels and restaurants catering to families. That's changing fast, and not just at budget places. When the tony Carlton offers a special kids program with savings and treats and the posh Four Seasons hosts "Tea Time for Tots" and serves milk and cookies at bedtime, others are sure to follow. But most hotels can at least help you find a baby-sitter; for Washingtonians a night out at a fashionable eatery is usually a night away from the kids—their own and other people's.

Even adults can get tired traipsing around the large Smithsonian museums. Bring a stroller for younger kids who may wear out easily (followed by the parents who end up having to carry them), although must leave it behind at the entrances to the White House and Washington Monument.

For kid-oriented fare, consult the Friday *Washington Post* "Weekend" section. Its "Carousel" listings include information on plays, puppet shows, concerts, story-telling sessions, nature programs, and other events for families. And tune in to WKDL, 1050 AM, D.C.'s first family-oriented radio station, with music and sightseeing news for children and parents.

Exploring

Pierre L'Enfant didn't design Washington's Mall with children in mind, but the concentration of monuments and museums surrounding the Mall couldn't be better for them. With most of the Smithsonian museums arranged around it, and the Washington Monument and Tidal Basin a few steps away, it should be every family's base camp.

Many Washington museums host exhibits designed for or appealing to children; helpful docents (trained guides) conduct kid-friendly tours. On the Mall are the **Discovery Room, Dinosaur Hall,** and **O. Orkin Insect Zoo** at the **National Museum of Natural History** and the **Hands On History Room** and **Hands On Science Room** at the **National Museum of American History.** The **National Air and Space Museum** is cool to kids. In front of the **Arts and Industries Building** stands an old-time carousel. The sound of the submarine dive Klaxon reverberating through the halls of the **Navy Museum** beckons children who love to push it and peer through the museum's operating periscopes. The **National Aquarium Touch Tank** is usually thronged by future ichthyologists. The **National Geographic Explorers Hall,** an interactive museum, quizzes kids about the Earth.

Many Washington museums have special printed children's guides to their collections, allowing kids to, for example, take pencil in hand and go on "scavenger hunts" to pick out the shapes and patterns in a work of modern art. Ask at the information desks.

The following Smithsonian museums have **diaper-changing facilities** in both men's and women's rooms: the Smithsonian Castle, the Freer Gallery, the Hirshhorn Museum, the National Museum of Natural History, the National Museum of American History, the National Air and Space Museum, the Renwick Gallery, and the National Museum of American Art. Metro stations have no rest rooms at all.

Here are some other attractions tailor-made for family visits.

Museums, Monuments, and Exhibits

Bureau of Engraving and Printing (☞ The Mall *in* Chapter 2). Any youngster who gets an allowance will enjoy watching money roll off the presses at the Bureau of Engraving and Printing. Kids and grown-ups who have ever wondered what a million dollars really looks like will never forget the awesome sight of a block of one million $1 bills on display in the visitors' center. It is huge. ☞ *Free.*

Capital Children's Museum. A former convent three blocks from Union Station is the site of this sprawling, decidedly hands-on museum. Everything is at kid level and just about everything is meant to be touched. That means children may "drive" a Metrobus, make Mexican hot chocolate, create their own old-time animations, weave their way through a maze, and fill a room with huge soap bubbles. Volunteer docents guide children and parents to different activity areas and oversee their young charges as they engage in such play as cooking tortillas or making paper flowers. The museum's focus is on how people in other cultures live, so there is an international flavor to many of the exhibits. Unlike the glitzier Smithsonian offerings, this museum seems a bit frayed around the edges. But it's a comfortable sort of wear and tear, achieved through the inquisitive hands of countless young visitors, and it makes the Capital Children's Museum seem like one huge playroom. ⊠ *800 3rd St. NE,* ☎ *202/543–8600.* ☞ *$6, children under 2 free.* ☉ *Daily 10–5.*

DAR Museum (☞ The White House Area *in* Chapter 2). Exhibits frequently explore how families lived in colonial times. Youngsters will especially love the free "Colonial Adventure" tours that are usually held the first and third Sundays of the month. Costumed docents lead children ages five to seven through the museum, explaining the exhibits and describing life in Colonial America. Make reservations at least 10 days in advance by calling 202/879–3239. ☞ *Free.*

J. Edgar Hoover Federal Bureau of Investigation Building (☞ Old Downtown and Federal Triangle *in* Chapter 2). The one-hour tour of the FBI building is not suitable for all children. One deterrent: The typical wait for admission is 4 hours. Another is that a special agent gives a live-ammo firearms demonstration in the building's shooting range, which may frighten younger children. Be this as it may, for older boys and girls, this sort of demonstration may well be the high point of their visit to the Capitol, and in fact the FBI building tour is one of the most popular tourist activities in the city. ☞ *Free.*

National Zoological Park (☞ Cleveland Park and the National Zoo *in* Chapter 2). The nation's zoo is one of the best, a must-see for families, with a new cheetah conservation area, a new of Amazon rain forest exhibit that looks like the real thing, and cuddly-looking Hsing-Hsing, the only giant panda in the United States. Rental strollers are available for when little legs wear out. ☞ *Free.*

Washington Dolls' House and Toy Museum (☞ Around Washington *in* Chapter 2). Antique toys and doll houses are on display, and accessories and kits are available for purchase. Most of the collection is behind glass, disappointing younger visitors; older kids will enjoy it more. ⌧ *$3 adults, $2 children under 14.*

The Washington Monument (☞ The Monuments *in* Chapter 2). You can't really say you've been to Washington until you've taken in the view from atop this 555-foot-tall obelisk. ⌧ *Free.*

The Arts

Washington has a lively arts scene for young and old alike. The museum community and the John F. Kennedy Center for the Performing Arts serve as a mecca for traveling troupes, and the home-grown talent isn't bad either, with children's concerts and plays entertainment staples for many a Washington family. Museums often host programs related to their exhibitions—African trickster stories at the National Museum of African Art, for example—and "serious" groups such as the National Symphony Orchestra and the Washington Chamber Symphony have special programs to woo young fans. Check the "Carousel" listings in the "Weekend" section of the *Washington Post* for special events that crop up during the year. For example, the **Ringling Bros. and Barnum & Bailey Circus** usually moves into the D.C. Armory for two weeks each April. Wolf Trap Farm Park hosts the **International Children's Festival,** with performers from around the world, early each September.

Adventure Theater. Adventure Theater produces such traditional plays and musicals as *Charlotte's Web, Robin Hood,* and *Aesop's Fables* weekends year-round at Glen Echo Park. Plays are aimed at children ages 4 to 12 and are presented in a 192-seat theater. The audience sits on carpeted steps, perfect for sprawling families. Reservations are suggested. ⌧ *7300 MacArthur Blvd., Glen Echo, MD,* ☎ *301/320–5331.*

Discovery Theater. Located in the West Hall of the Smithsonian's Arts and Industries Building, Discovery Theater is the setting for plays, puppet shows, and storytellers. Most presentations are for those in preschool through second grade, but some offerings are for children as old as 12. ⌧ *900 Jefferson Dr. SW,* ☎ *202/357–1500.*

F. Scott Black's Dinner Theatre. About an hour's drive from Washington (not far from Baltimore), F. Scott Black's Dinner Theatre occasionally has weekend matinee performances of children's shows such as *The Wizard of Oz* and *The Princess and the Magical Pea.* ⌧ *100 E. Chesapeake Ave., Towson, MD,* ☎ *410/321–6595.*

Hirshhorn Museum and Sculpture Garden (☞ The Mall *in* Chapter 2). The Hirshhorn screens free children's movies and cartoons most Saturday mornings at 11. Its collection of 4,000 paintings and drawings and 2,000 sculptures is sure to contain some artwork that children can relate to and enjoy. ⌧ *7th St. and Independence Ave. SW,* ☎ *202/ 357–2700.*

John F. Kennedy Center of the Performing Arts (☞ Foggy Bottom *in* Chapter 2). The Kennedy Center is the setting for more than 100 family events each year, including the **Imagination Celebration,** which runs from October through May. Year-round offerings include dance, music, storytelling, plays, and concerts for prekindergarten to high school-age kids. It's also the home base of the **National Symphony Orchestra,** whose Family Concerts are for children as young as three. Other concerts, which include "instrument petting zoos," are for youngsters six and up. ⌧ *New Hampshire Ave. and Rock Creek Pkwy. NW,* ☎ *202/467–4600; tour information, 202/416–8341.* ⌧ *Free.* ☉ *Daily*

10–9 or until last show lets out; box office Mon.–Sat. 10–9, Sun. and holidays noon–9; tour daily 10–1.

Now This! A musical-comedy improvisation group that brings things down to kid level, Now This! performs Saturday matinees. Children shout out suggestions to help the actors keep the show rolling. ⊠ *Omni Shoreham Hotel, Marquee Lounge, 2500 Calvert St. NW,* ☎ *202/ 745–1023.*

Puppet Co. Playhouse. In this theater in Glen Echo Park, Maryland, skilled puppeteers manipulate marionettes in classic plays and stories. ⊠ *7300 MacArthur Blvd.,* ☎ *301/320–6668.*

Saturday Morning at the National. A performance series for youngsters, Saturday Morning at the National has featured such acts as mimes, puppet shows, dance troupes, magicians, and children's theater groups. Performances are free but seating is first come, first served at the National Theatre Saturdays at 9:30 AM and 11 AM from October through March. ⊠ *1321 Pennsylvania Ave. NW,* ☎ *202/783–3372.*

Washington Chamber Symphony. The Washington Chamber Symphony gets children excited about classical music by providing workbooks, bringing kids on stage, marching the orchestra down the aisles, or having kids sing along with the proceedings. Its "Family Series" programs are for children as young as four; "Concerts for Young People" are for ages six and up. Most performances are at the Kennedy Center. A few suburban dinner theaters have children's weekend matinees to supplement their nighttime adult offerings. The plays—such favorites as *Jack and the Beanstalk, Little Red Riding Hood,* and *Beauty and the Beast*—usually include lunch or a snack. ☎ *202/452–1321.*

West End Dinner Theatre. In Alexandria, Virginia, a 20-minute drive from the Capitol, the West End Dinner Theatre often has Saturday matinees for children. Recent shows have included *Winnie the Pooh, Beauty and the Beast,* and *Aladdin.* ⊠ *4615 Duke St.,* ☎ *703/370–2500.*

Dining

When Washingtonians go out for a nice meal at a trendy downtown restaurant they usually leave the kids at home. That doesn't mean you need to check your children at the door, just that you shouldn't be surprised if you're one of the few obvious parents in attendance, especially in such neighborhoods as Adams-Morgan and Dupont Circle, where the restaurants cater to a young, single crowd. Most restaurants, however, stock booster seats and high chairs for kids who need a lift, and well-behaved babies are generally fawned upon wherever they go.

Inside the Beltway

For your own peace of mind you might want to eat somewhere with a loud dining room —the well-reviewed **Red Sage** and **Primi Piatti** (☞ Chapter 4) have noisy atmospheres—or at just about any Chinese restaurant (whose staffs seem especially tolerant of children).

Some other suggestions: **The American Café** chain (☞ Chapter 4), with many locations in the Washington area, has been keeping parents sane since it opened in 1979, with a children's menu kids can draw on (crayons provided). **Hamburger Hamlet** (⊠ 1601 Crystal Dr., Crystal City, VA, ☎ 703/413–0422) also lets kids express themselves on place mats. **T. G. I. Friday's** (⊠ 2100 Pennsylvania Ave. NW, ☎ 202/872–4344) is a down-to-earth restaurant offering hearty American fare; children's portions are available. **Geppetto** (⊠ 2917 M St. NW, ☎ 202/333–2602) is an Italian restaurant with irresistible carved marionettes as part of the decor. Teens and teens-in-training might enjoy the music and memorabilia of the **Hard Rock Café** (☞ Old Downtown and Federal Triangle *in* Chapter 2). Movie costumes and props (such as for a missile command center, complete with light-flashing console and radar tracking screen) glamorize the setting of **Planet Hollywood** (☞ Old Downtown and Federal Triangle *in* Chapter 2). For fast food a shade more interesting than hamburgers and fries, check out the food courts at Washington's four main malls: **Union Station** (☞ Capitol Hill *in* Chapter 2), **The Shops at National Place** (☞ The White House *in* Chapter 2 *and* the American Café *in* Chapter 4), **Georgetown Park** (☞ Georgetown *in* Chapter 2), and **The Pavilion at the Old Post Office** (☞ Old Downtown and Federal Triangle *in* Chapter 2).

Suburban Washington

Restaurants in the suburbs are generally friendlier places to bring children than their counterparts in the decidedly pinstripe-and-power-tie Capitol; prices are generally a bit cheaper as well. One standout is **The Calvert Grille** (⊠ 3106 Mount Vernon Ave., Alexandria, VA, ☎ 703/836–8425), specializing in barbecued baby-back ribs, which seats families in a back room equipped with toys and butcher paper so kids can draw on the tables. The often crowded '50s-style, meat-and-potatoes **Silver Diner** (⊠ 11806 Rockville Pike, Rockville, MD, ☎ 301/770–2828) has a basket of crayons and a pile of connect-the-dot place mats at the cash register. Budget travelers should check out **Chili's** (⊠ 11428A Rockville Pike, Rockville, MD, ☎ 301/881–8588), where anything on the children's menu is $1 on weekends. For interactive dining for the Nintendo generation, there's **Chuck E. Cheese** (⊠ several locations, including 6303 Richmond Hwy., Alexandria, VA, ☎ 703/660–6800).

A number of family-friendly hotels are worth considering, but with more and more hostelries introducing programs and touting their attractions for kids, you're bound to discover new ones if you check around when making reservations. The elegant, expensive **Carlton** has a Carlton Kids program with savings and treats. For a deluxe Georgetown locale, the **Four Seasons** offers children's menus, games, and activities, "Tea Time for Tots," and milk and cookies at bedtime. The **Holiday Inn Capitol Hill** may be inexpensive but it's location is great—with a million-dollar view of the Capitol building—and children under 18 stay free. The pricey **Omni Shoreham** has a weekend matinee cabaret for children and is near the National Zoo, as is the **Sheraton Washington.** The **Days Inn Connecticut Avenue** is away from the bustle of downtown, but only one Metro stop from the zoo. Several all-suite hotels are clustered in Foggy Bottom, including the **Embassy Suites** and two **Guest Quarters** hotels. In Georgetown, **Georgetown Suites** is spacious and reasonably priced.

Lodging

Washington has hotels for everyone, from the sightseer on a budget to the big spender on a junket. Luckily for families, children under 16 stay free in most hotels. When deciding on lodging with the little ones, here are some tips. Staying at an all-suite hotel will allow you to spread out and, if you prepare your meals in a kitchenette, keep costs down. A pool may be essential for a stay with kids; game rooms are a plus. Major convention hotels, and those on Capitol Hill and the waterfront, don't see as many families as those downtown, in Foggy Bottom, uptown, or in the Maryland and Virginia suburbs. The closer you are to a Metro stop, the quicker you can hit the sightseeing trail.

Washingtion has a growing number of family-friendly hotels. As more and more introduce programs and tout their attractions for kids, you're bound to discover new ones by checking around. The elegant **Carlton** has a Carlton Kids program with savings and treats. In Georgetown the deluxe **Four Seasons** offers children's menus, games, and activities, "Tea Time for Tots," and milk and cookies at bedtime. The **Holiday Inn Capitol Hill** is inexpensive but has a million-dollar view of the Capitol building; children under 18 stay free. The **Omni Shoreham** has a weekend matinee cabaret for children and is near the National Zoo, as is the **Sheraton Washington.** The **Days Inn Connecticut Avenue** is away from the bustle of downtown but only one Metro stop from the zoo. Several all-suite hotels are clustered in Foggy Bottom, including the **Embassy Suites** and two **Guest Quarters** hotels. In Georgetown, **Georgetown Suites** is spacious and reasonably priced.

Baby-Sitting Services

Most larger hotels and those with concierges can arrange baby-sitting with one of Washington's licensed, bonded child-care agencies. Rates are usually per hour, with a four-hour minimum, and you may need to pay the sitter's transportation costs. The average cost is around $10 an hour for one child, with additional children about $1 more per hour; some agencies charge more to sit for additional nonrelated children. Most agencies are happy to provide references; some sitters will even take kids sightseeing. Agencies can usually arrange last-minute child care but advance notice is appreciated.

WeeSit (✉ 10681 Oak Thrust Ct., Burke, VA 22015, ☎ 703/764–1542) works with many of the city's largest hotels. **Chevy Chase Babysitters** (✉ 10771 Middleboro Dr., Damascus, MD 20872, ☎ 301/916–2694) has been in business since 1960. **Mothers' Aides Inc.** (✉ Box 7088, Fairfax Station, VA 22039, ☎ 703/250–0700) counts schoolteachers among its sitters.

Parks and Playgrounds

Washington prides itself on its tree-lined streets; that green thumb extends to the city's parks. A patch of grass for picnicking or jogging or a watery spot for cooling hot feet is rarely far away.

The biggest stretch of parkland is Rock Creek Park (☞ Parks and Woodlands *in* Chapter 7). Start at the **Nature Center** (✉ 5200 Glover Rd. NW, ☎ 202/426–6829), where easily hiked trails lead off in all directions. A small room is filled with pelts, bones, feathers, and shells for naturalists-in-training to handle, and another with stuffed animals representative of the mid-Atlantic—foxes, squirrels, and other small mammals, as well as eagles, hawks, and other birds. On weekends, rangers lead nature walks, show and discuss live animals, and present films. The center's 70-seat planetarium introduces youngsters to the night sky with weekend shows at 1 PM for ages four and up, 4 PM for ages seven and up, and 3:45 PM on Wednesdays for ages four and up. Children also like the falling water of **Pierce Mill** (✉ Tilden St. and Park Rd. NW, ☎ 202/426–6908), where rangers grind grain into flour.

Running parallel to the Potomac is the Chesapeake & Ohio (C&O) Canal, a favorite spot for jogging and bicycling. Kids especially like the **mule-drawn barge rides,** which depart from spring through early autumn from Georgetown, as well as from the Great Falls Tavern Visitors Center on the Maryland side of the C&O Canal National Historic Park (☞ Parks and Woodlands *in* Chapter 7).

A small play area is close to the Capitol: the **Judicial Office Building** (✉ 2nd and E Sts. NE, beside Union Station), which has a modest but choice selection of play equipment behind it. The new generation of playgrounds—with lots of tubes and bridges—hasn't found its way into

Washington yet, but two in suburban Maryland are worth a trip. Both **Cabin John Regional Park** (✉ 7400 Tuckerman La., Rockville, MD, ☎ 301/299–0024) and **Wheaton Regional Park** (✉ 2000 Shorefield Rd., Wheaton, MD, ☎ 301/946–7033) include modern, terraced playgrounds with corkscrewing plastic slides, bouncing wooden bridges, sandboxes, and mazes. A bonus: Both have ice rinks and trains that operate seasonally, and there's even a carousel at Wheaton. Several members of the **Discovery Zone** franchise family have recently opened in the Maryland and Virginia suburbs. These indoor fitness centers are loaded with tunnels, ball bins, padded cubes and mats, and much more, all designed to let kids under 12 climb, jump, run, and basically go wild in their stocking feet. The cost is about $7 for two hours of play. Those closest to downtown D.C. are about 10 miles away at White Flint Mall (✉ 11301 Rockville Pike, 3rd floor, North Bethesda, MD, ☎ 301/231–0505) and Skyline Mall (✉ 5195A Leesburg Pike, Falls Church, VA, ☎ 703/379–6900).

Kite fliers can be found most windy weekends near the Washington Monument grounds. (Buy a kite at the National Air and Space Museum if you want to join them.) One of the oldest **miniature golf courses** in the country operates during the summer in East Potomac Park (☞ Parks and Gardens *in* Chapter 7). A good way to tire out rambunctious offspring is to let them work off some of their energy at the helm—and the pedals—of a paddleboat in the **Tidal Basin** (☞ The Monuments *in* Chapter 2) at the helm of a paddleboat.

Budding Paul Wylies and Nancy Kerrigans can practice their moves at two ice rinks close to the Mall. **The Sculpture Garden Outdoor Rink** is two blocks from the Hirshhorn Museum (✉ Constitution Ave. between 7th and 9th Sts. NW, ☎ 202/371–5340). The other option is the **Pershing Park Ice Rink** (✉ Pennsylvania Ave. between 14th and 15th Sts. NW, ☎ 202/737–6938). Rental skates are available. Both rinks operate seasonally.

Washington has no beaches, but **Adventure World** (✉ 13710 Central Ave., Largo, MD, ☎ 301/249–1500) is a 115-acre theme park in suburban Maryland that operates from late May through October (weekends only in May, September, and October). It has plenty—water slides, wave pool, kiddie ferris wheel, roller coaster, bumper cars—to keep small children occupied; more than 50 rides for older youngsters include three rollercoasters. Games and shows include a family-oriented song-and-dance show at the "Crazy Horse Saloon," magic shows, wild west stunt shows, even a circus show where the kids don costumes and perform on stage).

Shopping

Young visitors can leave Washington loaded with goodies, from souvenir T-shirts to paper models of the White House. Don't overlook the merchandise on the Mall. The Smithsonian museums have creatively stocked shops; many of the items are actually educational.

Favorite Smithsonian shops include those in the **National Museum of American History** (books, games), the **National Museum of Natural History** (dinosaur models, stuffed animals), and the **National Air and Space Museum,** where no kid can resist sampling the astronauts' freeze-dried ice cream sandwiches in foil pouches, even though they're messy and not particularly tasty.

Traditional allures are at **F.A.O. Schwarz,** the upscale toy store; the **Kid's Closet,** a children's clothing store in downtown D.C.; and the **Cheshire Cat,** a bookstore just for children (☞ Chapter 8). The latter also has occasional reading and story-telling sessions, and well-known children's book authors sometimes stop by to meet their readers.

The Great Train Store (✉ Union Station, 40 Massachusetts Ave. NE, ☎ 202/371–2881) has all manner of train sets, engineers' hats, and other choo-choo-related toys and memorabilia. **Al's Magic Shop** (✉ 1012 Vermont Ave. NW, ☎ 202/789–2800) has been catering to both magicians and pranksters for more than 50 years. **All Wound-Up** (✉ Pavilion at Old Post Office, 1100 Pennsylvania Ave. NW, ☎ 202/842–0635) sells scores of wind-up toys, model cars, and stuffed animals. Right next door, **Juggling Capitol** (☎ 202/789–1799) has everything juggling klutzes and experienced clowns might need. At the **ReUse** store (✉ 418 S. Washington St., Alexandria, VA, ☎ 703/549–0111) you'll find scraps of wood, old egg cartons, empty coffee cans, bits of yarn, bags of bottle caps, and other cast-off items designed to be recycled into children's art projects. Kids who want to pretend they're famous can get their likeness computer-superimposed on the cover of *National Geographic* (✉ National Geographic Explorers Hall, 17th and M Sts. NW, ☎ 202/857–7689). Put your face on a postage stamp, a $100 bill, or Mount Rushmore at the **National Museum of American History** (✉ 12th St. and Constitution Ave. NW, ☎ 202/357–2700).

4 Dining

By Deborah Papier

Updated by Holly Bass

ENJOY SUNNY AFRICAN pop music while you sample such delicacies as *moi-moi* (black-eyed peas, tomatoes, and corned beef) and *nklakla* (tomato soup with goat). Feast on *feijoada*, a rich Brazilian stew of black beans, pork, and smoked meats. Sample French specialties such as the delicious fish soup-stew called bouillabaisse, Italian favorites like fusilli broccoli with whole cloves of roasted garlic, Middle Eastern delicacies like succulent lamb kebobs and crisp vegetable fritters known as falafels, rich Spanish *Gállego* soup (full of white beans, potatoes, collard greens, and ham), crunchily addictive Vietnamese spring rolls, spicy Carolina shrimp (peel 'em and eat with steaming white grits beloved by southerners), and some of the finest marbled steaks and butter-soft roast beef this side of the Mississippi. For artful cusine in elegant settings, such restaurants as La Colline and the Little Inn at Washington (a 90-minute dive from the city through picturesque countryside) are world-renowned.

As the nation's capital, Washington finds itself playing host to an international array of visitors and newcomers. This constant infusion of new cultures means that District restaurants are getting better and better. (And sometimes, cheaper and cheaper: The sluggish economy of the early '90s has meant more reasonably priced fare and fixed-price specials in many of the city's top dining rooms.) Despite the dearth of ethnic neighborhoods and the kinds of restaurant districts found in many cities, you *can* find almost any type of food here, from Nepalese to Salvadoran to Ethiopian. Even the French-trained chefs who have traditionally set the standard in fine dining are turning to health-conscious New American cuisine, spicy Southwestern recipes, or bite-size appetizers called *tapas* for new inspiration.·

In the city's one officially recognized ethnic enclave, **Chinatown** (centered on G and H streets NW between 6th and 8th, with its own Metro station at Gallery Place), Burmese, Thai, and other Asian cuisines are adding new variety to the area's many traditional Chinese restaurants. The latter entice visitors with huge brightly-lit signs and offer such staples as beef with broccoli or kung pao chicken in a spicy sauce with roasted peanuts. But discriminating diners will find far better food at the smaller, less obvious restaurants like Full Kee or Li Ho's. A good rule of thumb is to look for recent reviews in the *Washingtonian Magazine, Washington Post, and Washington Times,* which proud owners display on doors or in windows.

Aside from Chinatown, there are seven areas of the city where restaurants are concentrated:

Most of the deluxe restaurants are **downtown** near K Street NW, also the location of many of the city's blue-chip law firms. These are the restaurants that feed off expense-account diners and provide the most elegant atmosphere, most attentive service, and often the best food. In the old downtown district, visitors with children can take advantage of the many sandwich shops geared to office workers to grab a quick bite during the day but will find far fewer choices evenings and weekends. However, the entire downtown area is in a state of flux gastronomically, with famed restaurants like Jean-Louis in the Watergate closing their doors and new ones blossoming. Trendy microbrewery/restaurants and cigar lounges are part of the new wave.

Another popular restaurant district is **Georgetown,** whose central intersection is Wisconsin Avenue and M Street. Here are some of the city's

It helps to be pushy in airports.

Introducing the revolutionary new TransPorter™ from American Tourister. It's the first suitcase you can push around without a fight. TransPorter's™ exclusive four-wheel design lets you push it in front of you with almost no effort–the wheels take the weight. Or pull it on two wheels if you choose. You can even stack on other bags and use it like a luggage cart.

Stable 4-wheel design.

TransPorter™ is designed like a dresser, with built-in shelves to organize your belongings. Or collapse the shelves and pack it like a traditional suitcase. Inside, there's a suiter feature to help keep suits and dresses from wrinkling. When push comes to shove, you can't beat a TransPorter™. For more information on how you can be this pushy, call 1-800-542-1300.

Shelves collapse on command.

American Tourister

Making travel less primitive.®

©1996 American Tourister®

Use your MCI Card® for the easy way to call when traveling.

MCI Calling Card

415 555 1234 2244
J.D. SMITH

Convenience on the road

- Your MCI Card® number is your home number, guaranteed.
- Pre-programmed to speed dial to your home.
- Call from any phone in the U.S.

MCI

1 - 8 0 0 - 7 5 4 - 8 9 4 1

http://www.mci.com

priciest houses as well as some of its cheesiest businesses, and its restaurants are similarly diverse, with white-tablecloth dining places next door to hole-in-the-wall joints. The closest Metro stop for all Georgetown restaurants is Foggy Bottom; the walk can still be substantial—15–20 minutes—depending on the place. Consult the Georgetown map before you set out. Restaurants in the adjacent **West End** are worth checking out as well. This area, bounded roughly by Rock Creek Park to the west, N Street to the north, 20th Street to the east, and K Street to the south, is increasingly bridging the gap between Georgetown and downtown restaurant zones.

An exuberantly diverse culinary competitor to Georgetown is **Adams-Morgan.** Eighteenth Street NW extending south from Columbia Road is wall-to-wall restaurants, with new ones opening so fast it's almost impossible to track them. Although the area has retained some of its Hispanic identity, the new eating establishments tend to be Asian, New American (traditional American ingredients given a French turn), Ethiopian, and Caribbean. Parking can be impossible on weekends. The nearest Metro stop—Woodley Park/Zoo—is a 10- to 15-minute walk; while it's a safe stroll at night, it may be more convenient to take a cab. **Woodley Park** has culinary temptations of its own, with a lineup of popular ethnic restaurants right by the Metro.

Just down the hill from 18th Street the **U Street** corridor begins. In the 1930s and 1940s this was the place to enjoy a late night drink and hear jazz greats like Duke Ellington, Billie Holliday, and Charlie Parker; they came to Washington from New York's Harlem district, then a nationally famous center of culture and the arts. After decades of neglect and devastation from the '60s riots, the U Street area has recently undergone a revitalization campaign. With some of the hippest bars in the District, quirky vintage stores, and numerous cafés, the neighborhood draws a young adult crowd day and night. U Street is home to several small clubs where DJs or live bands—playing everything from punk rock to rap to acid jazz (a fusion of jazz and danceable hiphop beats)—appear almost every night. Restaurants stay open late on weekend nights and offer good food at low prices, everything from burgers to gourmet pizza to Ethiopian dishes (eateries serving this African country's cuisine are abundant in the Capitol, and popular). The U Street vicinity is known for excellent fried fish spots like the Big Fish Deli and Webb's Southern Food; unfortunately they don't offer seating. Free parking is available after 8 PM in the Reeves Center Building on the corner of 14th and U streets.

South from U Street and north from K Street is **Dupont Circle,** around which a number of restaurants are clustered. Some of the city's best white-tablecloth restaurants serving Italian food can be found here. You'll find a variety of cafés, most with outdoor seating. The District's better gay-friendly establishments are here as well. Chains like Starbuck's and Hannibal's have put fancy coffee on every corner, but long-established espresso bars, like the 24-hour Afterwords (located within a book store), are a good source for breakfast and light or late fare. Those on 17th Street NW are especially popular with young adults.

Capitol Hill has a number of bar-eateries that cater to Congressional types in need of fortification after a day spent running the country. The dining possibilities on Capitol Hill are boosted by Union Station, which contains some decent—if pricey—restaurants like B. Smith's and America. There's also a large food court with fast food ranging from barbecue to sushi.

The restaurants in many of the city's luxury hotels are another source of fine dining. The Willard Hotel's formal dining room, the Mayflower's Nicholas, the Ritz-Carlton's Jockey Club, and the Morrison-Clark Inn's dining room are especially noteworthy. The cuisine is often artful and fresh, with special care given to ingredients, preparation, and presentation. Of course, such attention to detail comes at a price. One less expensive way to experience these nationally-recognized restaurants is a weekday lunch (☞ Chapter 5).

Outside the city limits intriguing restaurant districts also thrive. Happily, all are accessible by Metro. Downtown **Bethesda, Maryland,** offers a wealth of possibilities, among them spicy Southwestern dishes, classic Spanish cuisine, and good old American diner food. Some cognoscenti even think that Georgetown is losing business to Bethesda's tantalizing bistros. From Georgetown, Bethesda is a 20-minute drive up Wisconsin Avenue, or get off at the Bethesda Metro stop. Virginia has its ritzy Georgetown equivalent in quaint, historic **Old Town Alexandria,** and bragging rights to some of the Virginia's best Asian restaurants go to **Arlington,** where Wilson Boulevard is lined with popular Vietnamese establishments and branches of other D.C. restaurants. The King Street and Clarendon Metro stations respectively make these "gourmet ghettos" accessible to visitors.

CATEGORY	COST*
$$$$	over $35
$$$	$25–$35
$$	$15–$25
$	under $15

per person for a three-course meal, excluding drinks, service, and sales tax (10% in D.C., 4.5%–9% in VA, 5% in MD)

What to Wear
Gentlemen may be more comfortable wearing jackets and/or ties in $$$ and $$$$ restaurants, even when there is no formal dress code.

Adams-Morgan/Woodley Park

African
$ ✕ **Bukom Café.** Sunny African pop music, a palm-frond-and-*kente*-cloth decor, and a spicy West African menu brighten this narrow two-story dining room. Appetizers include moi-moi and *nklakla* (tomato soup with goat). Entrées range from lamb with melon seeds to *kumasi* (chicken in a peanut sauce) to vegetarian dishes such as *jollof* rice and fried plantains. Live music nightly and late hours (until 2 AM Wednesday, Thursday, and Sunday; until 3 AM Friday–Saturday) keep this place hopping, even by Adams-Morgan standards. ⊠ *2442 18th St. NW,* ☎ *202/265–4600. AE, D, MC, V. Closed Mon. No lunch Sun.*

Brazilian
$$ ✕ **Grill from Ipanema.** The Grill focuses on Brazilian cuisine, from spicy seafood stews to grilled steak and other hearty meat dishes. Appetizers include clams baked with hot peppers and cilantro and—for adventurous eaters—fried alligator. Traditional feijoada—a stew of black beans, pork, and smoked meat—is served Wednesday, Saturday and Sunday. ⊠ *1858 Columbia Rd. NW,* ☎ *202/986–0757. AE, D, DC, MC, V. No lunch weekdays.*

Ethiopian
$–$$ ✕ **Meskerem.** The cuisine of the East African country of Ethiopia
★   abounds in Adams-Morgan, but Meskerem is distinctive for its bright, appealingly decorated dining room and the balcony where you can eat

Ethiopian-style—seated on the floor on leather cushions, with large woven baskets for tables. Entrées are served on a large piece of *injera,* a sourdough flatbread; diners eat family style by scooping up mouth-ful-size portions of the hearty dishes with extra bread. Among Meskerem's specialties are delicious stews made with spicy *berbere* chili sauce, *kitfo,* a buttery beef dish served raw like steak tartare or very rare; and a tangy, green chili vinagrette potato salad. Combination plat-ters with several different meat or vegetable entrées are available as well. ⊠ *2434 18th St. NW,* ☎ *202/462–4100. AE, DC, MC, V.*

French

$$ ✕ **La Fourchette.** On a block in Adams-Morgan where new restaurants are opening almost weekly and closing just as fast, La Fourchette has stayed in business by offering good bistro or French-family-restaurant-style food (chicken in white wine sauce, rich beef stews) at reasonable prices. Most of the menu consists of daily specials and an early-bird fixed-price menu, but you can pretty much count on finding bouill-abaisse and rabbit on the list. La Fourchette looks the way a bistro should, with an exposed brick wall, a tin ceiling, bentwood chairs, and quasi-post-Impressionist murals. ⊠ *2429 18th St. NW,* ☎ *202/332–3077. AE, DC, MC, V. No lunch weekends.*

Italian

$ ✕ **Pasta Mia.** Pasta Mia's Southern Italian appetizers and entrées all cost a palatable $7–$9. Large bowls of steaming pasta are served with a generous layer of fresh grated parmesan. Best-sellers include fusilli broccoli with whole cloves of roasted garlic, rich fettuccine verde, and spicy penne arrabiata. *Tiramisù* served in a teacup with espresso-soaked ladyfingers is an elegant way to finish a meal. No wonder area chefs sneak in here on their nights off. ⊠ *1790 Columbia Rd. NW,* ☎ *202/328–9114. MC, V. No lunch.*

Malaysian

$$ ✕ **Straits of Malaya.** Just far enough away from Dupont Circle to be quaint, Straits of Malaya serves some of the most exotic food in Wash-ington—Malaysian/Singaporean cuisine that borrows from Chinese, Thai, and Indian cooking. Dishes—among them chicken satay (on skewers), five spice rolls, fiery *laksa* noodle soup, *udang goreng* (shrimp in a coconut milk sauce), and *poh pia* (shredded jicama stir-fried with vegetables)—are lovely combinations of sweet and pepper-hot spices. Dining on Straits' roof during the warm months is one of the city's finer pleasures. ⊠ *1836 18th St. NW,* ☎ *202/483–1483. AE, D, MC, V. No lunch weekends.*

Mediterranean

$$ ✕ **TomTom.** TomTom's trendy menu features pizza baked in a wood-burning oven and tapas of all sorts—not just traditional Spanish ap-petizers but also Italian and New American variations. The food can be quite good—green salads come topped with shrimp or grilled chicken and are fresh and generously portioned—but the real draw is the atmosphere. On warm nights the rooftop is packed and area artists set up easels to paint while patrons watch. Hip, artsy crowds wait al-most an hour on weekends for a table. ⊠ *2335 18th St. NW,* ☎ *202/588–1300. AE, D, DC, MC, V.*

Middle Eastern

$ ✕ **Mama Ayesha's Restaurant.** Journalists and politicians (autographed pictures of the last two presidents hang prominently) are known to fre-quent Ayesha's for the reasonably priced fare. At the family-run eatery, staples like chicken and lamb kebobs can be had for less than $10, bas-kets of complimentary pita bread are served hot, and the crisp falafels

SEE
ADAMS-MOR
WOODLEY PAR
DETAIL M

Aditi, **10**	Café Japone, **41**	Georgetown Café, **7**	Las Pampas, **9**
American Café, **63, 72**	Café Nema, **35**	Gerard's Place, **58**	Lauriol Plaza, **31**
Andalucia, **1**	Casa Africana, **37**	Hibiscus Cafe, **11**	Le Lion D'Or, **47**
Ben's Chili Bowl, **36**	Citronelle, **25**	i Ricchi, **44**	Li Ho, **66**
Bistro Français, **24**	City Lights of China, **30**	Imani Cafe, **76**	Little Viet Garden/ Queen Bee, **12**
Bombay Club, **56**	Coppis, **32**	Jaleo, **69**	Maison Blanche, **55**
Burma, **67**	Coco Loco, **65**	Kinkead's, **27**	Mango's, **33**
Cafe Asia, **49**	Cottonwood Cafe, **2**	La Brasserie, **73**	Marrakesh, **54**
Café Atlántico, **68**	Galileo, **50**	La Chaumière, **26**	The Monocle, **74**
Café Dalat, **19**	Georgia Brown's, **57**	La Colline, **71**	

Morton's of
Chicago, **17, 22**
Nora, **28**
Notte Luna, **59**
Obelisk, **39**
Occidental Grill, **61**
Old Ebbitt Grill, **60**
The Palm, **45**
Panjshir, **13**
Paolo's, **3, 14, 23**

Phillips Flagship, **64**
Pho 75, **20**
Pizzeria Paradiso, **40**
Polly's Café, **34**
Primi Piatti, **18, 53**
Red, Hot and
Blue, **4, 15, 48**
Red Sage, **62**
Rio Grande Cafe, **5, 16**
River Club, **21**

Sala Thai, **42**
Sam and Harry's, **46**
Sarinah Satay
House, **8**
701 Pennsylvania
Avenue, **70**
Sholl's Colonial
Cafeteria, **52**
Skewers/
Café Luna, **38**
Tabard Inn, **43**

Taberna del
Alabardero, **51**
Tastee Diner, **6**
Two Quail, **75**
Vincenzo al Sole, **29**

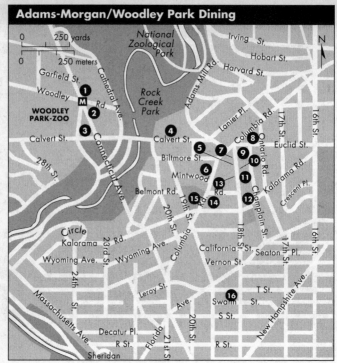

Adams-Morgan/Woodley Park Dining

(spicy vegetable fritters) are some of the best in town. ⊠ *1967 Calvert St. NW,* ☎ *202/232–5431. No credit cards.*

New American

$$$ ✕ **New Heights.** With its precise geometrical design softened by pastel colors, New Heights is one of Washington's most attractive restaurants specializing in New American cuisine, in which traditional American and more exotic food ingredients are combined in innovative ways. Salmon, a frequent offering, might be grilled with vegetables, swiss chard, and horseradish beurre blanc. Mustard-grilled quail in a port wine sauce might be accompanied by wild rice and croquettes made from quinoa, a high–protein grain from South America that tastes like couscous. With eleven large windows that let sunlight stream in, the restaurant is a good choice for Sunday brunch. Complimentary valet parking is an added benefit in area where parking can be difficult. ⊠ *2317 Calvert St. NW,* ☎ *202/234–4110. AE, D, DC, MC, V. No lunch Mon.–Sat.*

$$–$$$ ✕ **Cashion's Eat Place.** Cozy Cashion's feels like an inn from the 1940s South. Individual gaslights sit on each table, casting an amber glow, black-and-white family photos hang on the walls, and the dark wood floors look worn-in, even though the restaurant is only in its second year. Roast chicken, a steak entrée, and several fish dishes are menu staples. Meats are served in good portions and side dishes like garlicky mashed potatoes nicely round out a meal. Salads are towers of fresh whole leaves. Many dishes, from pasta to soup, are seasoned with ham. Dessert may be bread pudding made with croissants or a sinfully delicious cinnamon-chocolate mousse. Service can be leisurely. ⊠ *1819 Columbia Rd. NW,* ☎ *202/797–1819. MC, V. Reservations not accepted. Closed Mon. No lunch.*

Southwestern/Tex-Mex

$ ✗ **Peyote Café/Roxanne Restaurant.** Mexican influences on tradi-
tional southern food define the Southwestern menus at two connected
restaurants. Both offer great food, and you can order from either's menu
no matter where you sit. Twinkling lights, tables with bar stools, and
a rockin' jukebox attract a young crowd of primarily students and singles to the cozy Peyote Café. *Carne asada* (grilled rib-eye steak) is popular among carnivores. Not in the mood for meat? Choose from grilled
salmon, rotisserie-style "thunder" chicken, and "sweat hot fire" shrimp.
The Roxanne Restaurant features outdoor rooftop dining in warm
weather. ✉ *2319 18th St. NW,* ☎ *202/462–8330. Reservations not
accepted. AE, DC, MC, V. No lunch weekdays.*

Spanish

$ ✗ **El Rincon.** While South American El Rincon does serve black beans
and plantains, several entrées are actually Spanish. For example, Gállego soup—with white beans, potatoes, collard greens, and ham—is
filling and delicious, as is the crisply fried Spanish tortilla of sweet onion,
potato, and eggs. Though the quality of the food can be inconsistent,
locals like El Rincon for its low prices and generous portions (lobster
thermidor costs $9.95). ✉ *1826 Columbia Rd. NW,* ☎ *202/265–4943.
AE, MC, V.*

Thai

$ ✗ **Thai Town.** With its large, wooden booths and neon lighting, Thai
Town's ambience brings to mind a 50s-era diner. The restaurant's
food, however, is strictly traditional. Pad Thai, a flavorful mound of
noodles topped with shrimp, vegetables or shredded chicken or beef,
is the ever-popular Thai national dish, as are lemon grass soups and
curry preparations devoured from Thai Town's $6.95 all-you-can-eat
buffet. Patio seating is available. ✉ *2606 Connecticut Ave. NW,* ☎
202/387–8876. AE, DC, MC, V.

Trinidadian

$ ✗ **Islander.** Fancy it isn't; fantastic it is. Addie Green's authentic
★ Trinidadian eatery turns out some of Washington's most exciting and
satisfying food. Tangy soup made with vegetables and marinated fish,
delicious *accra* cod fritters, curried goat, tropical-herb-and-spice-mar-
inated calypso chicken, and the best and lightest dough-enveloped *rôti*
you'll ever taste will leave you delirious with pleasure. ✉ *1762 Columbia
Rd. NW, 2nd floor,* ☎ *202/234–4955. No credit cards. Closed Sun.
and Mon.*

Vietnamese

$$ ✗ **Saigon Gourmet.** Service is brisk and friendly at the popular,
French-influenced Saigon Gourmet. The upscale neighborhood pa-
trons return for the ultracrisp *cha-gio* (spring rolls), the savory *pho*
(beef broth), seafood soups, and the delicately seasoned and richly
sauced entrées. Shrimp Saigon mixes prawns and pork in a peppery
marinade, and another Saigon dish—grilled pork with rice crepes—
is a Vietnamese variation on Chinese *moo shu*. Bananas flambé make
for an entertaining dessert as the waiter seems to pour flames from
one plate to the other. ✉ *2635 Connecticut Ave. NW,* ☎ *202/265–
1360. AE, D, DC, MC, V.*

$ ✗ **Miss Saigon.** Green and mauve decor, black Art Deco accents, and
potted palms give Miss Saigon an intimate air. Begin with crisp egg rolls
or chilled spring rolls, then proceed to the daily specials, which usu-
ally feature the freshest seafood prepared in exciting ways. Careful at-
tention is paid to presentation as well as to seasoning. "Caramel"-cooked
meats are standouts, as are the grilled meats. Prices are moderate, es-
pecially for lunch, but you may have to order several dishes to have

your fill. ⊠ *1847 Columbia Rd. NW,* ☎ *202/667–1900. AE, MC, V. No lunch weekends.*

Capitol Hill

American

$$$ ✕ **Monocle.** The fireplaces and political portraits in a former pair of town houses add to the Monocle's aura of cozy tradition. The restaurant is still probably the best place in Washington for spotting members of Congress at lunch and dinner; its management keeps elected officials informed of when it's time to vote. The cooking—regional American cuisine—is adequate if unexciting and a so-so value, but the old-style Capitol Hill atmosphere, not the food, is the real draw here. Seafood is a specialty; try the crab cakes, and take advantage of the fresh fish specials. ⊠ *107 D St. NE,* ☎ *202/546–4488. AE, DC, MC, V. Closed weekends.*

$$ ✕ **Two Quail.** A welcome respite from the men's club atmosphere of traditional Capitol Hill eateries, this quaint, floral-pattern tearoom is tops among women for both romantic and power dining. The seasonal menu has both rich fare—apricot-and-sausage-stuffed pork chop, chicken stuffed with cornbread and pecans, game meats or filet mignon—and lighter, seafood pastas and meal-size salads. Service can be leisurely. ⊠ *320 Massachusetts Ave. NE,* ☎ *202/543–8030. AE, D, DC, MC, V. No lunch weekends.*

French

$$$ ✕ **La Brasserie.** One of Capitol Hill's most pleasant and satisfying restaurants, La Brasserie occupies two floors of adjoining town houses, with outdoor dining in season. The basically French menu changes seasonally, with such specials as poached salmon or breast of duck added daily. The crème brûlée, served cold or hot with fruit, is superb. ⊠ *239 Massachusetts Ave. NE,* ☎ *202/546–9154. AE, DC, MC, V.*

$$$ ✕ **La Colline.** Chef Robert Gréault has worked to make La Colline one
★ of the city's best French restaurants—and it is. The menu emphasizes seafood, with offerings ranging from simple grilled preparations to fricassées and gratins with imaginative sauces. Other items usually include duck with orange or cassis sauce and veal with chanterelle mushrooms. ⊠ *400 N. Capitol St. NW,* ☎ *202/737–0400. AE, DC, MC, V. Closed Sun. No lunch Sat.*

Seafood

$$ ✕ **Phillips Flagship.** Cavernous rooms and capacious decks overlook the Capitol Yacht Club's marina. There's a sushi bar (Mon.–Sat.), a party room with its own deck, catering rooms, and space for 1,400. Despite its size Phillips Flagship serves excellent seafood with dispatch. Succulent soft-shell crabs, large crab cakes, and blackened catfish are accompanied by chunky fresh vegetables cooked to crunchy perfection. ⊠ *900 Water St. SW,* ☎ *202/488–8515. AE, D, DC, MC, V.*

Southern

$ ✕ **Imani Café.** On the edge of historic Anacostia, one of the Capitol's oldest African-American communities, the Imani Café is already a neighborhood institution. Chicken or fish (baked or fried), spicy black-eyed peas, and peach cobbler are menu regulars. Baked macaroni and cheese and sweet iced-tea punch alone are worth the trip. A great way to end a visit to Frederick Douglass' house or the Smithsonian at Anacostia, with its changing exhibits on African-American culture, the Imani Café lets a family of four eat heartily for less than $30. ⊠ *1918 Martin Luther King Blvd.,* ☎ *202/678–4890. AE, MC, V.*

Downtown

American

$$$$ ✕ **Palm.** Food trends come and go, but the Palm pays no attention; it offers the same hearty food it always has—gargantuan steaks and Nova Scotia lobsters, several kinds of potatoes, and New York cheese-cake. Its plain decor is patterned after the New York original, and the businesslike air is matched by the pinstriped clientele. The Palm also offers a bargain lunch menu that includes shrimp, veal, and chicken salad. ⊠ *1225 19th St. NW,* ☎ *202/293–9091. AE, DC, MC, V. No lunch weekends.*

$$$$ ✕ **Sam and Harry's.** Sam and Harry's is understated, genteel, and packed at lunch and dinner. Although the miniature crab cakes are a good way to begin, the main attractions are the porterhouse and New York strip steaks served on the bone with a black bean garnish. For those who've sworn off beef, daily seafood specials include Maine lobster. End the meal with warm pecan pie laced with melted chocolate or an individual "turtle cake" full of caramel and chocolate and big enough for two. ⊠ *1200 19th St. NW,* ☎ *202/296–4333. AE, D, DC, MC, V. Closed Sun. No lunch Sat.*

$$ ✕ **Old Ebbitt Grill.** The Old Ebbitt Grill does more business than al-most any other eatery in town. People flock here to drink at the several bars, which seem to go on for miles, and to enjoy the oyster bar and carefully prepared bar food that includes buffalo chicken wings, hamburgers, and Reuben sandwiches. But this is not just a place for casual nibbling; the Old Ebbitt offers serious diners homemade pastas and daily specials that emphasize fish dishes and steak. Despite the crowds, the restaurant never feels cramped, thanks to its well-spaced, comfortable booths. Service can be slow at lunch. ⊠ *675 15th St. NW,* ☎ *202/347–4800. AE, DC, MC, V.*

$ ✕ **American Café.** The American Café empire, now three establishments strong, serves fresh, healthful food—but not health food—at affordable prices in a casual environment. Such sandwiches as roast beef on a huge croissant are still the mainstay of the café, with salads and snacks rounding out the regular menu. Intriguing specials might include fresh fish, seafood pie, chicken, and barbecued ribs. Service can be slow, but families and downtown diners on a budget find the American Cafés a lifesaver. ⊠ *Shops at National Place,* ☎ *202/626–0770;* ⊠ *227 Massa-chusetts Ave. NE,* ☎ *202/547–8500;* ⊠ *8601 Westward Center Dr., Vienna, VA,* ☎ *703/848–9488. AE, MC, V.*

$ ✕ **Sholl's Colonial Cafeteria.** Their slogan is, "Where good foods are prepared right, served right, and priced right"—and truer words were never spoken. Suited federal workers line up next to pensioners and visiting students to grab a bite at this Washington institution, where favorites include chopped steak, liver and onions, and baked chicken and fish. Sholl's is famous for its apple, blueberry, peach, and other fruit pies, but all the desserts are scrumptious and cost around $1. ⊠ *1990 K St. NW,* ☎ *202/296–3065. No credit cards.*

Asian

$ ✕ **Burma.** That Burma the country is bordered by India, Thailand, and
★ China gives some indication of the cuisine at Burma the restaurant, an exquisite jewel in fading Chinatown. Here curry and tamarind share pride of place with lemon, cilantro, and soy seasonings. Batter-fried eggplant and squash are deliciously paired with complex, peppery sauces. Green Tea Leaf and other salads, despite their odd-sounding names and ingredients, leave the tongue with a pleasant tingle. Such entrées as mango pork, tamarind fish, and Kokang chicken are equally satisfying. Bring a group and explore several options on the menu. The very reasonable prices (nothing is over $10) make this easy to do. ⊠

740 6th St. NW, ☎ *202/638–1280. AE, D, DC, MC, V. No lunch weekends.*

$ ✕ **Café Asia.** One of Washington's best pan-Asian restaurants, Café Asia presents Japanese, Chinese, Thai, Singaporean, Indonesian, Malaysian, and Vietnamese variations on succulent themes. Highlights include grilled shrimp paste on sugarcane, moist satays, spicy fish in banana leaves, and noodle soups. The dining area covers three floors, the decor is spartan, and the staff is small, but low prices and the chance to try many different types of food in one great place make waits worthwhile. ⊠ *1134 19th St. NW,* ☎ *202/659–2696. AE, DC, MC, V. Closed Sun.*

Chinese

$ ✕ **Li Ho/Full Kee.** Head for unassuming Li Ho if good food in satisfying portions is what you seek. Some locals prefer neighboring Full Kee, which has a competitive assortment of Cantonese-style roasted meats, but Li Ho's specialties—including duck soup with mustard greens and a Singapore-style rice noodle dish seasoned with curry and bits of meat—are favorites among the lunch-time crowd. ⊠ *501 H St. NW,* ☎ *202/289–2059. AE, MC, V.*

French

$$$$ ✕ **Le Lion D'Or.** Other French restaurants may flirt with fads, but Le
★ Lion D'Or sticks to the classics—or at any rate the neoclassics—and does them so well that its popularity remains undiminished year after year. If you've ever wondered why so many gourmets rave about French food, Le Lion D'Or's lobster soufflé, crepes with oysters and caviar, ravioli with foie gras, salmon with crayfish, and roast pigeon with mushrooms provide delectable answers. The fabulous dessert soufflés may be filled with raspberries or orange essence, or try the sinful chocolate soufflé surrounded by vanilla creme anglaise; all must be ordered in advance. ⊠ *1150 Connecticut Ave. NW (entrance on 18th St. NW),* ☎ *202/296–7972. Jacket and tie. AE, DC, MC, V. Closed Sun. No lunch.*

$$$$ ✕ **Maison Blanche.** A power-broker favorite, Maison Blanche owes its bipartisan popularity not only to its location near the White House and executive office buildings but also to its Old World elegance, the friendliness of the family that runs it, and its large repertoire of classic and modern French dishes, primarily fish. Exceptional are the rich lobster bisque, pastas, and mustard-seasoned rack of lamb. In addition, Maison Blanche goes to great lengths to obtain Dover sole, which it serves grilled or sauteed with butter and lemon. Although Dover sole is usually thought of as a British dish, Maison Blanche's version is the restaurant's most-ordered entrée. Warm caramel soufflé served with Armagnac liqueur ice cream is a popular dessert. ⊠ *1725 F St. NW,* ☎ *202/842–0070. AE, DC, MC, V. Closed Sun. No lunch Sat.*

Indian

$$–$$$ ✕ **Bombay Club.** One block from the White House, the beautiful Bom-
★ bay Club tries to re-create the kind of solace the Beltway elite might have found in a private club had they been 19th-century British colonials in India rather than late-20th-century Washingtonians. The bar, which serves hot hors d'oeuvres at cocktail hour, is furnished with rattan chairs and paneled with dark wood. The dining room, with potted palms and a bright blue ceiling above white plaster moldings, is elegant and decorous. The menu includes unusual seafood specialties and a large number of vegetarian dishes, but the real standouts are the breads and the seafood appetizers. ⊠ *815 Connecticut Ave. NW,* ☎ *202/659–3727. AE, DC, MC, V. No lunch Sat.*

International

$$$ ✗ **Coco Loco.** One of the hot spots in the "Pennsylvania Quarter" area, Coco Loco's big draw is Mexican tapas, appetizer-size snacks of endless variety that are generally washed down with wine or beer. Favorites include shrimp stuffed with white cheese and wrapped in bacon, red snapper with coconut milk and plantains, and *chiles rellenos* (stuffed chilis) in a tomato-cream puree. If you're into serious meat-eating, try the Brazilian-style *churrasqueria*—a parade of skewered grilled meats that are brought to your table and sliced right onto your plate. Wednesday through Saturday night, half the restaurant becomes an upscale nightclub. ⊠ *810 7th St. NW,* ☎ *202/289–2626. AE, DC, MC, V. Closed Sun. No lunch Sat.*

$$$ ✗ **Gerard's Place.** With a main dining room strikingly colored in gray
★ and burnt umber, Gerard's Place concentrates on such fresh, intriguingly prepared entrées as poached lobster with a ginger, lime, and Sauternes sauce; venison served with dried fruits and pumpkin and beetroot purees; and seared tuna with black olives and roasted red peppers. Desserts like the chocolate tear, a teardrop-shaped flourless chocolate cake veined with raspberry, are exquisite. ⊠ *915 15th St. NW,* ☎ *202/737–4445. AE, MC, V. Closed Sun. No lunch Sat.*

$$$ ✗ **701 Pennsylvania Avenue.** An eclectic cuisine drawn from Italy, France, Asia, and the Americas graces the menu of sleek 701 Pennsylvania Avenue, where an elegant meal might begin with tuna tartar topped with caviar, progress to grilled salmon in a ginger-soy broth with sesame noodles, and finish with orange-chocolate mousse. The restaurant's Caviar Lounge offers choices ranging from beluga to Alaskan keta and over 20 types of vodka. The fixed-price pretheater dinner ($21.95) is popular; if you're attending a performance at the Shakespeare Theatre this is a convenient, upper-crust choice. ⊠ *701 Pennsylvania Ave. NW,* ☎ *202/393–0701. AE, DC, MC, V. No lunch weekends.*

Italian

$$$$ ✗ **Galileo.** A spacious, popular restaurant boasting homemade every-
★ thing, from bread sticks to mozzarella, Galileo, in the Adams-Morgan neighborhood, offers risotto, a long list of grilled fish, a game bird dish (such as quail, guinea hen, or woodcock), and at least one or two beef or veal dishes. Preparations are generally simple. For example, the veal chop might be served with mushroom-and-rosemary sauce, the beef with black-olive sauce and polenta. ⊠ *1110 21st St. NW,* ☎ *202/293–7191. AE, D, DC, MC, V. No lunch weekends.*

$$$ ✗ **i Ricchi.** An airy dining room decorated with terra-cotta tiles, cream-
★ colored archways, and floral frescoes, i Ricchi is priced for expense accounts and remains a favorite of critics and upscale crowds for its earthy cuisine from the Northern Italian province of Tuscany. The spring/summer menu includes such offerings as rolled pork and rabbit roasted in wine and fresh herbs, and skewered shrimp; the fall/winter bill of fare brings grilled lamb chops, thick soups, and sautéed beef fillet. But whatever the calendar says, I Ricchi always feels like spring. ⊠ *1220 19th St. NW,* ☎ *202/835–0459. AE, DC, MC, V. Closed Sun. No lunch Sat.*

$$ ✗ **Notte Luna.** A glitzy power-lunch spot with a dramatic neon-accented black ceiling, Notte Luna has an open kitchen with a wood-burning pizza oven. Italian-restaurant staples of pasta, pizza, and veal dishes are on the menu, but with unexpected twists. You can order cracker-thin pizza topped with lamb sausage or pasta with grilled salmon. All meals start with crisp bread, cheese spread, and olives. Desserts, such as fresh berries or tiramisù, are always a treat. ⊠ *809 15th St. NW,* ☎ *202/408–9500. AE, MC, V. Closed Sun. No lunch Sat.*

$$ ✕ **Primi Piatti.** A meal at Primi Piatti—at the D.C. branch, at least—is like a rush-hour taxi ride in Rome: The crowds and the noise are overwhelming, but you'll never forget the trip. Here you get the real thing—not Americanized Italian—and the food is light and healthful to boot. Several kinds of fish—tuna with raisins and pine nuts is one preparation—as well as lamb and veal chops, sizzle each day on a wood-burning grill. Meats, also cooked on a rotisserie, are succulent; pastas and pizzas are rewarding, too. ✉ *2013 I St. NW,* ☎ *202/223–3600;* ✉ *8045 Leesburg Pike, Vienna, VA,* ☎ *703/893–0300. AE, DC, MC, V. No lunch weekends.*

Moroccan

$$ ✕ **Marrakesh.** A happy surprise is Marrakesh, a bit of Morocco in a part of the city better known for auto-supply shops. The menu is a fixed-price ($22) feast shared by everyone at your table and eaten without silverware (flatbread, served with the meal, is used as a scoop). Appetizers consist of a platter of three salads followed by *b'stella,* a chicken version of Morocco's traditional pigeon pie. For the first main course, choose from several chicken preparations. A beef or lamb dish is served next, followed by vegetable couscous, fresh fruit, mint tea, and pastries. Belly dancers put on a nightly show. Alcoholic drinks can really drive up the tab. ✉ *617 New York Ave. NW,* ☎ *202/393–9393. Reservations essential. No credit cards. No lunch.*

New American

$$$ ✕ **Occidental Grill.** In the stately Willard Hotel complex, the popular Occidental Grill offers innovative and artful dishes, attentive service, and photos of politicians past and present. Grilled options include poultry, steak, and fish; tuna, for instance, might be marinated in fresh herbs and garlic and served with a tomato *tapenade,* a condiment made with capers, anchovies, and olives. Salads and sandwiches are also available. ✉ *1475 Pennsylvania Ave. NW,* ☎ *202/783–1475. AE, DC, MC, V.*

$$–$$$ ✕ **Kinkead's.** Kinkead's multichambered dining room includes a downstairs pub with American-style tapas (a '90s buzzword when it comes to hors d'oeuvres) and other inexpensive fare. Upstairs, watch Kinkead and company turn out grilled dishes (the squid is scrumptious) with garden salsas, Southwest-inspired appetizers and seafood soups, and savory meat and fowl dishes. For a refreshing finish, the light cool tang of home-made sorbet is just the thing. ✉ *2000 Pennsylvania Ave. NW,* ☎ *202/296–7700. AE, DC, MC, V.*

South American

$$ ✕ **Café Atlántico.** Appetizers include conch fritters with tomato-mango ★   sauce and fresh guacamole made tableside by your waiter. Among the specialties are crepes with *cuitlacoche* (a rare truffle-like mushroom only found in South American cornfields) and Argentine grilled beef with garlicky *chimichurri* sauce. The flavorful feijoada salad features the same ingredients as the traditional Brazilian meat stew of the same name—minus the meat. Service is friendly and helpful. ✉ *8th and E Sts. NW,* ☎ *202/393–0812. Reservations not accepted. AE, D, DC, MC, V. No lunch weekends.*

Southern

$$–$$$ ✕ **Georgia Brown's.** The airy, curving dining room has white honeycomb windows and an unusual ceiling ornamentation of bronze ribbons. An elegant "New South" eatery, Georgia Brown's serves shrimp Carolina-style (with the head on and steaming grits on the side), grilled salmon and smoked-bacon green beans, beef tenderloin medallions with a bourbon-pecan sauce, and a thick rich she-crab soup. Fried green tomatoes, now part of the nation's culinary consciousness thanks to the 1991 movie of that name, are given the gourmet treatment.⊠ *950 15th St. NW,* ☎ *202/393–4499. AE, DC, MC, V. No lunch Sat.*

Southwestern/Tex-Mex

$$$ ✕ **Red Sage.** Near the White House is an upscale rancher's delight,
★ roping in the likes of George Bush and Bill Clinton for the tony chow. The multimillion-dollar decor has a barbed-wire-and-lizard theme and a pseudo-adobe warren of dining rooms. Upstairs is the chili bar and café, where thrifty trendsetters can enjoy the comparatively inexpensive sandwiches and appetizers. Downstairs, owner Mark Miller's Berkeley-Santa Fe background surfaces in elaborate, artful presentations such as grilled duck breast with *habanero* pepper and fig sausage, spicy lamb chops with wild-mushroom tamale, and red chili risotto—chilis, in fact, are everywhere. The limited selection of entrées includes lighter options as well. ⊠ *605 14th St. NW,* ☎ *202/638–4444. AE, D, DC, MC, V. No lunch Sun.*

Spanish

$$$ ✕ **Taberna del Alabardero.** The Spanish spoken in Taberna del Alabardero is a regal Castilian that matches the formal dining room and high-class service. Start with such appetizer-like tapas as fried calamari, proceed to a hefty bowl of gazpacho soup, and venture on to authentic paella, seafood casseroles, and elegant Spanish country dishes. The plush Old World decor and handsome bar create a romantic atmosphere. The clientele is similarly well-heeled and cosmopolitan. ⊠ *1776 I St. NW (entrance on 18th St.),* ☎ *202/429–2200. AE, D, DC, MC, V. Closed Sun. No lunch Sat.*

$$ ✕ **Jaleo.** A lively Spanish bistro, Jaleo encourages you to make a meal
★ out of its long list of hot and cold tapas snacks, although such entrées as grilled fish, seafood stew, and paella—which comes in three different versions—are just as tasty (and equally filling). Highlights of the appetizer-sized tapas are *gambas al ajillo* (sautéed garlic shrimp), fried potatoes with spicy tomato sauce, and *pinchitos* (a skewer of grilled chorizo) with garlic mashed potatoes. For dessert, don't miss the crisp and buttery apple charlotte and the not-too-tart, not-too-sweet lemon tart. ⊠ *480 7th St. NW,* ☎ *202/628–7949. AE, D, MC, V.*

Dupont Circle

Chinese

$$ ✕ **City Lights of China.** The Art Deco City Lights of China consistently
★ makes the top restaurant critics' lists every year. The traditional Chinese fare is excellent. Less common specialties are deftly cooked as well, among them lamb in a tangy peppery sauce and shark's fin soup. The mint green booths and elegant silk flower arrangements conjure up breezy spring days, even in the midst of a frenzied dinner rush. The delicious jumbo shrimp with spicy salt is baked in its shell before being quickly stirfried with ginger and spices. Seafood items tend to be especially pricy, but there are plenty of reasonably priced options on this extensive menu. ⊠ *1731 Connecticut Ave., NW,* ☎ *202/265-6688. AE, D, DC, MC, V.*

Italian

$$$ ✕ **Obelisk.** Obelisk's attractions are eclectic Italian cuisine and a small, fixed-price menu ($38) that includes both traditional dishes and chef Peter Pastan's imaginative innovations. Usually offered are one meat, one fish, and one poultry entrée. The meat is likely to be lamb, with garlic and sage or perhaps anchovies; fish might be a pompano stuffed with bay leaves; a typical poultry selection is the hardly typical pigeon with chanterelles. The minimally decorated dining room is tiny, with

tables so closely spaced that even whispers can be overheard. ⊠ *2029 P St. NW,* ☎ *202/872–1180. DC, MC, V. Closed Sun. No lunch.*

$$$ ✕ **Vincenzo al Sole.** Here's something rather rare: a restaurant that has
★ lowered its prices while continuing to offer many of the same dishes with no change in quality. The emphasis is on simply prepared seafood dishes such as *merluzzo alla calabrese* (roasted cod with capers and olives) and *branzino al salmoriglio* (grilled rockfish with oregano). The menu also includes meat and game dishes such as roast duck with polenta. Part of the dining room is in an airy, glass-roof courtyard. ⊠ *1606 20th St. NW,* ☎ *202/667–0047. AE, DC, MC, V. Closed Sun. No lunch Sat.*

$ ✕ **Pizzeria Paradiso.** Sharing a kitchen with the elite Italian restaurant Obelisk (☞ *above*), the petite Pizzeria Paradiso sticks to crowd-pleasing basics: pizzas, *panini* (sandwiches stuffed with Italian cured ham, sundried tomatoes and basil, or other ingredients) salads, and desserts. Although the standard pizza is satisfying, you can enliven things by ordering it with fresh buffalo mozzarella or unusual toppings such as potatoes, capers, and mussels. The sandwiches are assembled with homemade focaccia; gelato, an intensely flavored Italian ice cream, is also a house specialty. The trompe l'oeil ceiling adds space and light to a simple interior. ⊠ *2029 P St. NW,* ☎ *202/223–1245. DC, MC, V.*

Japanese

$$ ✕ **Café Japone.** Café Japone's dark interior has an alternative-scene edge. On some weeknights you're likely to find Japanese businessmen and students, happy from good food and bottles of hot sake, belting out the latest Asian pop songs while a karaoke sound system provides musical backup. On Wednesday and Friday nights, there's a live jazz band and a mellower crowd. The sushi is not a rave but its good. Steamed wontons and crispy fried *age dofu* (tofu in a soy broth) are tasty appetizers. Even nonvegetarians will enjoy the vegetable sushi plate; it pleases the eye as well as the palate and is like receiving a series of brightly colored presents wrapped in seaweed ribbon. ⊠ *2032 P St. NW,* ☎ *202/223–1573. AE, MC, V. No lunch.*

Middle Eastern

$ ✕ **Skewers/Café Luna.** As the name implies, the focus at Skewers is on kebabs, here served with almond-flaked rice or pasta. Lamb with eggplant and chicken with roasted pepper are the most popular variations, but vegetable kebabs and skewers of filet mignon and shrimp are equally tasty. With nearly 20 choices, the appetizer selection is huge. If the restaurant is too crowded, you can enjoy the cheap California eats (shrimp and avocado salad, mozzarella and tomato sandwiches, vegetable lasagna—except for salads, most offerings have Italian origins) downstairs at Café Luna (☎ 202/387–4005) or the reading room-coffeehouse upstairs at Luna Books (☎ 202/332–2543). ⊠ *1633 P St. NW,* ☎ *202/387–7400. AE, DC, MC, V.*

New American

$$$ ✕ **Nora.** Although it bills itself as an "organic restaurant," Nora is no collective-run juice bar. The food is sophisticated and attractive, like the quilt-decorated dining room. A good starter might be grilled marinated squid with orange cherry tomatoes and black olives. Entrées—roast monkfish with artichoke broth; rack of lamb with roast peppers, asparagus, and Swiss chard; and couscous risotto topped with wild mushrooms, spinach, and peppers, to name some past favorites—exemplify the chef's emphasis on well-balanced, complex ingredients. Chocolate soufflé cake with passion fruit ice cream and pear-and-blueberry cobbler with praline ice cream are among the sublime desserts. You may also want to try chef Nora Pouillon's Asia Nora in the West End. ⊠

2213 M St. NW, ☎ 202/797–4860; ✉ 2132 Florida Ave. NW, ☎ 202/462–5143. MC, V. Closed Sun. No lunch.

$$$ ✕ **Tabard Inn.** Named after the resting house in Chaucer's *Canterbury Tales*, the Tabard Inn has an old European feel: fading portraits, a mahogany-paneled main lounge, doilies, an upright piano. Similarly, the Tabard's New American cuisine mixes French, American, and other culinary styles. Reflecting the '60s values of its baby boomer clientele, produce and meat are free of hormones and pesticides. Appetizers have included shrimp-and-scallop cakes with chili-basil mayonnaise, and saffron lingine in a tomato-pepper fumet with salmon, oysters, and monkfish is a good example of a colorful main course. The strongest dishes are slightly dressed up classics like the grilled New York strip steak and sauteed soft shell crabs over wilted greens. For dessert warm strawberry-rhubarb crisp or white-chocolate cheesecake end dinner on a pleasing note. ✉ *1739 N St. NW, ☎ 202/833–2668. MC, V.*

South American/Spanish

$$ ✕ **Lauriol Plaza.** A charming corner enclave in upper Dupont Circle, Lauriol Plaza serves Latin American and Spanish dishes—seviche, paella, and so on—in winning combinations. Such rustic entrées as Cuban-style pork and *lomo saltado* (Peruvian-style strip steak with onions, tomatoes and fiery jalapeño peppers) are specialties. The simply decorated dining room, with white tablecloths and white walls enlivened by gilt-framed paintings, can get noisy; the alfresco terrace is preferable in good weather. ✉ *1801 18th St. NW, ☎ 202/387–0035. Reservations not accepted. AE, D, DC, MC, V.*

Thai

$–$$ ✕ **Sala Thai.** Who says Thai food has to be scalp-sweating hot? Sala Thai will make the food as spicy as you wish, but the chef is interested in flavor, not fire. Among the subtly seasoned offerings are *panang goong* (shrimp in curry-peanut sauce), chicken sautéed with ginger and pineapple, and flounder with a choice of four sauces. Mirrored walls and soft lights soften the ambience of this small downstairs dining room. ✉ *2016 P St. NW, ☎ 202/872–1144. AE, DC, MC, V.*

Georgetown/West End

American

$$$$ ✕ **Morton's of Chicago.** A national steak house chain that claims to serve the country's best beef, Morton's is always jumping, and it's certainly not the tacky vinyl-boothed dining room that keeps it busy. In the classic steak house tradition, Morton's emphasizes quantity as well as quality. The New York strip and porterhouse steaks, two of the most popular offerings, are well over a pound each. For diners with even larger appetites (or those sharing), there's a 3-pound porterhouse. Morton's menu also includes lamb, veal, chicken, lobster, and grilled fish. ✉ *3251 Prospect St., ☎ 202/342–6258. No lunch. ✉ 8075 Leesburg Pike, Vienna, VA, ☎ 703/883–0800. No lunch weekends. AE, DC, MC, V.*

$ ✕ **Georgetown Café.** With its unpretentious decor, cheap prices, and eclectic, lowbrow menu, the Georgetown Café is a bit of a neighborhood oddball. Students and blue-collar types are known to frequent the café for its offering of pizzas, gyros, and home-style American favorites like baked chicken and mashed potatoes. As one of D.C.'s few 24-hour operations, the Georgetown Café is also good for a late-night snack. ✉ *1523 Wisconsin Ave. ☎ 202/333–0215. D, MC, V.*

Argentine

$$ ✕ **Las Pampas.** Grilled fresh fish and a smattering of Tex-Mex staples supplement the traditional Argentine menu, which reflects that coun-

try's love of beef and its Continental heritage. Beef is fresh, not aged, and cooked over a special grill that simulates charcoal heat; the result is a firm-textured steak with a crusty surface and a juicy interior. New York strip steak and filet mignon are available from the grill, but the preferred choice is the *churrasco*, a special Argentine cut. ✉ *3291 M St. NW*, ☎ *202/333–5151. AE, DC, MC, V.*

Caribbean

$$ ✕ **Hibiscus Café.** African masks and multi-colored neon accents hang
★ from the ceiling of the modish restaurant, where weekend crowds are drawn by spicy jerk chicken, such blackened fish as grouper, shrimp curry, and flavorful soups (try the butternut-ginger bisque). Perfectly fried calamari and a generous piece of shark in a pocket of fried bread are paired with ginger sauce or tangy pineapple chutney to make delectable starters. Desserts—banana mousse with rum sauce, sweet potato-and-mango crumb pie—favor island fruits. The passion fruit punch is potent. Outdoor seating is available. ✉ *3401 K St. NW*, ☎ *202/965–7170. AE, D, MC, V. No lunch Sat., no dinner Sun. or Mon.*

French

$$$ ✕ **La Chaumière.** A favorite of Washingtonians seeking an escape from the hurly-burly of Georgetown, La Chaumière has the rustic charm of a French country inn, particularly during the winter, when its central stone fireplace warms the room. Fish stew, mussels, and scallops are on the regular menu, and there is usually a grilled fish special. The restaurant also has a devoted following for its meat dishes, which include such hard-to-find entrées as venison. Many local diners plan their meals around La Chaumière's rotating specials, particularly the couscous on Wednesday and the tasty boiled stew known as cassoulet on Thursday. ✉ *2813 M St. NW*, ☎ *202/338–1784. Reservations essential. AE, DC, MC, V. Closed Sun. No lunch Sat.*

$$ ✕ **Bistro Français.** Washington's chefs head for Bistro Français for the minute steak maître d'hôtel or the sirloin with herb butter. Among amateur eaters the big draw is the rotisserie chicken. Daily specials may include *suprême* of salmon with broccoli mousse and beurre blanc. The restaurant is divided into two parts—the café side and the more formal dining room; the café menu includes sandwiches and omelets in addition to entrées. The Bistro also offers $11.95 fixed-price lunches and $16.95 early and late-night dinner specials. It stays open until 3 AM Sunday–Thursday, 4 AM Friday and Saturday. ✉ *3128 M St. NW*, ☎ *202/338–3830. AE, DC, MC, V.*

Indian

$$ ✕ **Aditi.** Aditi's two-story dining room—with its burgundy carpets and chairs and pale, mint-colored walls with brass sconces—seems too elegant for a moderately priced Indian restaurant. The first floor is small, with a dramatic staircase leading to a larger room with windows that overlook the busy street. Tandoori and curry dishes are expertly prepared and, for those who like their Indian food on the mild side, not aggressively spiced; if you want your food spicy request it. Rice *biryani* entrées are good for lighter appetites. ✉ *3299 M St. NW*, ☎ *202/625–6825. AE, DC, MC, V.*

Indonesian

$$ ✕ **Sarinah Satay House.** A green door opens onto stairs that lead
★ down, then up and out into a lush, enclosed garden with real trees growing through the ceiling. Carved monkeys, parrots, and puppets add to the setting, where batik-clad waiters offer serenely unrushed service. The food at Sarinah Satay House is exquisite. Potato croquettes and the traditional *loempia* and *resoles* (crisp and soft spring rolls) come with a tangy, chili-spiked peanut dipping sauce, while the perfectly grilled

chicken satay is accompanied by a smoky-sweet peanut dip. At under $10, the combination *nasi rames*—chicken in coconut sauce, beef skewers, and spicy green beans with rice—is a bargain. ⊠ *1338 Wisconsin Ave. NW,* ☎ *202/337–2955. AE, D, DC, MC, V. Closed Mon. No lunch Sun.*

New American

$$$ ✕ **Citronelle.** The essence of California chic, Citronelle's glass-front
★ kitchen allows diners to see all the action as chefs scurry to and fro, creating culinary masterpieces. In an appetizer "tart" thinly sliced grilled scallops rest like pale white coins on puff pastry prettily surrounded by a tomato vinagrette. Loin of venison is served with an endive tart and garnished with dried apples. Leek-encrusted salmon steak is topped by a crisp fried-potato lattice. Desserts are equally luscious. The crunchy napoleon—layers of carmelized filo dough between creamy vanilla custard—is drizzled with butterscotch and dark chocolate. The hazelnut chocolate bar is another winner. A special chef's table gives lucky diners an inside view for a fixed price of $85. ⊠ *3000 M St. NW,* ☎ *202/625–2150. AE, DC, MC, V.*

$$$ ✕ **River Club.** Until someone invents a time machine, there is no better way to experience the Big Band era than to take a trip to the River Club, an Art Deco extravaganza in an out-of-the-way part of Georgetown. Decorated in ebony, silver, neon, and marble, the River Club is in fact a nightclub with a disc jockey who plays everything from '30s and '40s music to contemporary dance music; there's live music Wednesday, Thursday, and Saturday. Start your meal with Chinese smoked lobster; finish with layered white and dark chocolate mousse. Or stick with caviar and champagne. ⊠ *3223 K St. NW,* ☎ *202/333–8118. Jacket and tie. AE, DC, MC, V. Closed Mon. and Tues. No lunch.*

U Street

American

$ ✕ **Ben's Chili Bowl.** Long before U Street became a center of hipness, Ben's was offering patrons chili on hot dogs, chili on smoked sausages, chili on burgers, and chili just about any other way people like it. With its long faux-marble bar and shiny red-vinyl stools, it doesn't look like it has changed much. One concession to modern times is that Ben's offers turkey and vegetarian burgers, which some people find tastier than beef burgers, even though all three are cooked to the same deliciously unhealthy perfection on the grill. Add some cheese fries for a dollar more and you'll be in cholesterol heaven. Ben's is usually open until 2 or 3 AM. ⊠ *1213 U St. NW,* ☎ *202/667–0909. No credit cards.*

$ ✕ **Polly's Café.** Tables can be hard to come by on weekend nights at Polly's Café, a cozy U Street oasis with a fireplace. That's when locals come to swill beer, eat better-than-average bar food (burgers, nachos, chicken wings), and enjoy jukebox favorites from youth cultures of every era. A savory portobello mushroom "steak," crisp calamari, and Polly's own ample house salad are popular. At $6.50, Polly's hearty brunch is one of Washington's best values. ⊠ *1342 U Street NW,* ☎ *202/265–8385. D, DC, MC, V. No lunch weekdays.*

Caribbean

$–$$ ✕ **Mango's.** Wood tables washed in bold primary colors, high ceilings, artsy metalwork, and wall-size paintings enhance the pulsing energy of Mango's, an ultra-hip addition to U Street. The Caribbean-influenced fare is a fusion of many different ethnic cooking styles. Smoky caesar salad comes with plantain chips instead of croutons; coconut curried shrimp is paired with gingered vegetables. Other specialties include spicy pumpkin soup and orange-ginger chicken wings. Much of the produce is organically grown at a local farm. On weekend nights an early morning breakfast is served for exhausted clubhoppers. ✉ *2017 14th St. NW,* ☎ *202/332–2104. AE, MC, V. Closed Mon.*

International

$ ✗ **Café Nema.** The Café Nema's eclectic menu combines Somali, North African, and Middle Eastern cuisines. Entrées are simple but flavorful. Grilled chicken, lamb and beef kabobs, and salmon steak are paired with fresh vegetables and an outstanding curried Basmati rice pilaf that has bits of carmelized onion, whole cloves and raisins mixed in. The chef gives such appetizers as *sambousa* (flaky fried triangles of dough filled with curried vegetables or meat), hummus, and *baba ganoush* a distinct touch, making them taste slightly different (and better) from what similar restaurants offer. There's also a good selection of pastas, salads, and sandwiches. At $3.00, the generous, made-to-order falafel sandwich may well be the best bargain in the city. ✉ *1334 U St. NW,* ☎ *202/667–3215. AE, D, DC, MC, V.*

Italian

$$ ✗ **Coppi's Restaurant.** An Italian bicycling motif permeates popular Coppi's, from the posters and gear that hang on the walls down to the monogrammed racing shirts of the waitstaff. The wood-oven-baked pizzas are delicious and adventurous. When it appears as a special, the pizza *ai funghi di bosco* (white oysters, shiitake, and cremini mushrooms with Italian parsley, parmesan, olive oil and garlic) is a must. ✉ *1414 U St. NW,* ☎ *202/319–7773. AE, D, MC, V. No lunch.*

Maryland/Virginia Suburbs

Afghani

$$ ✗ **Panjshir.** Panjshir's Falls Church location favors a plush red and dark-wood decor, the Vienna branch is more into pinks. But both serve succulent kebabs of beef, lamb, and chicken, as well as fragrant stews (with and without meat) over impeccably cooked rice. Entrées come with Afghan salad (with a Green Goddess-like dressing) and hearty bread. ✉ *924 W. Broad St., Falls Church, VA,* ☎ *703/536–4566;* ✉ *224 Maple Ave. W, Vienna, VA,* ☎ *703/281–4183. AE, DC, MC, V. No lunch Sun.*

African

$ ✗ **Casa Africana.** Casa Africana specializes in food from the small West African country of Togo. Black-eyed peas are simmered in a gingery tomato sauce. Smoked bluefish is added to fresh salads. Melon-seed stew and chicken cooked in peanut sauce are also winners. Seafood is a specialty and comes fried, grilled, and stewed in a variety of spicy sauces. The restaurant also features an extensive list of meatless appetizers and side dishes, among them fried cassava, *klako* (plantain nuggets), and *ablo* (a steamed bread unique to Togo). Be sure to try the non-alcoholic, house-made ginger beer—it has a definite kick. ✉ *9411 Bonifant St., Silver Spring, MD,* ☎ *301/585–5659. AE, DC, MC, V. Closed Mon.*

American

$ ✗ **Tastee Diner.** The Tastees in Bethesda and Silver Springs, Maryland, are part of a dying breed in the Washington region. As 24-hour diners go, both are classics and sentimental favorites among many area residents. The warm feelings have less to do with the food than with the sense of old-fashioned community each place invokes. Meat loaf or a sandwich with coffee and pie run less than $5. Students and others on low budgets (or little sleep) ignore the dust, and relish the coffee, which flows endlessly. ✉ *7731 Woodmont Ave., Bethesda,*

MD, ☎ 301/652–3970. *Reservations not accepted. MC, V.* ⊠ *8516 Georgia Ave., Silver Spring, MD,* ☎ *301/589–8171. Reservations not accepted.*

Barbecue
$ ✗ **Red, Hot and Blue.** A chain with three D.C.-area locations, Red, Hot and Blue is a Memphis-style barbecue joint known for its ribs. They come "wet"—with sauce—or, when simply smoked, "dry." The delicious pulled-meat sandwiches and low prices lure hungry crowds. ⊠ *1120 19th St. NW,* ☎ *202/466–6731. Reservations not accepted. AE, MC, V.* ⊠ *1600 Wilson Blvd., Arlington, VA,* ☎ *703/276–7427. Reservations not accepted. AE, MC, V.* ⊠ *16811 Crabbs Branch Way, Gaithersburg, MD,* ☎ *301/948–7333. Reservations not accepted. MC, V.*

Italian
$$ ✗ **Paolo's.** Complimentary homemade bread sticks get meals at Paolo's off to a good crunchy start. Wise choices to follow might be the "beggar's purse" filled with wild mushrooms, spinach, and Taleggio cheese, or the grilled sea scallops. Then two of you can split a pizza from the wood-burning oven, with toppings that range from roasted vegetables to grilled chicken to rock shrimp scampi. Grilled meat entrées and a variety of pasta dishes (some low-fat) are also available. The Georgetown location is the noisiest. ⊠ *1801 Rockville Pike, Rockville, MD,* ☎ *301/984–2211;* ⊠ *11898 Market St., Reston, VA,* ☎ *703/318–8920;* ⊠ *1303 Wisconsin Ave. NW,* ☎ *202/333–7353. AE, DC, MC, V.*

New American
$$$$ ✗ **Inn at Little Washington.** The 90-minute drive takes you past rolling
★   hills and small farms in the Virginia countryside. Entering the inn, decorated like a luxurious English country manor, is like being swept into a Merchant-Ivory film. Dinner without wine costs $78 Sunday through Thursday, slightly more on weekends. After a first course of tiny canapes an excellent soup follows, perhaps chilled fruit or creamy leek. Trout smoked over applewood might come next, or medallions of veal with Virginia country ham and wild mushrooms, or roast venison with black currants and tart greens. Beautifully choreographed service makes the evening flow seamlessly. Desserts, which on warm evenings can be enjoyed in the garden, are fanciful and elegant. ⊠ *Middle and Main Sts., Washington, VA,* ☎ *540/675–3800. MC, V. Reservations essential. Closed Tues. except in May and Oct.*

Southwestern
$$ ✗ **Cottonwood Café.** As at its Boston counterpart, the stylish Cottonwood Café offers an innovative blend of Santa Fe, Texas, and New American dishes. The blue-cornmeal calamari appetizer is a must. Entrées are generous. Try "fire and spice" linguini with andouille sausage and shrimp, or "Barbacoa"—grilled chicken and shrimp marinated in barbecue sauce with baked banana, cheese, and a spicy sauce. ⊠ *4844 Cordell Ave., Bethesda, MD,* ☎ *301/656–4844. AE, DC, MC, V. No lunch Sun.*

$$ ✗ **Rio Grande Café.** Grilled quail, goat dishes (on Thursday), and other upscale Tex-Mex fare are worth braving Rio Grande's crowds. Crates of Mexican beer stacked against the walls add atmosphere, as does a perpetual-motion tortilla machine. ⊠ *4919 Fairmont Ave., Bethesda, MD,* ☎ *301/656–2981;* ⊠ *4301 N. Fairfax Dr., Arlington, VA,* ☎ *703/528–3131;* ⊠ *1827 Library St., Reston, VA,* ☎ *703/904–0703. AE, D, DC, MC, V.*

Spanish

$$ ✕ **Andalucia.** *Zarzuela*, a seafood stew, is one of Andalucia's traditional Spanish specialties. The spartan Rockville location (hidden in an office-and-shopping strip) was popular enough to spawn the more formally furnished Bethesda branch, which features a full tapas bar and a tempting dessert cart. Classical Spanish guitarists can be heard at both locations on weeknights. ⊠ *12300 Wilkins Ave., Rockville, MD,* ☎ *301/770–1880. AE, MC, V. Closed Mon.* ⊠ *4931 Elm St., Bethesda, MD,* ☎ *301/907–0052. AE, MC, V.*

Vietnamese

$ ✕ **Café Dalat.** In the heart of Arlington's "Little Saigon," Café Dalat offers incredibly low priced Vietnamese specialties in a far-from-fancy but clean and pleasant eatery.The service is known for an efficiency that nears light-speed. The lovely candy-cane shrimp dish could inspire a trip to Southeast Asia. *Da ram gung* is a sinus-clearing dish of simmered chicken and ginger. All the appetizers are winners, in particular the crispy spring rolls and the tangy Vietnamese shrimp salad in lemon vinaigrette. ⊠ *3143 Wilson Blvd., Arlington, VA,* ☎ *703/276–0935. MC, V.*

$ ✕ **Little Viet Garden/Queen Bee.** Although nearby Queen Bee (⊠ 3181 Wilson Blvd., ☎ 703/527–3444) has longer lines, Little Viet Garden's patrons swear by its crisp spring rolls; tasty beef-broth-and-glass-noodle soups; crispy crepes stuffed with chicken, shrimp, bean sprouts, and green onion; and beef tips and potato stir-fried with onion in a smoky sauce. In warm months reserve a table on the outdoor terrace bordered by a flowerbox-lined white fence. ⊠ *3012 Wilson Blvd., Arlington, VA,* ☎ *703/522–9686. AE, D, DC, MC, V.*

$ ✕ **Pho 75.** To refer to Pho 75's product as mere soup would be a disservice to the delightful procession of flavors that come with every mouthful—but that is essentially what pho is: a Hanoi-style beef soup packed with noodles and thinly sliced pieces of meat that are cooked in seconds by the steaming broth. A plate of fresh bean sprouts, mint leaves, lemon and green chilies comes with every order so that you may spice your feast-in-a-bowl as you wish. Pho comes in either a large ($4.95) or small ($4.25) bowl, a remarkable bargain either way. ⊠ *1711 Wilson Blvd., Arlington, VA,* ☎ *703/525–7355;* ⊠ *3103 Graham Rd., Ste. B, Falls Church, VA,* ☎ *703/204–1490;* ⊠ *1510 University Blvd., East Langley Park, MD,* ☎ *301/434–7844. No credit cards.*

5 Lodging

VISITORS WHO PLAN to spend the night, a week, or a month in D.C. will find a large variety of accommodations from which to choose. Hostelries include grand hotels with glorious histories, quiet Victorian inns, the hotel and motel chains common to every American city, and small independently operated hotels that offer little more than good location, a smile, and a comfortable, clean place to lay your head.

By Jan Ziegler

Updated by
Nancy Ryder

Because Washington is an international city, nearly all hotel staffs are multilingual. All hotels in the $$$ and $$$$ categories have concierges; some in the $$ group do, too. All the hotels we list are air-conditioned. All the large hotels and many of the smaller ones offer meeting facilities and special teleconferencing features for business travelers, ranging from state-of-the-art equipment to modest conference rooms with outside catering. Nearly all the finer hotels have superb restaurants whose traditionally high prices are almost completely justified.

Not all the city's hotels are included here; there are simply too many to list. Most of the major chains have properties in desirable locations throughout town and in the near suburbs. For a complete listing of hotels in the area, contact the Washington, D.C., Convention and Visitors Association (✉ 1212 New York Ave. NW, Washington, DC 20005, ☎ 202/789–7000). **Capitol Reservations** books rooms at more than 70 better hotels in good locations at rates 20%–40% off (☎ 202/452–1270 or 800/847–4832 from 9 to 6 weekdays); the company also sells packages with tours and meals. **Washington D.C. Accommodations** will book rooms in any hotel in town, with discounts of 20%–40% at about 40 locations (☎ 202/289–2220 or 800/554–2220 from 9 to 5 weekdays).

Reservations are crucial. Hotels are often full of conventioneers, politicians in transit, or families and school groups in search of cherry blossoms and monuments. If you're interested in visiting Washington at a calmer time—and if you can stand tropical weather—come in July or August, during the congressional recess. You may not spot many VIPs, but hotels will have more rooms to offer at lower rates, and you'll be able to relax. (August, however, is the busiest season for the Washington International Youth Hostel, so budget travelers should seek alternatives at this time.) Rates often drop in late December and January, too. Keep in mind also that rates can be significantly lower if they are part of a group, corporate, or weekend package. Also, some of the older hotels have a few smaller rooms that rent for prices in a lower category. It's always worth a call to check for special rates.

The hotel reviews here are grouped within neighborhoods according to price. Hotels' parking fees range from $5 to $15 a night, depending on how close to downtown you are.

CATEGORY	COST*
$$$$	over $190
$$$	$145–$190
$$	$100–$145
$	under $100

*All prices are for a standard double room, excluding room tax (13% in DC, 12% in MD, and 9.75% in VA) and $1.50 per night occupancy tax.

Bed-and-Breakfasts

Bed 'n' Breakfast Accommodations Ltd. of Washington, D.C. To find reasonably priced accommodations in small guest houses and private homes, this is a good source. ⊠ *Box 12011, Washington, DC 20005,* ☎ *202/328–3510.*

Bed and Breakfast League, Ltd. Here's a good place to write to for lovers of B&Bs seeking small guest houses and private homes with accommodations price to please. ⊠ *Box 9490, Washington, D.C. 20016-9490.*

Fodor's new toll-free lodging reservations hot line. Reserve a room in any property listed in Fodor's Washington, D.C. or any other Fodor's guide to any destination in the U.S. or the world by calling 1–800– FODORS–1 or 1–800/363–6771; 0800–89–1030 in Great Britain; 0014/800–12–8271 in Australia; or 1800–55–9101 in Ireland.

Capitol Hill

$$$$ ⊞ **Hyatt Regency on Capitol Hill.** Close to Union Station and the Mall, the elegant 11-story Hyatt Regency is a favorite of vacationing families and businesspeople. It contains a spectacular garden atrium with high-tech edges for which Hyatts are renowned. Suites on the south side have a view of the Capitol dome just a few blocks away, as does the rooftop Capitol View Club restaurant, which serves rack of lamb with coarse mustard crust and smoked Norwegian salmon with corn waffle, caviar, and cream, among other tempting staples. The 8,000-square-foot health club includes a glass-enclosed, 43-foot-long heated pool and open-air sun deck. ⊠ *400 New Jersey Ave. NW, 20001,* ☎ *202/737–1234 or 800/233–1234,* 𝗙𝗔𝗫 *202/393–5773. 834 rooms, 31 suites. 2 restaurants, 2 bars, room service, pool, health club, parking (fee). AE, DC, MC, V.*

$$$$ ⊞ **Washington Court.** Washington Court is one of the few luxury hotels in D.C. where three terraced tiers of polished steps leading to a skylit atrium make a truly grand entrance possible. The hotel shares its view of the Capitol with the Hyatt and others on the same street. ⊠ *525 New Jersey Ave. NW, 20001,* ☎ *202/628–2100 or 800/321– 3010,* 𝗙𝗔𝗫 *202/737–2641. 250 rooms, 15 suites. Restaurant, piano bar, room service, health club, parking (fee). AE, DC, MC, V.*

$$$ ⊞ **Phoenix Park Hotel.** Named after an historic park in Dublin, the Phoenix Park calls itself "the center of Irish hospitality in America"; it showcases the best the Emerald Isle has to offer. Near Union Station and only four blocks from the Capitol, the posh high-rise hostelry has an Irish club theme and is home to the Dubliner, one of Washington's best bars; leather, wood paneling, and leaded glass re-create the ambience of 18th-century Irish gentry. In warm weather it's open for alfresco dining; Irish entertainers perform nightly. The Powerscourt Restaurant, named after an Irish castle, is a favorite among Washington powerbrokers for its popular Celtic-Continental fare. A $23 million renovation in progress will add more than 70 new guest rooms and health club. ⊠ *520 N. Capitol St. NW, 20001,* ☎ *202/638–6900 or 800/824–5419,* 𝗙𝗔𝗫 *202/393–3236. 87 rooms, 3 penthouse suites. 2 restaurants, access to health club, laundry service, parking (fee). AE, DC, MC, V.*

$$ ⊞ **Bellevue Hotel.** The charming Bellevue Hotel has been in business since 1929, the year of the stock market crash. Its public rooms on the main floor have balconies and are modeled after great halls in manor houses of yore. Accommodations here are standard modest-hotel fare— some in need of refurbishment—but the staff is friendly. The location is convenient, near Union Station and major Metro stations and within six blocks of the Supreme Court and the Smithsonian museums. ⊠ *15 E St. NW, 20001,* ☎ *202/638–0900 or 800/327–6667,* 𝗙𝗔𝗫 *202/638– 5132. 138 rooms, 2 suites. Restaurant, bar, room service, library, free parking. AE, DC, MC, V.*

American Inn of
Bethesda, **2**

ANA Hotel, **32**

Bellevue Hotel, **65**

Best Western Rosslyn
Westpark, **12**

Capital Hilton, **48**

Capitol Hill Suites, **67**

Carlton Hotel, **49**

Crystal City
Marriott, **16**

Days Inn
Connecticut Avenue, **5**

Doubletree, **33, 38**

Embassy Row
Hotel, **27**

Embassy Suites, **30**

Four Seasons
Hotel, **22**

Georgetown
Dutch Inn, **19**

Georgetown Inn, **10**

Georgetown Suites, **21**

Governor's House
Hotel, **41**

Grand Hyatt, **55**

Hay-Adams Hotel, **50**

Henley Park Hotel, **57**

Holiday Inn Capitol
Hill, **63**

Holiday Inn
Central, **44**

Holiday Inn Chevy
Chase, **3**

Holiday Inn
Conference Center at
College Park, **60**

Hotel Anthony, **39**

Hotel Sofitel
Washington, **26**

Hotel Tabard Inn, **42**

Hotel Washington, **51**

Howard Johnson's
Kennedy Center, **36**

Howard Johnson's
National Airport, **14**

Hyatt Regency
Bethesda, **1**

Hyatt Regency on
Capitol Hill, **62**

Jefferson Hotel, **45**

J.W. Marriott, **53**

Kalorama Guest
House, **23**

Key Bridge
Marriott, **11**

$$ ☷ **Capitol Hill Suites.** On a quiet street behind the Library of Congress, Capitol Hill Suites is an all-suite hotel whose proximity to the House office buildings means that it is often filled with visiting lobbyists when Congress is in session. Its location near the Capitol South Metro stop makes it ideal for getting a feel for residential and official Washington in one convenient place. ⊠ *200 C St. SE, 20003,* ☎ *202/543–6000 or 800/424–9165,* FAX *202/547–2608. 152 suites. Kitchens, access to health club, parking (fee). AE, DC, MC, V.*

$ ☷ **Holiday Inn Capitol Hill.** For clean, comfortable, low-priced rooms with high-priced views, this is the place. A good value for budget-minded travelers (some rooms are $79), the Holiday Inn Capitol Hill offers the same magnificent views of the Capitol building as the pricier Hyatt, plus a convenient location. Children under age 18 stay free. ⊠ *415 New Jersey Ave. NW, 20001,* ☎ *202/638–1616 or 800/638–1116,* FAX *202/347–1813. 341 rooms, 5 suites. Restaurant, bar, room service, pool, parking (fee). AE, DC, MC, V.*

Downtown

$$$$ ☷ **Capital Hilton.** There are three reasons to stay at the Capital Hilton: location, location, and location. The place is always jumping because it's near the White House and many monuments; it's also in the middle of the K Street business corridor. The Twigs restaurant has better food and service than the on-site Trader Vic's; still, the ticky-tacky tropical theme of the latter is a tradition with some businesspeople and beloved by many leisure travelers as well. ⊠ *1001 16th St. NW, 20036,* ☎ *202/393–1000 or 800/445–8667,* FAX *202/639–5726. 515 rooms, 36 suites. 2 restaurants, room service, beauty salon, health club, laundry service and dry cleaning, parking (fee). AE, DC, MC, V.*

$$$$ ☷ **Carlton Hotel.** Entering the Carlton is like stepping into an updated Italian Renaissance mansion. In the opulent lobby—with its gilded ornamental ceiling and Louis XVI furnishings—you might run into Queen Elizabeth II or the chairman of the World Bank; the hotel has long been a favorite of leaders in business, politics, and society. In a bustling business sector near the White House, the Carlton offers cordial, dignified service. The ornate Allegro dining room—with hand-carved mahogany bar, Italian marble floor, and large Palladian windows—serves Continental cuisine; its buffet lunch and Sunday brunch get rave reviews. An exercise room is equipped with the latest gear. A Carlton Kids program offers savings and goodies; ask for details. ⊠ *923 16th St. NW, 20006,* ☎ *202/638–2626 or 800/325–3535,* FAX *202/638–4231. 183 rooms, 14 suites. Restaurant, bar, room service, exercise room, parking (fee). AE, DC, MC, V.*

$$$$ ☷ **Grand Hyatt.** Imagine a 1930s movie-musical set with a Mediterranean hillside village rising around a courtyard; a gazebo, curved lounge, and dining areas encircle a blue lagoon fed by waterfalls and containing a small island on which a pianist in formal attire plays Cole Porter tunes on a white grand piano. The Grand Hyatt has created just such a fanciful interior in a bustling high-rise hotel that compensates for the drabness of the neighborhood. Across the street from the Washington Convention Center and just steps away from downtown shopping and theaters, the location is convenient as well. ⊠ *1000 H St. NW, 20001,* ☎ *202/582–1234 or 800/233–1234,* FAX *202/637–4718. 889 rooms, 58 suites. 4 restaurants, 2 bars, room service, health club. AE, DC, MC, V.*

$$$$ ☷ **Hay-Adams Hotel.** An Italian Renaissance landmark a stone's throw
★ from the White House—rooms on the south side have a view to die for, worth making a reservation for well in advance to enjoy—the Hay-Adams has an eclectic grandeur inside: European and Oriental antiques;

Doric, Ionic, and Corinthian touches; carved walnut wainscotting; and intricate ornamental ceilings. It sits on the site of houses owned by statesman and author John Hay and diplomat and historian Henry Adams. The John Hay lounge seems to belong to an English Tudor residence. The Lafayette dining room serves "contemporary American" dishes. The hotel's afternoon tea is renowned. ⊠ *1 Lafayette Sq. NW, 20006,* ☎ *202/638–6600 or 800/424–5054,* ⨳ *202/638–2716. 125 rooms, 18 suites. 2 restaurants, bar, room service, laundry service and dry cleaning, parking (fee). AE, DC, MC, V.*

$$$$ ★ 🏨 **Jefferson Hotel.** Next door to the National Geographic Society and opposite the Russian Embassy, the Jefferson's undistinguished beaux-arts exterior is deceiving; inside this small luxury hotel, Federal-style finery abounds. The 100 rooms and suites are each unique in decor and furnished with antiques, original art, VCRs, and CD players; choose selections from the hotel's library or pack your own. The restaurant is a favorite of high-ranking politicos and film stars. Its American cuisine includes venison, spice-crusted swordfish, and prime rib. A high staff-to-guest ratio ensures outstanding service. Employees greet you by name; laundry is hand ironed and delivered in wicker baskets. ⊠ *1200 16th St. NW, 20036,* ☎ *202/347–2200 or 800/368–5966,* ⨳ *202/785–1505. 68 rooms, 32 suites. Restaurant, bar, room service, in-room VCRs, access to health club, laundry service, concierge, parking (fee). AE, DC, MC, V.*

$$$$ 🏨 **J. W. Marriott.** The large glossy Marriott has a prime location near the White House and next door to the National Theatre. The capacious, columned lobby includes a four-story atrium, marble and mahogany accents, Oriental rugs, and other artwork. Ask for a room on the Pennsylvania Avenue side or you may get a boring view. Guests have indoor access to the National Press Building and National Place, with 110 shops and more than 18 restaurants and cafés. ⊠ *1331 Pennsylvania Ave. NW, 20004,* ☎ *202/393–2000 or 800/228–9290,* ⨳ *202/626–6991. 722 rooms, 51 suites. 5 restaurants, bar, room service, indoor pool, exercise room, laundry service and dry cleaning, parking (fee). AE, DC, MC, V.*

$$$$ 🏨 **Madison Hotel.** Old World luxury and meticulous service prevail in the Madison (named for fourth U.S. president), which is why the signatures of presidents, prime ministers, sultans, and kings fill the guest register, as well as those of just plain well-to-do folks who appreciate punctilious European standards. Deceivingly contemporary on the outside, the 14-story building, four blocks from the White House, owns a world-class collection of antiques—a rare Chinese Imperial altar table and a Louis XVI palace commode are on display in the lobby. The Montpelier restaurant, specializing in continental cuisine, is art-filled and posh. ⊠ *15th and M Sts. NW, 20005,* ☎ *202/862–1600 or 800/424–8577,* ⨳ *202/785–1255. 318 rooms, 35 suites. 2 restaurants, bar, room service, exercise room, parking (fee). AE, DC, MC, V.*

$$$$ 🏨 **Stouffer Renaissance Mayflower.** Franklin Delano Roosevelt wrote "We have nothing to fear but fear itself" in Suite 776. J. Edgar Hoover dined here at the same table every day for 20 years. Ever since the 10-story Stouffer Renaissance Mayflower opened in 1925 for Calvin Coolidge's inauguration it has been making history makers (and leisure travelers) feel at home, and this national historic landmark, four blocks from the White House, continues to be a central part of Washington life. Sunlight spills into the majestic skylit lobby, causing the gilded trim to gleam; Oriental rugs splash the floors with color; sculpted cherubs prance around trees that brachiate into electrified candebra. Contemporary seafood is served amid silver, crystal, and artful flower arrangements at the Nicholas restaurant. ⊠ *1127 Connecticut Ave. NW, 20036,* ☎ *202/347–3000 or 800/468–3571,* ⨳ *202/466–9082. 660* *rooms, 81 suites. 2 restaurants, bar, room service, sauna, exercise room, shops, parking (fee). AE, DC, MC, V.*

$$$$ **⛨ Washington Renaissance Hotel.** Opposite the Washington Convention Center and near the "Pennsylvania Quarter," a slowly gentrifying area of restaurants and clubs, the 15-story Washington Renaissance Hotel is a completely equipped convention hotel primed for business travelers. The lobby's Chinese rock garden and fountain remind guests of their proximity to Chinatown; the nearby Techworld complex contains more than 50 shops. ⊠ *999 9th St. NW, 20001, ☎ 202/898–9000 or 800/228–9898, ⅨＸ 202/789–4213. 779 rooms, 21 suites. 3 restaurants, bar, deli, room service, indoor pool, health club, parking (fee). AE, DC, MC, V.*

$$$$ **⛨ Willard Inter-Continental.** "I am surely glad to be under your roof,"
★   declared Abraham Lincoln when entering the Willard Hotel on arrival in Washington as the nation's 16th president. Indeed, the Willard, whose present building dates from 1901, welcomed every American president from Franklin Pierce in 1853 to Dwight Eisenhower in the 1950s before closing after years of decline. The new Willard, a faithful renovation, is an opulent beaux arts feast to the eye, as the main lobby, with its spectacular proportions, great columns, huge chandeliers, mosaic floors, and elaborately carved ceilings attests. The hotel's formal eatery, the Willard Room, has won nationwide acclaim for its use of classic French and modern cuisine nouvelle techniques to enliven dishes from France, Germany, and the U.S. South. ⊠ *1401 Pennsylvania Ave. NW, 20004, ☎ 202/628–9100 or 800/327–0200, ⅨＸ 202/637–7326. 341 rooms, 38 suites. 2 restaurants, 2 bars, minibars, room service, health club, laundry service and dry cleaning, shops, meeting rooms, parking (fee). AE, DC, MC, V.*

$$$ **⛨ Henley Park Hotel.** A Tudor-style building adorned with 119 gar-
★   goyles, this National Historic Trust hotel with the charm of an English country house is unique in downtown Washington. The main eatery, Coeur de Lion, has a leafy atrium, stained glass windows, a pleasant English air, and a decidedly unEnglish menu in which such dishes as goat cheese-and-bell pepper ravioli and poached salmon with buckwheat noodles have Mediterranean and Asian accents. A bit far from the attractions of the Mall to walk and in a less-than-great neighborhood (take a cab after dark), Henley Park is nevertheless only a short ride on public transportation from the major sights; limousine service, gracious Old World atmosphere, and an attentive staff make it worth considering, especially if you like bed-and-breakfasts and country inns. ⊠ *926 Massachusetts Ave. NW, 20001, ☎ 202/638–5200 or 800/222–8474, ⅨＸ 202/638–6740. 79 rooms, 17 suites. Restaurant, bar, room service, access to health club, parking (fee). AE, DC, MC, V.*

$$$ **⛨ Marriott at Metro Center.** A marble lobby, art commissioned from Washington artists, and the popular Metro Grille and Bar—a handsome two-level facility decorated in mahogany, oak, brass, and marble that serves New American cuisine—are among the Marriott's virtues, plus its convenient Metro Center station location. Larger-than-average rooms are more comfortable than luxurious. ⊠ *775 12th St. NW, 20005, ☎ 202/737–2200, ⅨＸ 202/347–0860. 456 rooms, 12 suites. Restaurant, bar, room service, indoor pool, health club, laundry service and dry cleaning, parking (fee). AE, DC, MC, V.*

$$$ **⛨ Washington Vista Hotel.** A few blocks from the White House, Washington Convention Center, and K Street business corridor, the Washington Vista Hotel is designed to look like an urban town square with a garden-courtyard lobby flooded by light from a 130-foot window facing M Street. The hotel, host to Elizabeth Taylor, Kirk Douglas, and countless business travelers, gained undeserved notoriety as the site of Mayor Marion Barry's arrest in 1990. The buffet lunch at the Verandah is a bargain at $9.95. ✉ *1400 M St. NW, 20005,* ☎ *202/429–1700 or 800/847–8232,* ⬚ᴬˣ *202/728–0530. 386 rooms, 14 suites. 2 restaurants, 2 bars, room service, health club, baby-sitting, parking (fee). AE, DC, MC, V.*

$$ ⊞ **Governor's House Hotel.** Governor's House Hotel is only two blocks from Dupont Circle. The staff is friendly. Herb's Restaurant draws a lively professional and arty crowd. Families can take advantage of the 24 rooms with kitchenettes. ✉ *1615 Rhode Island Ave. NW, 20036,* ☎ *202/296–2100 or 800/821–4367,* ⬚ᴬˣ *202/331–0227. 152 rooms, 9 suites. Restaurant, bar, room service, pool, access to health club, parking (fee). AE, DC, MC, V.*

$$ ⊞ **Hotel Anthony.** A small hotel with a courteous staff, the Hotel Anthony offers the basics amid the K and L streets business district, close to the White House. Weekend rates are almost half price. ✉ *1823 L St. NW, 20036,* ☎ *202/223–4320 or 800/424–2970,* ⬚ᴬˣ *202/223–8546. 99 rooms. Restaurant, room service, access to health club, parking (fee). AE, DC, MC, V.*

$$ ⊞ **Hotel Washington.** Since opening in 1918 the Hotel Washington has
★ been known for its view. Washingtonians bring visitors to the outdoor rooftop bar for cocktails and a panorama that includes the White House grounds and Washington Monument. The oldest continuously operating hostelry in the city and now a national landmark, it sprang from the drawing boards of John Carrère and Thomas Hastings, who designed the New York Public Library. Some rooms look directly onto the White House lawn. Suite 506 is where Elvis Presley stayed on his trips to D.C. ✉ *515 15th St. NW, 20004,* ☎ *202/638–5900,* ⬚ᴬˣ *202/638–1594. 344 rooms, 16 suites. Restaurant, bar, deli, lobby lounge, room service, exercise room, laundry service and dry cleaning, business services. AE, DC, MC, V.*

$$ ⊞ **Morrison-Clark Inn Hotel.** A merger of two 1864 town houses, the
★ airy Victorian Morrison-Clark Hotel is a National Trust for Historic Preservation-designated Historic Hotel. One house has a 1917 Chinese Chippendale porch; Oriental touches echo throughout the public rooms, which include marble fireplaces and 14-foot-high mirrors with original gilding. Antique-filled rooms—some with bay windows, fireplaces, or access to a porch—have different personalities; one is called the "deer and bunny room" because of its decorative trim. The restaurant's New American–Southern cuisine has been roundly praised. ✉ *Massachusetts Ave. and 11th St. NW, 20001,* ☎ *202/898–1200 or 800/332–7898,* ⬚ᴬˣ *202/289–8576. 54 rooms. CP. Restaurant, room service, exercise room, laundry service and dry cleaning, parking (fee). AE, D, DC, MC, V.*

$ ⊞ **Holiday Inn Central.** Overlooking Scott Circle, the Holiday Inn has a fresh approach to elegance on a budget: a mix of generally spacious parlor suites and deluxe rooms and a bright, attractive lobby hosting a bar and the Avenue Café and Lounge. The rooftop pool is open in summer. The Dupont Circle Metro is three blocks away, although a cab is advised at night. ✉ *1501 Rhode Island Ave. NW, 20005,* ☎ *202/483–2000 or 800/465–4329,* ⬚ᴬˣ *202/797–1078. 183 rooms, 30 suites. Restaurant, bar, no-smoking floors, room service, pool, exercise room, shop, recreation room, laundry service, parking (fee). AE, DC, MC, V.*

$ ⊞ **Washington International AYH-Hostel.** This well-kept place has clean dormitory rooms with 250 bunk beds and a kitchen, laundry room, and living room. Single men and women are in separate rooms; families are given their own room if the hostel is not full. The hostel also sponsors tours, movies, and other programs. Register 24 hours a day, but play it safe and spring for a cab if you arrive at night. American Youth Hostels members pay $17 ($20 for nonmembers); the maximum stay is 15 days. Youthful European travelers predominate, and July–September is the busiest period. ✉ *1009 11th St. NW, 20001,* ☎ *202/737–2333,* ⅎᴬˣ *202/737–1508. 250 beds. Kitchen, shop, coin laundry. MC, V.*

Dupont Circle

$$$$ 🏨 **Ritz-Carlton.** The childhood home of Al Gore, the intimate Ritz-Carlton has an English hunt-club theme; rooms have views of Embassy Row or Georgetown and the National Cathedral. The pricey Jockey Club restaurant, with its half-timber ceilings, dark wood paneling, and red-checker tablecloths, draws the crowned heads of Washington. The Fairfax Bar is a cozy spot for a drink beside the fire (with piano entertainment some evenings). Guests have access to a nearby golf course, pool, and tennis courts. ✉ *2100 Massachusetts Ave. NW, 20008,* ☎ *202/293–2100 or 800/241–3333,* ⅎᴬˣ *202/466–9867. 174 rooms, 32 suites. Restaurant, bar, minibars, room service, in-room VCRs, massage, sauna, exercise room, meeting rooms. AE, DC, MC, V.*

$$$ 🏨 **Embassy Row Hotel.** Near Dupont Circle, in a neighborhood of grand houses now used mostly as embassies, museums, and galleries, the Embassy Row Hotel is convenient for both business and leisure travelers. The bar may be the coziest in Washington, and the food at Bistro Twenty-Fifteen, the hotel's restaurant, has made it a favorite of locals and tourists alike. The roof deck and pool offer fine views of the city. ✉ *2015 Massachusetts Ave. NW, 20036,* ☎ *202/265–1600 or 800/424–2400,* ⅎᴬˣ *202/328–7526. 168 rooms, 28 suites. Restaurant, bar, room service, pool, exercise room, parking (fee). AE, DC, MC, V.*

$$$ 🏨 **Hotel Sofitel Washington.** With the ambience of a European luxury
★   hostelry, the Hotel Sofitel Washington may be small, but its rooms are among the largest in any Washington hotel. The Trocadero Café serves three meals daily. ✉ *1914 Connecticut Ave. NW, 20009,* ☎ *202/797–2000 or 800/424–2464,* ⅎᴬˣ *202/462–0944. 108 rooms, 37 suites. Restaurant, bar, room service, access to health club, laundry service and dry cleaning, parking (fee). AE, DC, MC, V.*

$$$ 🏨 **Radisson Barceló Hotel.** The Radisson Barceló is convenient to Dupont Circle and Georgetown and its guest rooms are among the largest in town. The second-floor outdoor swimming pool, open only in summer, has a lovely setting—a brick courtyard enclosed by the walls of the hotel and the backs of a row of century-old town houses to the east. Southwest-Mediteranean fare is served at its Gabriel Restaurant. ✉ *2121 P St. NW, 20037,* ☎ *202/293–3100* ⅎᴬˣ *202/857–0134. 235 rooms, 65 suites. Restaurant, bar, room service, pool, sauna, exercise room, parking (fee). AE, DC, MC, V.*

$$$ 🏨 **Washington Hilton and Towers.** A busy convention hotel, the Wash-
★   ington Hilton is as much an event as a place to stay. You might run into a leading actor, cabinet official, or six busloads of towheaded teenagers from Utah in the lobby. Guest rooms are compact but light-filled, and the hotel is convenient, a short walk from the shops and restaurants of Dupont Circle and the Adams-Morgan neighborhood. ✉ *1919 Connecticut Ave. NW, 20009,* ☎ *202/483–3000 or 800/445–8667,* ⅎᴬˣ *202/265–8221. 1,062 rooms, 88 suites. 3 restaurants (1 seasonal), 2 bars, room service, pool, 3 tennis courts, health club, shops, parking (fee). AE, DC, MC, V.*

$$ 🏨 **Washington Courtyard by Marriott.** One of the city's best values for
★   budget travelers, Marriott's Washington Courtyard hotel is a good alternative for international tourists and businesspeople who can't find rooms at the Washington Hilton. Guest rooms on the west and south have good views. Coffee and cookies are served daily in the European-style lobby. ✉ *1900 Connecticut Ave. NW, 20009,* ☎ *202/332–9300*

or 800/842–4211, FAX *202/328–7039. 147 rooms. Restaurant, bar, pool, access to health club, parking (fee). AE, DC, MC, V.*

$ 🏨 **Hotel Tabard Inn.** Formed by a linkage of three Victorian town houses, the Hotel Tabard Inn is one of the oldest continuously running hostelries in D.C. Named after the inn in Chaucer's *Canterbury Tales*, it's furnished throughout with broken-in Victorian and American Empire antiques. Dim lighting and a genteel shabbiness strike some as off-putting, others as charming. Rooms have no TV, there's no room service, and what service there is can be uneven, but the quiet street, the quick walk to Dupont Circle and the K Street business district, and moderate prices for most rooms with private bath make early reservations advisable. ✉ *1739 N St. NW, 20036,* ☎ *202/785–1277,* FAX *202/785–6173. 40 rooms, 25 with bath. Restaurant. MC, V.*

Georgetown

$$$$ 🏨 **Four Seasons Hotel.** The Four Seasons Hotel may be a modern
★ brick-and-glass edifice amid Georgetown's 19th century Federal and Georgian row houses, but inside Old World elegance prevails; the rich mahogany paneling, antiques, spectacular flower arrangements, and impeccable service are hallmarks of a mecca for Washington's elite. Guest rooms offer a choice of views: of the old C&O Canal, the trees and streams of Rock Creek Park, the busy Georgetown street scene, or the quiet courtyard. The private nightclub Desirée is open to guests, as is what may be the poshest hotel health club in America (each Lifecycle machine has its own Walkman, TV, and VCR). The Four Seasons is kid-friendly, too, with children's menus, games, and activities, "Tea Time for Tots," and milk and cookies at bedtime. ✉ *2800 Pennsylvania Ave. NW, 20007,* ☎ *202/342–0444 or 800/332–3442,* FAX *202/342–1673. 160 rooms, 36 suites. 2 restaurants, bar, room service, pool, health club, nightclub, parking (fee). AE, DC, MC, V.*

$$$ 🏨 **Georgetown Dutch Inn.** Tucked away on a Georgetown side street, the modest all-suite Georgetown Dutch Inn has a homey ambience, a small lobby decorated with 18th-century touches, and rooms with family-room-style furnishings (sofa bed in the living room, walk-in kitchen); some lack bedroom windows. Complimentary Continental breakfast is served in the lobby. ✉ *1075 Thomas Jefferson St. NW, 20007,* ☎ *202/337–0900,* FAX *202/333–6526. 47 suites. CP. Room service, access to health club, free parking. AE, DC, MC, V.*

$$$ 🏨 **Latham Hotel.** A small Colonial-style hotel in a lively neighborhood, the Latham has rooms with a sleek, updated look that contrast with the redbrick, neocolonial exterior. Those on the M Street side have courtyard views overlooking the C&O Canal. The hotel is a favorite of Europeans, sports figures, and devotees of Georgetown. It's Citronelle restaurant (☞ Chapter 4) is among the best ✉ *3000 M St. NW, 20007,* ☎ *202/726–5000 or 800/368–5922,* FAX *202/337–4250. 143 rooms, 9 suites. Restaurant, bar, room service, pool, access to health club, parking (fee). AE, DC, MC, V.*

$$ 🏨 **Georgetown Inn.** With an atmosphere reminiscent of an old gentleman's sporting club, the Georgetown Inn is a small, quiet, intimate, European-style hotel with redbrick architecture and an 18th century flavor. At its Georgetown Bar & Grill everyone from shorts-clad tourists to pinstriped businesspeople can feel at home. ✉ *1310 Wisconsin Ave. NW, 20007,* ☎ *202/333–8900 or 800/424–2979,* FAX *202/625–1744. 95 rooms, 8 suites. Restaurant, bar, room service, exercise room, parking (fee). AE, DC, MC, V.*

$$ 🏨 **Georgetown Suites.** If you consider standard hotel rooms cramped and overpriced, the all-suite Georgetown Suites—in a redbrick courtyard one block south of M Street in the heart of Georgetown—is a find.

Suites vary in size but all have full kitchens, iron and ironing boards, hair dryers, and voice mail. Continental breakfast is free, as are local phone calls and long-distance access. You might have to carry your own bags and the Metro is a 10-minute walk away, but for comfort and value it's tops. Children under 12 stay free. ⊠ *1111 30th St. NW, 20007,* ☎ *202/298–7800 or 800/348–7203, FAX 202/333–5792. 138 suites. CP. Kitchens, exercise room, laundry service and dry cleaning, parking (fee). AE, DC, MC, V.*

Southwest

$$$$　🏨 **Loews L'Enfant Plaza.** Loews is an oasis of velvet and chintz in L'Enfant Plaza—a concrete, fortresslike collection of office buildings with underground shops and its own Metro stop. Travelers with government business stay here, too, in proximity to several agency headquarters and just down the street from Capitol Hill. Pets are allowed. Café Pierre serves an international menu at lunch and dinner. ⊠ *480 L'Enfant Plaza SW, 20024,* ☎ *202/484–1000 or 800/223–0888, FAX 202/646–4456. 348 rooms, 22 suites. 3 restaurants, 2 bars, room service, in-room VCRs, indoor pool, health club, parking (fee). AE, DC, MC, V.*

Northwest/Upper Connecticut Avenue

$$$$　🏨 **Omni Shoreham Hotel.** Resembling an old-time resort, the Omni
★　　Shoreham offers views of the jogging and bike paths of leafy Rock Creek Park and is close to the Adams-Morgan neighborhood, Dupont Circle, and the National Zoo. In back, a pool overlooks a sweeping lawn and woods beyond. Some of the large, light-filled rooms have fireplaces; half face the park. Comedienne Joan Cushing frequently holds forth in the Marquee Lounge, which has a weekend matinee cabaret for children. ⊠ *2500 Calvert St. NW, 20008,* ☎ *202/234–0700 or 800/834–6664, FAX 202/332–1373. 720 rooms, 50 suites. Restaurant, bar, snack bar, room service, pool, 3 tennis courts, basketball, exercise room, horseshoes, shuffleboard, shops, cabaret, parking (fee). AE, DC, MC, V.*

$$$$　🏨 **Sheraton Washington Hotel.** A veritable city on a hill, the Sheraton Washington is the largest hotel in town, with a courtyard graced by a modernistic fountain, an airy atrium, and plush sunken-seating areas in the lobby. It consists of an "old town"—a 1920s redbrick structure that used to be an apartment building—and a modern, convention-ready main complex. The 201 rooms and the public areas of the 10-story old section are furnished traditionally. Rooms in the newer section are contemporary, with chrome and glass touches. Most have a good view. ⊠ *2660 Woodley Rd. NW, 20008,* ☎ *202/328–2000 or 800/325–3535, FAX 202/234–0015. 1,380 rooms, 125 suites. 3 restaurants, bar, no-smoking rooms, room service, 2 pools, barbershop, exercise room, shops, baby-sitting, laundry service, meeting rooms, parking (fee). AE, DC, MC, V.*

$$　🏨 **Windsor Park Hotel.** Opposite the Chinese Embassy in the residential Kalorama neighborhood, the Windsor Park has small immaculate rooms. Continental breakfast is free. Street parking is almost nonexistent, but a garage is two blocks away. ⊠ *2116 Kalorama Rd. NW, 20008,* ☎ *202/483–7700 or 800/247–3064, FAX 202/332–4547. 39 rooms, 5 suites. CP. Refrigerators. AE, DC, MC, V.*

$　🏨 **Days Inn Connecticut Avenue.** If you prefer to stay away from the downtown bustle, Days Inn is on a wide avenue in a more residential area next door to the University of the District of Columbia. Rooms have standard hotel furnishings and may be small. The nearby Van Ness Metro is a quick way to get to the National Zoo. Several cafés are nearby. ⊠ *4400 Connecticut Ave. NW, 20008,* ☎ *202/244–5600 or 800/325–*

In case you want to see the world.

At American Express, we're here to make your journey a smooth one. So we have over 1,700 travel service locations in over 120 countries ready to help. What else would you expect from the world's largest travel agency?

do more®

http://www.americanexpress.com/travel

AMERICAN EXPRESS

Travel

In case you want to be welcomed there.

We're here to see that you're always welcomed at establishments everywhere. That's why millions of people carry the American Express® Card – for peace of mind, confidence, and security, around the world or just around the corner.

do more

Cards

In case you're running low.

We're here to help with more than 118,000 Express Cash locations around the world. In order to enroll, just call American Express before you start your vacation.

do more

Express Cash

And just in case.

We're here with American Express® Travelers Cheques
and Cheques *for Two*.® They're the safest way to carry
money on your vacation and the surest way to get a
refund, practically anywhere, anytime.
Another way we help you...

do more ®

Travelers Cheques

2525, FAX 202/244–6794. 150 rooms, 5 suites. Restaurant, room service, shops, parking (fee). AE, DC, MC, V.

$ ✦ **Kalorama Guest House.** Five separate turn-of-the-century town
★ houses—three on a quiet street in the Adams-Morgan neighborhood
and two in residential Woodley Park—compose the Kalorama Guest
House, with its comfortable atmosphere created by dark-wood walls;
hand-me-down antique oak furniture; traditional, slightly worn upholstery; brass or antique wooden bedsteads; and calico curtains. The
coffeepot is always on, the staff friendly, and guests have the run of
each house, its front parlor, and the areas where complimentary breakfast and afternoon aperitifs are served. Rooms range from large to tiny;
none has a phone or a TV. The inn in Adams-Morgan is steps from
the liveliest section of the neighborhood. The Woodley Park inn is near
the National Zoo. Both are a short walk to the Metro. ✉ *1854 Mintwood Pl. NW, 20009,* ☎ *202/667–6369,* FAX *202/319–1262. 2700;*
✉ *Cathedral Ave. NW, 20008,* ☎ *202/328–0860. 50 rooms, 30 with
bath, 5 suites. CP. AE, DC, MC, V.*

$ ✦ **Normandy Inn.** A small European-style hotel on a quiet street in the
★ exclusive embassy area of Connecticut Avenue, the Normandy is near
restaurants and some of the most expensive residential real estate in
Washington. Rooms are standard, functional, and comfortable; all
have refrigerators. Each Tuesday evening a wine-and-cheese reception
is held for guests. ✉ *2118 Wyoming Ave. NW, 20008,* ☎ *202/483–
1350 or 800/424–3729,* FAX *202/387–8241. 65 rooms, 10 suites. CP.
Refrigerators, room service, parking (fee). AE, D, MC, V.*

West End/Foggy Bottom

$$$$ ✦ **ANA Hotel.** The Japanese-owned ANA Hotel is a stylish combina-
★ tion of the contemporary and the traditional. About a third of the bright
airy rooms have a view of the central courtyard. The hotel's informal
restaurant, the Bistro, has the flavor of 19th-century Paris and contains an antique mahogany bar. A state-of-the-art health club includes
rowing machines, a cross-country ski simulator, treadmills, Cybex
equipment, a sauna, a steam room, and a pool. ✉ *2401 M St. NW,
20037,* ☎ *202/429–2400 or 800/228–3000,* FAX *202/457–5010. 407
rooms, 8 suites. 2 restaurants, bar, café, room service, beauty salon,
health club, parking (fee). AE, DC, MC, V.*

$$$$ ✦ **Park Hyatt.** With its neoclassical exterior and multicolored marble
lobby adorned with masterpieces by such Washington Color Painter
school artists as Kenneth Nolan, Gene Davis, and Paul Reed—plus works
by Matisse, Leger, Calder, and Picasso—the Park Hyatt is one of
Georgetown's toniest places to stay, with carpeting so thick you almost
bounce. Bronzes, chinoiserie, and a fortune teller at tea in the main-
floor lounge, which overlooks a lovely landscaped garden, are Old World
touches that offset the spareness of the hotel's design. The Park's
health club features an indoor pool with skylight, saunas, steam rooms,
Jacuzzi, and an exercise room stocked with the latest equipment. The
elegant, dramatically sunlit Melrose Restaurant serves contemporary
American cuisine with an emphasis on seafood. The Kennedy Center
is a 3-minute cab ride away. ✉ *1201 24th St. NW, 20037,* ☎ *202/789–
1234 or 800/233–1234,* FAX *202/457–8823. 93 rooms, 131 suites.
Restaurant, bar, outdoor café, room service, indoor pool, beauty salon,
massage, health club, parking (fee). AE, DC, MC, V.*

$$$$ ✦ **Watergate Hotel.** If you want to stay in the most important hotel
★ in modern American history, scene of the burglary that resulted in the
resignation of President Richard Nixon, here it is. The internationally
famous Watergate, its distinctive sawtooth design a landmark along
the Potomac, offers guests a taste of traditional English gentility. Guest

rooms are large; many have balconies and most have striking river views. Accustomed to serving the world's elite, the hotel also welcomes vacationing families and couples on getaway weekends—as long as price is no object. Next door is the Kennedy Center; Georgetown is a short walk away. Complimentary limousine service to Capitol Hill or downtown is available weekdays. ✉ *2650 Virginia Ave. NW, 20037,* ☎ *202/965–2300 or 800/424–2736,* ℻ *202/337–7915. 90 rooms, 146 suites. 2 restaurants, bar, room service, indoor pool, health club, parking (fee). AE, DC, MC, V.*

$$$ 🖵 **Embassy Suites.** Classical columns, plaster lions, huge Asian temple lights, and an atrium in which waterfalls gush, tall palms loom, and plants drip over balconies suggest the hanging gardens of Babylon reconstructed in a suburban shopping mall. Embassy Suites is in a fairly quiet West End enclave, within walking distance of Georgetown, the Kennedy Center, and Dupont Circle. Good for businesspeople and families alike, each suite has a refrigerator, microwave, and coffeemaker in addition to the usual amenities. The Italian restaurant, Panevino, gets favorable reviews.✉ *1250 22nd St. NW, 20037,* ☎ *202/857–3388 or 800/362–2779,* ℻ *202/293–3173. 318 suites. Full breakfast included. Restaurant, room service, indoor pool, health club, shop, recreation room, parking (fee). AE, D, DC, MC, V.*

$$$ 🖵 **Wyndham Bristol Hotel.** You don't get much of a view here but the location is excellent. Midway between the White House and Georgetown, the Wyndham is a favorite of movie and theater people because the Kennedy Center is just a few blocks away. Although the building is bordered on two sides by major thoroughfares, rooms are quiet. A cabinet full of Chinese porcelain is on display in the lobby. The rest of the hotel is English in decor. ✉ *2430 Pennsylvania Ave. NW, 20037,* ☎ *202/955–6400 or 800/996–3426; in Canada, 800/631–4200;* ℻ *202/775–8489. 202 rooms, 37 suites. Restaurant, bar, room service, health club, laundry service, parking (fee). AE, DC, MC, V.*

$$ 🖵 **Doubletree.** Two all-suite Doubletree hotels are in the Foggy Bottom area, each separately managed. All suites have a fully equipped walk-in kitchen with dishwasher and sofa sleeper as an extra bed. The staff is small and so are the lobbies, but the rooms are well furnished and comfortable. The New Hampshire Avenue location has an outdoor rooftop pool (a great spot for viewing fireworks on July 4). Both hotels are close to the Kennedy Center, Georgetown, and George Washington University. ✉ *801 New Hampshire Ave. NW, 20037,* ☎ *202/785–2000 or 800/424–2900,* ℻ *202/785–9485;* ✉ *2500 Pennsylvania Ave. NW, 20037,* ☎ *202/333–8060 or 800/424–2900,* ℻ *202/338–3818. 224 suites. Kitchens, room service, pool (New Hampshire Ave.), access to health club, library. AE, DC, MC, V.*

$$ 🖵 **River Inn.** This small all-suite hotel is steps from Georgetown, George Washington University, and the Kennedy Center. On the premises is the cozy Foggy Bottom Café. The best views are from the fourteen Potomac Suites, each of which has a full walk-in kitchen. The lobby is sleek and contemporary, but the room furnishings are homey and modest. This is a popular spot with parents of George Washington University students. ✉ *924 25th St. NW, 20037,* ☎ *202/337–7600 or 800/424–2741,* ℻ *202/625–2618. 127 suites. Restaurant, room service, use of pool at One Washington Circle and health club at Watergate. AE, DC, MC, V.*

$ 🖵 **Howard Johnson Kennedy Center.** The eight-story Howard Johnson lodge offers HoJo reliability in a location close to the Kennedy Center and Georgetown. Rooms are large and comfortable, and each has a refrigerator. ✉ *2601 Virginia Ave. NW, 20037,* ☎ *202/965–2700 or 800/654–2000;* ℻ *202/965–2700, Ext. 7910. 192 rooms. Restaurant, refrigerators, pool, laundry service, free parking. AE, DC, MC, V.*

Suburban Maryland

$-$$$ ☷ **Hyatt Regency Bethesda.** The atrium lobby, with glass elevators and ferns, is reminiscent of other Hyatt Regencies. So are the attentive service and the comfortable—if unremarkable—rooms. The sights of downtown Washington are about 15 minutes away by Metro. The adjacent Metro plaza has a small ice rink, open in winter, and an indoor food court. ⊠ *1 Bethesda Metro Center, Bethesda, MD 20814,* ☎ *301/657–1234 or 800/233–1234,* ⅎ *301/657–6453. 368 rooms, 13 suites. 2 restaurants, bar, room service, indoor pool, sauna, exercise room. AE, DC, MC, V.*

$$ ☷ **Holiday Inn Chevy Chase.** A short walk from the Friendship Heights Metro on the D.C. border, the Holiday Inn Chevy Chase is a comfortable hostelry in the heart of one of the area's most upscale shopping districts. While the on-site Julian's restaurant has deli fare, the nearby Chevy Chase Pavilion and Mazza Gallerie malls have expanded family dining options; a wealth of gourmet choices are one Metro stop away in Bethesda or a 15-minute car trip down Wisconsin Avenue into Georgetown. Families booking ahead can bring the rates down to the $ category and, as at all Holiday Inns, accompanying children under 18 stay free. ⊠ *5520 Wisconsin Ave., Chevy Chase, MD 20815,* ☎ *301/656–1500 or 800/465–4329,* ⅎ *301/656–5045. 206 rooms, 10 suites. Restaurant, room service, pool, health club. AE, DC, MC, V.*

$$ ☷ **Quality Hotel Silver Spring.** The convenient Quality Hotel Silver Spring is about three blocks north of Maryland's Silver Spring Metro station and close to the shops and restaurants in downtown Silver Spring, including the glossy new discount-oriented City Place complex. The marble and mahogany lobby, with many places to sit, is comfortable and intimate. ⊠ *8727 Colesville Rd., Silver Spring, MD 20910,* ☎ *301/589–5200 or 800/376–7666,* ⅎ *301/588–1841. 228 rooms, 28 suites. 2 restaurants, bar, room service, indoor pool, sauna, exercise room. AE, D, DC, MC, V.*

$ ☷ **American Inn of Bethesda.** At the less glamorous north end of downtown Bethesda, the American Inn sets no new standards for motel decor, but the rooms are clean, generally bright, and all have cable TV. The hotel houses two respectable restaurants: La Posada, a Mexican eatery, and El Caribe, which serves moderately priced Spanish/Latin American fare. Many other restaurants and nightclubs are within walking distance; the Bethesda Metro stop is a 10-minute walk away. ⊠ *8130 Wisconsin Ave., Bethesda, MD 20814,* ☎ *301/656–9300 or 800/323–7081,* ⅎ *301/656–2907. 75 rooms, 1 suite. CP. 2 restaurants, pool, laundry service, concierge. AE, D, DC, MC, V.*

$ ☷ **Holiday Inn Conference Center at College Park.** Close to the University of Maryland campus and NASA's Goddard Space Flight Center, this meetings-oriented Holiday Inn is also convenient for families. A complimentary shuttle takes guests to the Metro; downtown Washington is a 25-minute train ride away. An indoor pool, exercise room, and game room can keep kids (who stay free) occupied on nontouring days. ⊠ *10000 Baltimore Blvd. (Rte. 1), College Park, MD 20740,* ☎ *301/345–6700 or 800/441–4923,* ⅎ *301/441–4923. 222 rooms. Restaurant, bar, indoor pool, exercise room, recreation room, laundry service, meeting rooms. AE, DC, MC, V.*

$ ☷ **Ramada Inn-Rockville.** Also known as the Ramada Inn at Congressional Park, the Ramada Inn in Rockville, Maryland, is a seven-story hotel with a sturdy brick facade makes it look like an office building, but the decor inside is pleasantly cheery. Shuttle service is provided to area offices; the Twinbrook Metro stop (on the red line, about 30 minutes to downtown) is two blocks away across bustling Rockville Pike. In addition to an in-house eatery, fast food and upscale restaurants are nearby on the Pike. ⊠ *1775 Rockville Pike, Rockville, MD 20852,* ☎ *301/881–2300 or 800/255–1775,* FAX *301/881–9047. 160 rooms, 4 suites. Restaurant. AE, DC, MC, V.*

Suburban Virginia

$$$$ ⊞ **Morrison House.** The architecture and furnishings of the Morrison
★ House in Old Town Alexandria are so faithful to the style of the Federal period (1790–1820) that it's often mistaken for a renovation of a historic building rather than one built in 1985. Parquet floors, crystal chandeliers and sconces, and period furnishings re-create the atmosphere of a grand American house of 200 years ago. Guest rooms are an elegant blend of early American charm, with four-poster beds, armoires, and modern conveniences. The Elysium Restaurant serves Mediterranean-inspired cuisine. ⊠ *116 S. Alfred St., Alexandria, VA 22314,* ☎ *703/838–8000 or 800/367–0800,* FAX *703/684–6283. 42 rooms, 3 suites. 2 restaurants, access to health club. AE, DC, MC, V.*

$$$$ ⊞ **Ritz-Carlton, Pentagon City.** The 18-story Ritz-Carlton hotel may
★ tower above the trees in seemingly faraway Arlington, but its location at the Pentagon City Metro stop makes it more convenient to downtown Washington than many closer hotels. The decor looks to the Virginia horse country for its inspiration, and a $2 million collection of art and antiques, mostly from the 18th and 19th centuries, may be seen in the hotel's public spaces. Many rooms offer views of the monuments across the river. To use the hotel's fully equipped fitness center, just bring your sneakers—a full line of workout clothing, including swimsuits, is provided. The adjacent mall has cinemas, a food court, and 150 shops. ⊠ *1250 S. Hayes St., Arlington, VA 22202,* ☎ *703/415–5000 or 800/241–3333,* FAX *703/415–5060. 304 rooms, 41 suites. Restaurant, bar, room service, indoor pool, health club. AE, DC, MC, V.*

$$$ ⊞ **Crystal City Marriott.** A business hotel close to National Airport and the Pentagon, the Crystal City Marriott is in a thicket of office and apartment buildings. It's a good bet for families because the sights of the Mall are just minutes away by Metro. The lobby, with its lush plantings and marble floor, is more luxurious than the rooms. The atrium restaurant is light-filled and pleasant. ⊠ *1999 Jefferson Davis Hwy., Arlington, VA 22202,* ☎ *703/413–5500 or 800/228–9290,* FAX *703/413–0185. 336 rooms, 9 suites. Restaurant, 2 bars, room service, pool, health club, laundry service and dry cleaning, business services, meeting rooms. AE, DC, MC, V.*

$$$ ⊞ **Key Bridge Marriott.** Arlington's Key Bridge Marriott is a short walk across the Key Bridge to Georgetown; it's also near the Rosslyn Metro station for easy access to Washington's major sights. Many rooms have Washington views, as does the rooftop restaurant. Swim from the indoor to the outdoor pool via an underwater connection. At times, air traffic from Washington National can be noisy. ⊠ *1401 Lee Hwy., Arlington, VA 22209,* ☎ *703/524–6400 or 800/228–9290,* FAX *703/243–3280. 565 rooms, 20 suites. 2 restaurants, 2 bars, room service, indoor-outdoor pool, beauty salon, health club, shops. AE, DC, MC, V.*

$$ ⊞ **Best Western Rosslyn Westpark.** A dependable budget hotel, the Best Western Rosslyn Wespark is a five-minute walk from the Rosslyn Metro and a leisurely stroll or short drive from Georgetown, but the best thing about it may be the view of the Washington monuments from the Vantage Point restaurant's panoramic windows. Although the location, near Fort Myer and adjacent to Arlington National Cemetery, is very quiet at night, you can easily get to a wide variety of dining rooms and nightclubs along the orange line in Virginia or the blue and orange lines in Washington. A nice touch: free local calls. ⊠ *1900 N.*

Fort Myer Dr., Arlington, VA 22209, ☎ *703/527–4814 or 800/368–3408,* FAX *703/522–7480. 308 rooms. 2 restaurants, indoor pool, sauna, exercise room, laundry service and dry cleaning. AE, D, DC, MC, V.*

$ 📞 **Howard Johnson's National Airport.** Yes, it's an airport hotel, but despite it's remote-sounding locale, Howard Johnson's National Airport is only a mile from the monuments on the Mall, and you don't even have to walk: A complimentary shuttle goes to the Crystal City Metro stop (with several miles of underground shopping centers and offices). Rooms are standard but clean. The Olympic-size pool, like the on-site Bob's Big Boy restaurant, is a great draw for families. ✉ *2650 Jefferson Davis Hwy. (Rte. 1), Arlington, VA 22202,* ☎ *703/684–7200 or 800/278–2243,* FAX *703/684–3217. 278 rooms, 1 suite. Restaurant, pool, exercise room, laundry service, airport shuttle. AE, D, DC, MC, V.*

$ 📞 **Quality Inn Iwo Jima.** Within walking distance of the Iwo Jima memorial and the Rosslyn Metro, the Quality Inn Iwo Jima is a consistently well-regarded budget hotel offering easy access to Georgetown and the Pentagon-National Airport area. Rates drop in winter; there are discounts for senior citizens; and children under 18 stay free. ✉ *1501 Arlington Blvd. (Rte. 50), Arlington, VA 22209,* ☎ *703/524–5000 or 800/221–2222,* FAX *703/522–5484. 141 rooms. Restaurant, bar, room service, pool, exercise room, laundry service. AE, D, DC, MC, V.*

$ 📞 **Vienna Wolf Trap Motel.** A three-story motel in Vienna's low-rise downtown, close to the office complexes and giant retail centers of Tysons Corner, the Vienna Wolf Trap Motel is also just a quick bus or car ride from the Vienna Metro stop (on the orange line bus, 30 minutes by Metro from downtown). Room rates are extremely reasonable: $38 to $45. Though it faces a busy suburban shopping artery, the motel is set back far enough to block most noises. A number of restaurants are within walking distance. ✉ *430 Maple Ave. W, Vienna, VA 22180,* ☎ *703/281–2330,* FAX *703/281–2838. 115 rooms. Laundry service and dry cleaning. AE, DC, MC, V.*

6 Nightlife and the Arts

THE ARTS

By John F. Kelly

Updated by
Nancy Ryder

For most of its history, the Capitol has had one claim to fame: as the nation's historic center of political power. As for culture and the arts, Washington may as well have been a small town; there wasn't much. In the past 20 years, however, the cultural backwater has been transformed into a cultural capital. The Kennedy Center is a world-class venue, home of the National Symphony Orchestra and host to Broadway shows, ballet, modern dance, opera, and more. Washington even has its own "off Broadway": a half dozen or so plucky theaters spread out around the city that offer new twists on both old and new works. Several art galleries present highly regarded chamber music series. The service bands from the area's numerous military bases ensure an endless supply of martial music of the John Philip Sousa variety as well as rousing renditions of more contemporary tunes. Washington was the birthplace of *hardcore,* a socially aware form of punk rock music that has influenced young bands throughout the country. *Go-go*—infectious, rhythmic music mixing elements of rap, rhythm and blues, and funk—has been touted as the next big sound to go national but still seems confined largely to Washington.

Friday's *Washington Post* "Weekend" section is the best guide to events for the weekend and the coming week. The *Post's* daily "Guide to the Lively Arts" also outlines cultural events in the city. The *Washington Times* "Weekend" section comes out on Thursday. The free weekly *Washington CityPaper* hits the streets on Thursday and covers the entertainment scene well. You might also consult the "City Lights" section in the monthly *Washingtonian* magazine.

Tickets

Tickets to most events are available by calling or visiting each theater's box office.

Protix takes reservations for events at Wolf Trap and elsewhere in the city. It also has outlets in selected Woodward & Lothrop and Safeway stores. ☎ *703/218–6500.*

TicketMaster takes phone charges for events at most venues around the city. You can purchase TicketMaster tickets in person at all Hecht Company department stores. No refunds or exchanges are allowed. ☎ *202/432–7328 or 800/551–7328.*

TicketPlace sells half-price, day-of-performance tickets for selected shows; a "menu board" lists available performances. Only cash is accepted, and there's a 10% service charge per order. TicketPlace also is a full-price TicketMaster outlet. ⊠ *Lisner Auditorium, 730 21st St. NW,* ☎ *202/842–5387.* ☉ *Tues.–Fri. noon–4, Sat. 11–5. Tickets for Sun. and Mon. performances sold on Sat.*

Dance

Dance Place. A studio theater that presented its first performance in 1980, Dance Place hosts a wide assortment of modern and ethnic dance most weekends. ⊠ *3225 8th St. NE,* ☎ *202/269–1600.*

Joy of Motion. A dance studio by day, Joy of Motion is the home of several area troupes, including Michelle Ava and Company (modern dance), the Dupont Alley Dance Company (jazz), and TAPestry (you guessed it—tap). ⊠ *1643 Connecticut Ave. NW,* ☎ *202/387–0911.*

Mount Vernon College. An emerging center for dance in Washington, this women's liberal arts college presents dance companies in the fall and spring. Past participants in the dance series have included the troupes of Robert Small, Nancy Meehan, and Gus Solomons, Jr. ⊠ *2100 Foxhall Rd. NW,* ☎ *202/625–4655.*

Smithsonian Associates Program (☞ Smithsonian Institution, *below*). National and international dance groups often perform at various Smithsonian museums. ☎ *202/357–3030.*

Washington Ballet. In October, February, and May this company presents classical and contemporary ballets from the works of such choreographers as George Balanchine, Marius Petipa, and Choo-San Goh, mainly at the Kennedy Center and the Warner Theatre. Each December the Washington Ballet presents *The Nutcracker.* ☎ *202/362–3606.*

Film

AMC Union Station 9. Located on Capitol Hill, AMC Union Station 9 features nine screens and validated, three-hour parking at an adjacent parking lot. ⊠ *Union Station,* ☎ *202/842–3757.*

American Film Institute. More than 700 different movies—including contemporary and classic foreign and American films—are shown each year at the American Film Institute's theater in the Kennedy Center. Filmmakers and actors are often present to discuss their work. ⊠ *Kennedy Center, New Hampshire Ave. and Rock Creek Pkwy. NW,* ☎ *202/785–4600.*

Arlington Cinema 'N' Drafthouse. A suburban Virginia alternative to movie theaters in the Capitol, Arlington Cinema 'N' Drafthouse serves various libations and hot dogs, pizza, and other snacks to munch during its films. You must be 21 or over or with a parent to attend. ⊠ *2903 Columbia Pike, Arlington, VA,* ☎ *703/486–2345.*

Bethesda Theatre Café. If you find movie-theater seats a little too confining or the choice of soft drinks a little too soft, head for the Maryland suburbs where films are shown in a dinner-theater-like setting at Bethesda Theatre Café. Patrons sit at tables; a wait staff delivers pizza, hot dogs, nachos, and beer. You must be 21 or over or with a parent to attend. ⊠ *7719 Wisconsin Ave., Bethesda, MD,* ☎ *301/656–3337.*

Biograph. Washington's home for alternative cinema, the Biograph shows a mixture of first- run and repertory domestic and foreign films that share a non-mainstream niche. ⊠ *2819 M St. NW,* ☎ *202/333–2696.*

Cineplex Odeon Uptown. You don't find many like this old beauty anymore: one huge, multiplex-dwarfing screen, Art Deco flourishes instead of a bland boxy interior, a wonderful balcony, and—in one happy concession to modernity–crystalline Dolby sound. Other first-run movie theaters are clustered near Dupont Circle, in Georgetown, and around upper Wisconsin Avenue. ⊠ *3426 Connecticut Ave. NW,* ☎ *202/966–5400.*

Cineplex Odeon's West End 1–4 Closer to downtown than some other theaters, here's a convenient place to catch one of the latest hit films. ⊠ *23rd and L Sts. NW,* ☎ *202/293–3152.*

Filmfest DC. An annual citywide festival of international cinema, Filmfest DC takes place in late April and early May. ⊠ *Box 21396, 20009,* ☎ *202/274–6810.*

Hirshhorn Museum. For avant-garde and experimental film lovers, weekly movies—often first run documentaries, features, and short films—are shown free. ⊠ *8th and Independence Ave. SW,* ☎ *202/357–2700.*

Key. This four-screen theater specializes in foreign films and presents an annual animation festival. ⊠ *1222 Wisconsin Ave. NW,* ☎ *202/333–5100.*

Mary Pickford Theater. A 64-seat theater, the Mary Pickford shows classic and historically important films for free. ⊠ *Jefferson Bldg. of Library of Congress, 1st St. and Independence Ave. SE,* ☎ *202/707–5677.*

National Archives. Historical films are shown on a daily basis. Check the calendar of events for movie listings. ⊠ *8th and Constitution Aves. NW,* ☎ *202/501–5000.*

National Gallery of Art East Building. Usually *complementary* to exhibits, you can see classic and international films in the large auditorium. Tickets are free to the public. Pick up a film calendar at the museum for movie listings. ⊠ *4th and Constitution NW,* ☎ *202/737–4215.*

National Geographic Society. Educational films with a scientific, geographic, or anthropological focus are shown here weekly. ⊠ *17th and M Sts. NW,* ☎ *202/857–7588.*

West End 5, 6, 7. If you're in the mood for a movie and in the vicinity of downtown Washington, the West End is one of the more conveniently located multiplexes in the Capitol. ⊠ *23rd and M Sts. NW,* ☎ *202/452–9020.*

Music

Orchestra

National Symphony Orchestra. The season at the Kennedy Center extends from September to June. In summer the NSO performs at Wolf Trap and presents concerts on the West Lawn of the Capitol on Memorial Day and Labor Day weekends and on July 4. One of the cheapest ways to hear—if not necessarily see—the NSO perform in the Kennedy Center Concert Hall is to get a $10 "obstructed view" ticket. ⊠ *New Hampshire Ave. and Rock Creek Pkwy NW,* ☎ *202/416–8100.*

Concert Halls

DAR Constitution Hall. Constitution Hall was the home of the National Symphony Orchestra before the Kennedy Center was built. The 3,700-seat hall still hosts visiting performers, from jazz to pop to rap. ⊠ *18th and C Sts. NW,* ☎ *202/638–2661.*

George Mason University. The GMU campus in suburban Virginia is home to the ambitious Center for the Arts, a glittering complex that opened in 1990 and hosts a full range of performing arts events, from music to ballet to drama. There is a 1,900-seat concert hall, the 500-seat proscenium Harris Theatre, and the intimate 200-seat Black Box Theatre. Also on campus is the 9,500-seat Patriot Center, site of pop acts and sporting events. ⊠ *Rte. 123 and Braddock Rd., Fairfax, VA,* ☎ *703/993–8888, 703/993–3000, or 202/432–7328.*

John F. Kennedy Center for the Performing Arts. Any search for cultured entertainment should start at the John F. Kennedy Center for the Performing Arts. On any given night America's national cultural center may be hosting a symphony orchestra, a troupe of dancers, a Broadway musical, and a comedy whodunit. In other words, the "Ken-Cen" has a little of everything. It is actually five stages under one roof: the **Concert Hall,** home park of the National Symphony Orchestra; the 2,200-seat **Opera House,** the setting for ballet, modern dance, grand opera, and large-scale musicals; the **Eisenhower Theater,** usually used for drama; the **Terrace Theater,** a Philip Johnson–designed space that showcases chamber groups and experimental works; and the **Theater**

Lab, home to cabaret-style performances (since 1987 the audience-participation hit mystery, **Shear Madness,** has been playing here). ✉ *New Hampshire Ave. and Rock Creek Pkwy. NW,* ☎ *202/467–4600 or 800/444–1324.*

Lisner Auditorium. A 1,500-seat theater on the campus of George Washington University, Lisner Auditorium is the setting for pop, classical, and choral music. ✉ *21st and H Sts. NW,* ☎ *202/994–6800.*

Merriweather Post Pavilion. In Columbia, Maryland, an hour's drive north of Washington, Merriweather Post is an outdoor pavilion with some covered seating. It plays host in warmer months to big-name pop acts. ☎ *301/982–1800; off-season, 301/596–0660.*

National Gallery of Art. Free concerts by the National Gallery Orchestra, conducted by George Manos, plus performances by outside recitalists and ensembles, are held in the venerable West Building's West Garden Court on Sunday evenings from October to June. Most performances highlight classical music, though April's American Music Festival often features jazz. Entry is first-come, first-served. ✉ *6th St. and Constitution Ave. NW,* ☎ *202/842–6941 or 202/842–6698.*

Nissan Pavilion at Stone Ridge. Cellar Door Productions, the country's largest concert promoter, built its own 25,000-seat venue in 1995. In rural Virginia, about an hour from downtown Washington, the pavilion hosts all types of music. ✉ *7800 Cellar Door Dr., Gainesville, VA,* ☎ *703/549–7625 or 202/432–7328.*

Smithsonian Institution (☞ The Mall *in* Chapter 2). Many people think the Smithsonian museums are only repositories of fabulous objects. Not so. A rich assortment of music—both free and ticketed—is presented by the Smithsonian. American jazz, musical theater, and popular standards are performed in the National Museum of American History's Palm Court. In the third-floor Hall of Musical Instruments, musicians periodically perform on historic instruments from the museum's collection. The **Smithsonian Associates Program** (☎ 202/357–3030) offers everything from a cappella groups to Cajun zydeco bands; many perform in the National Museum of Natural History's Baird Auditorium. In warm weather performances are held in the courtyard between the National Portrait Gallery and the National Museum of American Art. ☎ *202/357–2700.*

USAir Arena. The home stadium for the Washington Capitals hockey and Washington Bullets basketball teams is also the area's top venue for big-name pop, rock, and rap acts. Formerly known as the Capital Centre, it seats 20,000. ✉ *1 Harry S. Truman Dr., Landover, MD,* ☎ *301/350–3400 or 202/432–7328.*

Wolf Trap Farm Park. Just off the Dulles Toll Road, about a half hour from downtown, Wolf Trap is the only national park dedicated to the performing arts. On its grounds is the **Filene Center,** an outdoor theater that is the scene of pop, jazz, opera, ballet, and dance performances each June through September. The rest of the year, the intimate, indoor **Barns at Wolf Trap** (☎ 703/938–2404) hosts folk, jazz, rock, chamber, opera, and other music. For tickets, call ProTix (☎ 703/218–6500). On summer performance nights, Metrorail operates a $3.50 round-trip shuttle bus between the West Falls Church Metro station and the Filene Center. The fare is exact change only and the bus leaves 20 minutes after the show, or no later than 11 PM, whether the show is over or not. ✉ *1551 Trap Rd., Vienna, VA,* ☎ *703/255–1900.*

Choral Music

Choral Arts Society. Founded in 1965, the 180-voice Choral Arts Society choir performs a varied selection of classical pieces at the Kennedy Center from September to April. Three Christmas sing-alongs are scheduled each December. ⊠ *New Hampshire Ave. and Rock Creek Pkwy. NW,* ☎ *202/244–3669.*

National Shrine of the Immaculate Conception. Choral and church groups frequently perform in the impressive settings here. ⊠ *Michigan Ave. and 4th St. NE,* ☎ *202/526–8300.*

Washington National Cathedral. Choral and church groups frequently perform in the impressive settings here. ⊠ *Wisconsin and Massachusetts Aves. NW,* ☎ *202/537–6200.*

Chamber Music

Corcoran Gallery of Art. Hungary's Takacs String Quartet and the Cleveland Quartet are among the chamber groups that appear in the Corcoran's Musical Evening Series, one Friday each month from October to May, with some summer offerings. Concerts are followed by a reception with the artists. ⊠ *17th St. and New York Ave. NW,* ☎ *202/638–3211.*

Folger Shakespeare Library. The Folger Shakespeare Library's internationally acclaimed resident chamber music ensemble, the Folger Consort, regularly presents a selection of instrumental and vocal pieces from the medieval, Renaissance, and Baroque periods, during a season that runs from October to May. ⊠ *201 E. Capitol St. SE,* ☎ *202/544–7077.*

National Academy of Sciences. Free performances by such groups as the Juilliard String Quartet and the Beaux Arts Trio are given October through May in the academy's acoustically nearly perfect 670-seat auditorium. ⊠ *2101 Constitution Ave. NW,* ☎ *202/334–2436.*

Phillips Collection. Duncan Phillips' mansion is more than an art museum. From September through May the long paneled music room hosts Sunday afternoon recitals. Chamber groups from around the world perform; May is devoted to performing artists from the Washington area. The concerts begin at 5 PM. For decent seats, arrive early. ⊠ *1600 21st St. NW,* ☎ *202/387–2151.*

Performance Series

Armed Forces Concert Series. From June to August, service bands from all four branches of the military perform Monday, Tuesday, Thursday, and Friday evenings, on the East Terrace of the Capitol and several nights a week at the Sylvan Theater (☞ *below*) on the Washington Monument grounds. The traditional band concerts include marches, patriotic numbers, and some classical music. The bands often perform at other locations throughout the year. ☎ *Air Force, 202/767–5658; Army, 703/696–3718; Navy, 202/433–2525; Marines, 202/433–4011.*

Carter Barron Amphitheater. On Saturday and Sunday nights from mid-June to August this lovely, 4,250-seat outdoor theater in Rock Creek Park hosts pop, jazz, gospel, and rhythm and blues artists such as Chick Corea, Nancy Wilson, and Tito Puente. The National Symphony Orchestra also performs, and for two weeks in June the Shakespeare Theatre presents a free play by the Bard. ⊠ *16th St. and Colorado Ave. NW,* ☎ *202/426–6837; off-season, 202/426–6893.*

District Curators. An independent, nonprofit organization, the District Curators group presents adventurous contemporary performers from around the world in spaces around the city. Past artists have included

Laurie Anderson, Philip Glass, the World Saxophone Quartet, and the Japanese dance troupe Sankai Juku. ☎ 202/783–0360.

Ft. Dupont Summer Theater. When it comes to music in Washington, even the National Park Service gets in on the act. NPS presents national and international jazz artists at 8:30 on Friday and Saturday evenings from mid-June to August at the outdoor Ft. Dupont Summer Theater. Wynton Marsalis, Betty Carter, and Ramsey Lewis are among the artists who have performed at free concerts in the past. ⊠ *Minnesota Ave. and F St. SE,* ☎ 202/426–7723 or 202/619–7222.

Sylvan Theater. Service bands from the four branches of the military perform alfresco at the Sylvan Theater from mid-June to August, Tuesday, Thursday, Friday, and Sunday nights. ⊠ *Washington Monument grounds,* ☎ 202/619–7225 or 202/619–7222.

Washington Performing Arts Society. An independent nonprofit organization, WPAS books high-quality classical music, ballet, modern dance, and some drama into halls around the city. Most of the shows—ranging from the Harlem Boys Choir to the Vienna Philharmonic—are held at the Kennedy Center. The **Parade of the Arts** series features shows with family appeal. ☎ 202/833–9800.

Opera

Mount Vernon College. The college's intimate Hand Chapel is the setting for otherwise rarely produced chamber operas each winter and spring. ⊠ *2100 Foxhall Rd. NW,* ☎ 202/625–4655.

Opera Theater of Northern Virginia. The three operas from the Opera Theater's season are sung in English and staged at an Arlington, Virginia, community theater. Each December the company presents a one-act opera especially for young audiences. ☎ 703/549–5039.

Summer Opera Theater Company. An independent professional troupe, the Summer Opera Theater Company mounts two fully staged productions each summer, one in June and one in July. ⊠ *Hartke Theater, Catholic University,* ☎ 202/526–1669.

Washington Opera. Seven operas—presented in their original languages with English supertitles—are performed each season (November–March) in the Kennedy Center's Opera House and Eisenhower Theater. Performances are often sold out to subscribers, but returned tickets can be purchased an hour before curtain time. Standing room tickets go on sale at the Kennedy Center box office each Saturday at 10 AM for the following week's performances. ☎ 202/416–7800 or 800/876–7372.

Theater

Commercial Theaters and Companies

Arena Stage. The city's most respected resident company (established 1950), the Arena was the first theater outside New York to win a Tony award. It presents a wide-ranging season in its three theaters: the theater-in-the-round Arena, the proscenium Kreeger, and the cabaret-style Old Vat Room. The ambitious New Voices series in the Old Vat allows audiences to see plays in development at reduced prices. ⊠ *6th St. and Maine Ave. SW,* ☎ 202/488–3300.

Ford's Theatre. Looking much as it did when President Lincoln was shot at a performance of *Our American Cousin,* Ford's is host mainly to musicals, many with family appeal. Dickens's *A Christmas Carol* is presented each holiday season. ⊠ *511 10th St. NW,* ☎ 202/347–4833.

Lincoln Theatre. From the 1920s to the 1940s, the Lincoln hosted the same performers as the Cotton Club and the Apollo Theatre in New York City: Cab Calloway, Lena Horne, Duke Ellington. The recently renovated 1,240-seater shows films and welcomes such acts as the Count Basie Orchestra and the Harlem Boys and Girls choir. ⊠ *1215 U St. NW,* ☎ *202/328–9177.*

National Theatre. Destroyed by fire and rebuilt four times, the National Theatre has operated in the same location since 1835. It presents pre- and post-Broadway shows. ⊠ *1321 E St. NW,* ☎ *202/628–6161.*

Shakespeare Theatre. Four plays—three by the Bard, another a classic from his era—are staged each year by the acclaimed Shakespeare Theatre troupe. In 1992 the troupe moved from its former home in the Folger Library to a new, state-of-the-art, 447-seat space. For two weeks each June the company has its own version of New York's Shakespeare in the Park: a free play under the stars at Carter Barron Amphitheatre (☞ *above*). ⊠ *450 7th St. NW,* ☎ *202/393–2700.*

Warner Theatre. One of Washington's grand theaters, the 1924 building received a complete face-lift in 1992. The renovated space now hosts road shows, dance recitals, and the occasional pop music act. ⊠ *13th and E Sts. NW,* ☎ *202/783–4000.*

Small Theaters and Companies

Spread out over the District, often performing in churches and other less-than-ideal settings, Washington's small theaters and companies are the places to see some beautifully staged and acted performances of plays and musicals that may be every bit as enthralling as their blockbuster counterparts—and often more daring. While such places have long labored in obscurity, fans of independent theater have enjoyed a veritable explosion of new companies in the last few years, many of which tackle difficult, controversial, and specialized subject matter. All compete quite fiercely for the Helen Hayes Award, Washington's version of the Tony. (Several acclaimed alternative stages are on 14th Street NW and near Dupont Circle; take a cab after dark.)

Gala Hispanic Theatre. The company produces Spanish classics as well as contemporary and modern Latin American plays in both Spanish and English. ⊠ *1625 Park Rd. NW,* ☎ *202/234–7174.*

Olney Theatre. Musicals, comedies, and summer stock are presented in a converted barn, an hour from downtown in the Maryland countryside. ⊠ *2001 Rte. 108, Olney, MD,* ☎ *301/924–3400.*

Signature Theatre. This plucky group burst upon the scene in 1990 with critically acclaimed productions of Stephen Sondheim musicals. In 1993 it moved from rented space to a 126-seat theater in a converted bumper-plating facility in suburban Virginia. Sondheim is still a favorite with Signature and Signature is said to be a favorite of Sondheim. ⊠ *3806 S. Four Mile Run Dr., Arlington, VA,* ☎ *703/820–9771.*

Source Theatre. The 107-seat Source Theatre presents established plays with a sharp satirical edge and modern interpretations of classics. Each July and August, Source hosts the Washington Theater Festival, a celebration of new plays, many by local playwrights. ⊠ *1835 14th St. NW,* ☎ *202/462–1073.*

Studio Theatre. An eclectic season of classic and offbeat plays is presented in this 200-seat theater, one of the nicest among Washington's small, independent companies. The upstairs, 50-seat Secondstage is home to particularly experimental works. ⊠ *1333 P St. NW,* ☎ *202/332–3300.*

Washington Stage Guild. Founded in 1985 and performing in historic Carroll Hall, Washington Stage Guild performs the classics as well as more contemporary fare. Shaw is a specialty. ⊠ *924 G St. NW,* ☎ *202/529–2084.*

Woolly Mammoth. Unusual, imaginatively produced shows have earned Wooly Mammoth good reviews and favorable comparisons to Chicago's Steppenwolf. ⊠ *1401 Church St. NW,* ☎ *202/393–3939.*

NIGHTLIFE

Even though the after-dark scene has contracted a bit in the last few years, Washington's nightlife still offers an array of watering holes, comedy clubs, discos, and intimate musical venues catering to a wide spectrum of customers, from proper political appointees to blue-collar regulars in from the suburbs. Many nightspots are clustered in a few key areas, simplifying things for the visitor who enjoys bar-hopping. Georgetown, in northwest Washington, leads the pack with an explosion of bars, nightclubs, and restaurants on M Street east and west of Wisconsin Avenue and on Wisconsin Avenue north of M Street. A half dozen Capitol Hill bars can be found on a stretch of Pennsylvania Avenue between 2nd and 4th streets SE. There is another high-density nightlife area around the intersection of 19th and M streets NW. Near the city's lawyer- and lobbyist-filled downtown, this neighborhood is especially active during happy hour.

As for music, Washington audiences are catholic in their tastes and so are Washington's music promoters. That means you can hear funk at a rock club, blues at a jazz club, and calypso at a reggae club. And it means big-name acts often perform at venues that also book Broadway shows and other nonmusical forms of entertainment. The music listings below are an attempt to impose order on this chaos. Your best bet is to consult Friday's "Weekend" section in the *Washington Post* and the free weekly *Washington CityPaper.* It's also a good idea to call clubs ahead of time to find out who's on that night and what sort of music will be played.

Acoustic/Folk/Country Clubs

Folklore Society of Greater Washington. Perhaps surprisingly, Washington has a very active local folk scene. For information on different folk events—from *contra* (a form of folk) dancing to storytelling to open sings—close call the recorded information line of the Folklore Society of Greater Washington. ☎ *202/546–2228.*

Afterwords. Afterwords could just as easily be called Forewords, shoehorned as it is in the Kramerbooks store, near Dupont Circle. Folkish acts entertain browsing bohemian bookworms as well as patrons seated at a cozy in-store café. ⊠ *1517 Connecticut Ave. NW,* ☎ *202/387–1462.* ☽ *Mon.–Thurs. 7:30 AM–1 AM, Fri. 7:30 AM–Mon. 1 AM.*

Birchmere. It may be in an unpretentious suburban strip mall, but Birchmere is one of the best places this side of the Blue Ridge Mountains to hear acoustic folk and bluegrass acts. Favorite sons the Seldom Scene are Thursday-night regulars. Audiences come to listen, and the management politely insists on no distracting chatter. ⊠ *3901 Mt. Vernon Ave., Alexandria, VA,* ☎ *703/549–5919. MC, V.* ☽ *Sun.–Thurs. 6:30 PM–11 PM, Fri. and Sat. 7 PM–12:30 AM.*

Junction. On the site of a former dinner theater, the Junction has two hardwood dance floors totaling more than 4,000 square feet. Local country and western fans consider it one of the best places to learn a two-step, and then practice it. ⊠ *1330 E. Gude Dr., Rockville, MD,* ☎ *301/217–5820. AE, D, MC, V.* 🖾 *Cover charge Fri. and Sat.* ☉ *Daily 11* AM*–2* AM.

Zed Restaurant. Can cowboy hats and boots peacefully co-exist in a city of Brooks Brothers suits? A visit to Zed proves that they can. Each evening, bands in this suburban Virginia night spot play hits from Nashville and other points south and west. Two-stepping is encouraged. ⊠ *6151 Richmond Hwy., Alexandria, VA,* ☎ *703/768–5558. AE, MC, V.* ☉ *Daily 11* AM*–2* AM.

Bars and Lounges

Bardo Rodeo. A Plymouth Fury crashing through the window of a converted car dealership sets the tone of this new suburban Virginia brew pub, which bills itself as the largest on the East Coast. It's a frenetic place—with loud music, mismatched furniture, and a sometimes lackadaisical approach to service—but it brews a changing assortment of stouts, ales, and bitters, and it has a wonderful approach to naming the food: Items on the menu have included "Honey, Where's the Keys to the Ducati?" (a pizza) and "She Was So Fine I'd Eat the Corn Out of Her Daddy's Garden" (a quesadilla). ⊠ *2000 Wilson Blvd., Arlington, VA,* ☎ *703/527–9399.* ☉ *Sat.–Wed. 4:30* PM*–2* AM*, Thurs. and Fri. 11:30* AM*–2* AM.

Brickskeller. A beer lover's mecca, Brickskeller is the place to go when you want something more exotic than a Bud Lite. More than 500 brands of beer are for sale—from Central American lagers to U.S. microbrewed ales. Bartenders oblige beer-can collectors by opening the containers from the bottom. ⊠ *1523 22nd St. NW,* ☎ *202/293–1885.* ☉ *Mon.–Thurs. 11:30* AM*–2* AM*, Fri. 11:30* AM*–3* AM*, Sat. 6* PM*–3* AM*, Sun. 6* PM*–2* AM.

Capitol City Brewing Company. Capitalizing on the microbrewery trend so popular elsewhere, Capitol City is the first brewery to operate in the District since Prohibition. A gleaming copper bar dominates the airy room, with metal steps leading up to where the brews are actually made. Capitol City makes everything from a bitter to a bock, though not all types are available at all times. As at a restaurant with a constantly changing menu, consult the brewmaster's chalkboard to see what's on tap. ⊠ *1100 New York Ave. NW,* ☎ *202/628–2222.* ☉ *Mon.–Sat. 11* AM*–2* AM*, Sun. 11* AM*–midnight.*

Champions. Walls covered with jerseys, pucks, bats, and balls, and the evening's big game on the big-screen TV—this popular Georgetown establishment is a sports lover's oasis. Ballpark-style food enhances the mood. ⊠ *1206 Wisconsin Ave. NW,* ☎ *202/965–4005.* ☉ *Mon.–Thurs. 5* PM*–2* AM*, Fri. 5* PM*–3* AM*, Sat. 11:30* AM*–3* AM*, Sun. 11:30* AM*–2* AM. *1-drink minimum Fri. and Sat. after 10* PM.

Dubliner. Snug paneled rooms, thick Guinness, and nightly live entertainment make Washington's premier Irish pub popular among Capitol Hill staffers. ⊠ *520 N. Capitol St. NW,* ☎ *202/737–3773.* ☉ *Sun.–Thurs. 11* AM*–1:30* AM*, Fri.–Sat. 11* AM*–2:30* AM.

15 Mins. A college-age clientele ventures downtown to enjoy the funky decorations, tiny dance floor, progressive music, and black lights that bathe the back room in an eerie, purplish glow. Blues bands, local new music bands, and obscure alternative music heroes such as Eugene Chadbourne and Marc Ribot play at the club or in the adjacent Rothschild's Cafeteria. The front room attracts after-work drinking types. As for the bar's unusual name, that's how long artist Andy Warhol predicted everyone would be famous in the future: 15 Mins. ✉ *1030 15th St. NW,* ☎ *202/408–1855.* ▢ *Cover charge.* ☾ *Mon.–Tues. 5 PM–2 AM, Wed.–Thurs. noon–2 AM, Fri. noon–3 AM, Sat. 8 PM–3 AM.*

Fishmarket. There's something different in just about every room of the Fishmarket, a multilevel, multiroom space in Old Town Alexandria, from piano bar crooner to ragtime piano shouter to guitar strummer. The operative word here is *boisterous.* Order the largest size if you like your beer in massive quantities; it comes in a glass big enough to wash your face in. ✉ *105 King St., Alexandria, VA,* ☎ *703/836– 5676.* ☾ *Mon.–Sat. 11:15 AM–1 AM, Sun. 11:15 AM–midnight.*

Food for Thought. Lots of Birkenstock sandals, natural fibers, and activist conversation give this Dupont Circle lounge and restaurant (vegetarian and organic meat) a '60s coffeehouse feel. Nightly folk music completes the picture. ✉ *1738 Connecticut Ave. NW,* ☎ *202/797– 1095.* ☾ *Mon.–Thurs. 11:30 AM–12:30 AM (closed Mon. 3–5), Fri. 11:30 AM–1:30 AM, Sat. noon–1:30 AM, Sun. 4 PM–12:30 AM.*

Hawk 'n' Dove. A friendly neighborhood bar in a neighborhood coincidentally dominated by the Capitol building, Hawk 'n' Dove's regulars include politicos, lobbyists, and well-behaved Marines from a nearby barracks. ✉ *329 Pennsylvania Ave. SE,* ☎ *202/543–3300.* ☾ *Sun.–Thurs. 10 AM–2 AM, Fri. and Sat. 10 AM–3 AM.*

Sign of the Whale. The best hamburger in town is available at the bar of a well-known post-preppie/neo-yuppie haven. ✉ *1825 M St. NW,* ☎ *202/785–1110.* ☾ *Sun.–Thurs. 11:30 AM–2 AM, Fri. and Sat. 11:30 AM–3 AM.*

Yacht Club. Enormously popular with well-dressed, middle-age singles, this suburban Maryland lounge is the brainchild of irrepressible entrepreneur and matchmaker Tommy Curtis, who measures his success by the number of engagements and marriages spawned at the Yacht Club. At last count it was approaching 70. ✉ *8111 Woodmont Ave., Bethesda, MD,* ☎ *301/654–2396. Jacket and tie (casual Wed.).* ☾ *Tues.–Thurs. 5 PM–1 AM, Fri. 5 PM–2 AM, Sat. 8 PM–2 AM.*

Cabarets

Capitol Steps. The musical political satire of the Capitol Steps, a group of current and former Hill staffers, is presented on Friday and Saturday at Chelsea's, a Georgetown nightclub, and occasionally at other spots around town. ✉ *1055 Thomas Jefferson St. NW; Chelsea's,* ☎ *202/298–8222; Capitol Steps, 703/683–8330.* ▢ *Cover charge.* ☾ *Fri. at 8 and Sat. at 7:30 most weeks. Reservations required.*

Gross National Product. After years of spoofing Republican administrations with such shows as *BushCapades* and *Man Without a Contra,* then aiming its barbs at the Democrats in *Clintoons,* the irreverent comedy troupe Gross National Product was most recently performing *On the Dole.* GNP stages its shows at Arena Stage's Old Vat Theater and at the Bayou in Georgetown. ☎ *202/783–7212 (GNP) for location and reservations, which are advised.* ▢ *Ticket charge.* ☾ *Shows Fri. 8 PM and Sat. 8 and 10 PM.*

Marquee Lounge. A cabaret in the Omni Shoreham Hotel, the Marquee Lounge is where political satirist and songster Mark Russell was ensconced for many years. Today funnywoman Joan Cushing assumes the character of quintessential Washington insider "Mrs. Foggy-bottom"and, with a small cast, pokes fun at well-known political figures in satirical skit and song. *Now This!,* a musical-comedy improv troupe, acts out audience suggestions every Thursday night, and various other cabaret offerings round out the schedule. ⊠ *2500 Calvert St. NW,* ☎ *202/745–1023. Reservations required.* 🎟 *Ticket charge.* ☉ *Joan Cushing Fri. and Sat. at 8, Now This! Thurs. at 8.*

Comedy Clubs

In the past few years the number of comedy groups in Washington that welcome, indeed rely on, the zany suggestions of audience members has mushroomed. These improvisation groups pop up at various venues, performing in the laughs-at-any-cost style of Chicago's Second City troupe, but many disappear as quickly as they appeared.

ComedySportz. Two teams of improv artists go to work to make you laugh three nights a week. ⊠ *Fun Factory, 3112 Mt. Vernon Ave., Alexandria, VA,* ☎ *703/684–5212. Reservations advised.* ☉ *Thurs.–Sat.*

Comedy Café. Local and national comics appear at the Comedy Café in the heart of downtown. Wednesday is open-mike night; Thursday is local talent; on Friday and Saturday name comedians headline. ⊠ *1520 K St. NW,* ☎ *202/638–5653.* 🎟 *Cover charge.* ☉ *Thurs. at 8:30; Fri. 8:30 and 10:30; Sat. 7, 9, and 11.*

Comedy Connection. With two locations in suburban Maryland, the Comedy Connection hosts comics six nights a week. Such black comedians as Franklin Ajaye, Sherman Hemsley, and Jimmie Walker call the Connection home when in town. ⊠ *312 Main St., Laurel, MD,* ☎ *301/490–1993.* ☉ *Thurs. at 9, Fri. and Sat. 8:30 and 10:45, Sun. 9.* ⊠ *1401 University Blvd., Hyattsville, MD,* ☎ *301/445–6700.* ☉ *Wed.–Fri. and Sun. at 8:30.* 🎟 *Cover charge and 2-drink minimum. No tennis shoes. Reservations advised.*

Garvin's Comedy Clubs. Garvin's is one of the oldest names in comedy in Washington and pioneered the practice of organizing comedy nights in suburban hotels. ⊠ *Westpark Hotel, 8401 Westpark Dr., Tysons Corner, VA.* ☉ *Fri. at 9, Sat. 8 and 10.* ⊠ *Augie's Restaurant, I–395 and S. Glebe Rd., Arlington, VA.* ☉ *Fri. and Sat. at 9. For both places,* ☎ *202/872–8880 (information and reservations, which are required).* 🎟 *Cover charge and drink minimum.*

Headliners. In 1994 Headliners moved from one bigger hotel space to two smaller ones. Now more intimate, the rooms are host to local and regional acts on weekdays and national talent on the weekends. ⊠ *Holiday Inn, 2460 Eisenhower Ave., Alexandria, VA,* ☎ *703/379–4242.* ☉ *Fri. at 9, Sat. 8:30 and 10:30.* ⊠ *Holiday Inn, 8120 Wisconsin Ave., Bethesda, MD,* ☎ *301/942–4242.* ☉ *Tues.–Thurs. at 8:30, Fri. and Sat. 8:30 and 10:30.* 🎟 *Cover charge. Reservations required.*

Improv. A new heavyweight on the Washington comedy scene, the Improv is descended from the club that sparked the stand-up boomlet in New York City and across the country. Name headliners are common. ⊠ *1140 Connecticut Ave. NW,* ☎ *202/296–7008.* 🎟 *Cover charge and 2-item (not necessarily drinks) minimum.* ☉ *Sun.–Thurs. at 8:30, Fri. and Sat. 8:30 and 10:30.*

Dance Clubs

Washington's dance clubs have taken a hint from their New York counterparts, transforming themselves nearly every night into different incarnations. Club owners rent their spaces to entrepreneurs who tailor the music and ambience to a certain type of crowd. Thus, a club might offer heavy "industrial" music on a Wednesday, host a largely gay clientele on a Thursday, and thump to the sounds of '70s disco on a Friday. It's best to call ahead or consult the often intriguing ads in the free weekly *Washington CityPaper*.

Chelsea's. Should a dance like the *lambada* ever again bubble up from South America, you'll find it at Chelsea's, an elegant Georgetown club near the C&O Canal. On Monday, there is Ethiopian music; Wednesday is world music night; hot Latin acts appear Thursday through Saturday; it's Persian music on Wednesday and Sunday. ⊠ *1055 Thomas Jefferson St. NW,* ☎ *202/298–8222.* ▨ *Cover charge Fri. and Sat.* ☉ *Wed., Thurs., and Sun. 9:30 PM–2 AM, Fri. and Sat. 9:30 PM–4 AM.*

Dancers. Located in suburban Maryland, Dancers' name is an apt description of the clientele as well as the club. This is no place for wallflowers; people come here to shake it. They're attracted to the 1,200-square-foot dance floor and the club's no-smoking, no-alcohol policy. Generally it's big bands on alternate Mondays, rhythm-and-blues bands on alternate Thursdays, swing dancing on Friday, and Latin sounds on Saturday. Good old (vintage '70s) disco finds its way into the mix, too. Dance lessons are usually offered early in the evening. ⊠ *4609 Willow La., Bethesda, MD,* ☎ *301/656–0595.* ▨ *Cover charge.* ☉ *Thurs.–Sat. 8 PM–12:30 AM; classes start at 7 PM.*

Fifth Column. A trendy, well-dressed crowd waits in line to dance to the latest releases from London and Europe on three floors of a disco that's actually a converted bank. Avant-garde art installations change every six months. ⊠ *915 F St. NW,* ☎ *202/393–3632.* ▨ *Cover charge.* ☉ *Mon. 9 PM–2 AM, Wed. and Thurs. 10 PM–2 AM, Fri. and Sat. 10 PM–3 AM.*

Kilimanjaro. Deep in ethnically diverse Adams-Morgan, Kilimanjaro specializes in "international" music from the Caribbean and Africa. Every Thursday there's a local reggae band, and there are occasional weekend shows. ⊠ *1724 California St. NW,* ☎ *202/328–3838.* ▨ *Cover charge.* ☉ *Wed.–Thurs. 5 PM–2 AM, Fri. 5 PM–4:30 AM, Sat. 8 PM–4 AM, Sun. 6 PM–2 AM.*

Ritz. Near the FBI Building is a downtown nightclub popular with the black professional crowd. The Ritz has five separate rooms of music, with DJs spinning everything from Top 40 and reggae in "Club Matisse" to house music in the upstairs "Freezone." ⊠ *919 E St. NW,* ☎ *202/638–2582. Jacket and tie Fri. and Sat. AE, MC, V.* ▨ *Cover charge.* ☉ *Wed. 9 PM–2 AM, Fri. 5 PM–3 AM, Sat. 9 PM–3 AM, Sun. 9 PM–2 AM.*

River Club. If you own a pair of spats, they wouldn't look out of place at the River Club, an elegant Georgetown supper club. Its Art Deco decor, like an Erté print come to life, serves as a backdrop for big band music from Doc Scantlin, Washington's answer to Cab Calloway, on Thursday nights. On Wednesday nights, enjoy the sounds of the Admirals. On weekends a DJ spins everything from Motown to big band. This is the perfect place for starring in your own Astaire and Rogers movie. ⊠ *3223 K St. NW,* ☎ *202/333–8118. Jacket and tie.* ▨ *Cover charge.* ☉ *Tues.–Thurs. 7 PM–2 AM, Fri. and Sat. 7 PM–3 AM.*

Tracks. A gay club with a large contingent of straight regulars, this warehouse-district disco has one of the largest dance floors in town and stays open late. ⊠ *1111 1st St. SE,* ☎ *202/488–3320.* ▨ *Cover charge.* ☉ *Thurs. 9 PM–4 AM, Fri. 8 PM–5 AM, Sat. 8 PM–6 AM, Sun. 4 PM–8 PM (tea dance) and 8 PM–4 AM.*

Zei. The latest attempt to be as hip as the Big Apple, Zei (pronounced "zee") is a New York–style dance club in a former electric power substation. It wants to attract "young, upscale politically aware women and men" with the relentless thump of Euro-Pop dance music and a design that includes a wall of television sets peering down on the proceedings. ⊠ *1415 Zei Alley NW (14th St. between H and I Sts. NW),* ☎ *202/842–2445. No tennis shoes.* ☒ *Cover charge.* ☉ *Wed. and Thurs. 10 PM–2 AM, Fri. and Sat. 10 PM–3 AM (call for occasional weeknight events).*

Jazz Clubs

Blues Alley. The restaurant turns out Creole cooking, while cooking on stage are such nationally known performers as Charlie Byrd and Ramsey Lewis. You can come for just the show, but those who come for a meal get better seats. ⊠ *Rear 1073 Wisconsin Ave. NW,* ☎ *202/337–4141.* ☒ *Cover charge and $7 food/drink minimum.* ☉ *Sun.–Thurs. 6 PM–midnight, Fri. and Sat. 6 PM–2 AM. Shows at 8 and 10, plus occasional midnight shows Fri. and Sat.*

Café Lautrec. The Toulouse-Lautrec decor, French food, and Gallic atmosphere are almost enough to convince you you're on the Left Bank of the Seine rather than the right bank of the Potomac. Cool cats play cool jazz nightly at Café Lautrec, with tap-dancing fixture Johne Forges hoofing atop tables most Fridays and Saturdays. ⊠ *2431 18th St. NW,* ☎ *202/265–6436.* ☒ *$6 minimum Tues. and Thurs.–Sun.* ☉ *Sun.–Thurs. 5 PM–2 AM, Fri. and Sat. 5 PM–3 AM.*

One Step Down. Low-ceilinged, intimate, and boasting the best jazz jukebox in town, One Step Down is a small club that books talented local artists and the occasional national act. The venue of choice for many New York jazz masters, the place is frayed and smoky, as a jazz club should be. Live music is presented Thursday–Monday. ⊠ *2517 Pennsylvania Ave. NW,* ☎ *202/331–8863.* ☒ *Cover charge and minimum.* ☉ *Mon.–Thurs. 10 AM–2 AM, Fri. 10 AM–3 AM, Sat. noon–3 AM, Sun. noon–2 AM.*

Takoma Station Tavern. In the shadow of the Metro stop that lends its name, the Takoma Station Tavern hosts such local favorites as Marshall Keys and Keith Killgo,with the occasional nationally known artist stopping by to jam. The jazz happy hours starting at 6:30 Wednesday through Friday pack the joint. There's reggae on Sundays. ⊠ *6914 4th St. NW,* ☎ *202/829–1999. No sneakers or athletic wear.* ☉ *Sun.–Thurs. 4 PM–2 AM, Fri. and Sat. 4 PM–3 AM.*

219 Basin Street Lounge. Across the Potomac in Old Town Alexandria above the 219 Restaurant, jazz combos perform Thursday through Saturday in an attractive Victorian-style bar. Musicians from local service bands often stop by to sit in. ⊠ *219 King St., Alexandria, VA,* ☎ *703/549–1141.* ☒ *Cover charge.* ☉ *Sun. 10 AM–10 PM, Mon.–Thurs. 11 AM–10:30 PM, Fri. 11 AM–11 PM, Sat. 8 AM–11 PM.*

Rock, Pop, and Rhythm and Blues Clubs

Bayou. In Georgetown, underneath the Whitehurst Freeway, the Bayou is a Washington fixture that showcases national acts on weeknights and local talent on weekends. Bands cover rock in all its permutations: pop rock, hard rock, soft rock, new rock, and classic rock. Tickets are available at the door or through TicketMaster. Occasional no-alcohol, all-ages shows allow those under 18 a chance to dance. ⊠ *3135 K St. NW,* ☎ *202/333–2897.* ☒ *Cover charge.* ☉ *Generally open daily 8 PM–2 AM.*

Grog and Tankard. A college-age crowd downs cheap pitchers of beer while listening to exuberant local bands in the Grog and Tankard, a small, comfortably disheveled night spot. ⊠ *2408 Wisconsin Ave.*

NW, ☎ 202/333–3114. ▣ *Cover charge after 9* PM. ☾ *Sun.–Thurs.*
5 PM–*2* AM, *Fri.–Sat. 5* PM–*3* AM.

9:30 Club. 9:30 is a trendy club booking an eclectic mix of local, national, and international artists, most of whom play what used to be
known as "new wave" music. The regulars dress to be seen, but visitors won't feel out of place. Get tickets at the door or through Ticket-
Master. ✉ *815 V St. NW,* ☎ *202/393–0930.* ▣ *Cover charge.* ☾ *Hrs
vary according to shows but generally open Sun.–Thurs. 7:30* PM-*midnight, Fri.–Sat. 9* PM–*2* AM.

Tornado Alley. Owner Mark Gretschel is a great booster of such "roots"
music as blues, Cajun, and zydeco. Resembling a high school gym, his
suburban Maryland Tornado Alley hosts such national cult favorites
as Koko Taylor, Wayne Toups and Zydecajun, Junior Wells, and
Clarence "Gatemouth" Brown, as well as such local heroes as ex-
Commander Cody guitarist Bill Kirchen. ✉ *11319 Elkin St., Wheaton,
MD,* ☎ *301/929–0795.* ▣ *Cover charge.* ☾ *Hrs vary according to
shows but generally open Tues.–Thurs. 5* PM–*1* AM, *Fri. and Sat. 5* PM–*2
AM, Sun. 5* PM–*1* AM.

Capitol Ballroom. With one of the largest venues for alternative and
rock music in Washington, the Capitol Ballroom holds 1,000 people
and brings in such bands as Ministry, Iggy Pop and Bad Religion. Depending on the act, tickets are available at TicketMaster or the door.
On a separate side of the club dancers can gyrate to a mix of dance
music mostly in the alternative genre. ✉ *1015 Half St. SE,* ☎ *202/554–
1500.* ▣ *Cover charge.* ☾ *Hrs vary according to show but generally
open at 7:00* PM *nightly. Dance club opens at 10:00* PM.

7 Outdoor Activities and Sports

THE OUTDOORS

By John F. Kelly

Updated by
Bruce Walker

Washington is a green and leafy city. Some neighborhoods are a full 10 degrees cooler than the rest of town on hot summer days. Of course, some of the best parks are monuments, meaning much of Washington's parkland is studded or embedded with inscribed slabs of stone. The city does have a few wild streaks, though: Rock Creek Park, the 1,800-acre swath of green that snakes through D.C. is home to native woodland, meadows, and all manner of fauna, from deer to shrews. The C&O Canal west of Georgetown blooms with wildflowers. Birds sing. An industrious beaver colony is fascinating to observe. Theodore Roosevelt Island, an 88-acre nature preserve in the Potomac across from the Kennedy Center, includes a variety of habitats—marshland, swampland, upland forests—that you can explore along 2½ miles of well-marked trails.

Cemeteries

Cemeteries have restrictions other great expanses of green do not. Jogging and picnicking, for example, are not permitted. You may, unfortunately, see some people thoughtlessly treading on graves and even the plaques they bear. Please be careful of where you walk. Even with such limits, cemeteries have an appeal unlike any other park. The history of those buried there and the art of the tombstones and memorials that mark their graves make for a rich sightseeing experience. Washington has its share of politicians' graves, but more fascinating are the surprises you'll discover in its cemeteries.

Arlington National Cemetery (☞ Arlington *in* Chapter 2). Once the estate of Robert E. Lee and his family, Arlington's 612 acres are a veritable Who's Who of the American military and politics. Buried here are several Kennedys, Audie Murphy, Joe Louis, Lee Marvin, Dashiell Hammett, and 250,000 other veterans.

Congressional Cemetery. Dating from 1807, the Congressional Cemetery was the first national cemetery created by the government. Notables buried here include U.S. Capitol architect William Thornton, Marine Corps march composer John Philip Sousa, Civil War photographer Mathew Brady, and FBI director J. Edgar Hoover. There are also 76 members of Congress, many of them buried under ponderous markers. A brochure for a self-guided walking tour is available at the office. ☒ *1801 E St. SE,* ☎ *202/543–0539.*

Glenwood Cemetery. Not far from Catholic University, Glenwood has its share of notable residents, including the artists Constantino Brumidi, responsible for much of the Capitol building's beauty (among other things, he painted the frescoes adorning the inside of the great dome), and Emanuel Leutze, painter of *Washington Crossing the Delaware,* one of the most famous paintings in American history. More striking are the tombstones of two more obscure citizens: Benjamin Greenup was the first firefighter killed on duty in Washington, and he's honored with an obelisk carved with his death scene. Teresina Vasco, a child who died at age 2 after playing with matches, is immortalized sitting in her favorite rocking chair. ☒ *2219 Lincoln Rd. NE,* ☎ *202/667–1016.*

Oak Hill Cemetery (☞ Georgetown *in* Chapter 2). Set on terraces stepping down to Rock Creek, Oak Hill may be the most beautiful cemetery in Washington. Among those buried here are John H. Payne, who earned immortality by penning a single operatic song *Home, Sweet*

Home; William Corcoran, founder of the Corcoran Gallery of Art; and Edwin M. Stanton, Lincoln's secretary of war.

Rock Creek Cemetery. Rock Creek, the city's oldest cemetery, is administered by the city's oldest church, St. Paul's Episcopal, which erected its first building in 1775. (What remains of the original structure is a single brick wall.) Many beautiful and imposing monuments are in the cemetery. The best known and most moving honors Marion Hooper "Clover" Adams, wife of historian Henry Adams; she committed suicide in 1885. Sculptor Augustus Saint-Gaudens created the enigmatic figure of a seated, shroud-draped woman, calling it *The Peace of God that Passeth Understanding,* though it's best known by the nickname "Grief." ☒ *Rock Creek Church Rd. and Webster St. NW,* ☎ *202/829–0585.*

Gardens

Bishop's Garden. A compact, traditional English-style garden, Bishop's Garden is on the grounds of the Washington Cathedral. Boxwoods, ivy, tea roses, yew trees, and an assortment of arches, bas-reliefs, and stonework from European ruins provide a restful counterpoint to the cathedral's Gothic towers. ☒ *Wisconsin and Massachusetts Aves. NW,* ☎ *202/537–6200.*

Brookside Gardens. At a rolling 50-acre display garden in suburban Maryland, formal seasonal displays of bulbs, annuals, and perennials and a sprawling azalea garden flourish. Inside, the two conservatories house—depending on the time of year—Easter lilies, tropicals, Japanese chrysanthemums, or poinsettia trees. ☒ *1500 Glenallan Ave., Wheaton, MD,* ☎ *301/949–8230.*

Constitution Gardens (☞ The Monuments, *in* Chapter 2). President Nixon once envisioned an oasis of greenery, eateries, and amusement park rides for the area south of Constitution Avenue between 17th and 23rd streets NW. While it never materialized, Constitution Gardens does offer paths winding through groves of trees, a lake, a memorial to signers of the Declaration of Independence, and the sobering Vietnam Veterans Memorial.

Dumbarton Oaks (☞ Georgetown *in* Chapter 2). Sculptured terraces, geometric gardens, fountains, arbors, pools, tree-shaded brick walks—such are the horticultural marvels on display on 10 acres of formal gardens, part of Dumbarton Oaks, a historic estate in the Georgetown neighborhood. Traditional English, Italian, and French styles are represented, forming one of the loveliest garden spots in the Capitol. ☒ *31st and R Sts. NW.* ☒ *Apr.–Oct. $3, Nov.–Mar. free.* ☉ *Apr.–Oct., daily 2–6; Nov.–Mar., daily 2–5; gardens and collections closed national holidays and Dec. 24.*

Hillwood Museum (☞ Around Washington *in* Chapter 2). The grounds of Marjorie Merriweather Post's 40-room Georgian-style mansion Hillwood House brim with fragrant attractions, among them a French-style parterre or ornamental garden, a rose garden, a formal Japanese garden, and paths that wind through azaleas and rhododendrons. There's a huge greenhouse in which 5,000 orchids bloom. The mansion is a museum filled with 18th- and 19th-century French and Russian decorative art. Children under 12 are not admitted to the house tour. Make reservations for the house tour well in advance. ☒ *4155 Linnean Ave. NW,* ☎ *202/686–5807.* ☒ *House and grounds $10, grounds only $2.* ☉ *House tour Mar.–Jan., Tues.–Sat. 9:30–3; grounds Mar.–Jan., Tues.–Sat. 9–5.*

Kahlil Gibran Memorial Garden. Dedicated in 1991, this tiny urban park combining Western and Arabian symbols is perfect for quiet contemplation. Limestone benches engraved with sayings from Gibran curve around a fountain and a bust of the Lebanese-born poet. ⊠ *3100 block of Massachusetts Ave. NW.*

Kenilworth Aquatic Gardens. Exotic water lilies, lotuses, hyacinths, and other water-loving plants thrive in this 12-acre sanctuary of quiet pools and marshy flats. In a pool near the visitor center bloom East Indian lotus plants grown from 350-year-old seeds recovered from a dry Manchurian lake-bed. The gardens are home to a variety of wetland animals, including turtles, frogs, muskrats, and some 40 species of birds. Early morning is the best time to visit, when day-bloomers are just opening and night-bloomers have yet to close. July is the best month to visit, as nearly everything is in bloom. ⊠ *Anacostia Ave. and Douglas St. NE,* ☎ *202/426–6905.* ▣ *Free.* ⊘ *Gardens daily 7–4; visitor center daily 8:30–4; Garden walk summer weekends at 9, 11, and 1.*

Lafayette Square (☞ The White House Area *in* Chapter 2). The White House faces this park bounded by Pennsylvania Avenue, Madison Place, H Street, and Jackson Place. An intimate oasis in the midst of downtown Washington, Layfayette square contains beautifully maintained trees and flower beds. Its five statues honor heroes of the American Revolution and the War of 1812.

Meridian Hill Park. Landscape architect Horace Peaslee created often-overlooked Meridian Hill Park after a 1917 study of the parks of Europe. As a result, it contains elements of parks in France (a long, straight mall bordered with plants), Italy (terraces and wall fountains), and Switzerland (a lower-level reflecting pool based on one in Zurich). It's also unofficially known as Malcolm X Park, renamed by the D.C. Council in the 1970s in honor of Malcolm X, who once spoke there. Drug activity once made it unwise to visit this park alone. It's somewhat safer now—President Clinton even paid a visit in 1994—but avoid it after dark. ⊠ *16th and Euclid Sts. NW,* ☎ *202/282–1063.*

Pershing Park (☞ The White House Area *in* Chapter 2). Inscribed granite slabs in a quiet, sunken garden, located at 15th Street and Pennsylvania Avenue, recount battles of World War I honoring General "Blackjack" Pershing, who commanded the American expeditionary force during the Great War. There's ice skating here in winter.

♻ **United States Botanic Gardens** (☞ Capitol Hill *in* Chapter 2). If you enjoy plants, trees, and flowers, the United States Botanic Gardens is one of the country's most spectacular examples of horticultural beauty. A peaceful, plant-filled oasis, its conservatory houses everything from exotic ferns to towering cacti to orchids in a profusion of tints, shades, and hues. ⊠ *1st St. and Maryland Ave. SW,* ☎ *202/225–8333.* ▣ *Free.* ⊘ *Daily 9–5.*

♻ **United States National Arboretum.** During azalea season (mid-April through May), this 444-acre oasis is a blaze of color. In the summer, clematis, ferns, peonies, rhododendrons, and roses bloom. For a relaxing stroll or scenic drive the arboretum is ideal. Also popular are the National Herb Garden and the National Bonsai Collection. ⊠ *3501 New York Ave. NE,* ☎ *202/245–2726.* ▣ *Free.* ⊘ *Daily 8–5, Bonsai Collection daily 10–3:30.*

West Potomac Park (☞ The Monuments *in* Chapter 2). Between the Potomac and the Tidal Basin, West Potomac Park is best known for its flowering cherry trees, in bloom only two weeks in April; most of the time West Potomac Park is just a nice place to relax, play ball, or admire the views at the Tidal Basin.

Parks

Audubon Naturalist Society. A self-guided nature trail winds through a verdant 40-acre estate and around the local Audubon Society's suburban Maryland headquarters (the estate is known as Woodend, as is the mansion, which was designed in the 1920s by Jefferson Memorial architect John Russell Pope). You're never very far from the trill of birdsong here, as the Audubon Society has turned the grounds into something of a private nature preserve, forbidding the use of toxic chemicals and leaving some areas in a wild, natural state. The bookstore stocks titles on conservation, ecology, and birding, as well as bird feeders and birdhouses. ⊠ *8940 Jones Mill Rd., Chevy Chase, MD,* ☎ *301/652–9188.* ☞ *Free.* ☉ *Grounds daily sunrise–sunset, bookstore Mon.–Wed. and Fri. 10–6, Thurs. 10–8, Sat. 9–5, Sun. noon–5.*

C&O Canal National Historical Park (☞ The C&O Canal and Great Falls *in* Chapter 9). Started in 1828, the C&O Canal was designed to link the growing Capitol with an expanding America. It stretched 184 miles to the west, with canal boats carrying loads of coal, timber, and wheat. Today it's a long, skinny park, with one end in Georgetown and the other in Cumberland, Maryland. Canoeists paddle the canal's "watered" sections; hikers and bikers use the 12-foot-wide towpath alongside it. In warmer months, hop a mule-drawn canal boat for a brief trip. The Great Falls Tavern Visitors Center in Maryland is a museum and headquarters for the rangers who manage the C&O Canal. Walk over a series of bridges to Olmsted Island in the middle of the Potomac; the view of the falls is spectacular. ⊠ *1057 Thomas Jefferson St. NW, Georgetown,* ☎ *202/653–5190;* ⊠ *Terminus of MacArthur Blvd., Great Falls, Potomac, MD,* ☎ *301/299–2026.* ☞ *$4 per vehicle.*

East Potomac Park. A 328-acre tongue of land, East Potomac Park hangs down from the Tidal Basin between the Washington Channel to the east and the Potomac River to the west. Facilities include playgrounds, picnic tables, tennis courts, swimming pools, a driving range, two nine-hole golf courses, and an 18-hole golf course (☞ Golf, *below*). The park's miniature golf course, built during the "midget golf" craze of the '20s, is the oldest in the area; its Art Deco–like architecture is a welcome contrast to the artificial, theme-park design of most subsequent courses. Double-blossoming cherry trees line Ohio Drive and bloom about two weeks after the single-blossoming variety that attracts throngs to the Tidal Basin each spring. *The Awakening*, a huge, fantastical sculpture of a man emerging from the ground, sits on Hains Point, at the tip of the park. Plans to build a "peace garden" here have plantings resembling a giant olive branch. ⊠ *Maine Ave. SW, heading west, or Ohio Dr., heading south (follow signs carefully),* ☎ *202/619–7222.* ☉ *Ohio Dr. closed to traffic on summer weekends and holidays 3 PM–6 AM.*

Ft. Washington Park. Built to protect the city from enemies sailing up the Potomac, this 1808 fort was burned by the British during the War of 1812. Rebuilt, it served as an Army post until 1945. The National Park Service maintains it now and holds historical programs there every weekend. A visit to the fort is the main attraction—and the view of Mount Vernon across the Potomac in Virginia. ⊠ *From Beltway (Rte. 95) take Indian Head Hwy. exit (Rte. 210) and drive 4½ mi south; look for sign on right,* ☎ *301/763–4600.*

Glen Echo Park (☞ The C&O Canal and Great Falls *in* Chapter 9). Once the site of the local Chautauqua Assembly, part of a 19th-century educational movement, Glen Echo Park was built in 1891 with the lofty goal of grooming adults of diverse ethnic backgrounds to be responsible citizens. Once an amusement park, it's now run by the National Park Service, which offers space to artists who conduct classes year-round and exhibit their work each month in a stone tower left over from the Chautauqua period. An antique carousel is open in the summer, and big-band and square dancing are in the Spanish ballroom. On weekends, Adventure Theater presents shows for children. ✉ *7300 MacArthur Blvd., Glen Echo, MD,* ☎ *301/492–6282.*

Glover-Archbold Park. Groves of beeches, elms, and oaks are at the 183-acre Glover-Archbold Park, part of the Rock Creek system. A 3.6-mile nature trail runs the length of Glover-Archbold, a gift to the city in 1924. ✉ *Garfield St. and New Mexico Ave. NW.*

Great Falls Park (☞ The C&O Canal and Great Falls *in* Chapter 9). The Potomac cascades dramatically over a steep, jagged gorge, creating the spectacle that gives this 800-acre Virginia park its name. Climbers scale the rock faces leading down to the water; experienced kayakers shoot the rapids. Watch both from the park's observation deck. Take a mule-drawn boat rides or follow blazed trails through the park, some with river views. A visitor center offers information on the park and on the ruins from two previous endeavors: George Washington's unsuccessful Patowmack Canal, designed to skirt unnavigable portions of the river, and Matildaville, a town founded by Henry "Light Horse Harry" Lee. Across the rapids is the C&O Canal National Historical Park (☞ *above*). Although the area is ideal for hiking, picnicking, climbing, and fishing, the rocks and the river are extremely dangerous here. The Park Service urges caution. ✉ *Rte. 193 (Georgetown Pike) and Old Dominion Dr., Great Falls, VA,* ☎ *703/285–2966.* ✇ *$4 per vehicle, $2 per person without vehicle.* ✆ *Park daily 7–dark; visitor center Mar.–Nov., daily 10–5, and Dec.–Feb., daily 10–4.*

Huntley Meadows. A 1,200-acre refuge in Alexandria, Huntley Meadows is a birder's delight. More than 200 species of fowl—from ospreys to owls, egrets to ibis—can be spotted here. Much of the park is wetlands, a favorite of aquatic species. A boardwalk circles through a marsh, putting visitors in sight of beaver lodges, and 3 miles of trails wend through the park, making it likely you'll spot deer, muskrats, and river otters. ✉ *3701 Lockheed Blvd., Alexandria, VA,* ☎ *703/768–2525.* ✇ *Free.* ✆ *Park usually daily dawn–dusk; visitor center usually Mar.–Dec., Mon. and Wed.–Fri. 9–5, weekends noon–5; Jan. and Feb., weekends noon–5.*

Rock Creek Park. The 1,800 acres of park on either side of Rock Creek have provided a cool oasis for Washington residents since Congress set them aside in 1890. Thirty picnic areas are scattered here. Bicycle routes and hiking and equestrian trails wind through the groves of dogwoods, beeches, oaks, and cedar. Rangers at the **Nature Center and Planetarium** introduce the park and list daily events. Guided nature walks leave from the center weekends at 3 (✉ south of Military Rd. at 5200 Glover Rd. NW, ☎ 202/426–6829). A highlight of the park is **Pierce Mill,** a restored 19th-century gristmill powered by the falling water of Rock Creek. National Park Service employees grind grain into flour and sell it to visitors (✉ Rock Creek Park at Tilden St. and Beach Dr., ☎ 202/426–6908). Other park features include **Ft. Reno, Ft. Bayard, Ft. Stevens,** and **Ft. DeRussy,** remnants of the original ring of forts that guarded Washington during the Civil War, and the **Rock Creek Park Golf Course,** an 18-hole public course (☞ Golf, *below*). ✉ *Be-*

tween 16th St. and Connecticut Ave. NW, ☎ *202/426–6829 or 202/882–7332.*

Theodore Roosevelt Island. An island wilderness-preserve in the Potomac River—including 2½ miles of nature trails through marshland, swampland, and upland forest—is an 88-acre tribute to the conservation-minded 26th president. Cattails, arrowarum, pickerelweed, willow, ash, maple, and oak all grow on the island, also a habitat for frogs, raccoons, birds, squirrels, and the occasional red or gray fox. A 17-foot bronze statue of Roosevelt was done by Paul Manship. A pedestrian bridge connects the island to a parking lot on the Virginia shore, accessible from the northbound lanes of the GW Memorial Pkwy. From downtown, take Constitution Ave. west across the Theodore Roosevelt Bridge to GW Memorial Pkwy. north and follow signs. ☎ *703/285–2598.* ▣ *Free.* ☉ *Island daily dawn–dusk.*

Zoos

⬡ **National Aquarium** (☞ Old Downtown and Federal Triangle *in* Chapter 2). Housed in the Department of Commerce Building, the National Aquarium, with tropical and freshwater fish, is the nation's oldest public aquarium.

⬡ **National Zoological Park** (☞ Cleveland Park and the National Zoo *in* Chapter 2). One of the foremost zoos in the world, the 160-acre zoo is known for its giant panda, Hsing-Hsing, and ambitious Amazonia ecosystem. Many animals are shown in naturalistic settings.

Organizations

Hikes and nature walks are listed in the *Washington Post*'s Friday "Weekend" section. Outings are sponsored by the following organizations:

Audubon Naturalist Society (☞ Parks, *above*). The society offers wildlife identification walks, environmental education programs, and— September through June—a weekly Saturday "bird walk" at its suburban Maryland headquarters. Birders interested in new local avian sightings will want to call the Audubon Society's Voice of the Naturalist tape (☎ 301/652–1088). ⊠ *8940 Jones Mill Rd., Chevy Chase, MD 20815,* ☎ *301/652–9188, Ext. 3006.*

Potomac-Appalachian Trail Club. The club sponsors hikes—usually free—on trails from Pennsylvania to Virginia, including the C&O Canal and the Appalachian Trail. ⊠ *118 Park St. SE, Vienna, VA 22180,* ☎ *703/242–0965.*

Sierra Club. Sierra Club offers regional outings (☎ 202/547–2326 or 202/547–5551).

SPORTS

When conversation turns to America's great sports towns, Washington isn't often high on the list. The honors usually go to New York, Los Angeles, or Boston. Nevertheless, the Capitol is home to an impressive variety of opportunities for both spectators and participants. National surveys show that residents are more active than the nation as a whole. In fact, they jog, cycle, swim, fish, lift weights, play tennis, and sail more than the residents of any other major U.S. city. Why? It may be that Washington's climate is generally mild year-round. The area's many parks, trails, and athletic facilities don't hurt, either. Whether you're coming for a week of sightseeing or a few days of business, bring your sweats. Monuments and boardrooms are just the start of what D.C. has to offer.

Participant Sports and Fitness

Bicycling

Bicycling is one of Washington's most popular activities for both locals and visitors. The numerous trails in the District and its surrounding areas are well maintained and clearly marked. Most of the paths described below in the section on jogging—the Mall, the Mount Vernon Trail, and Rock Creek Park—are also suitable for bikers.

ROUTES AND TRAILS

C&O Canal. For scenery, you can't beat the towpath that starts in Georgetown and runs along the C&O Canal into Maryland (☞ *Parks in* the Outdoors, *above*). You could pedal to the end of the canal, 184 miles away in Cumberland, Maryland, but most cyclists stop at Great Falls, 15 miles from where the canal starts. The towpath, a gravel-and-packed surface, is occasionally bumpy, but along the way you'll pass through wooded areas and see abundant flora and fauna and 19th-century locks from the canal's working days. Nearly all of the 89-mile-long towpath has recovered from the severe damage caused by heavy snows and subsequent flooding in 1996 and is now open to foot and bicycle traffic.

East Potomac Park. Cyclists interested in serious training might want to try the 3-mile loop around the golf course in East Potomac Park, Hains Point (entry is near the Jefferson Memorial)—a favorite training course for dedicated local racers and would-be triathletes. Restrict your workouts to the daytime; the area is not safe after dark.

RENTALS

Bicycles can be rented at the following locations:

Bicycle Exchange. Near the Mount Vernon Trail. ☒ *1506-C Belle View Blvd., Alexandria, VA,* ☎ *703/768–3444.*

Big Wheel Bikes. ☒ *1034 33rd St. NW, near C&O Canal Towpath, Georgetown,* ☎ *202/337–0254;* ☒ *315 7th St. SE, near Capitol Hill,* ☎ *202/543–1600;* ☒ *2 Prince St., near Mount Vernon Trail, Alexandria, VA,* ☎ *703/739–2300).*

Bikes & Books. Formerly Proteus Bicycle Shop. ☒ *2422 18th St. NW,* ☎ *202/332–6666;* ☒ *7945 MacArthur Blvd., near C&O Canal, Cabin John, MD,* ☎ *301/229–5900.*

City Bikes. Near the Rock Creek bike path. ☒ *2501 Champlain St. NW,* ☎ *202/265–1564.*

Fletcher's Boat House. ☒ *4740 Canal Rd., at Reservoir Rd.,* ☎ *202/244–0461.*

Metropolis Bike & Scooter. Also rents Rollerblades. ☒ *709 8th St. SE,* ☎ *202/543–8900.*

Thompson's Boat Center. ☒ *Virginia Ave. and Rock Creek Park, behind Kennedy Center,* ☎ *202/333–4861.*

INFORMATION AND ORGANIZATIONS

Washington Area Bicyclist Association. *The Greater Washington Area Bicycle Atlas,* published with the American Youth Hostels Association, and Michael Leccese's *Short Bike Rides in and Around Washington, D.C.* are invaluable. In addition, the Washington Area Bicyclist Association offers information and publications on cycling in the nation's capital. ✉ *818 Connecticut Ave. NW, Suite 300, 20006,* ☏ *202/872–9830,* ℻ *202/862–9762.*

Boating

Potomac River. Canoeing, sailing, and powerboating are all popular in the Washington, D.C. vicinity. Several places rent boats along the Potomac River north and south of the city. You can dip your oars just about anywhere along the Potomac for canoeing in the C&O Canal, sailing in the widening river south of Alexandria, even kayaking in the raging rapids at Great Falls, a 30-minute drive from the Capitol.

Mather Gorge. It's no accident that some of the best white-water kayakers and white-water canoeists in the country call Washington home; on weekends they practice below Great Falls in Mather Gorge, a canyon carved by the Potomac River just north of the city, above Chain Bridge. The water is deceptive and dangerous, and only top-level kayakers should consider a run there. It is, however, safe to watch the experts at play from a post above the gorge. For information, call the ranger stations at Great Falls, Virginia (☏ 703/285–2966) or Great Falls, Maryland (☏ 301/299–3613).

BOAT RENTALS

The two boathouses listed here are convenient for tourists.

Fletcher's Boat House. Rents rowboats and canoes. ✉ *4740 Canal Rd., at Reservoir Rd.,* ☏ *202/244–0461.*

Thompson's Boat Center. Rents canoes, rowboats, and rowing shells. ✉ *Virginia Ave. and Rock Creek Park, behind Kennedy Center,* ☏ *202/333–4861.*

Tidal Basin. On the east side of the Tidal Basin paddleboats are available during the summer (✉ in front of Jefferson Memorial, ☏ 202/484–0206). Even novices can rent Sunfish and Windsurfers—and, if you're an experienced sailor, larger craft—at **The Washington Sailing Marina** (✉ south of National Airport on George Washington Pkwy., ☏ 703/548–9027) and at the **Belle Haven Marina** (✉ south of Old Town Alexandria on George Washington Pkwy., ☏ 703/768–0018).

SAILING

Annapolis Sailing School. If you're really interested in sailing, consider taking a day trip to Annapolis, Maryland (about an hour's drive from Washington). Annapolis is one of the best sailing centers on the East Coast, and the Chesapeake Bay is one of the great sailing basins of the world. A good choice for lessons and rentals is the Annapolis Sailing School, a world-renowned school and charter company. ✉ *601 6th St.,* ☏ *410/267–7205.*

Fishing

The Potomac River is something of an environmental success story. Once dangerously polluted, it has rebounded in recent years, to the benefit of local fish and, therefore, local fisherman. Largemouth bass, striped bass, shad, and white and yellow perch are all down there somewhere, willing to take your bait.

FISHING SPOTS

Potomac River. A 5-mile stretch of the Potomac River—roughly from the Wilson Memorial Bridge in Alexandria south to Ft. Washington National Park—is one of the country's best spots for largemouth bass fishing. It has, in fact, become something of an East Coast mecca for anglers in search of this particular fish. The area around Fletcher's Boat House on the C&O Canal is one of the best spots for perch.

Delta Tackle. One of the best tackle shops in the Washington, D.C. area. ✉ *8580 Cinderbed Rd., #1800, Newington, VA,* ☎ *703/550–1471.*

Life Outdoors Unlimited. Simply renting a boat and going fishing in Washington is complicated because this stretch of the Potomac is divided among three jurisdictions: Virginia, Maryland, and the District of Columbia. Whose water you're fishing or which licenses you should have isn't always easy to deterimine. The solution: Hire a guide. Life Outdoors Unlimited, run by nationally known fisherman and conservationist Ken Penrod, is an umbrella group of area freshwater fishing guides. A dozen of the area's best guides are listed; for about $250 a day a guide sees to all your needs, from tackle to boats, and tells you which licenses are required. Penrod's guides are all pros who teach novices and guide experts. Call for details (☎ 301/937–0010). You maybe asked to leave a message; calls are usually returned the same evening.

INFORMATION

Gene Mueller, a nationally known hunting and fishing writer, has a column three times a week (Monday, Wednesday, and Friday) in the *Washington Times*. He takes readers' telephone calls Thursday mornings (☎ 202/636–3268). The "Fish Lines" column in Friday's *Washington Post* "Weekend" outlines where the fish are biting, from the Potomac to the Chesapeake Bay.

Golf

Serious golfers must resign themselves to driving out of the city to find a worthwhile course. None of the three public courses in town could be considered first-rate. Still, people line up to play here and at about 50 other local public courses, sometimes arriving as early as 2 AM to snare a tee time. (Some courses allow you to call ahead to reserve a tee time; call for details.)

PUBLIC COURSES WITHIN THE DISTRICT

East Potomac Park. This public course is a flat, wide, featureless, 6,303-yard, par-72 course. Its greatest claim to fame is that professional golfer and Washington resident Lee Elder got his start there. It also has two nine-hole courses and a driving range. Greens fees are $13.50 for 18 holes on weekdays, $9 for nine; weekends it's $17 and $10.50, respectively. One of the country's oldest miniature golf courses operates here during the summer. ✉ *Hains Point, East Potomac Park near Jefferson Memorial,* ☎ *202/863–9007.*

Langston Golf Course. Langston is a par-72, 6,300-yard course open to the public. It's popular, although its greens and fairways are poorly maintained; holes 8 and 9, by the Anacostia River, are challenging. Greens fees are $13.50 for 18 holes on weekdays, $9 for nine; weekends it's $17 and $10.50, respectively. ✉ *26th St. and Benning Rd. NE,* ☎ *202/397–8638.*

Rock Creek Park Golf Course. A 4,798-yard, par-65 public course, Rock Creek Park has an easy front nine, but its back nine holes are challenging. The tight, rolling, well-treed back nine make it the most attractive public course in the Capitol. Greens fees are $13.50 for 18 holes on weekdays, $9 for nine; weekends it's $17 and $10.50, respectively. ✉ *16th and Rittenhouse Sts. NW,* ☎ *202/882–7332.*

PUBLIC COURSES IN NEARBY SUBURBS

Enterprise. Maryland's 6,209-yard, par-72 golf course, 30 minutes by car from downtown Washington, has a reputation as the best-manicured public course in the Capitol area. Its well-landscaped layout gives it a country-club feel. The fee for 18 holes is $21 weekdays, $27 week-ends ⊠ *2802 Enterprise Rd, near Beltway in Prince George's County, Mitchellville, MD,* ☎ *301/249–2040.*

Northwest Park. About 30 minutes from town is a 6,732-yard, par-72 course that is extremely long and windy, making for slow play, but it is immaculately groomed. It also has a short-nine course. The fee for 18 holes is $18.50 weekdays, $23 weekends; the short-nine course is $10.50 and $12.50. ⊠ *15701 Layhill Rd., Wheaton, MD,* ☎ *301/598–6100.*

Penderbrook. If you are flying into or out of Dulles Airport and want to fit in a round of golf, try Penderbrook. A short but imaginative 5,927-yard, par-72 course, it is one of the best public courses in the area. The 5th, 11th, 12th, and 15th holes are exceptional. The weekday fee is $32 and the weekend fee is $42 for 18 holes. ⊠ *West Ox Rd. and I–66,* ☎ *703/385–3700.*

Reston National. A four-star, 6,480-yard, par-71 course widely considered the best public course in the metropolitan area, Reston National is about a half-hour drive from downtown Washington. Well maintained, it is heavily wooded but not too difficult for the average player. The fee is $36–$44 on weekdays and $55 weekends. ⊠ *11875 Sunrise Valley Dr., Reston, VA,* ☎ *703/620–9333.*

Health Clubs

The number of health clubs in the area has increased in recent years. All require that you be a member—or at least a member of an affiliated club—in order to use their facilities. Some hotels have made private arrangements with neighboring health clubs to enable guests to use the club's facilities (you may be charged a daily fee). Check with your hotel when making reservations. **The International Racquet Sports Association** has many member clubs in Washington. If you belong, present your membership card from your home club and pay a daily fee. The IRSA "Passport" lists member clubs.

National Capital YMCA. The National Capital YMCA offers basket-ball, weights, racquetball, squash, swimming, exercise equipment, and more. Some downtown hotels—the Hampshire Hotel, Canterbury Hotel, Howard Johnson Hotel & Suites, and Quality Inn—offer guests free one-day passes to the YMCA; your concierge has details. Members of an out-of-town Y show their membership card and pay a daily fee of $5 to $7, depending on the time of day; their guests are allowed for $15 to $25. ⊠ *1711 Rhode Island Ave. NW,* ☎ *202/862–9622.*

West End Executive Fitness Center. Guests at any Washington-area hotel may use the fabulous facilities the West End Executive Fitness Center at the ANA Hotel. All you need to do is show your hotel room key to the center's employees and pay a $20 daily fee ($5 to $10 for ANA guests). One of the fanciest fitness centers in Washington, the ANA is the place where celebrities like Cybill Shepherd, Holly Hunter, and Arnold Schwarzenegger come to get pumped. ⊠ *ANA Hotel, 2401 M St. NW,* ☎ *202/457–5070.*

Horseback Riding

Rock Creek Park Horse Center. Open all year, the Rock Creek Park Horse Center offers lessons and trail rides. The guided trail rides, for beginning riders 12 and up, are an hour long; the hours vary according to season. ⊠ *Military Rd. and Glover Rd. NW,* ☎ *202/362–0117.*

Ice Skating

Cabin John Regional Park. No matter if the weather is cold or hot, this year-round indoor rink in the Maryland suburbs is open for business.

Skate rentals are available. ⊠ *10610 Westlake Dr., Rockville, MD,* ☎ *301/365–0585.*

Mount Vernon Recreation Center. If you're in the neighborhood you might want to try this indoor, year-round suburban rink. Skates are rentable on site. ⊠ *2017 Belle View Blvd., Alexandria, VA,* ☎ *703/768–3222.*

Pershing Park Ice Rink. Pershing Park is one of Washington's most popular rinks. Skates can be rented on site. ⊠ *Pennsylvania Ave. between 14th and 15th Sts. NW,* ☎ *202/737–6938.*

Sculpture Garden Outdoor Rink. Each winter this rink reappears. Skates are rentable here, a convenience for visitors. ⊠ *Constitution Ave. between 7th and 9th Sts. NW,* ☎ *202/371–5340.*

Jogging

Members of Congress and Supreme Court justices may be spotted on **the Mall,** running loops around the monuments. Georgetown power brokers hoof it along the towpaths of the **C&O Canal** or on the meandering trails in **Rock Creek Park.** At lunchtime in Arlington, the Pentagon empties out along the **Mount Vernon Trail.** Even President Clinton jogs—usually on the White House's custom-built jogging track.

ROUTES, TRAILS, AND TRACKS

Downtown Washington and nearby northern Virginia offer some of the most scenic jogging trails in the country, and jogging is one of the best ways to take in the vistas of the city. Joggers unfamiliar with the city should not go out at night, and, even in daylight, it's best to run in pairs if you venture beyond the most public areas and the more heavily used sections of the trails.

C&O Canal. Maintained by the National Park Service, the 89-mile-long towpath is a favorite of runners and cyclists. The most popular loop— from a point just north of the Key Bridge in Georgetown to Fletcher's Boat House—is about 4 miles round-trip.

Mall. The loop around the Capitol and past the Smithsonian museums, the Washington Monument, the Reflecting Pool, and the Lincoln Memorial is the most popular of all Washington running trails. At any time of day, hundreds of joggers, speed walkers, bicyclists, and tourists can be seen making their way along the gravel pathways of this 4½-mile loop. For a longer run, veer south of the Mall on either side of the Tidal Basin and head for the Jefferson Memorial and East Potomac Park, the site of many races. Monday, Wednesday, and Thursday evenings at 6:30 the **Capitol Hill Runners** (☎ 301/283–0821) set off on a 4- to 8-mile run from the 1st Street SW garage entrance of the Rayburn House Office Building.

Mount Vernon Trail. Just across the Potomac in Virginia, the Mount Vernon Trail is a favorite with Washington runners. The northern (shorter) section begins near the pedestrian causeway leading to Theodore Roosevelt Island (directly across the river from the Kennedy Center) and goes past National Airport and on to Old Town Alexandria. This stretch is approximately 3½ miles one way. You can get to the trail from the District by crossing either the Theodore Roosevelt Bridge (at the Lincoln Memorial) or the Rochambeau Memorial Bridge (also known as the 14th Street Bridge, at the Jefferson Memorial). South of National Airport, the trail runs down to the Washington Marina. The final mile of the trail's northern section meanders through protected wetlands before ending in the heart of Old Town Alexandria. The longer, southern section of the trail (approximately 9 miles) takes you along the banks of the Potomac from Alexandria all the way to George Washington's home, Mount Vernon.

Rock Creek Park. A miraculously preserved bit of wilderness in the middle of Washington, Rock Creek Park has 15 miles of trails, a bicycle path, a bridle path, picnic groves, playgrounds, and a boulder-strewn rolling stream, from which it gets its name (the creek is not safe or pleasant for swimming). Starting at P Street on the edge of Georgetown, Rock Creek Park runs all the way to Montgomery County, Maryland. The most popular run in the park is a trail along the creek extending from Georgetown to the National Zoo (about a 4-mile loop). In summer, there is considerable shade, and there are water fountains at an exercise station along the way. The roadway is closed to traffic on weekends. On Sunday mornings, the **Fleet Feet Sports Shop** (☎ 202/387–3888), in the Adams-Morgan neighborhood near the National Zoo, sponsors 5-mile runs through Rock Creek Park and other areas.

INFORMATION AND ORGANIZATIONS

Gatorade/Road Runners Club of America Hotline. For general information about running and races in the Washington area, this is where to call (☎ 703/683–7722).

Road Runners Club of America. Your contact for running clubs in the region. ✉ *1150 S. Washington St., Suite 250, Alexandria, VA 22314,* ☎ *703/836–0558.*

Washington Post. Group runs and weekend races around Washington are listed in the Friday "Weekend" section's calendar.

Washington Times. The paper's Thursday calendar of events lists weekend races and group runs in the area.

Swimming

Aquatic Department, D.C. Department of Recreation. Washington has no beaches. If you want to swim, stay at a hotel with a pool. Once it was possible to swim at some hotel pools for a small fee; no longer. Health-club pools, too, are open only to members, though the downtown YMCA has a pool and welcomes members of out-of-town Ys—for a fee. The District of Columbia maintains eight public indoor pools, 20 large outdoor pools, and another 15 outdoor pools which are smaller but still fun for children. For more information and a list of public facilities, the D.C. Department of Recreation's Aquatic Department is the place to contact. ✉ *1230 Taylor St. NW, Washington, DC, 20011,* ☎ *202/576–6436.*

Tennis

Department of Recreation. Tennis, the sport of the rich, famous, and powerful, is extremely popular in Washington. The District maintains 144 outdoor courts, but since some are in seedy parts of town, check on the neighborhood in question before heading out. Call or write the Department of Recreation for a list of all city-run courts. Ask about specific courts as well. ✉ *3149 16th St. NW, Washington, DC, 20010,* ☎ *202/673–7646.*

Hains Point. With outdoor courts as well as courts under a bubble for wintertime play, Hains Point is one of the best places to play tennis in the Capitol region. Fees run from $15 to $24 an hour depending on the time and season. Make court reservations up to one week in advance. ✉ *East Potomac Park,* ☎ *202/554–5962.*

Rock Creek Tennis Center. Rock Creek has some of the finest clay and hard courts around town. Fees range from $3.25 to $24 an hour, depending on the time. Make reservations up to a week in advance. ✉ *16th and Kennedy Sts. NW,* ☎ *202/722–5949.*

Spectator Sports

TicketMaster. Tickets for all USAir Arena, Patriot Center, and Baltimore Arena events can be purchased through various Ticketmaster outlets in the Capitol region (☎ 202/432–7328 or 410/481–7328; outside of the D.C. and Baltimore areas, 800/551–7328).

Baseball

Baltimore Orioles. Washington doesn't have its own professional baseball team, so resident fans go to Baltimore to root for the Orioles in a beautiful new ballpark, **Oriole Park at Camden Yards.** It seats 48,000, with tickets ranging from $5 for bleacher seats to $25 for club level seats. ✉ *333 W. Camden St., Baltimore, MD,* ☎ *202/432–7328.*

Bowie Baysox. In 1994, the Bowie Baysox, the Orioles' Class AA farm team, opened a brand-new, 10,000-seat stadium in suburban Prince George's County, Maryland, about 45 minutes by car from Washington. Tickets range from $3 to $9. ✉ *Prince George's Stadium, Rtes. 50 and 301, Bowie, MD,* ☎ *301/805–6000.*

Frederick Keys. Head north of Washington up I–270 in Maryland to see the Oriole Class A Frederick Keys in action. Tickets range from $3 to $9, and children age 6 to 12 wearing Little League uniforms get in to Keys games free. ✉ *Harry Grove Stadium (Market St. exit from Rte. 70 or 270), Frederick, MD,* ☎ *301/662–0013.*

Hagerstown Suns. To watch the Toronto Blue Jay Class A Hagerstown Suns play, take I–270 north of the Capitol into Maryland. Tickets range from $3 to $9. ✉ *Municipal Stadium, 274 E. Memorial Blvd., Hagerstown, MD,* ☎ *301/791–6266.*

Prince William Cannons. If baseball à la Bull Durham is for you, Woodbridge, Virginia, is where to see the New York Yankees' Class A affiliate. Tickets range from $4.50 to $8.50. ✉ *G. Richard Pfitzner Stadium, south of Beltway,* ☎ *703/590–2311.*

Basketball

College Basketball. Among the Division I college basketball teams in the area, former NCAA national champion Georgetown University's Hoyas are the best known. Their home games are played at the USAir Arena (☎ 301/350–3400). Other Division I schools include the University of Maryland (☎ 301/314–7070), George Mason University (☎ 703/993–3000), George Washington University (☎ 202/994–3865), American University (☎ 202/885–3267), the U.S. Naval Academy (☎ 410/268–6060), and Howard University (☎ 202/806–7198).

Washington Bullets. The Washington Bullets' home games are held at the USAir Arena in Landover, Maryland, just outside the Beltway. Their schedule runs from September to April. Tickets range from $11 to $33. ✉ *USAir Arena near Landover Rd. and Beltway,* ☎ *301/622–3865; TicketMaster, 202/432–7328 or 800/551–7328.*

Football

College Football. Colleges around the Capitol offer an excellent alternative to perennially-booked-solid Redskins games for frustrated football fans. Teams from the University of Maryland (☎ 301/314–7070), the U.S. Naval Academy (☎ 410/268–6060) in Annapolis, and Howard University (☎ 202/806–7198) play full schedules.

Redskins. Washington is a football-crazy town—never, never say anything bad about the Redskins. Unfortunately, unless you're a close relative of the team's owner, getting tickets to a home game is tough. Since 1966, all Redskins games at the 55,750-seat Robert F. Kennedy Stadium on the eastern edge of Capitol Hill have been sold out to season-ticket holders. Tickets are occasionally advertised in the classified section of the Post, but expect to pay top dollar. Tickets to a Skins' preseason games in August may be easier to find. The situation will hopefully improve in 1997: A new, 78,600-seat stadium in Landover, Maryland, is being built. Construction has begun, but at press time a pending lawsuit concerning purported zoning violations blocks completion.

Horse Racing

Laurel Park. Maryland has a long-standing affection for the ponies. You can watch and wager on thoroughbreds at Laurel Park during a season that runs January to mid-March, June through July, and October through December. Race days are usually Tuesday and Thursday through Sunday. ⊠ *Rte. 198 and Race Track Rd., Laurel, MD,* ☏ *301/725–0400.*

Pimlico Race Course. On the third Saturday in May the Preakness Stakes is run at Baltimore's Pimlico Race Course. The course has additional thoroughbred racing from April through June, and July through the beginning of October. Race days are usually Tuesday and Thursday through Sunday. ⊠ *Hayward and Winner Aves., Baltimore, MD,* ☏ *410/542–9400.*

Rosecroft Raceway. Harness racing is just outside the Beltway at Rosecroft Raceway. Race days are usually Thursday through Sunday in a season that runs from February to mid-December. ⊠ *6336 Rosecroft Dr., Fort Washington, MD,* ☏ *301/567–4000.*

Ice Hockey

Washington Capitals. The Washington Capitals' season runs from October through April. In recent years the team has come close to greatness, but it has always choked at playoff time. Washingtonians love the Capitals, nonetheless. Home games are played at the USAir Arena. Tickets range from $12 to $45. ⊠ *Landover Rd. and Beltway,* ☏ *301/350–3400; TicketMaster, 202/432–7328 or 800/551–7328.*

8 Shopping

By Deborah
Papier

Updated by
Bruce Walker

AFRICAN MASKS LIKE THOSE inspiring Picasso . . . kitchenware as objects d'art . . . bargains on apparel by Christian Dior, Hugo Boss, and Burberrys . . . paisley scarves from India . . . toy trains from Switzerland . . . American and European antiques . . . books of every description . . . handicrafts from a dozen Native American tribes . . . music boxes by the thousand . . . textiles by the score . . . fine leather goods . . . love beads and diamonds—D.C. has something for shoppers of every political stripe. It wasn't always so. Once shopping here meant a trek to one of the suburban shopping malls offering far more than could be found in town. Visiting Bloomingdale's, Nordstrom, or Macy's still means going to Montgomery Mall or White Flint Mall in Bethesda, Maryland (the latter near the White Flint Metro), the twin megamalls in Tysons Corner, Virginia (reachable by bus but not subway), or the Fashion Centre mall at Pentagon City (Metro: Pentagon City).

In recent years, however, the city's own shopping scene has been revitalized. Although some longtime retailers have gone bankrupt, Filene's Basement (the Boston-based upscale fashion discounter) has moved in to fill the gap left by Raleighs' departure, and the remaining department stores have upgraded both their facilities and their merchandise. Many of the smaller one-of-a-kind shops have managed to survive urban renewal, designer boutiques are increasing, and interesting specialty shops and minimalls are popping up all over town. Weekdays downtown, street vendors offer a funky mix of jewelry, brightly patterned ties, buyer-beware watches, sunglasses, and African-inspired clothing, accessories, and art. Of course, T-shirts and Capital City souvenirs are always in plentiful supply, especially on the streets ringing *the* Mall.

On the discount scene, several major outlet centers are within 45 minutes of the city (including Potomac Mills, the mile-long mall off I–95 that bills itself as Virginia's leading tourist attraction); closer to the District, the off-price Nordstrom Rack and other discount shops are clustered in City Place mall, which opened in 1992 in downtown Silver Spring, Maryland (Metro: Silver Spring).

Store hours vary greatly. Play it safe. Call ahead. In general, Georgetown stores are open late and on Sunday; stores downtown that cater to office workers close at 6 PM and may not be open at all on Saturday or Sunday. Some stores extend their hours on Thursday.

Sales tax is 6%; major credit cards are accepted virtually everywhere.

Shopping Districts

Adams-Morgan. Scattered among the dozens of Latin, Ethiopian, and Caribbean restaurants in this most bohemian of Washington neighborhoods are a score of the city's most eccentric shops. If quality is what you seek it's a minefield; tread cautiously. Still, for the bargain hunter it's great fun. A word of caution—call ahead to verify hours. Adams-Morganites are often not clock-watchers, but you can be sure a weekend afternoon stroll will find a good representation of the shops open and a great few hours of browsing. Most of the shops are on 18th Street NW, between Columbia Road and California Avenue.

Chevy Chase Pavilion. Across from Mazza Gallerie, a major shopping district in the Capitol, is the newer, similarly upmarket Chevy Chase Pavilion. Its exclusive women's clothing stores include Joan & David and Steilmann European Selection (which carries Karl Lagerfeld's sportier KL line). Other specialty shops of note here are the Pottery

Washington Shopping

Ann Taylor, **3, 38, 52**

Appalachian
Spring, **52**

Beadazzled, **16**

Betsy Fisher, **26**

Britches of
Georgetown, **23**

Brooks Brothers, **35**

Burberrys, **29**

Chanel Boutique, **43**

Chapters, **39**

Charles Schwartz
& Son, **3**

Chenonceau
Antiques, **8**

Cherishables, **15**

Cheshire Cat, **5**

Chevy Chase Pavilion
(shopping center), **4**

Church's, **36**

Earl Allen, **41**

Eastern Market, **55**

Fahrney's, **44**

Fashion Centre at
Pentagon City, **44**

Filene's
Basement, **3, 33**

Forecast, **56**

Georgetown Leather
Design, **57**

Hecht's, **46**

Indian Craft
Shop, **42**

J. Press, **32**

John B. Adler, **45**

Kemp Mill
Music, **18, 34**

Khismet Wearable
Art, **10**

The Kid's Closet, **28**

Kitchen Bazaar, **6**

Kobos, **9**

Kramerbooks, **17**

Lammas Books, **19**

Lord & Taylor, **2**

Marston Luce, **25**

Mazza Gallerie
(shopping center), **3**

Moon, Blossoms and
Snow, **54**

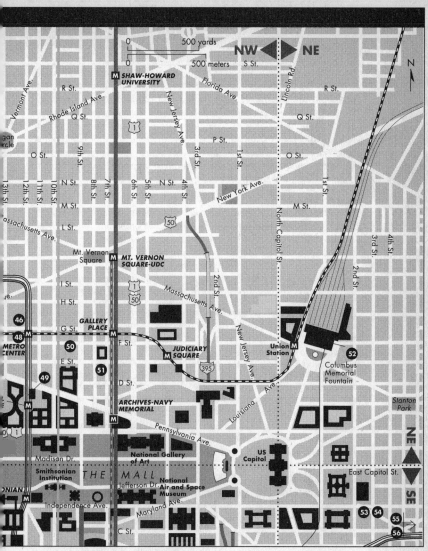

Barn, the National Cathedral Museum Shop, and Country Road Australia. ✉ *5335 Wisconsin Ave. NW,* ☎ *202/686–5335.*

Dupont Circle. You might call Dupont Circle a working-class version of Georgetown—blue collar instead of blue blood, not as well kept, with more apartment buildings than houses. But make no mistake: This is one of Washington's most vibrant neighborhoods, with a lively mix of shops and restaurants. Most of the action is on the major artery of Connecticut Avenue. The neighborhood has had its ups and downs. Today Dupont Circle is once again fashionable, and its many restaurants, offbeat shops, and specialty book and record stores lend it a distincive, cosmopolitan air. The street scene here is grittier than Georgetown's, with fewer teens and older shoppers and more twentysomethings and thirtysomethings.

Eastern Market. As the Capitol Hill area has become gentrified, additional unique shops and boutiques have sprung up in the neighborhood. Many are clustered around the 1873 building known as Eastern Market. Inside are produce and meat counters, plus the Market Five art gallery; outside are a farmer's market (on Saturdays) and a flea market (on weekends). Across 7th Street are Mission Traders (imported handicrafts), Antiques on the Hill (primarily furniture), and Forecast (women's clothing). ✉ *7th and C Sts. SE, 1 block north of Eastern Market Metro.*

Fashion Centre at Pentagon City. Just across the river in Virginia, a 10-minute ride on the Metro from downtown, is a four-story mall (including food court) with Macy's at one end and Nordstrom at the other. In between are such shops as Liz Claiborne and the Coach Store. ✉ *1100 S. Hayes St., Arlington, VA,* ☎ *703/415–2400.*

Georgetown. Georgetown remains Washington's favorite shopping area. This is the Capitol's center for famous citizens (*Washington Post* matriarch Katherine Graham and celebrity biographer Kitty Kelley are among the luminaries who call Georgetown home), as well as for restaurants, bars, nightclubs, and trendy shops. Though Georgetown is not on a subway line, and parking is impossible, people still flock here. The attraction (aside from the lively street scene) is the profusion of specialty shops in a charming, historic neighborhood. In addition to tony antiques, elegant crafts, and high-style shoe and clothing boutiques, the area offers wares that attract students and other less-well-heeled shoppers: books, music, and fashions from such popular chain stores as the Gap and Benetton.

Georgetown Park. The hub of Georgetown is the intersection of Wisconsin Avenue and M Street, with most of the stores lying to the east and west on M Street and to the north on Wisconsin. Near that intersection is Georgetown Park (✉ *3222 M St. NW,* ☎ *202/298–5577*), a three-level mall that looks like a Victorian ice-cream parlor inside. The pricey clothing and accessory boutiques and ubiquitous chain stores (such as Victoria's Secret) in the posh mall draw international tourists in droves. Next door to the mall is a branch of New York's premier gourmet food store, Dean & Deluca (✉ *3276 M St. NW,* ☎ *202/342–2500*).

Mazza Gallerie. A major shopping district is on upper Wisconsin Avenue straddling the Maryland border. Called the Mazza Gallerie, the four-level mall is anchored by the ritzy Neiman Marcus department store and a Filene's Basement. Its other stores include Williams-Sonoma's kitchenware and Laura Ashley Home. Other department stores are close by: Lord & Taylor and Saks Fifth Avenue (☞ Department Stores, *below*). ✉ *5300 Wisconsin Ave. NW,* ☎ *202/966–6114.*

Georgetown Shopping

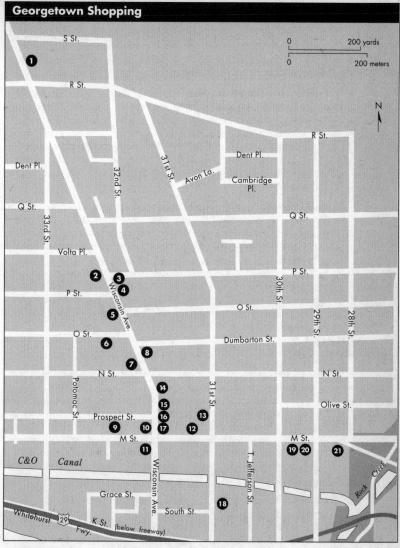

The American
Hand, **20**

Ann Taylor, **11**

Betsey Johnson, **8**

Britches Great
Outdoors, **17**

Britches of
Georgetown, **14**

Chevy Chase Pavilion
(shopping center), **4**

The Coach Store, **10**

Commander
Salamander, **5**

Earl Allen, **12**

F.A.O. Schwarz, **11**

Georgetown Antiques
Center, **19**

Georgetown
Park (mall), **11**

G.K.S. Bush, **21**

HMV Records, **16**

Little Caledonia, **4**

Martin's, **7**

Miller & Arney
Antiques, **1**

Old Print Gallery, **13**

Olsson's Books &
Records, **15**

Opportunity Shop, **3**

Orpheus Records, **9**

The Phoenix, **2**

Susquehanna, **6**

Yes!, **18**

Shops at National Place. The Shops takes up three levels, one of which is devoted to food stands. Although mainly youth-oriented (this is a good place to drop off teenagers weary of the Smithsonian and more in the mood to buy T-shirts), The Limited, Victoria's Secret, and The Sharper Image have stores here, too. ✉ *By Metro Center, 13th and F Sts. NW,* ☎ *202/783–9090.*

Pavilion at the Old Post Office. The city is justly proud of its Old Post Office Pavillion, a handsome shopping center in a historic building with 19th century origins. In addition to the 16 food vendors, there are 17 shops, among them Condor Imports (for South American and African clothing and crafts) and Juggling Capitol (for beginner to expert jugglers). The observation deck in the building's clock tower offers an excellent view of the city. ✉ *12th St. NW and Pennsylvania Ave.,* ☎ *202/ 289–4224.*

Union Station. One of the most delightful shopping enclaves in the Capitol, Union Station is resplendent with marble floors and gilded, vaulted ceilings. It's now both a working train station and a mall with three levels of stores—one with food stands and a cinema multiplex—and, appropriately, the Great Train Store, which offers train memorabilia and toy versions from the inexpensive to four-digit Swiss models. The east hall, reminiscent of London's Covent Garden, is filled with vendors of expensive and ethnic wares in open stalls. Christmas is an especially pleasant time to shop here. ✉ *Massachusetts Ave. NE near N. Capitol St.,* ☎ *202/371–9441.*

Department Stores

Filene's Basement. At this mecca for bargain hunters, steep discounts can be had on Christian Dior, Hugo Boss, Burberrys, and other designer men's and women's clothing labels. Off-price apparel, shoes, perfume, and accessories are offered as well. Neither of the Washington branches has a bargain-basement atmosphere. The downtown Filene's is especially well-appointed in wood and brass, with a handsome elevator to take you to the upper level. ✉ *1133 Connecticut Ave. NW,* ☎ *202/872– 8430. Metro: Farragut North.* ✉ *5300 Wisconsin Ave. NW,* ☎ *202/ 966–0208.*

Hecht's. The main downtown store is bright and spacious, and its sensible groupings and attractive displays of merchandise make shopping relatively easy on the feet and the eyes. The clothes sold here are a mix of conservative and trendy lines, with the men's department assuming increasing importance. Cosmetics, lingerie, and housewares are also strong departments. Sadly, one of the things that makes Hecht's Hecht's today is that it remains open; all its downtown neighbors—Garfinckel's and Woodward & Lothrop recently, Lansburgh's some years ago—have pulled up stakes. As a clothing/department store it's roughly comparable to Macy's. ✉ *12th and G Sts. NW,* ☎ *202/628–6661.*

Lord & Taylor. Lord & Taylor lets the competition be all things to all people while it focuses on nonutilitarian housewares and classic clothing by such designers as Anne Klein and Ralph Lauren. All clothing is designed and made in the United States. ✉ *5255 Western Ave. NW,* ☎ *202/362–9600.*

Neiman Marcus. If price is an object, this is definitely not the place to shop, although it's still fun to browse. Headquartered in Dallas, Neiman Marcus caters to customers who value quality above all. The carefully selected merchandise includes couture clothes, furs, precious jewelry, crystal, and silver. ⊠ *Mazza Gallerie, 5300 Wisconsin Ave. NW,* ☎ *202/966–9700.*

Saks Fifth Avenue. Though not technically a Washington department store since it is just over the Maryland line, Saks is nonetheless a Washington institution, a wide selection of European and American couture clothes; other attractions are the shoe, jewelry, fur, and lingerie departments. ⊠ *5555 Wisconsin Ave.,* ☎ *301/657–9000.*

Specialty Stores

Antiques and Collectibles

Chenonceau Antiques. The mostly American 19th- and 20th-century pieces on these two floors were selected by a buyer with an exquisite eye. Merchandise includes beautiful 19th-century paisley scarves from India and from Scotland, and 1920s glass lamps. ⊠ *2314 18th St. NW,* ☎ *202/667–1651.* ☽ *Fri.–Sun.*

Cherishables. American 18th- and 19th-century furniture and decorative arts are the featured attractions at Cherishables, with emphasis on the Federal period. ⊠ *1608 20th St. NW,* ☎ *202/785–4087.*

Georgetown Antiques Center. The center, in a Victorian town house, has two dealers who share space: Cherub Gallery (☎ 202/337–2224) specializes in Art Nouveau and Art Deco, and **Michael Getz Antiques** (☎ 202/338–3811) sells fireplace equipment and silverware. ⊠ *2918 M St. NW.*

G. K. S. Bush. G. K. S. Bush sells formal 18th- and early 19th-century American furniture and related works. ⊠ *2828 Pennsylvania Ave. NW,* ☎ *202/965–0653.*

Marston Luce. Focusing on American folk art, including quilts, weather vanes, and hooked rugs, Marston Luce also carries home and garden furnishings, primarily American, but some English and French as well. ⊠ *1314 21st St. NW,* ☎ *202/775–9460.*

Miller & Arney Antiques. English, American, and European furniture and accessories from the 18th and early 19th centuries give Miller & Arney Antiques a museum gallery air. Oriental porcelain adds splashes of color. ⊠ *1737 Wisconsin Ave. NW,* ☎ *202/338–2369.*

Old Print Gallery. The Capitol's largest collection of old prints and maps (including Washingtoniana) is housed in the Old Print Gallery. ⊠ *1220 31st St. NW,* ☎ *202/965–1818.*

Opportunity Shop of the Christ Child Society. A Georgetown thrift shop, Opportunity Shop sells vintage clothing and good-quality household goods. Consigned fine antiques at moderate prices are available on the second floor ⊠ *1427 Wisconsin Ave. NW,* ☎ *202/333–6635.*

Retrospective. A small shop crammed with high-quality furniture and accessories, mostly from the '40s and '50s, Retrospective is a place where you can still buy the princess phone that lit up your nightstand in 1962 and the plates your mother served her meat loaf on. ⊠ *2324 18th St. NW,* ☎ *202/483–8112.*

Susquehanna. The largest antiques shop in Georgetown, Susquehanna specializes in American furniture and paintings. ⊠ *3216 O St. NW,* ☎ *202/333–1511.*

Uniform. The best of the vintage clothing and household accessories shops in the Adams-Morgan neighborhood, Uniform has a vast assortment from the '50s and '60s: piles of fatigue, Nehru, and tie-died shirts, Sergeant Pepper jackets, navy pea coats, and all sorts of other formerly ordinary stuff now prized as icons of a bygone era. You'll also find lava lamps, pillbox hats, feathered mules with Lucite heels, and plateware that could have been props for the Jetsons. ✉ *2407 18th St. NW,* ☎ *202/483–4577.*

Books

Chapters. A "literary bookstore," Chapters eschews cartoon collections and diet guides, filling its shelves instead with serious contemporary fiction, classics, and poetry. ✉ *1512 K St. NW,* ☎ *202/347–5495.*

Cheshire Cat. This bookstore for children carries a selection of records, cassettes, posters, and books on parenting. ✉ *5512 Connecticut Ave. NW,* ☎ *202/244–3956.*

Kramerbooks. Open 24 hours on weekends, Kramerbooks shares space with a café that has late-night dining and weekend entertainment. The stock is small but well-selected ✉ *1517 Connecticut Ave. NW,* ☎ *202/387–1400.*

Lammas Books. A selection of music by women as well as women's and lesbian literature is for sale here. ✉ *1426 21st St. NW,* ☎ *202/775–8218.*

Mystery Books. Mystery Books has Washington's largest collection of detective, crime, suspense, and spy fiction. They deliver "Crime and Nourishment" gift baskets anywhere in the United States (☎ *800/955–2279*). ✉ *1715 Connecticut Ave. NW,* ☎ *202/483–1600.*

Olsson's Books & Records. A large and varied collection can be found at the Olsson chain. Hours vary significantly from store to store. ✉ *1239 Wisconsin Ave. NW,* ☎ *202/338–9544;* ✉ *1307 19th St. NW,* ☎ *202/785–1133;* ✉ *1200 F St. NW,* ☎ *202/347–3686;* ✉ *418 7th St. NW,* ☎ *202/638–7610.*

Second Story Books. A mecca for bibliophiles that encourages hours of browsing, this used-books (and records) emporium is located on Dupont Circle. ✉ *2000 P St. NW,* ☎ *202/659–8884.*

Trover Books. The latest political volumes and out-of-town newspapers are here. ✉ *221 Pennsylvania Ave. SE,* ☎ *202/547–2665.*

Vertigo Books. Just south of Dupont Circle, Vertigo Books emphasizes international politics, world literature, and African-American studies. ✉ *1337 Connecticut Ave. NW,* ☎ *202/429–9272.*

Yawa. Featuring a large collection of African and African-American fiction and nonfiction, magazines, and children's books, Yawa also sells ethnic jewelry, crafts, and greeting cards. ✉ *2206 18th St. NW,* ☎ *202/ 483–6805.*

Yes! A bookstore geared to self-development, Yes! has an unusual stock of volumes on philosophies of the world, meditative disciplines, and mental, physical, and spiritual health. ✉ *1035 31st St. NW,* ☎ *202/338–7874.*

Children's Clothing and Toys

F.A.O. Schwarz. F.A.O. Schwarz is the most upscale of toy stores, carrying such items as a toy car (a Mercedes, of course) that costs almost as much as the real thing. Among the other imports are stuffed animals (many larger than life), dolls, and children's perfumes. ✉ *Georgetown Park, 3222 M St. NW,* ☎ *202/342–2285.*

Kid's Closet. The downtown choice for baby clothes and shower gifts, The Kid's Closet also stocks some togs for older children. ✉ *1226 Connecticut Ave. NW,* ☎ *202/429–9247.*

Crafts and Gifts

American Hand. For one-of-a-kind functional and nonfunctional pieces by America's foremost ceramic artists, this is a wonderful place. The American Hand also carries limited edition objects for home and office, such as architect-designed dinnerware. ⊠ *2906 M St. NW,* ☎ *202/965–3273.*

Appalachian Spring. Appalachian Spring's two Washington stores sell traditional and contemporary crafts, including quilts, jewelry, weavings, pottery, and blown glass. ⊠ *1415 Wisconsin Ave. NW,* ☎ *202/337–5780;* ⊠ *Union Station,* ☎ *202/682–0505.*

Beadazzled. Head to Beadazzled for a truly dazzling array of ready-to-string beads, jewelry, and books on craft history and techniques. ⊠ *1522 Connecticut Ave. NW,* ☎ *202/265–2323.*

Fahrney's. Starting out as a pen bar in the Willard Hotel, a place to fill your fountain pen before embarking on the day's business, Fahrney's today sells pens in silver, gold, and lacquer by the world's leading manufacturers. ⊠ *1430 G St. NW,* ☎ *202/628–9525.*

Indian Craft Shop. Handicrafts, including jewelry, pottery, sand paintings, weavings, and baskets from a dozen Native American tribes—including Navajo, Pueblo, Zuni, Cherokee, Lakota, and Seminole—are for sale. Items range from inexpensive jewelry (for as little as $6) on up to collector-quality antiques costing $1,000 or more. ⊠ *Dept. of Interior, 1849 C St. NW, Room 1023,* ☎ *202/208–4056.*

Martin's. Martin's is a long-established Georgetown purveyor of china, crystal, and silver. ⊠ *1304 Wisconsin Ave. NW,* ☎ *202/338–6144.*

Moon, Blossoms and Snow. Moon, Blossoms and Snow concentrates on wearable art. In addition to hand-painted, hand-woven garments, the store sells contemporary American ceramics, glass, jewelry, and wood. ⊠ *225 Pennsylvania Ave. SE,* ☎ *202/543–8181.*

Music Box Center. An exquisite specialty store, the Music Box Center provides listening opportunities via more than 1500 music boxes that play 500 melodies. ⊠ *918 F St. NW,* ☎ *202/783–9399.*

Phoenix. The Phoenix sells Mexican crafts, including folk art, silver jewelry, fabrics, and native and contemporary clothing in natural fibers. ⊠ *1514 Wisconsin Ave. NW,* ☎ *202/338–4404.*

Skynear and Company. The owners of Skynear and Company travel the world to find the unusual—and do: an extravagant assortment of rich textiles, furniture, and home accessories for the art of living. ⊠ *2122 18th St. NW,* ☎ *202/797–7160;* ⊠ *Mazza Gallerie, 5300 Wisconsin Ave. NW,* ☎ *202/362–7541.*

Jewelry

Charles Schwartz & Son. A full-service jeweler, Charles Schwartz specializes in precious stones in traditional and modern settings. Fine watches are also offered. ⊠ *Mazza Gallerie, 1213 Connecticut Ave. NW,* ☎ *202/363–5432.*

Pampillonia Jewelers. Traditional designs in 18-karat gold and platinum are found here, including many pieces for men. ⊠ *Mazza Gallerie,* ☎ *202/363–6305;* ⊠ *1213 Connecticut Ave. NW,* ☎ *202/628–6305.*

Tiny Jewel Box. The Tiny Jewel Box features well-chosen estate jewelry, contemporary jewelry, and unique gifts. ⊠ *1143 Connecticut Ave. NW,* ☎ *202/393–2747. Metro: Farragut North.*

Kitchenware

Little Caledonia. Little Caledonia has nine rooms crammed with thousands of unusual and imported items for the home. Candles, cards, fabrics, and lamps round out the stock of decorative kitchenware. ⊠ *1419 Wisconsin Ave. NW,* ☏ *202/333–4700.*

Leather Goods

Coach Store. For fine leather, the Coach Store carries a complete (and expensive) line of well-made handbags, briefcases, belts, and wallets. ⊠ *1214 Wisconsin Ave. NW,* ☏ *202/342–1772.*

Georgetown Leather Design. Most of the leather goods in this collection—including jackets, briefcases, wallets, gloves, and handbags—are custom-made for the store. ⊠ *Fashion Centre at Pentagon City, 1100 S. Hayes St., Arlington, VA,* ☏ *703/418–6702.*

Men's and Women's Clothing

Britches Great Outdoors. The casual version of Britches of Georgetown, Britches Great Outdoors has filled many Washington closets with rugby shirts and other sportswear. ⊠ *1225 Wisconsin Ave. NW,* ☏ *202/333–3666.*

Burberrys. Burberrys made its reputation with the trench coat, but this British company also manufactures traditional men's and women's apparel. ⊠ *1155 Connecticut Ave. NW,* ☏ *202/463–3000.*

Commander Salamander. As much entertainment as funky shopping—leather, chains, silver skulls—it's open until 10 on weekends. ⊠ *1420 Wisconsin Ave. NW,* ☏ *202/337–2265.*

Forecast. If you favor a classic, contemporary look in clothing, Forecast should be in your future. ⊠ *218 7th St. SE,* ☏ *202/547–7337.*

John B. Adler. A longtime Washington clothier, John B. Adler offers the Ivy League look in suits, sport coats, and formal and casual wear. ⊠ *901 15th St. NW (entrance on I St.),* ☏ *202/842–4432.*

Kobos. A rainbow of clothing and accessories imported from West Africa is for sale at Kobos, plus a small selection of African music. ⊠ *2444 18th St. NW,* ☏ *202/332–9580.*

Men's Clothing

Britches of Georgetown. Britches carries an extensive selection of traditional but trend-conscious designs in natural fibers. ⊠ *1219 Connecticut Ave. NW,* ☏ *202/347–8994;* ⊠ *1247 Wisconsin Ave. NW,* ☏ *202/338–3330.*

Brooks Brothers. The oldest men's store in America, Brooks Brothers has sold traditional formal and casual clothing since 1818. It is the largest men's specialty store in the area and has a small women's department as well. ⊠ *1840 L St. NW,* ☏ *202/659–4650;* ⊠ *5504 Wisconsin Ave.,* ☏ *301/654–8202.*

J. Press. J. Press was founded in 1902 as a custom shop for Yale University. It is a resolutely traditional clothier: Shetland wool sport coats are a specialty. ⊠ *1801 L St. NW,* ☏ *202/857–0120.*

Music

HMV Records. A new two-story music store in Georgetown, HMV Records specializes in rock but also has a large selection of classical music. ⊠ *1229 Wisconsin Ave. NW,* ☏ *202/333–9292.*

Kemp Mill Music. This local chain store, with even more suburban locations than it has in Washington proper, sells popular-music CDs and cassettes at low prices. ⊠ *1518 Connecticut Ave. NW,* ☎ *202/332–8247;* ⊠ *1900 L St. NW,* ☎ *202/223–5310.*

Olsson's Books & Records. Here's a full line of compact discs and cassettes, with a good classical and folk music selection. Hours vary significantly from store to store. ⊠ *1239 Wisconsin Ave. NW,* ☎ *202/338–9544;* ⊠ *1307 19th St. NW,* ☎ *202/785–1133;* ⊠ *1200 F St. NW,* ☎ *202/347–3686;* ⊠ *418 7th St. NW,* ☎ *202/638–7610.*

Orpheus Records. Orpheus Records specializes in new and used jazz and blues records. ⊠ *3249 M St. NW,* ☎ *202/337–7970.*

Serenade Record Shop. A full-catalogue music store, the Serenade Record Shop is especially strong in classical music. ⊠ *1800 M St. NW,* ☎ *202/452–0075.*

Tower Records. The 16,000-square-foot Tower Records offers Washington's best selection of music in all categories, plus videos and laser discs. ⊠ *2000 Pennsylvania Ave. NW,* ☎ *202/331–2400;* ⊠ *Rockville, MD,* ☎ *301/468–8901;* ⊠ *Vienna, VA,* ☎ *703/893–6627.*

Shoes

Church's. Church's is an English company whose handmade men's shoes are noted for their comfort and durability. ⊠ *1820 L St. NW,* ☎ *202/296–3366.*

Shoe Scene. The fashionable, moderately priced shoes for women found here are direct imports from Europe. ⊠ *1330 Connecticut Ave. NW,* ☎ *202/659–2194.*

Women's Clothing

Ann Taylor. Ann Taylor sells sophisticated fashions for the woman who has broken out of the dress-for-success mold. The store also has an excellent shoe department. ⊠ *1720 K St. NW,* ☎ *202/466–3544;* ⊠ *3222 M St. NW,* ☎ *202/338–5290;* ⊠ *5300 Wisconsin Ave. NW,* ☎ *202/244–1940;* ⊠ *Union Station,* ☎ *202/371–8010.*

Betsey Johnson. This shop sells fanciful frocks for the young and restless. ⊠ *1319 Wisconsin Ave. NW,* ☎ *202/338–4090.*

Betsy Fisher. *Tasteful* is the word that best describes Betsy Fisher's clothing; it appeals to women of all ages. ⊠ *1224 Connecticut Ave. NW,* ☎ *202/785–1975.*

Chanel Boutique. The Willard Hotel annex is where to find goodies from the legendary house of fashion. ⊠ *1455 Pennsylvania Ave. NW,* ☎ *202/638–5055.*

Earl Allen. Catering to the professional woman, Earl Allen offers conservative but distinctive dresses and sportswear, much of it made exclusively for this shop with two locations in the Capitol. ⊠ *3109 M St. NW,* ☎ *202/338–1678;* ⊠ *1825 I St. NW,* ☎ *202/466–3437.*

Khismet Wearable Art. Original fashions and traditional garments designed by Millée Spears, who lived in Ghana, fill colorful Khismet. Spears uses ethnic textiles both for garments suitable for the office and for an evening out. ⊠ *1800 Belmont Rd. NW,* ☎ *202/234–7778.*

Rizik Bros. Rizik Bros. is a Washington institution combining designer clothing and accessories with expert service. The sales staff is trained to find just the right style from the large inventory, and prices are right. Take the elevator up from the northwest corner of Connecticut and L streets. ⊠ *1100 Connecticut Ave. NW,* ☎ *202/223–4050.*

9 Side Trips

THE C&O CANAL AND GREAT FALLS

By Michael
Dolan

Updated by
Nancy Ryder

In the 18th and early 19th centuries, the Potomac River was the main transport route between Cumberland, Maryland, one of the most important ports on the nation's frontier, and the seaports of the Chesapeake Bay. Tobacco, grain, whiskey, furs, iron ore, timber, and other commodities were sent down the Potomac from Cumberland to the ports of Georgetown and Alexandria, which served as major distribution points for both domestic and international markets.

Although it served as a vital link with the country's western territories, the Potomac did have some drawbacks as a commercial waterway: Rapids and waterfalls along the 190 miles between Cumberland and Washington made it impossible for traders to navigate the entire distance by boat. Just a few miles upstream from Washington, the Potomac cascaded through two such barriers—the breathtakingly beautiful Great Falls and the less dramatic but no less impassable Little Falls.

To help traders move goods between the eastern markets and the western frontier more efficiently, 18th-century engineers proposed that a canal with a series of elevator locks be built parallel to the river. The first such canal was built at the urging of George Washington, who actually helped found a company just for this purpose. In 1802, after 17 years of work, his firm opened the Patowmack Canal on the Virginia side of the river.

In 1828 Washington's canal was replaced by the **Chesapeake & Ohio (C&O) Canal,** which had been dug along the opposite shore. The C&O stretched from the heart of Washington to Cumberland. Starting near what is now the intersection of 17th Street and Constitution Avenue NW (the public rest room there was originally a lock house), the C&O moved barges through 75 locks.

Ironically, the C&O Canal began operation the same day as the Baltimore & Ohio Railroad, the concern that eventually put the canal out of business. The C&O route to the west nevertheless did prove to be a viable alternative for traders interested in moving goods through the Washington area and to the lower Chesapeake. During the mid-19th century, the canal boats carried as many as a million tons of merchandise a year. The C&O Canal stopped turning a profit in 1890 but remained in business until 1924, when a disastrous storm left it in ruins. Ownership then shifted to the B&O Railroad, which sold the canal to the federal government in 1938 for $2 million. In 1939 the canal became part of the National Capital Parks System.

In the 1950s a proposal to build a highway over the canal near Washington was defeated by residents of the Palisades, a neighborhood that overlooks the waterway. Since 1971 the canal has been a national park, providing Washingtonians and visitors with a window into the past and a marvelous place to pursue recreational activities.

The twin parks of **Great Falls**—on either side of the river 13 miles northwest of Georgetown—are also now part of the National Park system. The 800-acre park on the Virginia side is a favorite place for outings for local residents and is easily accessible by tourists. The steep, jagged falls roar into a narrow gorge, providing one of the most spectacular scenic attractions in the East.

Exploring

Numbers in the margin correspond to points of interest on the C&O Canal and Great Falls map.

❸ Chain Bridge. Named for the chains that held up the original structure, the Chain Bridge links the District with Virginia. The bridge was built to enable cattlemen to bring Virginia herds to the slaughterhouses along the Potomac on the Maryland side. During the Civil War the bridge was guarded by Union troops stationed at earthen fortifications along what is now Potomac Avenue NW. The Virginia side of the river in the area around Chain Bridge is known for its good fishing and narrow, treacherous channel.

Clara Barton House. Near Glen Echo Park, the Clara Barton House is one of the most striking Victorian structures in Glen Echo. It has been preserved as a monument to the founder of the American Red Cross. Barton moved here toward the end of her life, using the place for a while to store Red Cross supplies and as the organization's head-quarters. Today the building is furnished with original period artifacts. ⊠ *5801 Oxford Rd., Glen Echo, MD,* ☎ *301/492–6245.* 🎟 *Free.* ☉ *Daily 10–5; guided tour hourly on the ½ hr.*

❷ Fletcher's Boat House. For renting canoes and bicycles and purchasing fishing tackle and D.C. fishing licenses, Fletcher's Boat House is good. Fishermen often congregate here to fish for shad, perch, catfish, striped bass, and other freshwater species. ⊠ *4740 Canal Rd., at Reservoir Rd.,* ☎ *202/244–0461.* ☉ *Spring, daily 5:30 AM–5 PM; summer, weekdays 7:30 AM–7:30 PM, weekends 5:30 AM–7:30 PM.*

❶ Georgetown. The towpath along the canal in Georgetown passes traces of that area's industrial past, such as the Godey Lime Kilns near the mouth of Rock Creek, as well as the fronts of numerous houses that date from 1810. From April through early November mule-drawn barges leave for 90-minute trips from the Foundry Mall on Thomas Jefferson Street NW, half a block south of M Street. No reservations are required for the public trips. ☎ *202/653–5190 or 301/299–2026; group reservations and rates, 301/299–3613.* 🎟 *$5.*

Glen Echo. A charming village of Victorian houses, Glen Echo was founded in 1891 when brothers Edwin and Edward Baltzley fell under the spell of the Chautauqua movement promoting liberal education among the masses. The brothers sold land and houses to further their dream, but the Glen Echo Chautauqua lasted only one season. Their compound served a stint as an amusement park and is now run by the National Park Service as an arts and cultural center.

❹ Glen Echo Park. Noted for its whimsical architecture, including a stone tower left from the Chautauqua period, Glen Echo Park is also famed for its splendid 1921 Dentzel carousel. From late spring to early fall you can buy a cheap trip into the past, complete with music from a real calliope. The park is also the site of frequent folk festivals, and dances are held in the ornate Spanish Ballroom. For scheduling information, check the "Weekend" section in Friday's *Washington Post* or the free weekly *Washington CityPaper.* ⊠ *7300 MacArthur Blvd.,* ☎ *301/492–6282.*

❺ Great Falls Tavern. On the Maryland side of Great Falls Park, the Great Falls Tavern features displays of canal history and a platform from which to look at the falls. Better yet, walk over the Olmsted Bridges out to a small island in the middle of the river for a spectacular view. On the canal walls are "rope burns" caused by decade upon decade of fric-

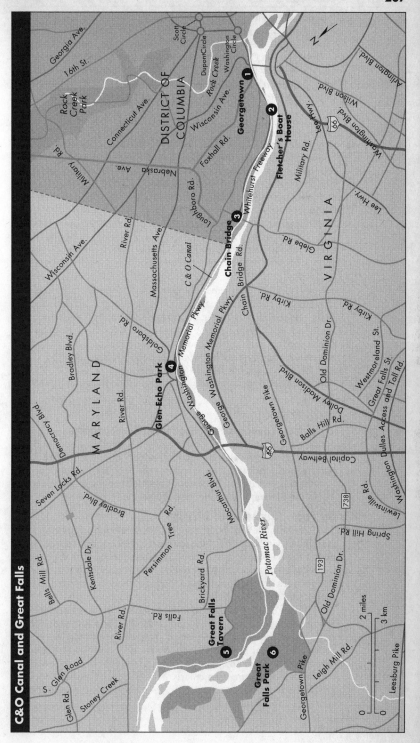

tion from barge lines. Half a mile west a flood marker shows how high the Potomac can go—after a hurricane in 1972 the river crested far above the ground where visitors stand. Canal barge trips start here between April and October (☞ Guided Tours, *below*). The tavern ceased being a hostelry long ago, so if you're hungry head for the snack bar a few paces north of the tavern. ⊠ *Great Falls Park,* ☎ *301/299–2026; tavern and museum, 301/299–3613.* ⊠ *$4 per vehicle, $2 per person without vehicle, good for 7 days for MD and VA sides of park.* ☉ *Park daily sunrise–sunset, tavern and museum daily 9–5.*

❻ **Great Falls Park.** The Virginia side of Great Falls Park is not accessible from the Maryland side but offers the best views of the Potomac, as well as trails leading past the old Patowmack Canal and among the boulders lining the edge of the falls. Horseback riding is permitted but you can't rent horses in the park. Trail maps are available at the visitor center, also a starting point for various tours (☞ Guided Tours, *below*). Swimming and wading are prohibited, but you can fish (a Virginia, Maryland, or D.C. license is required for anglers 16 and older), climb rocks (climbers must register at the visitor center beforehand), and go white-water kayaking (*below* the falls only, and only by experienced boaters). From craggy aeries overlooking the river and from several artificial platforms you can watch helmeted kayakers and climbers test their skills against the river and the rocks. As is true all along this stretch of the river, the currents are deadly. Despite frequent signs and warnings, each year some visitors dare the water and lose. Avoid even the most benign-looking ripple. ☎ *703/285–2966.* ⊠ *$4 per vehicle, $2 per person without vehicle, good for 7 days for MD and VA sides of park.* ☉ *Daily 8 AM–sunset.*

Getting Around

By Car
To reach the Virginia side of Great Falls Park, take the scenic and winding Route 193 (Exit 13 off Route 495, the Capitol Beltway) to Route 738, and follow the signs. It takes about 25 minutes to drive to the park from the Beltway. You can get to the Maryland side of the park by following MacArthur Boulevard from Georgetown or by taking Exit 41 off the Beltway, following the signs to Carderock.

By Foot, Canoe, and Bicycle
The C&O Canal Park and its towpath are favorite destinations for joggers, bikers, and canoeists. The towpath has only a slight grade, which makes for a leisurely ride or hike. Most recreational bikers consider the 13 miles from Georgetown to Great Falls an easy ride; at only one short stretch of rocky ground near Great Falls do bikers need to carry their cycles. You can also take a bike path that parallels MacArthur Boulevard for much of the distance to the Maryland side of the park. Storm damage has left parts of the canal dry, but many segments remain intact and navigable by canoe. You can rent canoes or bicycles at **Fletcher's Boat House,** just upriver from Georgetown (☞ Exploring, *above*). In winter the canal sometimes freezes solid enough to allow for ice skating; during particularly hard freezes it's possible to skate great distances along it, occasionally interrupting your stride for short clambers around the locks.

Guided Tours

Great Falls Park Visitor Center and Museum. A tour of the visitor center and museum at Great Falls Park in Virginia takes 30 minutes. Staff members conduct special tours and walks year-round. Visitors are encouraged to take self-guided tours along well-marked trails, including one that follows the route of the old Patowmack Canal. ⊠ *Park,* ☎ *703/285–2966.*

Great Falls Tavern. On the Maryland side of Great Falls Park, the old Great Falls Tavern serves as a museum and a headquarters for the rangers who manage the C&O Canal. During warm weather, replicas of the old mule-drawn boats carry visitors along this stretch of the canal; similar trips also begin in Georgetown. History books and canal guides are on sale at both parks as well as at many bookstores in the District. ⊠ *Park,* ☎ *301/299–2026.*

Inn at Glen Echo. A charming pink cottage located next to Glen Echo Park, the Inn at Glen Echo specializes in American cuisine with an emphasis on seafood dishes. Live jazz can be heard in the bar on weekends. Entrées range from $14 to $19. ⊠ *6119 Tulane Ave., Glen Echo, MD,* ☎ *301/229–2280. AE, MC, V.*

Old Angler's Inn. Facing the woods above the C&O Canal, diners can sit out on the flagstone terrace in good weather or inside the tavern in cold. The American contemporary includes duck, rack of lamb, venison and soft-shell crabs. ⊠ *10801 McArthur Blvd., Glen Echo, MD,* ☎ *301/299–9097. AE, D, DC, MC, V.*

ANNAPOLIS, MARYLAND

Although it has long since been overtaken by Baltimore as the major Chesapeake port, **Annapolis** is still a popular destination for oyster catchers and yachting aficionados, and on warm sunny days the City Dock is thronged with billowing sails set strikingly against a background of redbrick waterfront buildings, mostly shops and restaurants. Annapolis's enduring nautical reputation derives largely from the presence of the **United States Naval Academy,** whose handsomely uniformed students grace the city streets in their summer whites and winter navy-blues (the *real* navy blue, which is practically black). October sailboat and powerboat shows attract national attention, keeping local hotels and restaurants full even after the summer tourist season has ended.

In 1649 a group of Puritan settlers relocated from Virginia to a spot at the mouth of the Severn River; the community that they called Providence is now an upscale residential area. Lord Baltimore—who held the Royal charter to settle Maryland—named the area around the new town Anne Arundel County, after his wife; in 1684 Anne Arundel Town was established, across from Providence, on the south side of the Severn. Ten years later, Anne Arundel Town became the capital of Maryland and was renamed Annapolis—for Princess Anne, who later became queen. Annapolis received its city charter in 1708.

Annapolis—not the better-known Baltimore—is the state capital. One of the country's largest assemblages of 18th-century architecture (including 50 pre-Revolutionary buildings) recalls the city's days as a major port, particularly for the export of tobacco. In fact, in 1774 local patriots matched their Boston counterparts (who had thrown their famous tea party the previous year) by burning the *Peggy Sue,* a ship loaded with taxed tea. A decade later, in 1783 and 1784, Annapolis served as the nation's first peacetime capital. Annapolis's waterfront orientation enables visitors to do the city justice in a single well-planned day.

Exploring

Numbers in the margin correspond to points of interest on the Annapolis map.

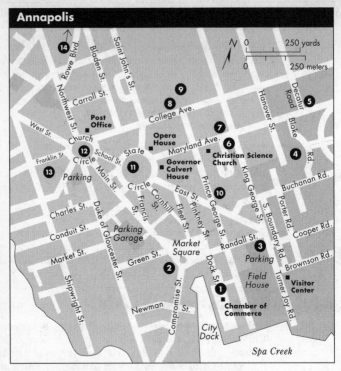

Annapolis

⑬ **Banneker-Douglass Museum of Afro-American Life.** On Franklin Street,
the Banneke-Douglass Museum of Afro-American Life, an ivy-covered
redbrick former church, houses changing exhibits, lectures, films, and
literature that convey a picture of the African-American experience in
Maryland. ⊠ *84 Franklin St.,* ☎ *410/974–2894.* ⊠ *Free.* ☉ *Tues.–Fri.
10–3, Sat. noon–4.*

❼ **Chase-Lloyd House.** Across the street from the famous Hammond-Harwood House is another well-known residence designed by the Colonial architect William Buckland: the Chase-Lloyd House, with its
gracefully massive facade—sheer except for a center third beneath a
pediment. In 1774 the tobacco planter and revolutionary Edward
Lloyd IV completed work begun five years earlier by Samuel Chase, a
Supreme Court justice and future signer of the Declaration of Independence. The first floor is open to the public and contains more of
Buckland's handiwork, including a parlor mantelpiece with tobacco
leaves carved into the marble. The house is furnished with a mixture
of 18th-, 19th-, and 20th-century pieces. The staircase parts dramatically around a Palladian window (an arched, triple window whose center segment is taller than its flanks). For more than 100 years the
house has served as a home for elderly Episcopalian women. ⊠ *22 Maryland Ave.,* ☎ *410/263–2723.* ⊠ *$2.* ☉ *Mar.–Dec., Tues.–Sat. 2–4.;
Jan. and Feb., Tues., Fri., and Sat. 2–4.*

❻ **Hammond-Harwood House.** The three-story redbrick Hammond-Harwood House is near the U.S. Naval Academy on Maryland Avenue.The
house is the only verifiable full-scale example of the work of William
Buckland, the most prominent Colonial architect at the time of his death,
in 1774—the year in which the house was completed. Buckland was
famous for his interior woodwork, which may also be seen in the
Chase-Lloyd House across the street and in George Mason's Gunston

Hall in Lorton, Virginia. Exquisite moldings, cornices, and other carvings appear throughout, including garlands of roses above the front doorway. These were meant to be part of the manorial wedding present from Matthias Hammond, a lawyer and revolutionary, to his fiancée, who jilted him before the project was finished. Hammond never married, and he died in 1784. The Harwoods took over the house toward the turn of the century. Today the house is furnished with 18th-century pieces, and the garden is tended with regard to period authenticity. ✉ *19 Maryland Ave.,* ☎ *410/269–1714.* 🎫 *$4; combination ticket with Paca House (☞ below) $9; call for group rates.* 🕐 *Mon.–Sat. 10–4, Sun. noon–4.*

⑭ **Helen Avalynne Tawes Garden.** The 6-acre Helen Avalynne Tawes Garden, next to the Tawes State Office Building Complex, is planted with flora from different regions of the state, evoking Western Maryland's mountain forests and the marshland along the Chesapeake; the ponds host various fish, fowl, and amphibians. Naturally, the state flower, the black-eyed Susan, is well represented. Call for information on weekday tours. ✉ *580 Taylor Ave.,* ☎ *410/974–3717.* 🎫 *Free.* 🕐 *Daily dawn–dusk.*

❶ **Information Booth.** Start your Annapolis visit at the redbrick information booth, operated by the **Annapolis–Anne Arundel County Conference and Visitors Bureau,** to obtain maps and brochures. The booth is on the city dock, adjacent to the harbormaster's office. Outside, impressive motor- and sail-craft moor at the edges of Dock Street and Market Place. Shops, restaurants, and bars populate the dock area. ☎ *410/268–8687.* 🕐 *Apr.–Oct., daily 10–5.* ✉ *26 West St.* 🕐 *Daily 9–5.*

NEED A BREAK?

The reconstructed **Market House pavilion**—originally a collection of mid-19th-century market stalls in the center of Market Square—now sells baked goods, fast food, and fish (prepared or to cook at home). There's no seating; set up your picnic anywhere on the dock.

---

❷ **Maritime Museum.** On Main Street by the dock, the Maritime Museum occupies a warehouse that stored supplies for the Revolutionary Army during the War of Independence, when the city was a vital link in the supply chain. Exhibits pertain to the history of maritime commerce in Annapolis and include artifacts of Colonial-era trade and a diorama of the city's waterfront in the 18th century. ✉ *77 Main St.,* ☎ *410/268–5576.* 🎫 *Free.* 🕐 *Apr.–Oct., daily 9–5; Nov.–Mar., daily 10–4.*

⑪ **Maryland State House.** The domed Maryland State House, completed in 1780, is the oldest state capital in continuous legislative use and the only one where the U.S. Congress has sat. During 1783 and 1784 when Congress convened here, it accepted the resignation of General George Washington as commander in chief of the Continental Army, and it ratified the Treaty of Paris with the king, concluding the War of Independence. Both of these matters were determined in the Old Senate Chamber, which is filled with intricate woodwork (featuring the ubiquitous tobacco motif) attributed to William Buckland, the best-known Colonial architect. Also decorating this room is Charles Willson Peale's painting *Washington at the Battle of Yorktown,* considered the masterpiece of the Revolutionary War period's finest portrait artist. The state Senate and House now hold their sessions in two other chambers in the building. Also on the grounds is the oldest public building in Maryland, the minuscule redbrick **Treasury,** built in 1735. ✉ *State Circle,* ☎ *410/974–3400.* 🎫 *Free.* 🕐 *Daily 9–5; visitor center weekends 10–4; ½-hr tour daily at 11 and 3.*

⑫ **St. Anne's Church.** School Street leads you to the center of Church Circle, where you'll see the Episcopal St. Anne's Church, the third church of that name on that spot. The first, built in 1704, was torn down in 1775. The second, built in 1792, burned down in 1858; however, parts of the walls survived and were incorporated into the present structure, which was built in 1859. The parish was founded in 1692, and King William III donated the communion silver. The churchyard contains the grave of the last Colonial governor, Sir Robert Eden. ⊠ *Church Circle,* ☎ *410/267–9333.* ☏ *Free.* ☉ *Daily 7:30–6.*

NEED A
BREAK?

A saloon and oyster bar along the historic City Dock, **McGarvey's Saloon and Oyster Bar** (⊠ 8 Market Space, ☎ 410/263–5700), is an atmospheric choice for seafood, steaks, and other American favorites.

Annapolis's first brew pub, the **Ram's Head Tavern** (⊠ 33 West St., ☎ 410/268–4545), serves award-winning chili, sandwiches, and salads, as well as bottled beer from more than two dozen countries or one of their very own.

As part of the eighteenth century Maryland Inn, the **Treaty of Paris Restaurant** (⊠ 16 Church Circle, ☎ 410/263–2641) serves continental fare in a period-style restaurant.

❽ **St. John's College.** Here is the alma mater of Francis Scott Key, lyricist of *The Star Spangled Banner.* However, since 1937, the college has been best known as the birthplace of the controversial Great Books curriculum that includes reading the works of great authors from Homer to Freud. Conservative thinkers maintain that the curriculum conveys the basic knowledge a college-educated person should know. Those on the left consider it politically incorrect because works by "dead white European males" predominate while those of women, ethnic minorities, gays, and other marginalized groups are excluded. Climb the gradual slope of the long, brick-paved path to the impressive golden ❾ cupola of **McDowell Hall,** the third-oldest academic building in the country, just as St. John's is the third-oldest college in the country (after Harvard and William and Mary). Founded as King William's School in 1696, the school was chartered under its current name in 1784. The enormous tulip poplar called the **Liberty Tree,** on the lawn fronted by College Avenue, is possibly 600 years old. In its shade colonists and Indians made treaties in the 17th century, revolutionaries rallied in the 18th century, Union troops encamped in the 19th century, and commencement takes place every spring. The **Elizabeth Myers Mitchell Art Gallery** (☎ 410/626–2556), on the east side of Mellon Hall, presents a variety of exhibits and special programs related to the fine arts. Down King George Street toward the water is the **Carroll-Barrister House,** now the college admissions office. The house was built in 1722 at Main and Conduit streets and was moved onto campus in 1957. Charles Carroll—not the signer of the Declaration, but his cousin—who helped draft Maryland's Declaration of Rights, was born here. Free tours are available by appointment. ☎ *410/263–2371.*

★ ❸ **United States Naval Academy.** From the information booth (☞ *above*), cross Market Square and follow Randall Street a few blocks to reach the United States Naval Academy. By the gate at King George Street is Ricketts Hall, where you can join a guided tour and get literature. The academy, established in 1845 on the site of a U.S. Army fort, occupies 329 scenic riverside acres, earning it the dubious title of "country club on the Severn" from its West Point rivals. In the center of the ❹ campus the bronze-dome, interdenominational **U.S. Naval Chapel** contains the crypt of the Revolutionary War hero John Paul Jones, the

⑤ naval officer who, in an engagement with a British ship, uttered the famous declaration, "I have not yet begun to fight!" The **museum in Preble Hall** tells the story of the U.S. Navy, with displays of miniature ships and flags from the original vessels. Periodic full-dress parades and (in warmer months) daily noontime musters of the midshipmen take place at various spots around campus, but the most remarkable sight may be the sample student quarters open to the public—they're quite a bit neater than the typical college dorm! ☎ *410/263–6933.* 🖾 *Free.* 🖾 *Tour $5.* ☉ *Visitor center daily 9–4; 1-hr tour June–Aug. every ½ hr, Mon.–Sat. 9:30–3:30, Sun. 12:30–3:30; Mar.–May and Sept.–Nov. hourly, Mon.–Sat. 10–3, Sun. 12:30–3; Dec.–Feb., Mon.–Sat. at 11 and 1, Sun. 12:30 and 2:30.*

⑩ **William Paca House and Garden.** The William Paca House was built in 1765; the garden originally was finished in 1772 and gradually restored in this century. These comprise the estate of William Paca, a signer of the Declaration of Independence and governor of Maryland from 1782 to 1785. Inside, the main floor (furnished with 18th-century antiques) retains its original Prussian-blue and soft-gray color scheme. The second floor contains a mixture of 18th- and 19th-century pieces. The adjacent 2-acre garden provides a longer perspective on the back of the house, plus worthwhile sights of its own: a Chinese Chippendale bridge, a pond, a wilderness area, and formal arrangements. ⊠ *186 Prince George St.,* ☎ *410/263–5553.* 🖾 *House and garden $6; house only $4; garden only $3; combination ticket for Paca House and garden and Hammond-Harwood House (☞ above) $9.* ☉ *House and garden Jan. and Feb., Fri. and Sat. 10–4, Sun. noon–4; Mar.–Dec., Mon.–Sat. 10–4, Sun. noon–4.*

Getting Around

No regular train or bus service connects Washington to Annapolis. The drive (east on U.S. Route 50, to the Rowe Boulevard exit) normally takes 35–45 minutes, but if you travel between 3:30 and 6:30 PM budget two hours for rush-hour traffic.

Parking spots on Annapolis's historic downtown streets are rare, but there's a free lot at the Navy–Marine Corps Stadium (to the right of Rowe Boulevard as you enter town from Route 50), from which a shuttle (☎ 410/263–7964) heads to downtown for 75¢.

Guided Tours

Chesapeake Marine Tours, Inc. Cruises offered by Chesapeake Marine Tours depart from the Annapolis dock in good weather. Tours range from 40 minutes to 7½ hours, extending as far as St. Michael's, a preserved 18th-century fishing village and yachting mecca on the eastern shore of the bay. ☎ *410/268–7600 or 301/261–2719.* 🖾 *$6–$35.*

Historic Annapolis Foundation. "Acoustiguide" audio-tape-enriched walking tours of the city's historic district, prepared by the Historic Annapolis Foundation (☎ 410/267–7619) and narrated by Walter Cronkite, are available at the **Maritime Museum** (☞ *above*). 🖾 *$7.*

Three Centuries Tours. Costumed guides from Three Centuries Tours wear colonial dress and take visitors to the State House, St. John's College, and the Naval Academy. ☎ *410/263–5401.* 🖾 *$7.*

MOUNT VERNON, WOODLAWN, AND GUNSTON HALL

Long before Washington was planned, the shores of the Potomac had been divided into plantations by wealthy traders and gentleman farmers. Most traces of the Colonial era were obliterated as the Capitol grew in the 19th century, but several splendid examples of plantation architecture remain on the Virginia side of the Potomac just 15 miles or so south of the District. The three mansions described in this section can easily be visited in a single day: **Mount Vernon,** the home of George Washington and one of the most popular sites in the area; **Woodlawn,** the estate of Washington's granddaughter; and **Gunston Hall,** the home of George Mason, author of the document on which the Bill of Rights was based. On hillsides overlooking the river, these estates offer magnificent vistas and bring a bygone era to vivid life.

Exploring

Numbers in the margin correspond to points of interest on the Mount Vernon, Woodlawn, and Gunston Hall map.

Mount Vernon

★ ❶ **Mount Vernon.** Mount Vernon and the surrounding lands had been in the Washington family for nearly 90 years by the time George inherited it all in 1761. Before taking over command of the Continental Army, Washington was a yeoman farmer managing the 8,000-acre plantation, of which more than 3,000 acres were under cultivation. He also oversaw the transformation of the main house from an ordinary farm dwelling into what was for the time a grand mansion.

The main house with its red roof is elegant though understated. The exterior is made of yellow pine painted and coated with layers of sand— "rusticated," in the language of the day—to resemble white-stone blocks.

The inside of the building is more ornate, especially the formal receiving room with its molded ceiling decorated with agricultural motifs. Throughout the house are other, smaller symbols of the owner's eminence, such as a key to the main portal of the Bastille, presented to Washington by the Marquis de Lafayette, and Washington's presidential chair. Small groups of visitors are ushered from room to room, each of which is staffed by a guide who describes the furnishings and answers questions.

The real (often overlooked) treasure of Mount Vernon is the view from around back: Beneath a 90-foot portico (George Washington's contribution to architecture), the home's dramatic riverside porch looks out on an expanse of lawn that slopes down to the Potomac. In springtime the view of the river (a mile wide at the point at which it passes the plantation) is framed by the blossoms of wild plum and dogwood. Ships of the United States and foreign navies always salute when passing the house.

Tours of the sprawling grounds are self-guided. Visitors are free to visit the plantation workshops, the kitchen, the carriage house, the gardens, reconstructions of the slave quarters, and, down the hill toward the boat landing, the tomb of George and Martha Washington. Among the souvenirs sold at the plantation are stripling boxwoods that began life as clippings from bushes planted in 1798, the year before Washington died. The tour of house and grounds takes about two hours. A limited number of wheelchairs is available at the main gate. ⊠ *8 mi south of Alexandria, at southern end of George Washington Pkwy.,*

Mount Vernon, Woodlawn, and Gunston Hall

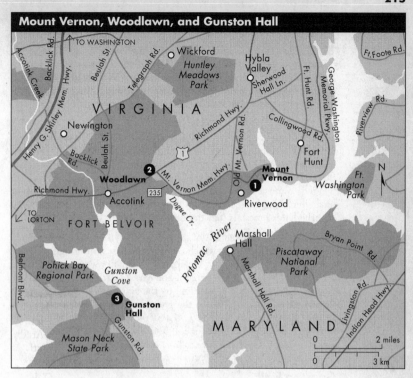

☎ 703/780–2000. 🎫 $7. ⊙ Mar., daily 9–5; Apr.–Aug., daily 8–5;
Sept. and Oct., daily 9–5; Nov.–Feb., daily 9–4.

NEED A
BREAK?

Mt. Vernon Inn (☎ 703/780–2000), on the grounds of the estate, is
often crowded but you can't beat the location. The inn has atmosphere
too. Waiters and waitresses dress in period garb and serve regional
Virginia dishes. *AE, MC, V.*

With a view of the Potomac River, the **Cedar Knoll Inn on the Potomac
Restaurant** (⊠ 9030 Lucia La., ☎ 703/799–1501) is exactly one mile
north of Mt. Vernon. Diners can enjoy Mediterranean cuisine with such
dishes as paella, trout, and salmon. *AE, D, DC, MC, V.*

Woodlawn

Pope-Leighey House. Designed by Frank Lloyd Wright and built in 1940,
the Pope-Leighey House sits on the grounds of the historic Woodlawn
estate 3 miles from Mount Vernon (☞ *above*). Wright's modernist design in cypress, brick, and glass offers a peculiar counterpoint to the
Georgian stylings of Woodlawn. Not to every taste, it *is* an architectural education. The structure originally stood in nearby Falls Church,
Virginia; it was rescued from the path of a highway and moved to the
Woodlawn grounds in 1964. ⊠ *3 mi west on Rte. 235 from Mount
Vernon,* ☎ 703/780–4000. 🎫 *$5; combination ticket for Woodlawn
and Pope-Leighey House $10.* ⊙ *Jan. and Feb., weekends 9:30–4;
Mar.–Dec., daily 9:30–4:30; tour every ½ hr (last tour at 4).*

❷ **Woodlawn.** Three miles from Mount Vernon on Route 1, the Woodlawn Plantation occupies a piece of ground that was originally part of
the Mount Vernon estate; even today you can see the red roof of Washington's home from Woodlawn. The house at Woodlawn was built for
Washington's step-granddaughter, Nellie Custis, who married his fa-

vorite nephew, Lawrence Lewis. (Lewis had come to Mount Vernon from Fredericksburg to help Uncle George manage his five farms.)

The Lewises' home, completed in 1805, is noteworthy from an architectural standpoint. It was designed by William Thornton, a physician and amateur architect from the West Indies who drew up the original plans for the Capitol (☞ Capitol Hill *in* Chapter 2). Like Mount Vernon, the Woodlawn house is made wholly of native materials, including the clay for its bricks and the yellow pine used throughout the interior.

In the tradition of Southern riverfront mansions, Woodlawn has a central hallway that provides a cool refuge during the summer. At one corner of the passage is a bust of George Washington set on a pedestal so that the crown of the head is at 6'2"—Washington's actual height. Elsewhere is a music room with a ceiling two feet higher than any other in the building, built that way to improve the acoustics for the harp and clavichord recitals that the Lewises and their children enjoyed.

After Woodlawn passed out of the Lewis family's hands it was owned by a Quaker community, which established there a meetinghouse and the first integrated school in Virginia. Subsequent owners included the playwright Paul Kester and Senator and Mrs. Oscar Underwood of Alabama. The property was acquired by the National Trust for Historic Preservation in 1957. Also on the grounds of Woodlawn is the Pope-Leighey House (☞ *above*). ⊠ *3 mi west on Rte. 235 from Mount Vernon,* ☎ *703/780–4000.* ☜ *$6; combination ticket for Woodlawn and Pope-Leighey House $10.* ☉ *Jan. and Feb., weekends 9:30–4; Mar.–Dec., daily 9:30–4:30; tour every ½ hr (last tour at 4).*

Gunston Hall

❸ Gunston Hall. Unlike Mount Vernon, Gunston Hall, 15 miles away in Lorton, is rarely crowded with visitors. This was the home of a lesser-known George: George Mason—gentleman farmer, captain of the Fairfax militia, and author of the Virginia Declaration of Rights. Mason was one of the framers of the Constitution but refused to sign the final document because it did not prohibit slavery, adequately restrain the powers of the federal government, or include a bill of rights.

Completed in 1759, Gunston Hall is built of native brick, black walnut, and yellow pine. The architectural style of the time demanded absolute balance in all structures. Hence the "robber" window on a second-floor storage room and the fake door set into one side of the center hallway. The house's interior, with its carved woodwork in styles from Chinese to Gothic, has been meticulously restored, with paints made from the original formulas and with carefully carved replacements for the intricate mahogany medallions in the moldings.

The formal gardens are famous for their boxwoods, some of which were planted in the 1760s and have now grown to be 12 and 14 feet high. In Mason's day boxwood was used as a garden border because its acrid smell repelled deer. A tour of Gunston Hall takes 30 minutes. ☎ *703/550–9220.* ☜ *$5.* ☉ *Daily 9:30–5, last tour at 4:30.*

Getting Around

By Bicycle

An asphalt bicycle path leads from the Virginia side of Memorial Bridge (adjacent to the Lincoln Memorial), past National Airport and through Alexandria all the way to Mount Vernon. The trail is steep in places, but a biker in moderately good condition can make the 16-mile trip in less than two hours. Bicycles can be rented at several locations in Washington (☞ Bicycling *in* Chapter 7).

By Boat

An especially pleasant way to travel down the Potomac is to cruise on the *Potomac Spirit,* which makes the 4½-hour trip from Washington to Mount Vernon Tuesday–Sunday, twice daily from mid-June through August and once daily from September through October and late March to mid-June. ✉ *Boats leave from Pier 4, 6th and Water Sts. SW,* ☎ *202/554–8000.* 🎫 *Roundtrip $22.*

By Car

To get to Mount Vernon from the Capitol Beltway (Route 495), take exit 1 onto the George Washington Memorial Parkway, and follow the signs. From downtown Washington, cross into Arlington on either Key Bridge, Memorial Bridge, or the 14th Street bridge, and drive south on the George Washington Memorial Parkway toward National Airport. Proceed past the airport and through Alexandria straight to Mount Vernon. The trip from Washington takes about a half hour.

To reach Woodlawn and Gunston Hall you need a car. From Mount Vernon, continue south on the George Washington Parkway to Route 1. The entrance to Woodlawn is straight across from the exit; to reach Gunston Hall, turn left and follow the signs.

By Subway and Bus

You can get to Mount Vernon from the District by taking one Metro and one bus each way. From downtown, take the yellow line train to Huntington ($1.50–$2.05, depending on the time of day). Then catch Fairfax County Connector Bus 101/Ft. Hunt to Mt. Vernon (50¢). Bus 101 leaves Huntington once an hour and operates Monday–Sunday 6:30 AM–8:15 PM, Saturday 7:20 AM–7:30 PM, Sunday 9:30–6. Returning to Huntington from Mt. Vernon, the bus will be marked 101/HUN-TINGTON. ☎ *703/339–7200 for schedule information.*

Guided Tours

Gray Line Tours. Gray Line runs half-day trips to Mount Vernon and Old Town Alexandria. Buses depart daily at 8:30 AM from Union Station. ☎ *301/386–8300.* 🎫 *$22.*

Tourmobile. Tourmobile offers trips to and from Mount Vernon. Tours depart from April through October, daily at 10 AM, noon, and 2 PM from Arlington Cemetery and the Washington Monument. Reservations must be made in person one hour before departure. ☎ *202/554–5100.* 🎫 *$16.50; 2-day combination ticket for Mount Vernon and several sites in Washington $25.50.*

FREDERICKSBURG, VIRGINIA

On land once favored by Indian tribes as fishing and hunting ground, the compact city of Fredericksburg, near the falls of the Rappahannock River, figured prominently at crucial points in the nation's history, particularly during the Revolutionary and Civil wars. Just 50 miles south of Washington on I–95, Fredericksburg is today a popular day-trip destination for history buffs. The town's 40-block **National Historic District** contains more than 350 original 18th- and 19th-century buildings, including the house George Washington bought for his mother, Mary Washington; James Monroe's law office; the Rising Sun Tavern; and Kenmore, the magnificent 1752 plantation home of George Washington's sister. The town is a favorite with antiques collectors, who enjoy cruising the dealers' shops along Caroline Street.

Although its site was visited by explorer Captain John Smith as early as 1608, the town of Fredericksburg wasn't founded until 1728. Established as a frontier port to serve nearby tobacco farmers and iron miners, Fredericksburg took its name from England's crown prince at the time, and the streets still bear names of members of his family: George, Caroline, Sophia, Princess Anne, Hanover, William, and Amelia.

George Washington knew Fredericksburg well, having grown up just across the Rappahannock on Ferry Farm. He lived there from age 6 to 16, and the legends about chopping down a cherry tree and throwing a coin across the Rappahannock—later mythologized as the Potomac—go back to this period of his life. In later years Washington often returned to visit his mother here on Charles Street.

Fredericksburg prospered in the decades after independence, benefiting from its location midway along the 100-mile path between Washington and Richmond, an important intersection of railroad lines and waterways. When the Civil War broke out in 1861, Fredericksburg became the linchpin of the Confederate defense of Richmond and, as such, the inevitable target of Union assaults. In December 1862, Union forces attacked Fredericksburg in what was to be the first of four major battles fought in and around the town. In the battle of Sunken Road, Confederate defenders sheltered by a stone wall at the base of Marye's Heights mowed down Union soldiers by the thousands as they charged across the fields on foot and on horseback.

By war's end, the fighting in Fredericksburg and in battles at nearby Chancellorsville, the Wilderness, and the Spotsylvania Court House had claimed more than 100,000 dead or wounded. Fredericksburg's cemeteries hold the remains of 17,000 soldiers from both sides. Miraculously, despite heavy bombardment and house-to-house fighting, much of the city remained intact.

A walking tour through the town proper takes three to four hours; battlefield tours each can take that long. The short hop across the Rappahannock to Chatham Manor is well worth it, if for no other reason than that the site offers a splendid view of all of Fredericksburg.

Exploring

Numbers in the margin correspond to points of interest on the Fredericksburg map.

⓫ Chatham Manor. A fine example of Georgian architecture, Chatham Manor was built between 1768 and 1771 by William Fitzhugh on a site overlooking the Rappahannock River and the town of Fredericksburg. Fitzhugh, a noted plantation owner, frequently hosted such luminaries of his day as George Washington and Thomas Jefferson. During the Civil War, Union forces commandeered the house and converted it into a headquarters and hospital. President Abraham Lincoln visited there to confer with his generals; Clara Barton and the poet Walt Whitman tended the wounded. After the war the house and gardens were restored by private owners and eventually donated to the National Park Service. Concerts often are held here during the summer. ⊠ *Chatham La., Stafford County (take William St. across bridge and follow signs approximately ½ mi),* ☎ *703/373–4461.* ☜ *Free.* ☉ *Daily 9–5.*

❹ Confederate Cemetery. The Confederate Cemetery contains the remains of more than 2,000 soldiers (most of them unknown) as well as the graves of generals Dabney Maury, Seth Barton, Carter Stevenson, Daniel Ruggles, Henry Sibley, and Abner Perrin. ⊠ *1100 Washington Ave., near Washington Ave. and Amelia St.* ☉ *Daily dawn–dusk.*

❼ Fredericksburg Area Museum and Cultural Center. Housed in an 1816 building once used as a market and town hall, this museum's six permanent exhibit galleries tell the story of the area from prehistoric times through the Revolutionary and Civil wars to the present. Displays include dinosaur footprints from a nearby quarry, Native American artifacts, an 18th-century plantation account book with an inventory of slaves, and Confederate memorabilia. ✉ *907 Princess Anne St.,* ☎ *703/371–3037.* ▩ *$3.* ☉ *Mar.–Nov., Mon.–Sat. 9–5, Sun. 1–5; Dec.–Feb., Mon.–Sat. 10–4, Sun. 1–4.*

★ ❷ **Fredericksburg Battlefield Visitor Center.** At this informative tourist facility you can learn about Fredericksburg's role in the Civil War by attending the succinct slide show and then moving on to displays of soldiers' art and battlefield relics. Park rangers lead frequent walking tours of the area. The center offers tape-recorded tour cassettes ($2.75 rental, $4.25 purchase) and maps showing how to reach hiking trails at the nearby Wilderness, Chancellorsville, and Spotsylvania Court House battlefields (all within 15 miles of Fredericksburg). Just outside is Sunken Road, where from December 11 to 13, 1862, General Robert E. Lee led his troops to a bloody but resounding victory over Union forces attacking across the Rappahannock; 18,000 men from both sides died in the clash. Much of the stone wall that hid Lee's sharpshooters has been rebuilt, but 100 yards from the visitor center part of the original wall looks out on the statue *The Angel of Marye's Heights* by Felix de Weldon. This memorial honors Sergeant Richard Kirkland, a South Carolinian who risked his life to bring water to wounded foes; he later died at the Battle of Chickamauga. ✉ *Lafayette Blvd. at Sunken Rd.,* ☎ *703/373–6122.* ☉ *Mid-June–Labor Day, daily 8:30–6:30; Sept. 3–mid-June, weekdays 9–5, weekends 9–6.*

❶ **Fredericksburg Visitor Center.** Stop by the Fredericksburg Visitor Center for booklets and pamphlets on local history, information on restaurants and lodging, and an orientation slide show. You can get parking passes here, good for a whole day in what would normally be two-hour zones. Also available are money-saving Hospitality Passes to city attractions. A pass to seven sites costs $16 for adults, $6 for those 6–18; the costs of any four sites are $11.50 and $4, respectively. The center is in a structure that was built in 1824 as a residence and confectionery; during the Civil War it was used to hold prisoners. ✉ *706 Caroline St.,* ☎ *703/373–1776 or 800/678–4748.* ☉ *Mid-June–Labor Day, daily 9–7; Sept. 2–mid-June, daily 9–5.*

❽ **Home of Mary Washington.** On Fredericksburg's Charles Street is the post-White House residence of America's first first lady, a modest white-painted house that George purchased for her in 1772. She spent the last 17 years of her life there, tending the charming garden where her boxwood still flourishes and where many a bride and groom now exchange their vows. Inside, displays include many of Mrs. Washington's personal effects, as well as period furniture and, in the garden, plants she herself started. ✉ *1200 Charles St.,* ☎ *703/373–1569.* ▩ *$3.* ☉ *Mar.–Nov., daily 9–5; Dec.–Feb., daily 10–4.*

❿ **Hugh Mercer Apothecary Shop.** Offering a close-up view of 18th- and 19th-century medicine, including instruments and procedures that would have served a torturer well during the Spanish Inquisition, the Hugh Mercer Apothecary Shop was established in 1771 by Dr. Mercer, a Scotsman who served as a brigadier general of the Revolutionary Army (he was killed at the Battle of Princeton). General George S. Patton of World War II fame was one of Mercer's great-great-great-grandsons. Dr. Mercer might have been more careful than most other Colonial physicians, yet his methods will make you cringe. A costumed hostess will explicitly describe amputations and cataract operations before the discovery of anesthetics. You will also hear about therapeu-

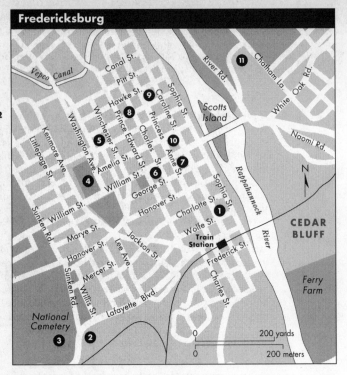

tic bleeding and see the gruesome devices used in Colonial dentistry. ⊠ *1020 Caroline St., at Amelia St.,* ☏ *703/373–3362.* 🎫 *$3.* ☉ *Mar.–Nov., daily 9–5; Dec.–Feb., daily 10–4.*

❻ James Monroe Museum and Memorial Library. A tiny one-story building where the man who was to be the fifth president of the United States practiced law from 1787 to 1789, the James Monroe Museum and Memorial Library contains many of Monroe's possessions, collected and preserved by his family until this century. They include a mahogany dispatch-box used during the negotiation of the Louisiana Purchase and the desk on which Monroe signed the doctrine named for him. ⊠ *908 Charles St.,* ☏ *703/899–4559.* 🎫 *$3.* ☉ *Mar.–Nov., daily 9–5; Dec.–Feb., daily 10–4.*

★ ❺ Kenmore. Kenmore was the home of Fielding Lewis, a patriot, plantation owner, and brother-in-law of George Washington. (Lewis sacrificed much of his fortune to operate a gun factory that supplied the American forces during the Revolution.) Kenmore's plain exterior belies the lavish interior; these have been called some of the most beautiful rooms in America. The plaster moldings in the ceilings are outstanding and even more ornate than Mount Vernon's. Of equal elegance are the furnishings, which include a large standing clock that belonged to Mary Washington. Across the street are fine examples of Victorian architecture and a monument to Mary Washington, as well as the entrance to the Confederate Cemetery. After the 60-minute tour visitors to Kenmore are served tea and gingerbread baked according to a Washington family recipe. ⊠ *1201 Washington Ave.,* ☏ *703/373–3381.* 🎫 *$5.* ☉ *Mar.–Nov., daily 9–5; Dec., daily 10–4; Jan. and Feb., Sat. 10–4, Sun. noon–4.*

❸ National Cemetery. The National Cemetery is the final resting place of 15,000 Union casualties, most of whom were never identified. ⊠

Lafayette Blvd. and Sunken Rd., ☏ *703/373–6122.* ☼ *Daily sunrise–sunset.*

NEED A
BREAK? At the **Irish Brigade** (✉ 1005 Princess Anne St., ☏ 703/371-9413), American and traditional Irish dishes as well as vegetarian meals served daily.

Set in a 1771 Georgian style house, **Le Lafayette** (✉ 623 Caroline St., ☏ 703/373-6895), serves French fare Tuesday through Sunday.

Stop for a gourmet sandwich or a slice of quiche at the **Made in Virginia Store Deli** (✉ 101 William St., ☏ 703/371-2233). If you have a sweet tooth, the rich desserts are not to be missed.

❾ **Rising Sun Tavern.** In 1760 George Washington's brother Charles built as his home what became the Rising Sun Tavern, a watering hole for such pre-Revolutionary patriots as the Lee brothers; Patrick Henry, the patriot and pamphleteer who wrote, "give me liberty or give me death"; and first- and third-presidents-to-be Washington and Jefferson. A "wench" in period costume leads the tour without stepping out of character. From her perspective you watch the activity—day and night, upstairs and down—at this busy institution. In the taproom you are served spiced tea. ✉ *1304 Caroline St.,* ☏ *703/371–1494.* ▱ *$3.* ☼ *Mar.–Nov., daily 9–5; Dec.–Feb., daily 10–4.*

Getting Around

By Bus

Greyhound Line buses (☏ 202/289–5160 or 800/231–2222) depart several times a day from Washington to Fredericksburg. A round-trip ticket is $29. Buses stop at a station on alternate Route 1, about 2 miles from the center of town; cabs are available there.

By Car

To get to Fredericksburg from the District, take I–95 south to Route 3, turn left, and follow the signs. The drive takes about an hour one way, except during rush hour.

By Train

Amtrak trains bound for Fredericksburg depart six times daily from Washington's Union Station and take about an hour (☏ 202/484–7540 or 800/872–7245). The Fredericksburg railroad station is near the historic district (Caroline St. and Lafayette Blvd). A round-trip ticket from Washington costs $20.

Guided Tours

Contact the tour coordinator at the **Fredericksburg Visitor Center** (☞ *above*) to arrange a group tour of the city as well as of battlefields and other historic sites in the area. Reservations are required. The **Fredericksburg Department of Tourism** (in the Visitor Center) publishes a booklet that includes a short history of Fredericksburg and a self-guided tour covering 29 sights.

10 Portraits of Washington

HISTORY AT A GLANCE

1608   Captain John Smith sails from Jamestown up the Potomac river. Colonization follows.

1775–83   American Revolutionary War.

1788   U.S. Constitution ratified.

1789   New York is the capital. George Washington becomes the first U.S. president.

1790   Philadelphia is now the capital; but in return for the South's assumption of the North's Revolutionary War debt, George Washington will select a Southern capital site.

1792   White House construction begins.

1793   Capitol Building construction begins.

1800   Congress relocates from Philadelphia; John Adams, elected in **1797,** moves into an unfinished White House.

1803   The city's population is 3,000.

1812–15   War of 1812. In **1814,** British burn Washington, including such landmarks as the White House and the Capitol; storms save the city from total destruction.

1846   Smithsonian Institution established.

1861–65   Civil War. Lincoln assassinated in **1865.**

1862   Lincoln issues the Emancipation Proclamation abolishing slavery.

1900   The city's population is 300,000.

1912   Cherry trees, gifts from Japan, are planted.

1914–18   World War I (United States enters in **1917**).

1919–33   Prohibition begins with the passage of the Volstead Act; it's repealed by FDR 14 years later.

1929–39   Great Depression.

1939–45   World War II (United States enters in **1941**).

1943   Pentagon completed.

1945   On July 16, the first atomic explosion occurs in a test at Alamagordo, New Mexico.

1950–53   Korean War.

1962   Cuban Missile Crisis.

1963   The U.S. Military Assistance Command is set up in South Vietnam, beginning America's involvement in what would become known as the Vietnam War.

1963   President Kennedy assassinated in Dallas.

1969   After $25 billion spent on the U.S. space program, Neil Armstrong and Buzz Aldrin of Apollo 11 are the first humans to walk on the moon.

1972   Watergate break-in.

1973   The U.S. signs the Paris peace accords ending the Vietnam War.

1974   Citing "political" difficulties arising from the Watergate break-in, President Nixon resigns.

1981   A crazed youth named John Hinkley attempts to assassinate President Reagan.

1976 Metrorail service begins.

1990 The city's population is 570,000.

1991 The Soviet Union's government and economy continue to crumble. In **1992**, President Bush and Russian president Boris Yeltsin issue a joint statement officially ending the Cold War on February 1.

1995–6 Federal employees furloughed twice between November and January as a result of budget battles between Republican dominated Congress and President Clinton.

PRESIDENTS

1. George Washington (1789–97)
2. John Adams (1797–1801)
3. Thomas Jefferson (1801–09)
4. James Madison (1809–17)
5. James Monroe (1817–25)
6. John Quincy Adams (1825–29)
7. Andrew Jackson (1829–37)
8. Martin Van Buren (1837–41)
9. William Henry Harrison (March 4–April 4, 1841—died in office)
10. John Tyler (1841–45)
11. James Knox Polk (1845–49)
12. Zachary Taylor (1849–50—died in office)
13. Millard Fillmore (1850–53)
14. Franklin Pierce (1853–57)
15. James Buchanan (1857–61)
16. Abraham Lincoln (1861–65—assassinated)
17. Andrew Johnson (1865–69)
18. Ulysses Simpson Grant (1869–77)
19. Rutherford Birchard Hayes (1877–81)
20. James Abram Garfield (Mar.–Sept. 1881—assassinated)
21. Chester Alan Arthur (1881–85)
22. (Stephen) Grover Cleveland (1885–89)
23. Benjamin Harrison (1889–93)
24. (Stephen) Grover Cleveland (1893–97)
25. William McKinley (1897–1901—assassinated)
26. Theodore Roosevelt (1901–1909)
27. William Howard Taft (1909–13)
28. (Thomas) Woodrow Wilson (1913–21)
29. Warren Gamaliel Harding (1921–23—died in office)
30. (John) Calvin Coolidge (1923–29)
31. Herbert Clark Hoover (1929–33)
32. Franklin Delano Roosevelt (1933–45—died in office)
33. Harry S. Truman (1945–53)
34. Dwight David Eisenhower (1953–61)
35. John Fitzgerald Kennedy 1961–63—assassinated)
36. Lyndon Baines Johnson (1963–69)
37. Richard Milhous Nixon (1969–74—resigned from office)
38. Gerald Rudolph Ford (1974–77)
39. James Earl (Jimmy) Carter (1977–81)
40. Ronald Wilson Reagan (1981–89)
41. George Herbert Walker Bush (1989–93)
42. William Jefferson (Bill) Clinton (1993–)

SPEAKING OF WASHINGTON

WASHINGTON, D.C., is a bit like the weather: Everybody likes to talk about it. Unlike the weather though, we can do something about Washington. Every few years Americans are invited to throw the bums out and usher a new crop of bums in. And there's no doubt these politicians will form some opinion of their new home.

Politicians, poets, presidents, First Ladies, humorists, foreign visitors—they've all put pen to paper in expressing their opinion of the city that literally rose from the swamp.

"That Indian swamp in the wilderness." —Thomas Jefferson, circa 1789

"A century hence, if this country keeps united, it will produce a city though not so large as London, yet of magnitude inferior to few others in Europe."—George Washington, 1789

"May the spirit which animated the great founder of this city, descend to future generations."—John Adams, 1800

"I had much rather live in the house at Philadelphia. Not one room or chamber is finished of the whole. It is habitable by fires in every part, 13 of which we are required to keep daily or sleep in wet or damp places."—Abigail Adams, 1800 (after moving into the White House)

"This boasted [Pennsylvania] Avenue is as much a wilderness as Kentucky. Some half-starved cattle browsing among the bushes present a melancholy spectacle to the stranger . . . . So very thinly is the city peopled that quails and other birds are constantly shot within a hundred yards of the Capitol."—Charles W. Jansen, 1806

"This embryo capital, where Fancy sees / Squares in morasses, obelisks in trees; / Which second-sighted seers, ev'n now, adorn / With shrines unbuilt, and heroes yet unborn. / Though nought but woods, and Jefferson they see, / Where streets should run, and sages *ought* to be." —Thomas Moore, 1806

"Washington has certainly an air of more magnificence than any other American town. It is mean in detail, but the outline has a certain grandeur about it."—James Fenimore Cooper, 1838

"In democratic communities the imagination is compressed when men consider themselves; it expands indefinitely when they think of the state. Hence it is that the same men who live on a small scale in cramped dwellings frequently aspire to gigantic splendor in the erection of their public monuments. The Americans have traced out the circuit of an immense city on the site which they intend to make their capital, but which up to the present time is hardly more densely peopled than Pontoise, though, according to them, it will one day contain a million inhabitants. They have already rooted up trees for 10 miles around lest they should interfere with the future citizens of this imaginary metropolis. They have erected a magnificent palace for Congress in the center of the city and have given it the pompous name of the Capitol."—Alexis de Tocqueville, 1840

"This town looks like a large straggling village reared in a drained swamp." —George Combe, 1842

"It is sometimes called the City of Magnificent Distances but it might with greater propriety be termed the City of Magnificent Intentions . . . . Spacious avenues that begin in nothing and lead nowhere; streets, a mile long, that only want houses, roads, and inhabitants; public meetings that need but a public to be complete; and ornaments of great thoroughfares, which only lack great thoroughfares to ornament—are its leading features. One might fancy the season over and most of the houses gone out of town forever with their masters."—Charles Dickens, 1842

"I . . . found the capital still under the empire of King Mud . . . . Were I to say that it was intended to be typical of the condition of the government, I might be considered cynical."—Anthony Trollope, 1862

"Washington is the paradise of gamblers, and contains many handsome and elegantly-fitted-up establishments. It is said at least one hundred of these 'hells' were in full blast during the war."—Dr. John B. Ellis, 1870

"Why, when I think of those multitudes of clerks and congressmen—whole families of them—down there slaving away and keeping the country together, why then I know in my heart there is something so good and motherly about Washington, that grand old benevolent National Asylum for the Helpless."—Mark Twain, 1873

"One of these days this will be a very great city if nothing happens to it."—Henry Adams, 1877

"Wherever the American citizen may be a stranger, he is at home here."—Frederick Douglass, 1877

"Washington is no place in which to carry out inventions."—Alexander Graham Bell, 1887

"But taking it all in all and after all, Negro life in Washington is a promise rather than a fulfillment. But it is worthy of note for the really excellent things which are promised."—Paul Laurence Dunbar, 1900

"In Washington there is no life apart from government and politics: it is our daily bread; it is the thread which runs through the woof and warp of our lives; it colors everything."—A. Maurice Low, 1900

"What you want is to have a city which every one who comes from Maine, Texas, Florida, Arkansas, or Oregon can admire as being something finer and more beautiful than he had ever dreamed of before."— James Bryce, 1913

"Things get very lonely in Washington sometimes. The real voice of the great people of America sometimes sounds faint and distant in that strange city. You hear politics until you wish that both parties were smothered in their own gas."—Woodrow Wilson, 1919

"Congress has been writing my material for years and I am not ashamed of what I have had. Why should I pay some famous Author, or even myself, to sit down all day trying to dope out something funny to say on the Stage? . . . No, sir, I have found that there is nothing as funny as things that have happened . . . Nothing is so funny as something done in all seriousness . . . Each state elects the most serious man it has in the District . . . He is impressed with the fact that he is leaving Home with the idea that he is to rescue his District from Certain Destruction, and to see that it receives its just amount of Rivers and Harbors, Postoffices and Pumpkin Seeds. Naturally, you have put a pretty big load on that man . . . It's no joking matter to be grabbed up bodily from the Leading Lawyer's Office of Main Street and have the entire populace tell you what is depending on you when you get to Washington."—Will Rogers, 1924

"Washington . . . is the symbol of America. By its dignity and architectural inspiration . . . we encourage that elevation of thought and character which comes from great architecture."—Herbert Hoover, 1929

"Of my first trip to the top of the Washington Monument, which must have been made soon after it was opened in 1888, I recall only the fact that we descended by walking down the long, dark steps, and it seemed a journey without end. There was in those days a bitter debate as to whether a baseball thrown from the top of the monument could be caught by a catcher on the ground, and my father was much interested and full of mathematical proofs that it couldn't be done. Some time later it was tried, and turned out to be very easy."—H. L. Mencken, 1936

"Living in contemporary Washington, caught literally and physically in L'Enfant's dream, and encountering on every hand the brave mementos of Washington, Jefferson, Jackson, Lincoln and Roosevelt, is to live as close as possible to both the source and the climax of the major sequences of the human story."—George Sessions Perry, 1946

"Washington isn't a city, it's an abstraction."—Dylan Thomas, 1950

"There are a number of things wrong with Washington. One of them is that everyone has been too long away from home."—Dwight D. Eisenhower, 1955

"Whatever we are looking for, we come to Washington in millions to stand in silence and try to find it."—Bruce Catton, 1959

"Washington is a literal cesspool of crime and violence."—Sen. James O. Eastland, 1960

"A city of southern efficiency and northern charm."—John F. Kennedy, 1960

"Every dedicated American could be proud that a dynamic experience of democracy in his nation's capital had been made visible to the world."—Martin Luther King, Jr., 1963

"Washington is several miles square and about as tall, say, as the Washington Monument, give or take a little. It is surrounded on all four sides by reality."—Arthur Hoppe, 1975

"One of my earliest recollections of Washington is of a tragicomic speech by Michigan Congressman Fred Bradley, protesting that all the wining and dining was getting him down. 'Banquet life is a physical and mental strain on us hardly imaginable to the folks back home,' said the distraught Bradley. 'The strain is terrific.' He was dragooned into attending altogether too many parties, he complained; but his appeal for fewer invitations was greeted with guffaws. Three weeks later Representative Bradley, age forty-nine, dropped dead. The official diagnosis was heart failure."—Jack Anderson, 1979

"As we quietly approached our new home, I told Rosalyn with a smile that it was a nice-looking place. She said, 'I believe we're going to be happy in the White House.' We were silent for a moment, and then I replied, 'I just hope that we never disappoint the people who made it possible for us to live here.' Rosalyn's prediction proved to be correct, and I did my utmost for four solid years to make my own hope come true."—Jimmy Carter, 1982, from *Keeping Faith: Memoirs of a President*

"The first thing that struck me about the White House was how cold it was. The country was still suffering from the energy crisis, and President Carter had ordered that the White House thermostats be turned down."—Nancy Reagan, 1989, from *My Turn*

"I think all of us are beginning to understand Washington better and get a more realistic sense of how it works. I have a clearer idea in my own mind what it will take to make the arguments that will change the government's direction. The problems are not quite as overwhelming and undefined as when we started off our 'Agenda for Change'—I feel liberated."—Hillary Rodham Clinton, 1993, from *Hillary Rodham Clinton: A First Lady for Our Time*

—Compiled by John F. Kelly

SO YOU WANT TO BE A WASHINGTON INSIDER

RICH AND POOR. Black and white. Politicians. Diplomats. Labor unionists. Lobbyists. Bureaucrats. Spies. Immigrants. Eggheads. P.R. flacks. Journalists. Lawyers galore. They all come together in an polymorphous place called the District of Columbia. The city's denizens range from bagel-chomping political activitists and smooth-talking executives with careful hair and red power ties to tourists speaking Spanish or Swahili and elderly Anacostia women scraping to get by. All are subsumed in some way by politics. New York has Wall Street. Los Angeles has Hollywood. Washington has the White House, the Capitol, and the Supreme Court. The focus on political power is what sets the city apart. Elusive yet undeniably distinct, Washington has a personality—or personalities—all its own. Passionate? Yes. Intense? Yes. Neurotic? Yes.

Remember that smart kid who asked too many questions in 10th-grade math class? Or that obnoxiously eager senior class president? Now imagine tens of thousands of them—political science and economics majors in college—fully grown and just as obnoxious, flocking to Washington, only now they vie for the attention of cabinet secretaries instead of classmates.

Maybe that was a low blow. Try to get used to it. In Washington, it's part of the normal exchange of pleasantries. Those who aspire to insider status must know who to praise and who to condemn during the most politically potent hour of the day: happy hour. Elsewhere you may be known for what you drive; here you are known for who you support or condemn. The atmosphere is preening, chesslike, aboil with pinstriped ambition.

Ironically, the best advice on how to be a player in D.C. was penned centuries before the Capitol (and the country) existed. Free of illusion and based on the keenest insights, Niccolò Machiavelli's *Prince* shrewdly lays out the timeless principles of wresting and keeping power: it is better to be feared than to be loved; it is sometimes merciful to be cruel; do not put public applause before the retention of power. Washington power brokers need to have such dicta embedded in their genetic codes. To see the various *intrigues du jour* played out for public edification and amusement, tune in to the Sunday morning news shows: the Roman colosseums of the Digital Era.

Would-be insiders must first learn to act the part. The 10 rules of etiquette (or laws of the jungle) we're about to disclose are, as the CIA likes to stamp on its documents, for "Eyes Only." A true insider holds the cards close to the chest; information being the coin of the realm, one doesn't normally give it away for free. Profligate bean spillers risk the ultimate Capitol punishment: an empty mailbox at invitation time for a celebrity-packed White House soirée.

1. *Become a "position-dropper."* Elsewhere, name-dropping to enhance the public perception of one's importance may be the norm. In Washington people would never be so vulgar; here they position-drop. Position is everything in the Capitol, and the small talk at a reception is always a bit strained until basic information on one's geographical proximity to people who really count is exchanged. You might say you live next to a certain prestigious diplomat or regularly dine with a columnist from the *Washington Post*. Until such associations are declared, simply telling someone your name is— well, meaningless.

2. *Create an air of mystery about your connections.* On the other hand, you may augment your caché by coyly refusing to reveal the name of the important Washington personage with whom you identify. Known as the "Deep Throat Ploy," the intent is to create a sense of intrigue about one's totem and by association about oneself. You might, for example, make vague mention of some "very good friend" who's an influential aide to a certain powerful senator, and add that you occasionally exchange pleasantries in an underground parking garage. If the name

is not forthcoming, fellow insiders won't pry. Some connections are like money; publicity invites theft.

3. *Invite the right sort of people to your fêtes.* The consummate insider not only knows important people, he or she periodically sets them out for public exhibition complete with a wet bar and hors d'oeuvres. To make a decent impression, your circle of friends should at minimum include a cabinet secretary's chief of staff or an ambassador from an oil-rich country, preferrably one of each. A high-ranking naval officer also makes a lovely statement; dress whites break up the monotony of all those dark suits.

4. *Have a good opening line.* If you come from Boston or Milwaukee or Tuscon, family, church or recreational preferences might seem a fit topic of conversation after you've been introduced to someone new. In Washington social intercourse is for schmoozing and networking in pursuit of city's twin obsessions: getting power, and then getting more. You can always tell which party guests have more well-rounded interests. They're the ones marooned at the punch bowl with no one to talk to. To avoid the same fate, try this ice breaker; it's practically foolproof: "I work for the (insert your company name here). That's all I can tell you about it." Nothing arouses curiosity like announcing you have a secret. Just be aware that half of Washington is using the same ploy.

5. *Get out and socialize.* You can't be an insider by staying inside. Elsewhere, it's rumored that men and women get together after hours for pleasure. This has people in Washington scratching their heads. Socializing in the Capitol is not mere recreation. Like breathing, it's fundamental. If you're not doing it you can hardly be said to be alive. The true insider needs a daily fix of power-socializing. Having the right people at your own affairs will elicit a fistful of invitations to everyone else's tony little do's. Those elegant rectangles of paper are like molecules of air; without them, everything else in life ceases to matter.

6. *Let people think you're popular.* No matter how benign the person you are talking with may seem, never admit to having only one invitation to a dinner party or cocktail reception on a given night. Elsewhere, such honesty may be appealing. In Washington you might as well break into a chorus of "I'm a Loser." Effect an aura of surface calm beneath which you subtly and genteely seem beset by the social demands important people make of you. A day or two later, invitations will arrive in the mail. Project an air of having just come from one function and of readying yourself for another. Cellular phones were made for this purpose. Arrange to have yours ring often in public and your postal carrier will soon complain about the sudden surge in the volume of your mail.

7. *Leave your human frailties at home.* No self-respecting Washington insider would admit to passing up a social engagement out of simple human fatigue or an even more primitive desire to spend a quiet evening at home. In D.C., it's just not done, not when there are new connections to make, careers to advance, and the ambitions of others to feed or crush. Have your priorities straight or it will be noted. Here insomnia isn't a disorder; it's a gift.

8. *Look the part.* Be brilliant in Washington, but not in what you wear. For the upwardly mobile insider, a strict dress code, unwritten but universally observed and stringently enforced, favors high necklines and pearls for women, dark suits for men. Peacocks and politics don't mix. Trendy East Village togs may fit right into New York's "gorgeous mosaic" at Lincoln Center. At Washington's Kennedy Center, Dolce & Gabana suits that show off your bodacious bod will provoke frowns and gasps. Some insiders may secretly envy your sartorial liberation, although they'll never admit it. Officially, expect to be treated like Hester Prynne.

9. *Pack your credentials.* Rare distinction is important here. Because everyone has to wear the same clothes, if person A wasn't brokering a Middle East peace treaty and person B wasn't striving to save snail darters and spotted owls, you'd never know who was who. Job titles should be so long listeners need to take notes. You might be a lobbyist with the International Association of Amusement Parks and Attractions or the chairperson of a foundation on opportunities for iron works development in Eastern Europe. The more words, the merrier.

10. *If you can't tell a good lawyer joke, start practicing.* Lawyer jokes evoke explosions of laughter among Washington's elite. There's no surer way to grease the social wheels. The Capitol is alleged to have more lawyers per capita than anyplace on the planet, and after a few bottles of wine or bourbon or both the dinner conversation may turn giddy. Lawyer jokes soon follow. In fact, lawyers, trying to be self-deprecating and humorous, may be the first to tell them. An example:

> Question: What are three lawyers at the bottom of the Potomac River?

> Answer: A good start.

Seinfeld they're not. The sad truth is that the lawyer jokes floating around Washington are little better than elephant jokes. Be the life of the party. Your lawyer jokes are bound to be better. While listening to someone else tell one of these groaners, it's crucial that you not moan or roll your eyes. Let a subtle Giaconda smile play upon your lips; incline your head in a detectable nod. The people who insist on telling these jokes and laughing uproariously are, after all, just what you aspire to be: rich, powerful, brilliant insiders. But they're nerds. It's congenital. Really, they're trying.

Seamlessly acting the part is the first rung on the ladder budding insiders must ascend. Camouflage has advantages. It frees you to observe already established pros at close quarters without disturbing them as they enact their exotic rituals. Remember that imitation is the sincerest form of flattery. Ape outstandingly and you could end up a lobbyist, chief of protocol, or special prosecutor before your vacation is over. What a postcard that would make! And if you have good lawyer jokes, don't sell yourself short. Every two years House seats are up for grabs; often they are won by people with less.

—Anna Borgman, Neil Chesanow,
and Stephen Wolf

EDIFICE TREKS

WASHINGTON probably produces more words than any other city in the world. Politicians orate, pundits speculate, and commentators narrate. But Washington's words have a peculiarly fleeting quality. They're copied into notebooks, transferred to computer screens, then set into type and bound into reports that are filed on shelves and forgotten. They're printed in newspapers that yellow and turn to dust. Words are spat out in sound bytes on the evening news, then released into the ether, lost forever. In the wordy war of politics, a paper trail is something best avoided.

But there is a stone trail in Washington, too: The words someone felt were important enough not just to commit to parchment, paper, or videotape, but to engrave in sandstone, marble, or granite. On the buildings of Washington are noble sentiments and self-serving ones, moving odes and contemplative ones.

A reading tour of Washington's inscriptions amounts to a classical education. The inscriptions, lofty in position and tone, are taken from the Bible, from the Greeks and Romans, from poets and playwrights, from presidents and politicians. When viewing Washington's inscriptions, soaking up what is in most cases a perfect union of poesy and architecture, it's easy to see why the words "edifice" and "edify" spring from the same root.

Lesson one starts in Union Station, that great Beaux Arts bathhouse on Capitol Hill. Architect Daniel Burnham's 1908 train station is encrusted with carvings that do everything from romantically outline the development of the railroad to offer lessons in both humility and hospitality.

On the western end of the shining white Vermont granite structure, above the entrance to the Metro, is written (in all capital letters, as most inscriptions are):

He that would bring home the wealth of the Indies must carry the wealth of the In-

dies with him. So it is in travelling. A man must carry knowledge with him if he would bring home knowledge.

A bit heavy to digest when dashing for the Metroliner on a rainy Monday morning, but worth mulling over once a seat is found.

At the other end of the station is the perfect sentiment for the returning hero:

Welcome the coming, speed the parting guest. Virtue alone is sweet society. It keeps the key to all heroic hearts and opens you a welcome in them all.

These are just two of the half dozen inscriptions on Union Station. Above allegorical statues by Louis Saint-Gaudens that stand over the main entrance are inscriptions celebrating the forces that created the railroads, including this set singing the praises of fire and electricity:

Fire: greatest of discoveries, enabling man to live in various climates, use many foods, and compel the forces of nature to do his work. Electricity: carrier of light and power, devourer of time and space, bearer of human speech over land and sea, greatest servant of man, itself unknown. Thou has put all things under his feet.

So inspirational were these and the other Union Station inscriptions thought that the Washington Terminal Company, operators of the station, once distributed free pamphlets imprinted with them. This probably saved more than a few sore necks.

Union Station's inscriptions were selected by Charles William Eliot, who was president of Harvard University. According to John L. Andriot's "Guide to the Inscriptions of the Nation's Capital," Eliot borrowed from such sources as the Bible, Shakespeare, Alexander Pope, and Ralph Waldo Emerson. Eliot also penned his own epigrams, a seemingly modest skill until you start to wonder what you'd come up with when confronted with a big blank wall that will bear your words forever.

Eliot wrote the two inscriptions on the City Post Office right next to the station. The inscriptions, facing Massachusetts Avenue, describe the humble letter carrier as a:

Carrier of news and knowledge, instrument of trade and industry, promoter of mutual acquaintance of peace and of goodwill among men and nations . . . and a . . . Messenger of sympathy and love, servant of parted friends, consoler of the lonely, bond of scattered family, enlarger of the common life.

It's said that President Woodrow Wilson edited these inscriptions, unaware that the Ivy League wordsmith Eliot had written them. Like all good editors, Wilson improved them.

Rocks and Hard Places

Behind every inscription in Washington is the person who carved it, the man or woman who put chisel or pneumatic drill to stone and, with a sharp eye and a steady hand, made the most lasting of impressions.

Ann Hawkins is one such carver. (You can admire her chisel work throughout the National Gallery of Art. She did the names on the Patrons' Permanent Fund in the east building, a roll call of philanthropists.)

"There are two comments I get from people who watch me carve and they make perfect symmetry," says Hawkins. "Half the people say 'Oh, that looks so tedious. You must have a lot of patience.' But I also get 'That looks *fun.*' And they wish they could do it."

Hawkins studied four years before she could carve well enough to take her first paying commission. She's been carving professionally since 1982, and in that time she's decided that stones are "living, breathing things." And each one is different. Sandstone is soft. Slates can be brittle and hard, with knots in them almost like wood. White Vermont marble feels sugary and crumbles a bit at the first stroke. Tennessee pink marble is chunky and firm.

There are a lot of things a stone carver has to take into account before striking the first blow, Hawkins says. "The nature of the stone, the light the inscription will re-

ceive, the weathering of the stone, how large the letters will be, what distance they'll be viewed from."

The most important part of carving, she says, is the layout of the inscription. The letters must be spaced correctly, not bunched too tightly together as if they were typeset, but spread comfortably and handsomely. The inscription must look as if it is *of* the stone, not *on* the stone.

Hawkins draws the letters on paper that—"after being measured from every direction" to make sure it's straight—is taped to the stone over sheets of typewriter carbon paper. She then outlines the inscription, transferring it to the stone. With a tungsten-carbide-tip chisel she starts hammering, sometimes working her way around the edges of the letter, sometimes starting in the center and working out. She turns and shifts the blade, roughing the letter in at first, then finishing it, aiming for the perfect V-shape indentation that is the mark of a hand-carved inscription. (Inscriptions that are machine sandblasted through a stencil have a round center.) As in everything from squash to Frisbee, it's all in the wrist.

If the inscription is outside, the sun will provide the contrast necessary for the letters to be read. As the rays rake across the inscription, the shadows will lengthen, making the words pop. If the inscription is indoors, Hawkins paints the inside of the letters with a lacquer that's mixed with pigment, deepening the color of the stone.

Triangular Logic

If a walk around Washington's inscriptions is a classical education, a perambulation of Federal Triangle is the civics lesson. The limestone cliffs of the Triangle, stretching from their base at 15th Street down Pennsylvania and Constitution avenues, are inscribed with mottoes that immediately conjure up a nobler time.

The walls fairly sing with inscriptions, enjoining passersby to be eternally vigilant (it's *the price of liberty; Study the past,* says the National Archives), and to heed Thomas Jefferson and *Cultivate peace and commerce with all* (on the Commerce Building and an example of one of the tenets of good epigram selection: Try to work the name of the building into at least one inscription).

The Federal Triangle inscriptions also provide justification for the buildings that they decorate and government departments they praise. The inscription on the Internal Revenue Service headquarters on Constitution Avenue is not Dante's *Abandon all hope ye who enter here,* but Oliver Wendell Holmes's *Taxes are what we pay for a civilized society.* Just in case you were wondering what you were paying for every April 15.

Likewise, on the Justice Department we have:

Justice is the great interest of man on earth. Wherever her temple stands there is a foundation for social security, general happiness and the improvement and progress of our race.

While Justice certainly has its share of letters (including this bit of Latin: *Lege atque ordine omnia fiunt*—"By law and order all is accomplished"), the award for the most verbose structure must go to the Commerce Department Building. Stretched out along 14th Street, eight stories up and spread out over hundreds of feet, is this edifying ode:

The inspiration that guided our forefathers led them to secure above all things the unity of our country. We rest upon government by consent of the governed and the political order of the United States is the expression of a patriotic ideal which welds together all the elements of our national energy promoting the organization that fosters individual initiative. Within this edifice are established agencies that have been created to buttress the life of the people, to clarify their problems and coordinate their resources, seeking to lighten burdens without lessening the responsibility of the citizen. In serving one and all they are dedicated to the purpose of the founders and to the highest hopes of the future with their local administration given to the integrity and welfare of the nation.

It's a mouthful. But it's also redolent of a time that seems almost hopelessly naive now, a time when we could use words like "national energy" and "purpose of the founders" without smirking. This passage and two other long ones were created especially for the building, composed, it is believed, by Royal Cortissoz, for 50 years the influential art critic of the *New York Tribune* (and author of this much pithier epigram from the Lincoln Memorial: *In this temple as in the hearts of the people for whom he saved the union the memory of Abraham Lincoln is enshrined forever.*).

You can imagine Washingtonians in the 1930s watching as the inscriptions were going up in Federal Triangle, trying to guess what would be said, as if a huge game of hangman were being played. At least one Washingtonian wasn't thrilled with what he saw. In 1934, when the giant Commerce Department Building was in its final stages of construction, one Thomas Woodward wrote a letter to a friend in the Department of Justice, expressing his dismay. The letter was addressed to Charles W. Eliot II, son of the Harvard president who composed the Union Station and City Post Office epigrams. The younger Eliot forwarded the letter of complaint to Charles Moore, chairman of the Commission of Fine Arts, the body responsible—then as now—for reviewing the design of government building projects. Moore allowed as how his commission hadn't been consulted on the inscriptions. The younger Eliot followed up with a salvo of his own to Moore, stating that the inscriptions "seem to be thoroughly bromidic and uninteresting—a lost opportunity."

Eliot had a point. The Commerce Department inscriptions are lecturing rather than inspirational, long and sour rather than short and sweet. Moore must have forgotten that he once wrote: "Inscriptions are an art in themselves. They should be monumental and express in few words a great sentiment."

Still, there can be poetry in even the longest of inscriptions. Consider this moving sentiment, carved on the hemicycle of the Post Office Department building, facing 14th Street:

The Post Office Department, in its ceaseless labors, pervades every channel of commerce and every theatre of human enterprise, and while visiting as it does kindly, every fireside, mingles with the throbbings of almost every heart in the land. In the amplitude of its beneficence, it ministers to all climes, and creeds, and pursuits, *with the same eager readiness and with equal fullness of fidelity. It is the delicate ear trump through which alike nations and families and isolated individuals whisper their joys and their sorrows, their convictions and their sympathies to all who listen for their coming.*

What is it about the Post Office that inspires the most poignant inscriptions? And to whom do we talk about getting "ear trump" back into common usage?

Oops . . .

What do you do if you're a stone carver and you make a mistake? After all, the expression "carved in stone" isn't much good if fixing a typo on a chunk of marble is as easy as depressing the backspace key. Ann Hawkins: "If I got a chip, there are epoxy resins I could apply. . . . It's very rare to make a mistake, unless you do something stupid."

On big projects, boo-boos can be lopped out entirely, the offending block of stone cut out and replaced with a "dutchman," a fresh piece that's inserted like a patch and—hopefully—carved correctly. There's no dutchman in what is perhaps the city's most obvious mistake. Inscribed in three sections on the north wall of the Lincoln Memorial is Abraham Lincoln's second Inaugural address. Twenty lines down in the first block of words is a phrase that concludes: "WITH HIGH HOPES FOR THE EUTURE." The poor stone carver added an extra stroke to the *F,* transforming it into an *E.* Because the inscription is inside—away from the sunshine and its shadows—it would be virtually unreadable if the insides of the letters weren't painted black. And so, the bottom stroke of the *E* was left unpainted, making the best of a bad situation.

Back to the Stone Age

The capital's official buildings, monuments, and memorials urge us in various ways to remember the past or strive toward a more perfect future. None of the blank verse, mottoes, or maxims, though, are as moving as what appears on a V-shape set of black granite panels set into the ground near the Lincoln Memorial. The inscription isn't made up of words at all, but it's as moving as any sonnet.

Etched into the stone of the Vietnam Veterans Memorial are the names of the more than 58,000 Americans killed in that war. The names weren't carved high atop a pediment out of reach but were sandblasted delicately into the wall. Washington's other inscriptions might be meant to provide edification from a distance, but this memorial is designed to be touched, its inscriptions traced with unsteady fingers. And behind the names we see ourselves, reflected in the stone as true as any mirror.

Which leads us to the state of stone carving in Washington today. Most newer buildings in Washington aren't graced with inscriptions. While a building named after a famous American might once have warranted an inscribed quotation from that person, today we have the James Forrestal Federal Building and the William McChesney Martin, Jr. Federal Reserve Board Building with nary a peep from either gentleman.

Gone, too, is the specially commissioned aphorism meant to enlighten or fire. Inscriptions like those on the Justice and Commerce department buildings—whether you consider them quaint optimism or naive bluster—are in short supply these days.

After all, the 1990s aren't like the 1930s, the period of Washington's big inscription boom. This is supposed to be the time of little, quiet government, not big, loud government. Why should government buildings assault the eyes of pedestrians and motorists with jingoistic slogans and propagandist mottoes? Shouldn't the feds just get out of our hair?

Perhaps, but somehow when we were willing to not only stand behind our words but carve them immutably into the living stone, it suggested we believed in them a little more, thought them worth remembering, no matter how self-evident or self-aggrandizing they seemed.

We don't seem to do much of that anymore. Maybe it's time to read the writing on the walls.

—John F. Kelly

THE FEDERAL GOVERNMENT: HOW OUR SYSTEM WORKS

NEW YORK MAY BE the fashion capital of the United States and Los Angeles the center of entertainment, but government—and power—is the name of the game in Washington.

The federal government is a major employer, an important landlord, and a source of contracts, contacts, or conversation for Washingtonians. It is a patron of the arts and a provider for the needy. To some, pervasive government is what's wrong with Washington. To others, it's what's right.

The federal government occupies some of the choicest real estate in town, yet pays no taxes to the District of Columbia. On the other hand, although citizens of the District *do* pay taxes, they could not vote until some 20 years ago. This has changed; now they can help elect the president, but still they have only a nonvoting delegate in Congress.

In Washington, the "separation of powers" doctrine becomes more than just a phrase in the Constitution. A visit here gives you a chance to see the legislative, executive, and judicial branches of government in action; to see how the system of checks and balances works. As Boswell put it, you have an opportunity, "instead of thinking how things may be, to see them as they are."

The Legislative Branch

In Pierre L'Enfant's 18th-century plan for the city of Washington, the U.S. Capitol and the White House were just far enough away from each other on Pennsylvania Avenue to emphasize the separation of powers between the legislative and executive branches. L'Enfant chose Jenkins Hill as the site for the Capitol; it is the focal point of an area now called Capitol Hill.

Guided tours of the Capitol leave from the Rotunda almost continuously from 9 AM to 3:45 PM daily throughout the year. The Senate side of the Capitol faces Constitution Avenue, while the House side can be approached from Independence Avenue.

Drop by the office of your senator or representative to pick up passes to the Visitors Galleries. Without a pass, you are not permitted to watch the proceedings. There are two Senate office buildings at First and Constitution Avenue NE, named, respectively, for former senators Everett Dirksen and Richard Russell. A third, honoring Senator Philip A. Hart, opened in November 1982 at Second and Constitution NE.

The House office buildings, named for former Speakers Joseph Cannon, Nicholas Longworth, and Sam Rayburn, are located in that order along Independence Avenue between First Street SE, and First Street SW. It is generally agreed by residents and visitors alike that the Rayburn Building is the least attractive and, at $75 million, one of the most expensive structures in the city.

According to the Constitution, "the Congress shall assemble at least once in every year, and such meeting shall begin at noon on the 3rd day of January, unless they shall by law appoint a different day." In the years before air-conditioning, Congress usually recessed during the summer and reconvened in the fall. Today, however, with congressional calendars more crowded and air-conditioning commonplace, sessions frequently last much longer. It is not unusual for the House and/or Senate to sit through the summer and well into the fall.

Congressional sessions usually begin at noon; committee meetings are generally held in the morning. Check the *Washington Post's* "Today in Congress" listings to find out what is going on.

Don't be surprised to see only a handful of senators or members of Congress on the floor during a session. Much congressional business dealing with constituent problems is done in committees or in offices. When a vote is taken during a session, bells are rung to summon absent members to the floor.

To save time, many senators and members of Congress make the brief trip between their offices and the Capitol on the congressional subway. Visitors may ride, too. The Senate restaurant in the Capitol—famed for its bean soup—is open to the public at all times. Cafeterias in the Rayburn, Longworth, and Dirksen office buildings are also open to visitors. Watch the hours, however. From 11:30 AM to 1:15 PM, only members of Congress and their staffs are admitted.

There are two senators from each state, who are elected for six-year terms; the 435 members of the House serve for two years. Senate and House members receive an annual salary of $133,600.

How a Bill Becomes Law

Legislation is a complicated, time-consuming process. Here, briefly, is the usual legislative procedure in the House of Representatives.

Such a brief summary cannot possibly convey the intrigue, the drama, and the behind-the-scenes maneuvering by members, their staffs, and lobbyists involved in the legislative process. Often the stakes are high and the battles hard fought.

The Executive Branch

The White House is at 1600 Pennsylvania Avenue NW, the most prestigious address in the country. However, its first occupant, Abigail Adams, was disappointed in the damp, drafty "President's Palace." She complained that it had "not a single apartment finished" and "not the least fence, yard, or other convenience without." On the other hand, Thomas Jefferson found the house "big enough for two emperors, one Pope, and the grand lama"—and still unfinished.

When Franklin Delano Roosevelt became president in 1932, the entire White House staff consisted of fewer than 50 people. Today, approximately 1,800 people work for the executive office of the president. They are crammed into offices in the east and west wings of the White House and in the ornate Executive Office Building (formerly the State, War, and Navy Building), adjacent to the White House to the west on Pennsylvania Avenue.

The president's annual salary is $200,000; the vice president receives $160,600. They are elected for a four-year term. If the president dies or becomes incapacitated, the vice president is next in line of succession. He is followed, in order, by the Speaker of the House of Representatives, the president pro tempore of the Senate, the secretaries of state, treasury, and defense, the attorney general, the postmaster general, and the secretaries of the interior, agriculture, commerce, labor, health and human services, housing and urban development, transportation, energy, education, and veterans affairs.

The Judicial Branch

Traditionally, the opening session of the Supreme Court, on the first Monday in October, marks the beginning of Washington's social season, and the quadrennial inaugural festivities add to the excitement. The inaugural week in January usually includes a star-studded gala, as well as receptions honoring the new president, vice president, and their spouses.

The Supreme Court meets from October through June in a Corinthian-column white-marble building at First Street and Maryland Avenue NE. Until 1935, the justices used various rooms in the Capitol. For a while, in the 19th century, they met in taverns and boardinghouses. You can see the Old Supreme Court Chamber on the ground floor of the Capitol.

Approximately 5,000 cases are submitted for appeal each year, and the justices choose about 3%—roughly 160 cases in all—those which raise constitutional questions or affect the life or liberty of citizens.

Justice Felix Frankfurter said, "The words of the Constitution are so unrestricted by their intrinsic meaning or by their history or by tradition or by prior decisions that they leave the individual Justice free, if indeed they do not compel him, to gather meaning not from reading the Constitution but from reading life."

In the courtroom, the nine black-robed justices are seated in high-back black leather chairs in front of heavy red velvet draperies. Lawyers for each side present their oral arguments, with the justices often interjecting questions or comments.

Generally, the court sits for two weeks and then recesses for two weeks to do research and write opinions.

They are on the bench Monday, Tuesday, and Wednesday from 10 AM to noon and from 1 to 3 PM from October through April and they usually hear about four cases a day. During this first part of the term, the justices meet privately every Wednesday afternoon and all day Friday to discuss the cases they have heard that week and to take a preliminary vote on decisions.

The chief justice assigns different members to write the opinions. If the chief justice is on the minority side in a particular case, however, the senior justice in the majority assigns the opinion. Any justice may write his or her own opinion, agreeing or disagreeing with the majority. During the remainder of the term, in May and June, the justices usually meet every Thursday to decide on releasing their opinions.

Monday is "Decision Day," probably the most interesting time to visit the Supreme Court. That is when the justices announce their decisions and read their opinions.

Throughout the year, in the courtroom, staff members give a brief lecture about the court Monday through Friday, every hour on the half-hour from 9:30 AM to 3:30 PM. Lectures are not given on holidays or when the justices are on the bench hearing cases.

Supreme Court justices are appointed by the president with the advice and consent of the Senate. They serve for life or, as the Constitution says, "during good behavior."

Associate justices receive $161,100 per year; the chief justice's salary is $171,500. After 10 years of service, justices may resign or retire with full pay.

Lobbyists

Virtually every special-interest group in the country, as well as a sprinkling of foreign governments, is represented by someone who "lobbies" for its cause in Washington—some say that the word comes from President Grant's time. He used to escape the White House for brandy and a cigar in the lobby of the Willard Hotel, where interested parties would try to bend his ear. Today's lobbyists frequently conduct their business over luncheons, cocktails, and dinners, as well as on the golf courses or tennis courts of suburban country clubs.

Lobbyists' backgrounds are as diverse as the causes they represent. They are usually lawyers, public relations executives, or former congressional staff members. Many were once members of Congress or high government officials from all over the United States who have developed "Potomac fever"; that is, they do not return home but find being a Washington representative the ideal way to continue to influence public policy.

Sometimes, it appears that every group is well represented here except the average citizen. Under those circumstances, if you have a pet project, discuss it with your senator or member of Congress—he or she is your lobbyist. In doing so—like Washington's highly skilled and well-paid lobbyists—you would simply be exercising your First Amendment rights to express your beliefs and influence your government.

—Betty Ross

BOOKS AND MOVIES

CLASSIC WASHINGTON novels include *Democracy,* by Henry Adams, and Gore Vidal's *Washington, D.C.* Edward P. Jones's critically acclaimed *Lost in the City* is a collection of short stories about black Washingtonians. Margaret Leach's *Reveille in Washington* re-creates the city during the Civil War; E. J. Applewhite comments on the architecture of the city in *Washington Itself;* Louis A. Halle's *Springtime in Washington* is the definitive look at the flora and fauna of the capital; and in *Ear on Washington,* gossip columnist Diana McClellan recounts some of the town's juicier stories. *Literary Washington,* by David Cutler, explores past and contemporary writers who have lived in and written about the city. Sites and stories relating to the capital's African-American history are presented in *The Guide to Black Washington,* by Sandra Fitzpatrick and Maria R. Goodwin. Characters in Margaret Truman's mysteries have been found murdered everywhere from the Smithsonian to the Supreme Court.

For detailed, full-color maps of Washington, D.C., and its surroundings, pick up Fodor's *Flashmaps.* A more selective listing of attractions, dining, and lodging can be found in Fodor's slimmer, smaller, *Pocket Washington, D.C.*

For some reason, movies about Washington always seem to be about power and/or corruption. In the Frank Capra classic, *Mr. Smith Goes to Washington,* Jefferson Smith (Jimmy Stewart) is chosen to replace a recently deceased senator. He goes to Washington, naively thinking he is going there to work for the good of the people, but soon learns that those who appointed him have their own motives. The film version of *All the President's Men* (based on the book by the same title), starring Robert Redford and Dustin Hoffman, is the story of two *Washington Post* reporters, Bob Woodward and Carl Bernstein, whose investigation into the break-in at the Democratic National Committee's office in the Watergate Hotel led to the resignation of President Richard M. Nixon. When Henry Fonda is named Secretary of State, his Communist past threatens his confirmation in the film *Advise and Consent,* based on the book by Allen Drury. In *Seven Days in May,* a hawkish general (Burt Lancaster) plots to overthrow the president (Frederic March). One of the general's aides (Kirk Douglas) learns of the plot and saves both the day and democracy.

Born Yesterday was first made in 1950, with Broderick Crawford as a corrupt junk tycoon who comes to Washington with his unsophisticated girlfriend (a performance that won Judy Holliday the Academy Award) to create a scrap iron cartel. Reporter William Holden is hired to educate her. When she discovers that Crawford is using her, Holliday turns the tables. The film was remade in 1993 with John Goodman, Melanie Griffith, and Don Johnson.

Other recent movies set (at least partially) in Washington include: *No Way Out,* the story of a secretary of defense (Gene Hackman) who tries to shift the blame of a murder to an alleged Soviet spy (Kevin Costner); the comedy *Dave,* which stars Kevin Kline as a presidential look-alike who is asked to fill in for the president during social functions, but ends up taking on all his duties; *In the Line of Fire,* starring Clint Eastwood as a secret service agent assigned to protect the president against psycho stalker John Malkovich; and *Patriot Games,* with Harrison Ford as an upstanding intelligence officer who learns of an illicit war on drugs.

INDEX

✕ = restaurant, ⊞ = hotel

Fodor's Travel Publications

Available at bookstores everywhere, or call 1–800–533–6478, 24 hours a day.

Gold Guides

U.S.

Alaska	Florida	New Orleans	Santa Fe, Taos, Albuquerque
Arizona	Hawai'i	New York City	
Boston	Las Vegas, Reno, Tahoe	Pacific North Coast	Seattle & Vancouver
California		Philadelphia & the Pennsylvania Dutch Country	The South
Cape Cod, Martha's Vineyard, Nantucket	Los Angeles		U.S. & British Virgin Islands
	Maine, Vermont, New Hampshire	The Rockies	
The Carolinas & the Georgia Coast	Maui & Lāna'i	San Diego	USA
			Virginia & Maryland
Chicago	Miami & the Keys	San Francisco	Washington, D.C.
Colorado	New England		

Foreign

Australia	Europe	Montréal & Québec City	Scotland
Austria	Florence, Tuscany & Umbria	Moscow, St. Petersburg, Kiev	Singapore
The Bahamas			South Africa
Belize & Guatemala	France	The Netherlands, Belgium & Luxembourg	South America
Bermuda	Germany		Southeast Asia
Canada	Great Britain	New Zealand	Spain
Cancún, Cozumel, Yucatán Peninsula	Greece	Norway	Sweden
	Hong Kong	Nova Scotia, New Brunswick, Prince Edward Island	Switzerland
Caribbean	India		Thailand
China	Ireland		Tokyo
Costa Rica	Israel	Paris	Toronto
Cuba	Italy	Portugal	Turkey
The Czech Republic & Slovakia	Japan	Provence & the Riviera	Vienna & the Danube
Eastern & Central Europe	London	Scandinavia	
	Madrid & Barcelona		
	Mexico		

Fodor's Special-Interest Guides

Caribbean Ports of Call	Halliday's New Orleans Food Explorer	Sunday in New York	Where Should We Take the Kids? Northeast
The Complete Guide to America's National Parks	Healthy Escapes	Sunday in San Francisco	Worldwide Cruises and Ports of Call
Family Adventures	Kodak Guide to Shooting Great Travel Pictures	Walt Disney World, Universal Studios and Orlando	
Gay Guide to the USA	Net Travel	Walt Disney World for Adults	
Halliday's New England Food Explorer	Nights to Imagine	Where Should We Take the Kids? California	
	Rock & Roll Traveler USA		

Escape to ancient cities and

journey to *exotic islands with*

CNN Travel Guide, a wealth of valuable advice. Host

Valerie Voss will take you to

all of your favorite destinations,

including those off the beaten

path. Tune-in to your passport to the world.

CNN TRAVEL GUIDE
SATURDAY 12:30 PMᴇᴛ   SUNDAY 4:30 PMᴇᴛ

CNN✈
Airport Network

Your
Window
To The
World
While You're
On The
Road

Keep in touch when you're traveling. Before you take off, tune in to CNN Airport Network. Now available in major airports across America, CNN Airport Network provides nonstop news, sports, business, weather and lifestyle programming. Both domestic and international. All piloted by the top-flight global resources of CNN. All up-to-the minute reporting. And just for travelers, CNN Airport Network features two daily Fodor's specials. "Travel Fact" provides enlightening, useful travel trivia, while "What's Happening" covers upcoming events in major cities worldwide. So why be bored waiting to board? **TIME FLIES WHEN YOU'RE WATCHING THE WORLD THROUGH THE WINDOW OF CNN AIRPORT NETWORK!**

WHEREVER YOU TRAVEL, *H*ELP IS NEVER FAR AWAY.

From planning your trip to providing travel assistance along the way, American Express® Travel Service Offices are always there to help.

Washington, D.C.

American Express Travel Service
1150 Connecticut Avenue N.W.
202/457-1300

American Express Travel Service
Mazza Gallerie, 5300 Wisconsin
3rd Floor, N.W.
202/362-4000

Travel

http://www.americanexpress.com/travel

American Express Travel Service Offices
are located throughout the United States.
For the office nearest you, call 1-800-YES-AMEX.